CONTENTS

International cases are denoted 🌐.

BECOMING FAMILIAR WITH FINANCIAL REPORTING

Basics, Tools, and the Persistence of Earnings

Basics—Interpretation and Preparation of Financial Statements

Tools—Discounted Cash Flow

Tools—Basic Valuation and the Persistence of Earnings

Tools—Cash Basis versus Accrual Basis Reporting

Evaluating Financial Reporting Disclosures

Balance Sheet Components and Issues in the Quality of Earnings

Assets

Liabilities

Owners' Equity

Intercorporate Investments

Financial Statement Analysis

CASES IN FINANCIAL REPORTING

An Integrated Approach
with an Emphasis on Earnings Quality and Persistence

Fifth Edition

D. Eric Hirst
Red McCombs School of Business
UNIVERSITY OF TEXAS AT AUSTIN

Mary Lea McAnally
Mays Business School
TEXAS A&M UNIVERSITY

Upper Saddle River, NJ 07458

Senior Acquisitions Editor: Wendy Craven
VP/Editorial Director: Jeff Shelstad
Project Manager: Kerri Tomasso
Manufacturing Buyer: Michelle Klein
Cover Design: Jayne Conte
Printer/Binder: Banta-Harrisonburg

Credits and acknowledgments borrowed from other sources and reproduced, with permission, in this textbook appear on appropriate page within text.

Pearson Education LTD.
Pearson Education Singapore, Pte. Ltd
Pearson Education, Canada, Ltd
Pearson Education–Japan
Pearson Education Australia PTY, Limited
Pearson Education North Asia Ltd
Pearson Educación de Mexico, S.A. de C.V.
Pearson Education Malaysia, Pte. Ltd

10 9 8 7 6 5 4 3 2 1
0-13-188120-5

CASES IN ALPHABETICAL ORDER

PREFACE

This book is a collection of financial accounting cases designed to help you become a user of financial reports. Learning accounting is very much like learning a new language. The best way to learn any language is to immerse oneself in the language and to converse with many people. Conversations speed up language acquisition and teach the nuances of the language. Conversations strengthen language skills and build breadth. This collection creates a set of conversational opportunities. You will learn accounting by reading financial statements and by responding to topical questions about those financials. By reading and using many different companies' financial statements, you will speed-up your acquisition of accounting concepts and skills. By observing the nuances of financial reporting, you will quickly learn to speak "accounting," the language of business.

These materials bridge a void in introductory financial statement materials at both the undergraduate and the graduate level. Typically, students are required to read a textbook chapter and do some exercises to ensure concept comprehension. Assigned end of chapter material, however, is often not sufficiently challenging to students with stronger analytical abilities. Questions often focus on financial statement preparation rather than, as appropriate for many students, financial statement use. At the other extreme, unstructured discussion cases can leave students with a weak grasp of the mechanics and subtleties of financial accounting. The cases here fill the void.

Each case deals with a specific financial accounting topic within the context of one (or more) corporation's financial statements. Each case contains financial statement information (a balance sheet, income statement, statement of cash flows, and footnotes) and a set of directed questions pertaining to one or two specific financial accounting issues. You will use the financial statement information to infer and interpret the economic events underlying the numbers. Some cases are accompanied by a related article taken from the business press. In those instances, information from the article is incorporated into the questions in the case. Some cases involve two or three companies within an industry and the case questions focus on intercompany comparisons of financial information. Some cases include industry-level information that you will use to assess the performance or position of the case company. Numerous cases are based on international companies.

WHAT MAKES THESE MATERIALS UNIQUE

These materials have a proven track record. The book was developed from the course materials used since 1991 at the University of Texas at Austin. The course (a semester-long, compulsory, first-year introductory class) has been extremely well-received by students each semester it is taught. The course consistently receives among the highest student evaluations in the UT and Texas A&M M.B.A. cores. The cases have been used with success internationally at ITESM in Mexico City and INSEAD in Fontainebleau, France.

Several unique features distinguish this casebook:

Financial Statement Diversity—This book comprises 33 cases. We believe that you will appreciate the exposure to many different companies and quickly learn that, while financial statements do not all look the same, you *can* understand and use them all.

Current Financial Statements—The cases are very current; primarily dated 2001 through 2004. This affords you the opportunity to read and use pertinent and timely financial information. Some older cases have been included because they explicate a concept particularly well or because they demonstrate an uncommon trend.

International Financial Statements—Cases cover companies from Canada, France, Germany, India, Japan, Mexico, the Netherlands, the UK, and Taiwan as well as from the U.S. Many of the U.S. companies are major multinationals. The globalization of business necessitates your facility with financial statements other than those prepared in accordance with U.S. GAAP. The international cases will help you understand some of the recent harmonization efforts between the International Accounting Standards Board and the U.S. Financial Accounting Standards Board. Some international cases require you to recast the financials to U.S. GAAP. Thus, you will become a sophisticated user of financial information.

Learning Objectives—Cases are prefaced with a set of learning objectives. These become your learning goals as you work through the cases. The focus of each case is made clear through these objectives.

Corporate Descriptions—Each case focuses on one or two sets of financial statements. A brief description of the companies in the case is designed to remind you that accounting information is used in specific business contexts. Reported financial accounting numbers are the result of a series of complex, professional estimates and judgments. Many of these are influenced by industry practice. Correctly reading and interpreting financial information is predicated on your awareness of a company's business and industry.

THE 'CPA' APPROACH—CONCEPTS, PROCESS, AND ANALYSIS

As in prior editions, the questions are organized in "C.P.A." order.

Concepts The typical case begins with a set of conceptual questions. As we introduce each topic area, we want to ensure that you are familiar with the vocabulary and the broader concepts before moving into the specific application to the case-corporation. These general questions focus each case on its topic area. For example, the Continental case on leases begins with the conceptual questions "what is a lease?" Several cases make explicit reference to the concept statements of the Financial Accounting Standards Board. These concept questions call for factual responses that you are likely to easily provide. For those wanting to read the Concepts Statements or the Financial Accounting Standards, all are available at www.fasb.org.

Process Before you become a sophisticated consumer of accounting information you need an understanding of the accounting process and the basics of financial statement preparation. Thus, the second set of questions in each case focuses on the process. Process questions require you to retrieve specific information from the financial statements and to manipulate the information via calculations, journal entries, and T-accounts. It is at this point that many textbook exercises end. However, we believe that the accounting process is not the end but the means by which you will build a firm understanding of how financial accounting works the way it does.

Analysis With a strong understanding of the concepts and a solid knowledge of the accounting cycle, you are ready for higher level analytical questions. These questions have you synthesize, analyze, interpret information and formulate and defend your opinion on accounting policies, standards, and corporate behavior. Thus, analysis questions sharpen your higher-order thinking skills. In the 5th edition, there is increased use of the DuPont model of ROE analysis across cases.

By grouping the case questions into the C.P.A. categories, the text has broad audience. Taken alone, the Concept and Process questions are perfectly aimed at undergraduate introductory financial accounting classes. Because many M.B.A. students have taken some accounting and most have had some business experience, they are better prepared to handle the Analysis questions even at the introductory level. Several topics (e.g. pensions, leases, marketable securities, deferred taxes) included in this casebook are not typically covered in an introductory course. These can be used at the intermediate level for undergraduate and M.B.A. classes. For intermediate and financial statement analysis courses, the Concept questions can be used by your instructor to start class discussion. Taking up these questions first ensures that you are on firm ground before you tackle the more challenging Analysis questions. The full set of financial statements included with each case affords you and your class instructor the opportunity to explore issues the Analysis questions do not touch upon.

NEW IN THE 5TH EDITION

In keeping with the contemporary flavor of the earlier editions, we have added a dozen new companies to the book (Vodafone, Rhodia, Kohl's, Caterpillar, Deere, CNH Global, Tasty Baking, Dr. Reddy's Laboratories, Rite Aid, Continental Airlines, International Speedway, and Chico's). We reviewed all of the continuing cases with an eye to improving their clarity. To that end, we reorganized the questions in several cases (Food Lion, Taiwan Semiconductor and Wachovia). We have included financial ratios and questions about management's incentives and motives in arriving at accounting choices in many cases. Several cases now include industry-level information. As well, we have included tables to many cases to guide the quantitative analysis especially when the questions require comparisons across years, to industry averages, or among firms. We continue to include a significant number of non-U.S. companies, denoted 🌍 in the table of contents.

HOW TO USE THESE MATERIALS

We've designed these cases to be used in conjunction with an introductory, intermediate, or financial statement analysis textbook. The order in which material is presented by your instructor does not affect the relevance of the cases. Each case stands alone and while some cases naturally precede others, there is no prescribed order.

As you use these materials, notice two main themes—earnings persistence and the quality of earnings. The first third of the cases in the book relate to the framework of financial reporting. In these cases you are acquiring skills in basic financial statement preparation, and in understanding how financial statements aid in the investment decision process. In achieving the latter, we emphasize how financial statements classify items and how such classifications are important in the prediction of the nature, uncertainty, and timing of future cash flows. Thus, we introduce the notion of earnings *persistence* and how it affects firm valuation. The remainder of the cases explores the accounting issues for the major financial statement line items. We place particular emphasis on the latitude and judgment management has in arriving at the reported numbers and the economic consequences of their choices. This introduces the notion of the *quality* of earnings. The cases are designed to help you acquire the skills necessary to identify quality of earnings issues and learn how to deal with them (for example, by restating the financials under different assumptions or accounting methods).

INSTRUCTOR RESOURCES

A solutions manual with teaching notes is available to qualified instructors. Please visit the support site on the web at www.prenhall.com/accounting.

These cases can be custom published through Prentice Hall Custom Business Resources. For more information on custom publishing, visit http://www.pearsoncustom.com/database/busmain.html or contact your Prentice-Hall sales representative.

ACKNOWLEDGMENTS

We thank a number of people. First, the University of Texas at Austin, Texas A&M University, and INSEAD students who have used prior versions of the cases, have provided tremendous feedback. Each semester, they tell us how to improve the cases, and we listen. Second, our teaching assistants have helped craft some of the best questions in the book. Special thanks are due to A&M doctoral students Janell Blazovich, Ryan Huston and William Strawser who helped develop case questions and more importantly, related solutions. Bob May provided invaluable help in organizing and structuring the package as a whole. Feedback from reviewers, including Ashiq Ali (Arizona), Ellen Engel (Chicago), Robert Hartman (Iowa), Philip Lewis (Northern Kentucky), John Neill (Abilene Christian) and Pamela Stuerke (Rhode Island) is also appreciated. Finally, the crew at Prentice Hall, including Wendy Craven, kept the project going and saw it to completion. Thanks to all!

Although we have made every effort to avoid errors, any that remain are solely our responsibility. Should you have any suggestions for improving this product, we can be reached as follows:

Eric Hirst	Eric.Hirst@mccombs.utexas.edu
Mary Lea McAnally	MMcAnally@mays.tamu.edu

ABOUT THE AUTHORS

D. Eric Hirst, Ph.D., is Professor at the Red McCombs School of Business at the University of Texas at Austin. He received his Ph.D. from the University of Minnesota and M.Acc. and B.A. from the University of Waterloo. He worked as a Chartered Accountant with experience in public practice. His research on auditor, investor, and analyst judgment has been published in *The Journal of Accounting Research, The Accounting Review, Contemporary Accounting Research, The Journal of Financial Statement Analysis, Accounting Horizons, Auditing: A Journal of Practice & Theory, The International Tax Journal, CA Magazine, Organizational Behavior and Human Decision Processes* and others. At UT, Professor Hirst teaches financial accounting and financial statement analysis in the MBA and Executive M.B.A. programs. He has received numerous faculty-determined and student-initiated teaching awards at the University of Texas at Austin and INSEAD.

Mary Lea McAnally, Ph.D., CA, CIA is Associate professor of Accounting at Mays Business School at Texas A&M University. She obtained her Ph.D. from Stanford University and B.Comm. from the University of Alberta. She is a Chartered Accountant (Canada) with experience in public practice and industry. She is also a Certified Internal Auditor. Her research interests include capital markets, accounting and disclosure in regulated environments, and accounting for risk. She has published articles in *The Journal of Accounting and Economics, The Journal of Accounting Research, The Accounting Review, Contemporary Accounting Research, Accounting Horizons, The Journal of Accounting, Auditing, and Finance,* and *Financial Analysts Journal.* At Texas A&M, Professor McAnally teaches financial accounting in the M.B.A. and executive programs. She has received numerous faculty-determined and student-initiated teaching awards at the University of Texas and Texas A&M University.

ASICS Corporation—Understanding Financial Statements

From small beginnings in 1949, ASICS Corporation has grown into one of Japan's foremost manufacturers of general sporting goods and equipment. Today, with some of the industry's most advanced research facilities, a diversified manufacturing base, and a network of operations that spans the United States, Europe, Australia, and Asia, ASICS is a globally oriented company actively pursuing worldwide expansion. The name ASICS derives from anima sana in corpore sano, *a Latin phrase expressing the ancient ideal of a sound mind in a sound body. This concept is central to our role as a manufacturer of general sporting goods and researcher in the field of total health and fitness.* (from the 2002 ASICS Corporation annual report)

Learning Objectives

- Become familiar with a set of financial statements and the notes thereto.
- Perform a basic analysis and interpretation of the financial statements.
- Recognize the role of estimation in the preparation of financial statements.

Refer to the 2002 ASICS Corporation financial statements.

 Concepts 

a. What is the nature of ASICS' business? That is, based on what you know about the company and on the accompanying financial statements, how does ASICS make money?

b. What financial statements are commonly prepared for external reporting purposes? What titles does ASICS give these statements? What does "consolidated" mean?

c. How often do publicly traded corporations (including ASICS, whose shares trade on the Tokyo, Osaka, and Nagoya stock exchanges in Japan) typically prepare financial statements for external reporting purposes?

d. Speculate on who uses the financial statements ASICS prepares.

e. Who are ASICS' external auditors? What sort of audit opinion did ASICS receive in 2002? In your own words, what does the opinion mean? Why is the audit report dated several months after ASICS' year end?

 Analysis 

A company's financial statements can be analyzed in many ways. Return on equity (ROE) is a widely-used measure of profitability that compares the profit the company made during the period (net income) to the resources invested in the company (shareholders' equity). The DuPont model systematically breaks ROE into components. One form of the model is:

$$\text{ROE} = \frac{\text{NI}}{\text{EBT}} \times \frac{\text{EBT}}{\text{EBIT}} \times \frac{\text{EBIT}}{\text{Sales}} \times \frac{\text{Sales}}{\text{Total Assets}} \times \frac{\text{Total Assets}}{\text{Common Equity}}$$

where NI is net income, EBT is earnings before tax, and EBIT is earnings before interest and tax.

- NI / EBT measures the proportion of earnings before tax that is kept by the company.
- EBT / EBIT measures the effect of interest; it indicates the proportion of earnings before interest and tax that is retained after paying interest. It should be considered together with the leverage

component (Total Assets / Common Equity). Further analysis of this component includes average interest rates on debt (and on investments if interest expense is reported net of interest income).

- EBIT / Sales measures the company's operating return on sales; it can be broken down into further subcomponents such as the gross margin percent. Preparing common-size income statements will help you analyze this component. This component and the next form the 'guts' of the model—did the managers operate the firm profitably?
- Sales / Total Assets measures asset utilization; it can be broken down into further subcomponents such as accounts receivable turnover, inventory turnover, and plant asset turnover. This is another key component—did the managers use the assets efficiently?
- Total Assets / Common Equity measures the effect of leverage on ROE. Note that this ratio equals 1 + the debt-equity ratio (i.e., Total Liabilities / Total Common Equity). Subcomponents include the current and quick ratios. Together with the interest component of ROE, you can look at times interest earned and other fixed charge ratios.

Note that once the common terms cancel ROE is Net Income divided by the firm's Common Equity (the book value of what the shareholders have invested and reinvested in the firm). ROE, its components, and further subcomponents can be compared across time, firms, and to expectations, making it a very powerful tool.

f. Use the DuPont model to calculate ASICS' ROE and its components for 2001 and 2002. Comment on the results.

g. Construct common-size income statements and balance sheets for 2001 and 2002. Common-size income statements scale each income statement line item by *net* sales. Common-size balance sheets are created by dividing each figure on a given year's balance sheet by that year's total assets, thereby creating a balance sheet on a 'percent of assets' basis.

h. Refer to the common-size income statements to answer the following questions.

   i. What are ASICS' major sources of revenues? That is, what products generate the bulk of its sales? Do the financial statements and notes thereto provide such detailed data? In your opinion, should they?

   ii. What are ASICS' major expenses?

   iii. Was ASICS profitable during 2002? Explain your definition of "profitable."

i. Refer to the common-size balance sheets to answer the following questions.

   i. What are ASICS' major investments? That is, what are its major assets?

   ii. How has ASICS financed (i.e. paid for) these investments? That is, what are ASICS' major liabilities and equities?

j. Refer to the statement of cash flows. Did ASICS generate cash from operations during 2002? What were some significant uses of ASICS' cash during the year?

k. Refer to the notes to the Consolidated Financial Statements.

   i. Several notes refer to "significant" amounts. What does ASICS mean by this term?

   ii. The notes to the financial statements discuss the accounting choices and principles used in ASICS' financial statements. Review those notes and list as many of the estimates underlying the financial statements as you can. Are any accounts "estimate-free?"

Consolidated Balance Sheets

ASICS Corporation and Consolidated Subsidiaries
March 31, 2002 and 2001

ASSETS	Millions of yen 2002	Millions of yen 2001	Thousands of U.S. dollars (Note 1) 2002
Current assets:			
Cash and cash equivalents	**¥ 10,526**	¥ 11,500	**$ 79,142**
Short-term investments	**1,991**	1,061	**14,970**
Notes and accounts receivable:			
Trade	**41,325**	41,499	**310,714**
Unconsolidated subsidiaries and affiliates	**1,580**	1,137	**11,880**
Less allowance for doubtful receivables	**(1,188)**	(1,642)	**(8,932)**
Inventories (Note 4)	**26,598**	26,558	**199,985**
Short-term loans	**63**	59	**473**
Deferred income taxes (Note 11)	**1,052**	983	**7,910**
Other current assets	**3,943**	3,287	**29,647**
Total current assets	**85,890**	84,442	**645,789**
Property, plant and equipment:			
Land (Note 5)	**5,623**	5,621	**42,278**
Buildings and structures (Note 5)	**23,383**	22,948	**175,812**
Machinery and equipment	**11,633**	11,843	**87,466**
Construction in progress	**—**	19	**—**
Less accumulated depreciation	**(24,792)**	(24,213)	**(186,406)**
Property, plant and equipment, net	**15,847**	16,218	**119,150**
Investments and long-term receivables:			
Investments in securities (Note 3):			
Unconsolidated subsidiaries and affiliates	**4,448**	4,742	**33,444**
Other	**5,472**	5,408	**41,143**
Long-term receivables	**1,006**	1,334	**7,564**
Deferred income taxes (Note 11)	**246**	171	**1,850**
Other assets	**3,206**	2,761	**24,105**
Less allowance for doubtful receivables	**(1,374)**	(1,162)	**(10,331)**
Total investments and other assets	**13,004**	13,254	**97,775**
	¥114,741	¥113,914	**$862,714**

See accompanying notes to consolidated financial statements.

LIABILITIES AND STOCKHOLDERS' EQUITY	Millions of yen 2002	2001	Thousands of U.S. dollars (Note 1) 2002
Current liabilities:			
Short-term bank loans (Note 5)	**¥ 11,896**	¥ 14,125	**$ 89,444**
Current portion of long-term debt (Note 5)	**3,246**	2,467	**24,406**
Notes and accounts payable:			
Trade	**21,147**	21,206	**159,000**
Unconsolidated subsidiaries and affiliates	**180**	301	**1,353**
Construction	**54**	88	**406**
Accrued income taxes (Note 11)	**292**	367	**2,195**
Accrued expenses	**5,662**	5,375	**42,571**
Other current liabilities	**3,987**	3,853	**29,978**
Total current liabilities	**46,464**	47,782	**349,353**
Long-term liabilities:			
Long-term debt (Note 5)	**13,160**	12,722	**98,947**
Deferred income taxes (Note 11)	**268**	667	**2,015**
Accrued retirement benefits (Note 6)	**5,987**	4,921	**45,015**
Other long-term liabilities	**1,495**	2,361	**11,241**
Total long-term liabilities	**20,910**	20,671	**157,218**
Minority interests	**1,855**	1,595	**13,947**
Contingent liabilities (Note 7)			
Stockholders' equity:			
Common stock:			
Authorized—600,000,000 shares			
Issued—213,962,991 shares at March 31, 2002 and 2001	**23,972**	23,972	**180,241**
Additional paid-in capital	**21,066**	34,495	**158,391**
Land revaluation reserve (Note 12)	**(398)**	—	**(2,992)**
Retained earnings (deficit)	**1,675**	(13,856)	**12,594**
Unrealized holding gain on securities	**340**	971	**2,556**
Translation adjustments	**(1,141)**	(1,716)	**(8,579)**
Less treasury stock, at cost (27,044 shares at March 31, 2002 and 143 shares at March 31, 2001)	**(2)**	(0)	**(15)**
Total stockholders' equity	**45,512**	43,866	**342,196**
	¥114,741	¥113,914	**$862,714**

Consolidated Statements of Income

ASICS Corporation and Consolidated Subsidiaries
Years ended March 31, 2002 and 2001

	Millions of yen		Thousands of U.S. dollars (Note 1)
	2002	2001	**2002**
Net sales	**¥128,901**	¥126,446	**$969,180**
Cost of sales	**82,938**	81,276	**623,594**
Gross profit	**45,963**	45,170	**345,586**
Selling, general and administrative expenses (Note 10)	**42,480**	42,078	**319,398**
Operating income	**3,483**	3,092	**26,188**
Other income (expenses):			
Interest and dividend income	**219**	174	**1,647**
Interest expenses	**(1,256)**	(1,391)	**(9,444)**
Equity in earnings of affiliates	**98**	207	**737**
Settlement money for trademark infringement	**111**	—	**835**
Loss on valuation of investments in securities	**(562)**	(369)	**(4,226)**
Other, net	**841**	414	**6,323**
	(549)	(965)	**(4,128)**
Income before income taxes and minority interests	**2,934**	2,127	**22,060**
Income taxes (Notes 3 and 11):			
Current	**759**	668	**5,707**
Deferred	**(101)**	(422)	**(759)**
	658	246	**4,948**
Income before minority interests	**2,276**	1,881	**17,112**
Minority interests in net income of consolidated subsidiaries	**153**	141	**1,150**
Net income	**¥ 2,123**	¥ 1,740	**$ 15,962**

See accompanying notes to consolidated financial statements.

Consolidated Statements of Stockholders' Equity

ASICS Corporation and Consolidated Subsidiaries
Years ended March 31, 2002 and 2001

		Millions of yen					
	Number of shares of common stock	Common stock	Additional paid-in capital	Land revaluation reserve	Retained earnings (deficit)	Unrealized holding gain on securities	Translation adjustments
Balance at March 31, 2000	213,962,991	¥23,972	¥34,495	¥ —	¥(15,569)	¥ —	¥ —
Net income					1,740		
Bonuses to directors and corporate auditors					(27)		
Net change in unrealized holding gain on securities						971	
Net change in translation adjustments							(1,716)
Balance at March 31, 2001	213,962,991	23,972	34,495	—	(13,856)	971	(1,716)
Net income					**2,123**		
Bonuses to directors and corporate auditors					**(21)**		
Reversal of additional paid-in capital			**(13,429)**		**13,429**		
Net change in land revaluation reserve (Note 12)				**(398)**			
Net change in unrealized holding gain on securities						**(631)**	
Net change in translation adjustments							**575**
Balance at March 31, 2002	**213,962,991**	**¥23,972**	**¥21,066**	**¥(398)**	**¥ 1,675**	**¥340**	**¥(1,141)**

		Thousands of U.S. dollars (Note 1)					
	Number of shares of common stock	Common stock	Additional paid-in capital	Land revaluation reserve	Retained earnings (deficit)	Unrealized holding gain on securities	Translation adjustments
Balance at March 31, 2001	213,962,991	$180,241	$259,361	$ —	$(104,180)	$7,301	$(12,902)
Net income					**15,962**		
Bonuses to directors and corporate auditors					**(158)**		
Reversal of additional paid-in capital			**(100,970)**		**100,970**		
Net change in land revaluation reserve (Note 12)				**(2,992)**			
Net change in unrealized holding gain on securities						**(4,745)**	
Net change in translation adjustments							**4,323**
Balance at March 31, 2002	**213,962,991**	**$180,241**	**$158,391**	**$(2,992)**	**$ 12,594**	**$2,556**	**$ (8,579)**

See accompanying notes to consolidated financial statements.

Consolidated Statements of Cash Flows

ASICS Corporation and Consolidated Subsidiaries
Years ended March 31, 2002 and 2001

	Millions of yen		Thousands of U.S. dollars (Note 1)
	2002	2001	2002
Operating activities:			
Income before income taxes and minority interests	**¥ 2,934**	¥ 2,127	**$22,060**
Adjustments to reconcile net income before income taxes and minority interests to net cash provided by operating activities:			
Depreciation and amortization	**1,236**	1,282	**9,293**
Decrease in allowance for doubtful receivable	**(258)**	(446)	**(1,940)**
Increase in accrued retirement benefits	**999**	802	**7,511**
Loss on revaluation of investments in securities	**562**	369	**4,226**
Settlement money for trademark infringement	**(111)**	—	**(835)**
Interest and dividend income	**(219)**	(174)	**(1,647)**
Interest expenses	**1,257**	1,391	**9,451**
Equity in earnings of affiliates	**(98)**	(207)	**(737)**
Loss on disposal of property, plant and equipment	**78**	22	**587**
Gain on sale of property, plant and equipment	**(9)**	(4)	**(67)**
Other, net	**(109)**	299	**(820)**
Decrease (increase) in operating assets:			
Notes and accounts receivable	**1,336**	1,422	**10,045**
Inventories	**1,181**	1,045	**8,880**
Other operating assets	**(46)**	59	**(346)**
Increase (decrease) in operating liabilities:			
Notes and accounts payable	**(857)**	1,263	**(6,443)**
Accrued consumption taxes	**(2)**	(67)	**(15)**
Other operating liabilities	**(245)**	(538)	**(1,842)**
Bonuses to directors and corporate auditors	**(21)**	(28)	**(158)**
Subtotal	**7,608**	8,617	**57,203**
Interest and dividends received	**282**	239	**2,120**
Interest paid	**(1,234)**	(1,372)	**(9,278)**
Settlement money for trademark infringement	**111**	—	**835**
Income taxes paid	**(1,060)**	(712)	**(7,970)**
Net cash provided by operating activities	**5,707**	6,772	**42,910**
Investing activities:			
Increase in time deposits	**(162)**	—	**(1,218)**
Proceeeds from time deposits	**100**	0	**752**
Purchase of property, plant and equipment	**(651)**	(719)	**(4,895)**
Proceeds from sale of property, plant and equipment	**108**	896	**812**
Purchase of securities	**(2,598)**	(74)	**(19,534)**
Proceeds from sale of securities	**16**	150	**120**
(Increase) decrease in short-term loans	**(103)**	55	**(774)**
Increase in long-term loans receivable	**(310)**	(39)	**(2,331)**
Collection of long-term loans receivable	**64**	38	**481**
Other, net	**(861)**	10	**(6,474)**
Net cash (used in) provided by investing activities	**(4,397)**	317	**(33,061)**
Financing activities:			
Decrease in short-term bank loans, net	**(3,285)**	(3,702)	**(24,699)**
Proceeds from long-term debt	**3,516**	1,200	**26,436**
Repayment of long-term debt	**(2,521)**	(2,600)	**(18,955)**
Proceeds from issuance of bonds	**—**	3,121	**—**
Proceeds from sale of treasury stock	**2**	5	**15**
Purchases of treasury stock	**(5)**	(5)	**(38)**
Cash dividends paid to minority interests	**(20)**	(83)	**(150)**
Other, net	**(152)**	(69)	**(1,143)**
Net cash used in financing activities	**(2,465)**	(2,133)	**(18,534)**
Effect of exchange rate changes on cash and cash equivalents	**181**	214	**1,361**
Net (decrease) increase in cash and cash equivalents	**(974)**	5,170	**(7,324)**
Cash and cash equivalents at beginning of year	**11,500**	6,330	**86,466**
Cash and cash equivalents at end of year	**¥10,526**	¥11,500	**$79,142**

See accompanying notes to consolidated financial statements.

Notes to Consolidated Financial Statements

ASICS Corporation and Consolidated Subsidiaries
March 31, 2002

1 BASIS OF PRESENTATION OF CONSOLIDATED FINANCIAL STATEMENTS

ASICS Corporation (the "Company") and its domestic consolidated subsidiaries maintain their books of account in conformity with financial accounting standards generally accepted and applied in Japan and its overseas subsidiaries in conformity with those of their countries of domicile.

The accompanying consolidated financial statements have been prepared in accordance with accounting principles and practices generally accepted and applied in Japan, which may differ in certain material respects from accounting principles and practices generally accepted in countries and jurisdictions other than Japan, and are compiled from the consolidated financial statements prepared by the Company as required by the Securities and Exchange Law of Japan. Certain modifications to the format have been made to facilitate understanding by readers outside Japan.

The U.S. dollar amounts in the accompanying consolidated financial statements have been translated from yen amounts solely for convenience and, as a matter of arithmetic computation only, at the rate of ¥133=US$1.00, the rate of exchange prevailing on March 31, 2002. This translation should not be construed as a representation that the yen amounts have been, could have been, or could in the future be, converted into U.S. dollars at the above or any other rate.

Certain reclassifications of previously reported amounts have been made to conform the consolidated statement of income for the year ended March 31, 2001 to the 2002 presentation. Such reclassification had no effect on net income and stockholders' equity.

2 SUMMARY OF SIGNIFICANT ACCOUNTING POLICIES

a. Principles of Consolidation

The accompanying consolidated financial statements include the accounts of the Company and its significant subsidiaries (the "Group"). All significant intercompany transactions and accounts have been eliminated in consolidation. Foreign consolidated subsidiaries are consolidated on the basis of fiscal years ending December 31, which differs from the balance sheet date of the Company. As a result, adjustments have been made for any significant intercompany transactions which took place during the period between the year-ends of these foreign consolidated subsidiaries and the year-end of the Company.

Up to the year ended March 31, 2001, investments in two affiliates including H.D.C. Corporation were accounted for by the equity method, under which the Group includes its share in the income or loss of this company in consolidated net income and records its investments at cost adjusted for its share of income or loss and dividends received.

Effective the year ended March 31, 2002, the equity method was not applied to H.D.C. Corporation due to the fact that the Company underwrote a loan guarantee for H.D.C. in the fiscal year under review, and it was judged providing an allowance for doubtful receivables for anticipated losses related to indemnity rights would be more appropriate to reflect actual status.

Other subsidiaries and affiliates are not significant in terms of their total assets, net income or loss and retained earnings or accumulated deficit. Accordingly, these other subsidiaries and affiliates are not consolidated or accounted for by the equity method. Investments in such subsidiaries and affiliates are stated at cost. The excess of cost over the underlying net assets at the respective dates of acquisition is, in general, amortized over a period of five years on a straight-line basis, except that immaterial amounts are charged to income as incurred.

b. Foreign Currency Translation

All monetary assets and liabilities denominated in foreign currencies are translated into yen at the rates of exchange in effect at the balance sheet date and gain or loss on each translation is credited or charged to income.

Revenue and expense items arising from transactions denominated in foreign currencies are generally translated into yen at the rates in effect at the respective transaction dates. Foreign exchange gain and loss are credited or charged to income in the period in which such gain or loss is recognized for financial reporting purposes.

The financial statements of the foreign subsidiaries are translated into yen at the rates of exchange in effect at the balance sheet date except that the components of stockholders' equity are translated at their historical exchange rates.

Effective April 1, 2000, the Company and its domestic consolidated subsidiaries adopted a revised accounting standard for foreign currency translation. The effect of the adoption of the revised standard on the consolidated financial statements was immaterial for the year ended March 31, 2001. Due to a change effective the year ended March 31, 2001 in the regulations relating to the presentation of translation adjustments, the Company has presented foreign currency translation adjustments as a component of stockholders' equity and minority interests in consolidated subsidiaries (instead of as a component of assets or liabilities) in its consolidated financial statements.

c. Cash and Cash Equivalents

For the purposes of the consolidated statements of cash flows, cash and cash equivalents consist of cash on hand, deposits with banks withdrawable on demand and short-term investments which are readily convertible to cash subject to an insignificant risk of any change in their value and which were purchased with an original maturity of three months or less.

d. Investments in Securities

Through March 31, 2000, securities listed on stock exchanges were principally stated at the lower of cost or market, cost being determined by the moving average method, except for securities held by certain consolidated subsidiaries and certain securities other than listed securities which were valued at cost.

Effective April 1, 2000, the Company and its domestic consolidated subsidiaries have adopted the "Accounting Standard for Financial Instruments" issued by the Business Accounting Deliberation Council of Japan. The new standard requires that securities be classified into three categories: trading securities, held-to-maturity debt securities and other securities.

Under the new standard, trading securities, consisting of debt and marketable equity securities, are stated at fair value. Gain and loss, both realized and unrealized, are charged to income. Held-to-maturity debt securities are stated at their amortized cost. Marketable securities classified as other securities are carried at fair value with changes in unrealized holding gain or loss, net of the applicable income taxes, reported as a separate component of stockholders' equity. Non-marketable securities classified as other securities are carried at cost determined by the moving average method.

As of April 1, 2000, the Company and its domestic consolidated subsidiaries assessed their intent to hold their securities included in short-term investments and investments in securities, classified their securities as "other securities" and accounted for these securities at March 31, 2001 in accordance with the new standard referred to above. As a result, short-term investments increased by ¥945 million and investments in securities and other assets decreased by ¥30 million and ¥915 million, respectively.

e. Inventories

Inventories are stated principally at cost determined by the first-in, first-out method.

f. Property, Plant and Equipment

Depreciation of property, plant and equipment is principally computed by the declining-balance method over the useful lives of the respective assets except that the straight-line method is applied to buildings (except for structures attached to the buildings) acquired subsequent to April 1, 1998. Significant renewals and additions are capitalized at cost. Maintenance and repairs are charged to income as incurred.

g. Allowance for Doubtful Receivables

Up to the year ended March 31, 2000, the Company and its domestic consolidated subsidiaries provided an allowance for doubtful receivables principally at an estimated aggregate amount of probable bad debts plus the maximum amount permitted to be charged to income under the Corporation Tax Law of Japan.

Effective April 1, 2000, the Company and its domestic consolidated subsidiaries have adopted a new accounting standard for financial instruments. Under the new accounting standard, the Company and its domestic consolidated subsidiaries have provided an allowance for doubtful receivables in an amount calculated based on their historical experience of bad debts on ordinary receivables plus an additional estimate of probable specific bad debts from customers experiencing financial difficulties.

h. Retirement Benefits

The Group has non-contributory defined benefit pension plans and retirement benefit plans.

Through March 31, 2000, accrued retirement benefits for employees were stated at the amount which would be required to be paid if all employees covered by the plans voluntarily terminated their employment with their respective company at the balance sheet date. However, a portion of the amount paid from the pension plan was excluded from the above calculation.

Effective April 1, 2000, the Company and its domestic consolidated subsidiaries have adopted the "Accounting Standard for Retirement Benefits" issued by the Business Accounting Deliberation Council of Japan. In accordance with this new standard, accrued retirement benefits have been provided based on the amount of the projected benefit obligation reduced by the pension plan assets at fair value as of March 31, 2001. The net retirement benefit obligation at transition of ¥4,748 million is being amortized by the straight-line method over 15 years.

Unrecognized past service cost is amortized principally by the straight-line method over five years, which is within the estimated average remaining years of service of the eligible employees.

Actuarial gain or loss is being amortized in the year following the year in which the gain or loss is recognized, principally by the straight-line method over 11 years, which is within the estimated average remaining years of service of the eligible employees.

The effect of the adoption of the new standard for retirement benefits was to increase loss before income taxes and minority interests for the year ended March 31, 2001 by ¥1,056 million over the amount which would have been recorded under the method applied in the previous year.

i. Leases

Noncancelable lease transactions are accounted for as operating leases whether such leases are classified as operating or finance leases, except that leases which stipulate the transfer of ownership of the leased property to the lessee are accounted for as finance leases.

j. Research and Development Costs and Computer Software

Research and development costs are charged to income as incurred. Expenditures relating to computer software developed for internal use are charged to income as incurred, except if these are deemed to contribute to the generation of future income or cost savings. Such expenditures are capitalized as assets and amortized by the straight-line method over the useful life of the software, generally a period of five years.

k. Income Taxes

Income taxes are calculated on taxable income and charged to income on an accrual basis. Certain temporary differences exist between taxable income and income reported for financial statement purposes, which enter into the determination of taxable income in a different period.

l. Derivatives and Hedging Activities

Derivative financial instruments are utilized by the Group principally in order to manage certain risks arising from adverse fluctuations in foreign currency exchange rates and interest rates. The Company has established a control environment which includes policies and procedures for risk assessment, including an assessment of the effectiveness of the hedging, and for the approval, reporting and monitoring of transactions involving derivatives. The Group does not hold or issue derivatives for speculative trading purposes.

The Group is exposed to certain market risks arising from their forward foreign exchange contracts and swap agreements. The Group is also exposed to the risk of credit loss in the event of nonperformance by the counterparties to the currency and interest-rate contracts; however, the Group does not anticipate nonperformance by any of these counterparties, all of whom are financial institutions with high credit ratings.

In accordance with a new accounting standard for financial instruments which became effective April 1, 2001, derivative positions are carried at fair value with any changes in unrealized gain or loss charged or credited to operations, except for those which meet the criteria for deferral hedge accounting under which unrealized gain or loss is deferred as an asset or a liability. Receivables and payables hedged by qualified forward foreign exchange contracts are translated at the corresponding foreign contract exchange rates.

3 INVESTMENTS IN SECURITIES

Information regarding other securities with market value at March 31, 2002 and 2001 is summarized as follows:

	Millions of yen						Thousands of U.S. dollars		
	2002			2001			**2002**		
	Acquisition costs	Carrying value	Unrealized gain (loss)	Acquisition costs	Carrying value	Unrealized gain (loss)	Acquisition costs	Carrying value	Unrealized gain (loss)
Securities whose carrying value exceeds their acquisition cost:									
Equity securities	**¥2,137**	**¥2,780**	**¥643**	¥2,413	¥4,069	¥1,656	**$16,068**	**$20,902**	**$4,835**
Others	**404**	**408**	**4**	10	10	0	**3,038**	**3,068**	**30**
Subtotal	**2,541**	**3,188**	**647**	2,423	4,079	1,656	**19,106**	**23,970**	**4,865**
Securities whose carrying value does not exceed their acquisition cost:									
Equity securities	**905**	**860**	**(45)**	1,071	985	(86)	**6,805**	**6,466**	**(338)**
Corporate bonds	**1,900**	**1,885**	**(45)**	—	—	—	**14,286**	**13,947**	**(338)**
Others	**226**	**197**	**(28)**	102	94	(8)	**1,699**	**1,481**	**(211)**
Subtotal	**3,031**	**2,912**	**(118)**	1,173	1,079	(94)	**22,790**	**21,894**	**(887)**
Total	**¥5,572**	**¥6,100**	**¥529**	¥3,596	¥5,158	¥1,562	**$41,896**	**$45,864**	**$3,978**

The carrying value of other securities without market value at March 31, 2002 and 2001 was as follows:

	Millions of yen		Thousands of U.S. dollars
	2002	2001	**2002**
Money trust in commingle funds	**¥ 901**	¥ 910	**$6,774**
Unlisted equity securities (except for equity securities traded on the OTC market)	**178**	178	**1,338**
Unlisted foreign debt securities	**71**	70	**534**
	¥1,150	¥1,158	**$8,646**

At March 31, 2002, the redemption schedule for other securities by maturity date was as follows:

	Millions of yen			Thousands of U.S. dollars		
	Due in one year or less	Due after one year through five years	Due after five years through ten years	Due in one year or less	Due after one year through five years	Due after five years through ten years
Corporate bonds	¥900	¥—	¥1,000	$6,767	$ —	$7,519
Beneficial securities of investment trust	—	75	10	—	564	75
	¥900	¥75	¥1,010	$6,767	$564	$7,594

4 INVENTORIES

The following is a summary of inventories at March 31, 2002 and 2001:

	Millions of yen		Thousands of U.S. dollars
	2002	2001	**2002**
Finished products	**¥24,471**	¥24,542	**$183,993**
Work in process	**444**	419	**3,338**
Raw materials and supplies	**1,683**	1,597	**12,654**
	¥26,598	¥26,558	**$199,985**

5 SHORT-TERM BANK LOANS AND LONG-TERM DEBT

The average annual interest rates on short-term bank loans were 3.2% and 6.5% for the years ended March 31, 2002 and 2001, respectively.

Long-term debt at March 31, 2002 and 2001 consisted of the following:

	Millions of yen		Thousands of U.S. dollars
	2002	2001	**2002**
2.56% yen secured bonds, due 2005	**¥ 3,000**	¥ 3,000	**$ 22,556**
2.74% yen secured bonds, due 2006	**2,000**	2,000	**15,038**
1.22% yen unsecured bonds, due 2008	**1,600**	1,600	**12,030**
1.12% yen unsecured bonds, due 2008	**800**	800	**6,015**
1.60% yen unsecured bonds, due 2008	**800**	800	**6,015**
Loans, primarily from banks, due 2003–2005, at interest rates ranging from 1.4% to 3.8%, secured	**310**	460	**2,331**
Loans, primarily from banks, due 2003–2007, at interest rates ranging from 1.0% to 4.9%, unsecured	**7,896**	6,529	**59,368**
	16,406	15,189	**123,353**
Current portion of long-term debt	**(3,246)**	(2,467)	**(24,406)**
	¥13,160	¥12,722	**$ 98,947**

The aggregate annual maturities of long-term debt subsequent to March 31, 2002 are summarized as follows:

	Millions of yen	Thousands of U.S. dollars
Years ending March 31:		
2003	¥ 3,246	$ 24,406
2004	2,961	22,263
2005	1,704	12,812
2006	3,235	24,323
2007	2,060	15,489
2008 and thereafter	3,200	24,060
	¥16,406	$123,353

Assets pledged at March 31, 2002 as collateral for short-term bank loans of ¥150 million (US$1,128 thousand), bonds of ¥5,000 million (US$37,594 thousand) and long-term loans of ¥160 million (US$1,203 thousand) are summarized as follows:

	Millions of yen	Thousands of U.S. dollars
Land	¥4,070	$30,602
Buildings and structures, at book value	3,316	24,932
	¥7,386	$55,534

6 ACCRUED RETIREMENT BENEFITS

The following table sets forth the funded and accrued status of the Group's defined benefit plan at March 31, 2002 and 2001:

	Millions of yen		Thousands of U.S. dollars
	2002	2001	**2002**
Retirement benefit obligation	**¥(20,604)**	¥(18,814)	**$(154,917)**
Plan assets at fair value	**7,749**	7,739	**58,263**
Unfunded retirement benefit obligation	**(12,855)**	(11,075)	**(96,654)**
Unrecognized net retirement benefit at transition	**4,115**	4,432	**30,940**
Unrecognized actuarial loss	**3,445**	1,722	**25,902**
Unrecognized past service cost	**(692)**	—	**(5,203)**
Accrued retirement benefits	**¥ (5,987)**	¥ (4,921)	**$ (45,015)**

The components of retirement benefit expenses for the years ended March 31, 2002 and 2001 are outlined as follows:

	Millions of yen		U.S. dollars
	2002	2001	**2002**
Service cost	**¥1,149**	¥1,103	**$ 8,639**
Interest cost	**555**	496	**4,173**
Expected return on plan assets	**(238)**	(258)	**(1,789)**
Amortization of net retirement benefit obligation at transition	**223**	223	**1,677**
Recognized net actuarial loss	**157**	—	**1,180**
Retirement benefit expenses	**¥1,846**	¥1,564	**$13,880**

The retirement benefit expenses of its consolidated subsidiaries calculated by the simplified method have been included in service cost in the above table.

Assumptions used in accounting for the retirement benefit plans for the years ended March 31, 2002 and 2001 were as follows:

	2002	2001
Discount rate	**3.0%**	3.5%
Expected rate of return on plan assets	**3.5%**	3.5%

7 CONTINGENT LIABILITIES

Contingent liabilities at March 31, 2002 and 2001 were as follows:

	Millions of yen		Thousands of U.S. dollars
	2002	2001	**2002**
Trade notes receivable discounted	**¥1,764**	¥2,149	**$13,263**
Guarantees of bank loans of an unconsolidated subsidiary	**—**	33	**—**

8 LEASES

The Group leases machinery and equipment and other assets. The following pro forma amounts represent the acquisition costs (including the interest portion), accumulated depreciation and net book value of the leased assets as of March 31, 2002 and 2001, which would have been reflected in the balance sheets if finance lease accounting had been applied to the finance leases currently accounted for as operating leases.

	Millions of yen						Thousands of U.S. dollars		
	2002			2001			**2002**		
	Machinery and equipment	Other	Total	Machinery and equipment	Other	Total	Machinery and equipment	Other	Total
Acquisition costs	**¥2,218**	**¥29**	**¥2,247**	¥2,400	¥60	¥2,460	**$16,677**	**$218**	**$16,895**
Accumulated depreciation	**(1,180)**	**(23)**	**(1,203)**	(1,291)	(44)	(1,335)	**(8,872)**	**(173)**	**(9,045)**
Net book value	**¥1,038**	**¥ 6**	**¥1,044**	¥1,109	¥16	¥1,125	**$ 7,805**	**$ 45**	**$ 7,850**

Lease payments relating to finance leases accounted for as operating leases amounted to ¥545 million (US$4,098 thousand) and ¥563 million for the years ended March 31, 2002 and 2001, respectively. These accounts were equal to the depreciation expenses of the leased assets computed by the straight-line method over the respective lease terms.

Future minimum payments (including the interest portion thereon) subsequent to March 31, 2002 under finance leases other than those which transfer the ownership of the leased property to the Group are summarized as follows:

	Millions of yen	Thousands of U.S. dollars
Due within one year	¥ 449	$3,376
Due after one year	595	4,474
Total	¥1,044	$7,850

9 DERIVATIVES AND HEDGING ACTIVITIES

The outstanding interest rate swaps at March 31, 2002 and 2001 were as follows:

	Millions of yen				Thousands of U.S. dollars	
	2002		2001		2002	
	Notional amount	Unrealized loss	Notional amount	Unrealized loss	Notional amount	Unrealized loss
Interest rate swaps:						
Variable-rate into fixed-rate obligations	**¥1,850**	**¥19**	¥1,950	¥(16)	**$13,910**	**$143**
Variable-rate into variable-rate obligations	**390**	**2**	700	(6)	**2,932**	**15**

The outstanding interest rate options at March 31, 2002 and 2001 were as follows:

	Millions of yen				Thousands of U.S. dollars	
	2002		2001		2002	
	Notional amount	Unrealized gain (loss)	Notional amount	Unrealized gain (loss)	Notional amount	Unrealized gain (loss)
Interest rate options:						
Interest rate caps purchased	**¥1,155**	**¥ 0**	¥1,630	¥ 0	**$8,684**	**$ 0**
Interest rate caps sold	**750**	**(1)**	800	(5)	**5,639**	**(6)**
Interest rate floors sold	**1,155**	**(17)**	1,580	(28)	**8,684**	**(128)**
Interest rate caps purchased/interest rate floors sold	**180**	**(3)**	240	(4)	**1,353**	**(23)**

10 RESEARCH AND DEVELOPMENT COSTS

Research and development costs included in selling, general and administrative expenses for the years ended March 31, 2002 and 2001 were ¥387 million ($2,910 thousand) and ¥394 million, respectively.

11 INCOME TAXES

Income taxes applicable to the Company and its domestic consolidated subsidiaries consist of corporation, inhabitants' and enterprise taxes. The statutory tax rate in Japan for the years ended March 31, 2002 and 2001 was, in the aggregate, approximately 41.7%.

The effective tax rates reflected in the consolidated statements of income for the years ended March 31, 2002 and 2001 differ from the above statutory tax rate for the following reasons:

	2002	2001
Statutory tax rate:	**41.7%**	41.7%
Permanently nondeductible expenses	**2.8**	4.1
Permanently nontaxable dividends received	**(1.9)**	(2.8)
Inhabitants' per capita taxes	**1.5**	2.1
Foreign tax credits	**3.3**	4.1
Utilization of tax loss carryforwards	**(30.8)**	(85.3)
Change in valuation allowance	**(3.4)**	27.0
Tax losses of consolidated subsidiaries	**10.5**	15.4
Dividends received from consolidated subsidiaries	**2.1**	9.7
Equity in earnings of affiliates	**(1.3)**	(4.0)
Other	**(2.1)**	(0.5)
Effective tax rate	**22.4%**	11.5%

Deferred income taxes reflect the net tax effect of the temporary differences between the carrying amounts of the assets and liabilities for financial reporting purposes and the corresponding amounts for income tax purposes. The significant components of the Group's deferred tax assets and liabilities at March 31, 2002 and 2001 are summarized as follows:

	Millions of yen		Thousands of U.S. dollars
	2002	2001	**2002**
Deferred tax assets:			
Allowance for doubtful receivables	**¥ 1,439**	¥ 1,633	**$10,820**
Accrued retirement benefits	**1,758**	1,270	**13,218**
Tax loss carryforwards	**7,175**	9,925	**53,947**
Other	**1,595**	1,344	**11,992**
Gross deferred tax assets	**11,967**	14,172	**89,977**
Less valuation allowance	**(10,669)**	(13,018)	**(80,218)**
Total deferred tax assets	**1,298**	1,154	**9,759**
Deferred tax liabilities:			
Unrealized holding gain on securities	**268**	667	**2,015**
Total deferred tax liabilities	**268**	667	**2,015**
Net deferred tax assets	**¥ 1,030**	¥ 487	**$ 7,744**

In assessing the deferred tax assets, management of the Company considers whether it is more likely than not that some portion or all of the deferred tax assets will not be realized. The ultimate realization of deferred tax assets is entirely dependent upon the generation of future taxable income in specific tax jurisdiction during the periods in which those temporary differences become deductible. Although realization is not assured, management considered the projected future taxable income in making this assessment. Based on these factors, management believes it is more likely than not that the Company will realize the benefits of these deductible differences, net of the existing valuation allowance at March 31, 2002.

12 LAND REVALUATION

At March 31, 2002, ASICS Trading Co., Ltd., an affiliate of the Company, revalued its land held for business use.

The differences on the land revaluation have been accounted for as land revaluation reserve under stockholders' equity at ¥398 million (US$2,992 thousand), the Company's share in this affiliate.

13 AMOUNTS PER SHARE

The computation of basic net income per share is based on the weighted average number of shares of common stock outstanding during each year.

Net assets per share are based on the number of shares of common stock outstanding at the year-end.

	Millions of yen		Thousands of U.S. dollars
	2002	2001	**2002**
Net income	**¥212.74**	¥205.01	**$1.60**
Net assets	**9.92**	8.13	**0.07**

14 SEGMENT INFORMATION

(1) Industry Segments

The Group is primarily engaged in the manufacture and sale of sports products in Japan and overseas. As most of consolidated net sales were related to sports and leisure products, the disclosure of business segment information has been omitted.

(2) Geographic Segments

The domestic and foreign operations of the Group for the years ended March 31, 2002 and 2001 are summarized as follows:

	Millions of yen						
2002	Japan	United States of America	Europe	Other areas	Total	Eliminations/ corporate	Consolidated
Net sales:							
Sales to customers	**¥81,373**	**¥20,798**	**¥24,529**	**¥2,201**	**¥128,901**	**¥ —**	**¥128,901**
Intersegment	**2,108**	**14**	**7**	**2,268**	**4,397**	**(4,397)**	**—**
Total sales	**83,481**	**20,812**	**24,536**	**4,469**	**133,298**	**(4,397)**	**128,901**
Operating expenses	**82,065**	**19,672**	**23,666**	**4,275**	**129,678**	**(4,260)**	**125,418**
Operating income	**¥ 1,416**	**¥ 1,140**	**¥ 870**	**¥ 194**	**¥ 3,620**	**¥ (137)**	**¥ 3,483**
Assets	**¥86,446**	**¥ 9,803**	**¥17,862**	**¥2,918**	**¥117,029**	**¥(2,288)**	**¥114,741**

	Millions of yen						
2001	Japan	United States of America	Europe	Other areas	Total	Eliminations/ corporate	Consolidated
Net sales:							
Sales to customers	¥84,917	¥18,226	¥21,145	¥2,158	¥126,446	¥ —	¥126,446
Intersegment	1,827	5	21	1,976	3,829	(3,829)	—
Total sales	86,744	18,231	21,166	4,134	130,275	(3,829)	126,446
Operating expenses	85,271	17,256	20,771	3,929	127,227	(3,873)	123,354
Operating income	¥ 1,473	¥ 975	¥ 395	¥ 205	¥ 3,048	¥ 44	¥ 3,092
Assets	¥89,625	¥ 8,823	¥15,564	¥2,575	¥116,587	¥(2,673)	¥113,914

	Thousands of U.S. dollars						
2002	Japan	United States of America	Europe	Other areas	Total	Eliminations/ corporate	Consolidated
Net sales:							
Sales to customers	**$611,827**	**$156,376**	**$184,428**	**$16,549**	**$ 969,180**	**$ —**	**$969,180**
Intersegment	**15,849**	**105**	**53**	**17,053**	**33,060**	**(33,060)**	**—**
Total sales	**627,676**	**156,481**	**184,481**	**33,602**	**1,002,240**	**(33,060)**	**969,180**
Operating expenses	**617,029**	**147,910**	**177,940**	**32,143**	**975,022**	**(32,030)**	**942,992**
Operating income	**$ 10,647**	**$ 8,571**	**$ 6,541**	**$ 1,459**	**$ 27,218**	**$ (1,030)**	**$ 26,188**
Assets	**$649,970**	**$ 73,707**	**$134,300**	**$21,940**	**$ 879,917**	**$(17,203)**	**$862,714**

(3) Overseas Sales

Overseas sales, which include export sales of the Company and its domestic consolidated subsidiaries and sales (other than exports to Japan) of the foreign consolidated subsidiaries, for the years ended March 31, 2002 and 2001 are summarized as follows:

	Millions of yen		Thousands of U.S. dollars
	2002	2001	**2002**
Overseas sales:			
North America	**¥ 20,810**	¥ 18,244	**$156,466**
Europe	**24,383**	21,020	**183,331**
Other areas	**3,270**	3,045	**24,586**
Total	**¥ 48,463**	¥ 42,309	**$364,383**
Consolidated net sales	**¥128,901**	¥126,446	**$969,180**
Overseas sales as a percentage of consolidated sales:			
North America	**16.2%**	14.5%	
Europe	**18.9**	16.6	
Other areas	**2.5**	2.4	
Total	**37.6%**	33.5%	

Independent Auditor's Report

The Board of Directors and Stockholders
ASICS Corporation:

We have audited the consolidated balance sheets of ASICS Corporation and consolidated subsidiaries as of March 31, 2002 and 2001, and the related consolidated statements of income, stockholders' equity and cash flows for the years then ended, all expressed in yen. Our audits were made in accordance with auditing standards, procedures and practices generally accepted and applied in Japan and, accordingly, included such tests of the accounting records and such other auditing procedures as we considered necessary in the circumstances.

In our opinion, the accompanying consolidated financial statements, expressed in yen, present fairly the financial position of ASICS Corporation and consolidated subsidiaries at March 31, 2002 and 2001, and the results of their operations and their cash flows for the years then ended, in conformity with accounting principles and practices generally accepted in Japan applied on a consistent basis.

As described in Note 2, ASICS Corporation and consolidated subsidiaries have adopted new accounting standards for foreign currency translation, financial instruments, and retirement benefits effective April 1, 2000, in the preparation of their consolidated financial statements.

The U.S. dollar amounts in the accompanying consolidated financial statements with respect to the year ended March 31, 2002 are presented solely for convenience. Our audit also included the translation of yen amounts into U.S. dollar amounts and, in our opinion, such translation has been made on the basis described in Note 1.

Shin Nihon & Co.

Osaka, Japan
June 27, 2002

See Note 2 (a) which explains the basis of preparation of the consolidated financial statements of ASICS Corporation under Japanese accounting principles and practices.

Nike—Basic Ratio Analysis

Nike, Inc. designs, develops, and markets, both domestically and internationally, a wide variety of athletic and leisure footwear and apparel for competitive and recreational uses. Nike is based in Beaverton, Oregon.

Learning Objectives

- Become familiar with basic financial analysis of the return on equity.
- Compare ROE components over time.
- Interpret basic solvency and profitability ratios and subcomponents of the DuPont model.

Refer to the 2002 Consolidated Financial Statements of Nike, Inc.

Concepts

A company's financial statements can be analyzed in many ways. Return on equity (ROE) is a widely-used measure of profitability that compares the profit the company made during the period (net income) to the resources invested in the company (shareholders' equity). The DuPont model systematically breaks ROE into components. One form of the model is:

$$\text{ROE} = \frac{\text{NI}}{\text{EBT}} \times \frac{\text{EBT}}{\text{EBIT}} \times \frac{\text{EBIT}}{\text{Sales}} \times \frac{\text{Sales}}{\text{Total Assets}} \times \frac{\text{Total Assets}}{\text{Common Equity}}$$

where NI is net income, EBT is earnings before tax, and EBIT is earnings before interest and tax.

- NI / EBT measures the proportion of earnings before tax that is kept by the company.
- EBT / EBIT measures the effect of interest; it indicates the proportion of earnings before interest and tax that is retained after paying interest. It should be considered together with the leverage component (Total Assets / Common Equity). Further analysis of this component includes average interest rates on debt (and on investments if interest expense is reported net of interest income).
- EBIT / Sales measures the company's operating return on sales; it can be broken down into further subcomponents such as the gross margin percent. Preparing common-size income statements will help you analyze this component. This component and the next form the 'guts' of the model—did the managers operate the firm profitably?
- Sales / Total Assets measures asset utilization; it can be broken down into further subcomponents such as accounts receivable turnover, inventory turnover, and plant asset turnover. This is another key component—did the managers use the assets efficiently?
- Total Assets / Common Equity measures the effect of leverage on ROE. Note that this ratio equals 1 + the debt-equity ratio (i.e., Total Liabilities / Total Common Equity). Subcomponents include the current and quick ratios. Together with the interest component of ROE, you can look at times interest earned and other fixed charge ratios.

Note that once the common terms cancel ROE is Net Income divided by the firm's Common Equity (the book value of what the shareholders have invested and reinvested in the firm). ROE, its components, and further subcomponents can be compared across time, firms, and to expectations, making it a very powerful tool.

✧ Analysis ✧

a. Using the information in Nike's 2002 financial statements, compute the following:

   i. Nike's return on equity in 2002 and 2001 (use the DuPont model to calculate the components of ROE). Comment on any major changes.

   ii. Common-size income statements for 2000-2002 and common-size balance sheets for 2002 and 2001. Common-size income statements scale each income statement line item by *net* sales. Common-size balance sheets are created by dividing each figure on a given year's balance sheet by that year's total assets, thereby creating a balance sheet on a 'percent of assets' basis.

   iii. Return on assets for fiscal 2002 and 2001. Return on assets is defined as: $\frac{\text{Net Income} + \text{Interest Expense (1 - tax rate)}}{\text{Total Assets}}$. You can estimate the tax rate by dividing "income taxes" on the income statement by "income before taxes and cumulative effect of accounting change."

   iv. Current ratio at May 31, 2002 and 2001. Current ratio is defined as: $\frac{\text{Current Assets}}{\text{Current Liabilities}}$.

   v. Working capital at May 31, 2002 and 2001. Working capital is defined as: *current assets less current liabilities*.

b. Did Nike earn more or less income between 2000 and 2002? Use the common-size income statements to determine the major reasons for the change.

c. Evaluate the trend in Nike's profitability over the three years. (*Hint*: Simply comparing net income year to year ignores the changing level of assets or shareholders' equity used to generate the income. To determine whether Nike's profitability changed, assess whether Nike's return on assets and ROE increased or decreased.)

d. How much cash did Nike have at May 31, 2002?

e. Was Nike in a position to pay its short-term obligations at May 31, 2002? What was Nike's current ratio at May 31, 2002? Did Nike have positive working capital? Use the common-size balance sheets to explore major changes between fiscal 2001 and fiscal 2002.

f. Were Nike's operations a source or a use of cash in fiscal 2002?

g. What were Nike's major sources and uses of cash in fiscal 2002?

NIKE, INC.
CONSOLIDATED STATEMENTS OF INCOME

	Year Ended May 31,		
	2002	2001	2000
	(In millions, except per share data)		
Revenues	$9,893.0	$9,488.8	$8,995.1
Costs and expenses:			
Cost of sales	6,004.7	5,784.9	5,403.8
Selling and administrative	2,820.4	2,689.7	2,606.4
Interest expense (Notes 4 and 5)	47.6	58.7	45.0
Other income/expense, net (Notes 1, 10 and 11)	3.0	34.1	20.7
Total costs and expenses	8,875.7	8,567.4	8,075.9
Income before income taxes and cumulative effect accounting change	1,017.3	921.4	919.2
Income taxes (Note 6)	349.0	331.7	340.1
Income before cumulative effect of accounting change	668.3	589.7	579.1
Cumulative effect of accounting change, net of income taxes of $3.0 (Note 1)	5.0	—	—
Net income	$ 663.3	$ 589.7	$ 579.1
Basic earnings per common share — before accounting change (Notes 1 and 9)	$ 2.50	$ 2.18	$ 2.10
Cumulative effect of accounting change	0.02	—	—
	$ 2.48	$ 2.18	$ 2.10
Diluted earnings per common share — before accounting change (Notes 1 and 9)	$ 2.46	$ 2.16	$ 2.07
Cumulative effect of accounting change	0.02	—	—
	$ 2.44	$ 2.16	$ 2.07

The accompanying notes to consolidated financial statements are an integral part of this statement.

NIKE, INC.

CONSOLIDATED BALANCE SHEETS

	May 31, 2002	May 31, 2001
	(In millions)	
ASSETS		
Current Assets:		
Cash and equivalents	$ 575.5	$ 304.0
Accounts receivable, less allowance for doubtful accounts of $77.4 and $72.1	1,807.1	1,621.4
Inventories (Note 2)	1,373.8	1,424.1
Deferred income taxes (Notes 1 and 6)	140.8	113.3
Prepaid expenses and other current assets (Note 1)	260.5	162.5
Total current assets	4,157.7	3,625.3
Property, plant and equipment, net (Note 3)	1,614.5	1,618.8
Identifiable intangible assets and goodwill, net (Note 1)	437.8	397.3
Deferred income taxes and other assets (Notes 1 and 6)	233.0	178.2
Total assets	$6,443.0	$5,819.6
LIABILITIES AND SHAREHOLDERS' EQUITY		
Current Liabilities:		
Current portion of long-term debt (Note 5)	$ 55.3	$ 5.4
Notes payable (Note 4)	425.2	855.3
Accounts payable (Note 4)	504.4	432.0
Accrued liabilities (Note 15)	768.3	472.1
Income taxes payable	83.0	21.9
Total current liabilities	1,836.2	1,786.7
Long-term debt (Notes 5 and 14)	625.9	435.9
Deferred income taxes and other liabilities (Notes 1 and 6)	141.6	102.2
Commitments and contingencies (Notes 13 and 15)	—	—
Redeemable Preferred Stock (Note 7)	0.3	0.3
Shareholders' Equity:		
Common Stock at stated value (Note 8):		
Class A convertible — 98.1 and 99.1 shares outstanding	0.2	0.2
Class B — 168.0 and 169.5 shares outstanding	2.6	2.6
Capital in excess of stated value	538.7	459.4
Unearned stock compensation	(5.1)	(9.9)
Accumulated other comprehensive loss	(192.4)	(152.1)
Retained earnings	3,495.0	3,194.3
Total shareholders' equity	3,839.0	3,494.5
Total liabilities and shareholders' equity	$6,443.0	$5,819.6

The accompanying notes to consolidated financial statements are an integral part of this statement.

NIKE, INC.

CONSOLIDATED STATEMENTS OF CASH FLOWS

	Year Ended May 31,		
	2002	2001	2000
		(In millions)	
Cash provided (used) by operations:			
Net income	$ 663.3	$ 589.7	$ 579.1
Income charges not affecting cash:			
Depreciation	223.5	197.4	188.0
Deferred income taxes	15.2	79.8	36.8
Amortization and other	53.1	16.7	35.6
Income tax benefit from exercise of stock options	13.9	32.4	14.9
Changes in certain working capital components:			
Increase in accounts receivable	(135.2)	(141.4)	(82.6)
Decrease (increase) in inventories	55.4	(16.7)	(311.8)
Decrease in other current assets and income taxes receivable	16.9	78.0	61.2
Increase (decrease) in accounts payable, accrued liabilities and income taxes payable	175.4	(179.4)	178.4
Cash provided by operations	1,081.5	656.5	699.6
Cash provided (used) by investing activities:			
Additions to property, plant and equipment and other	(282.8)	(317.6)	(419.9)
Disposals of property, plant and equipment	15.6	12.7	25.3
Increase in other assets	(39.1)	(42.5)	(51.3)
Increase in other liabilities	3.5	5.1	5.9
Cash used by investing activities	(302.8)	(342.3)	(440.0)
Cash provided (used) by financing activities:			
Proceeds from long-term debt issuance	329.9	—	—
Reductions in long-term debt including current portion	(80.3)	(50.3)	(1.7)
(Decrease) increase in notes payable	(431.5)	(68.9)	505.1
Proceeds from exercise of stock options and other stock issuances	59.5	56.0	23.9
Repurchase of stock	(226.9)	(157.0)	(646.3)
Dividends — common and preferred	(128.9)	(129.7)	(133.1)
Cash used by financing activities	(478.2)	(349.9)	(252.1)
Effect of exchange rate changes	(29.0)	85.4	48.7
Net increase in cash and equivalents	271.5	49.7	56.2
Cash and equivalents, beginning of year	304.0	254.3	198.1
Cash and equivalents, end of year	$ 575.5	$ 304.0	$ 254.3
Supplemental disclosure of cash flow information:			
Cash paid during the year for:			
Interest	$ 54.2	$ 68.5	$ 45.0
Income taxes	262.0	173.1	221.1
Non-cash investing and financing activity:			
Assumption of long-term debt to acquire property, plant and equipment	—	—	$ 108.9

The accompanying notes to consolidated financial statements are an integral part of this statement.

NIKE, INC.

CONSOLIDATED STATEMENTS OF SHAREHOLDERS' EQUITY

	Common Stock				Capital in Excess of Stated Value	Unearned Stock Compensation	Accumulated Other Comprehensive Loss	Retained Earnings	Total
	Class A		Class B						
	Shares	Amount	Shares	Amount					
	(In millions, except per share data)								
Balance at May 31, 1999	100.7	0.2	181.6	2.7	334.1	—	(68.9)	3,066.5	3,334.6
Stock options exercised			1.3		38.7				38.7
Conversion to Class B Common Stock	(1.5)		1.5						
Repurchase of Class B Common Stock			(14.5)	(0.1)	(17.3)			(627.1)	(644.5)
Dividends on Common stock ($.48 per share)								(131.5)	(131.5)
Issuance of shares to employees			0.5		13.5	(13.5)			—
Amortization of unearned compensation						1.8			1.8
Comprehensive income:									
Net income								579.1	579.1
Foreign currency translation (net of tax expense of $1.2)							(42.2)		(42.2)
Comprehensive income							(42.2)	579.1	536.9
Balance at May 31, 2000	99.2	0.2	170.4	2.6	369.0	(11.7)	(111.1)	2,887.0	3,136.0
Stock options exercised			2.9		91.0				91.0
Conversion to Class B Common Stock	(0.1)		0.1						—
Repurchase of Class B Common Stock			(4.0)		(4.8)			(152.2)	(157.0)
Dividends on Common stock ($.48 per share)								(129.6)	(129.6)
Issuance of shares to employees			0.1		6.7	(6.7)			—
Amortization of unearned compensation						7.3			7.3
Forfeiture of shares from employees					(2.5)	1.2		(0.6)	(1.9)
Comprehensive income:									
Net income								589.7	589.7
Foreign currency translation and other (net of tax benefit of $2.4)							(41.0)		(41.0)
Comprehensive income							(41.0)	589.7	548.7
Balance at May 31, 2001	99.1	$0.2	169.5	$ 2.6	$459.4	$ (9.9)	$(152.1)	$3,194.3	3,494.5
Stock options exercised			1.7		72.9				72.9
Conversion to Class B Common Stock	(1.0)		1.0						
Repurchase of Class B Common Stock			(4.3)		(5.2)			(232.5)	(237.7)
Dividends on Common stock ($.48 per share)								(128.6)	(128.6)
Issuance of shares to employees and others			0.2		13.2	(1.9)			11.3
Amortization of unearned compensation						6.5			6.5
Forfeiture of shares from employees			(0.1)		(1.6)	0.2		(1.5)	(2.9)
Comprehensive income (Note 12):									
Net income								663.3	663.3
Other comprehensive income (net of tax benefit of $17.4):									
Foreign currency translation							(1.5)		(1.5)
Cumulative effect of change in accounting principle (Note 1)							56.8		56.8
Adjustment for fair value of hedge derivatives							(95.6)		(95.6)
Comprehensive income							(40.3)	663.3	623.0
Balance at May 31, 2002	98.1	$0.2	168.0	$ 2.6	$538.7	$ (5.1)	$(192.4)	$3,495.0	$3,839.0

The accompanying notes to consolidated financial statements are an integral part of this statement.

Club Méditerranée S. A.—International GAAP

Club Méditerranée S. A. is a French business corporation established in 1957. It fully develops and manages holiday centers and the centers' activities. More generally, this consists of all industrial, commercial, and financial operations involving both stocks in the centers and shares of real estate.

Learning Objectives

- Read a set of foreign financial statements.
- Observe the differences between French and U.S. GAAP.
- Restate foreign financial statements to U.S. presentation format.
- Evaluate liquidity and solvency using simple ratios.

Refer to the 2001 financial statements of Club Méditerranée S. A. (Club Med).

✧ Concepts ✧

a. The balance sheet of Club Med is presented in a format that differs from that of U.S. companies.

   i. What notable differences exist with respect to the ordering of the assets and liabilities?

   ii. What differences are there with respect to the columns of data presented?

   iii. What other differences do you note?

   iv. Prepare the 2001 balance sheet for Club Med in accordance with U.S. GAAP presentation. Leave the amounts in euros. (*Hint*: Notes 2-15 and 2-16 provide useful information.)

b. The income statement for Club Med also differs from U.S. GAAP income statements.

   i. List some of the notable differences.

   ii. Which of Club Med's accounting principles would you be interested in reading about before you relied on their income statement?

✧ Analysis ✧

c. Based on your answer to part *a*, calculate the October 31, 2001 working capital balance and the current ratio for Club Med. Was the company in a position to pay its short-term obligations at October 31, 2001? Explain.

   Working capital is defined as: *current assets less current liabilities*.

   Current ratio is defined as: $\frac{\text{Current Assets}}{\text{Current Liabilities}}$.

Consolidated Balance Sheet at October 31

millions of euros

ASSETS	Note	Oct. 31, 2001	Oct. 31, 2000	Oct. 31, 1999
Intangible assets		**245**	**195**	**173**
Goodwill	2.1	115	101	100
Other	2.2	130	94	73
Tangible assets		**1,017**	**1,156**	**926**
Land	2.3	118	156	137
Property and equipment	2.3	715	777	646
Other	2.3	184	223	143
Financial assets	2.4	**92**	**86**	**95**
Investments in companies accounted for by the equity method	2.5	10	13	33
Other investments, loans and advances	2.6	9	9	15
Deposits	2.7	62	50	35
Other (loans)	2.7	11	14	12
TOTAL FIXED ASSETS		1,354	1,437	1,194
Inventories	2.8	31	32	27
Trade receivables	2.9	58	85	52
Other receivables	2.9	158	208	104
Marketable securities	2.10	18	11	12
Bank and cash	2.10	108	111	90
TOTAL CURRENT ASSETS		373	447	286
Deferred taxes	2.11	49	2	1
Prepaid expenses and deferred charges	2.17	54	70	48
TOTAL ASSETS		1,830	1,956	1,529

millions of euros

LIABILITIES AND SHAREHOLDERS' EQUITY	Note	Oct. 31, 2001	Oct. 31, 2000	Oct. 31, 1999
Common stock		77	68	59
Additional paid-in capital		562	462	434
Reserves		171	268	5
Group net (loss) income		(70)	59	38
Shareholders' equity	2.12	**740**	**857**	**536**
Minority interests	2.13	**14**	**27**	**16**
Provisions for contingencies and charges		**186**	**117**	**143**
Deferred taxes	2.11	40	0	0
Other provisions for contingencies and charges	2.14	146	117	143
Bonds	2.15	129	129	288
Bank loans and other debt	2.15	393	416	206
Trade payables		120	116	101
Amounts received for future vacations		79	133	128
Other liabilities	2.16	125	146	92
Total debt		**846**	**940**	**815**
Accrued expenses and deferred income	2.17	44	15	19
TOTAL LIABILITIES AND SHAREHOLDERS' EQUITY		1,830	1,956	1,529

Consolidated Statement of Operations, *years ended October 31*

millions of euros

	Note	2001	2000	1999
Revenues	3.1	**1,985**	**1,889**	**1,478**
Other operating income	3.2	37	56	25
Total revenues		**2,022**	**1,945**	**1,503**
Purchases		(922)	(898)	(658)
External services	3.3	(530)	(471)	(400)
Payroll expenses		(390)	(356)	(298)
Other operating expenses		(46)	(50)	(39)
Depreciation and amortization		(88)	(82)	(67)
Provisions (net)		4	15	30
Operating expense		**(1,972)**	**(1,842)**	**(1,432)**
Operating income		**50**	**103**	**71**
Net financial expense	3.4	**(33)**	**(13)**	**(17)**
Income from continuing operations, before tax		**17**	**90**	**54**
Net income (loss) from equity companies	3.5	0	2	(2)
Income before tax, exceptional items and amortization of goodwill		**17**	**92**	**52**
Net exceptional expense	3.6	(71)	(14)	(2)
Income tax	3.7	(6)	(10)	(5)
Amortization of goodwill	3.8	(8)	(7)	(6)
Net (loss) income before minority interests		**(68)**	**61**	**39**
Minority interests	3.9	(2)	(2)	0
Group net (loss) income		**(70)**	**59**	**39**

	Note	2001	2000	1999
Net (loss) income per share – primary (in euros)	3.10	**(3.74)**	**3.44**	**2.50**
Net (loss) income per share – diluted (in euros)	3.10	**(3.74)**	**3.34**	**2.68**

Consolidated Statement of Cash Flows, years ended October 31

millions of euros

	Note	2001	2000	1999
Cash flows from operations				
Net (loss) income before minority interests		(68)	60	39
Depreciation, amortization and provisions for impairment in value	4.1	110	87	76
Net (gain) loss on sales of assets	4.2	(19)	(24)	(4)
Other	4.3	(6)	(7)	2
CASH FLOW		**17**	**116**	**113**
Change in working capital requirement [1]		52	(138)	(31)
NET CASH PROVIDED (USED) BY OPERATING ACTIVITIES		**69**	**(22)**	**82**
Capital expenditure	4.4			
Acquisition of intangible assets		(23)	(29)	(16)
Acquisition of tangible assets		(133)	(254)	(164)
Acquisition of financial assets		(59)	(35)	(85)
Cash acquired		(24)	0	21
Total investments		(239)	(318)	(243)
Cash flows from asset disposals	4.5			
Proceeds from disposals of fixed assets		106	117	21
Proceeds from disposals of financial assets		12	9	0
Total asset disposals		**118**	**126**	**21**
NET CASH USED BY INVESTING ACTIVITIES		**(121)**	**(192)**	**(222)**
NET CASH USED, BEFORE FINANCING ACTIVITIES		**(52)**	**(214)**	**(141)**
Cash flows from financing activities				
Capital increases		106	188	22
Dividends paid		(25)	(10)	0
NET CASH PROVIDED BY FINANCING ACTIVITIES		**81**	**178**	**22**
Impact of change in exchange rates		(2)	0	(4)
Impact of changes in scope of consolidation on net indebtedness	4.6	0	5	0
DECREASE (INCREASE) IN NET INDEBTEDNESS		**27**	**(31)**	**(123)**
Net indebtedness at beginning of year		(423)	(392)	(269)
Net indebtedness at end of year		(396)	(423)	(392)

(1) Including increase (decrease) in short-term provisions for contingencies and charges, treated as accrued expenses.

2-15 Bonds, bank loans and other debt

These items can be analyzed as follows:

millions of euros

	Oct. 31, 2001	Oct. 31, 2000
Bonds with equity warrants	**129**	**129**
Bank loans and debts		
Short-term bank loans and overdrafts	114	243
Current maturities of long-term debt	43	27
Long-term debt	236	146
Total bank loans and debts	**393**	**416**
Total	**522**	**545**

2-15-1 Analysis of debt by category

millions of euros

	Oct. 31, 2001	Oct. 31, 2000
Bonds	**129**	129
Obligations under capital leases	**79**	91
Bank borrowings	**184**	56
Other borrowings, deposits received and accrued interest	**16**	26
Bank overdrafts	**114**	243
Total	**522**	**545**

2-15-2 Analysis of debt by maturity

millions of euros

	Oct. 31, 2001	Oct. 31, 2000
Less than one year (including bank overdrafts)	**161**	**170**
Beyond one year		
2001-2002	-	47
2002-2003	146	151
2003-2004	18	18
2004-2005 (1)	156	115
2005-2006	8	8
Beyond	33	36
Total due beyond one year	**361**	**375**
Total	**522**	**545**

(1) Including confirmed line of credit (note 1-7-2).

2-15-3 Analysis of debt by repayment currency

millions of euros

	Oct. 31, 2001	Oct. 31, 2000
Euro zone currencies	459	431
US dollars	25	69
Other	38	45
Total	**522**	**545**

2-15-4 Analysis of debt by interest rate

millions of euros

	Oct. 31, 2001	Oct. 31, 2000
Fixed rate debt	182	178
Variable rate debt (1)	340	367
Total	**522**	**545**

(1) Variable rate debt totaling 175 million euros had been hedged as of October 31, 2001, to fix the rates on 3-month Euribor-indexed debt for the following year at between 3.30% and 3.56%.

2-16 Other liabilities

millions of euros

	Oct. 31, 2001	Oct. 31, 2000
Accrued charges	27	31
Accrued payroll expenses	46	43
Accrued taxes	33	35
Other	19	37
Total	**125**	**146**

The decrease in other liabilities is due in part to the buyback of part shares in the Club Med 2 cruise ship.

2-17 Prepaid expenses and deferred charges/ Accrued expenses and deferred income

These items broke down as follows:

millions of euros

	Oct. 31, 2001	Oct. 31, 2000
Prepaid expenses	52	67
Deferred charges	2	3
Prepaid expenses and deferred charges	**54**	**70**
Deferred income (1)	44	14
Accrued expenses and deferred income	**44**	**14**

(1) The increase in this item corresponds to memberships taken out by customers of the Gymnase Club Group, which was included in the scope of consolidation during the year.

Food Lion, Inc.—Preparation of Financial Statements

Food Lion, Inc. operates a chain of retail food supermarkets in fourteen states, principally located in the Southeast. The company competes with national, regional, and local supermarket chains, supercenters, discount food stores, single unit stores, convenience stores and warehouse clubs. The company's stores sell a wide variety of groceries, produce, meats, dairy products, seafood, frozen food, deli/bakery and non-food items such as health and beauty aids and other household and personal products. Warehousing and distribution facilities, including a transportation fleet, are also owned and operated by the company. On December 28, 1996, 1,112 Food Lion stores were in operation employing 27,924 full-time and 45,246 part-time workers. After a series of mergers and acquisitions, in 1999 the company adopted the name Delhaize America and is one of the nation's largest supermarket companies.

Learning Objectives

- Determine how economic events affect a company's financial statements.
- Record economic events and prepare a simple set of financial statements.
- Understand the concepts of accrual, deferral, and reclassification.

To complete this case you need to develop a simple computerized spreadsheet. The structure of the spreadsheet follows after the case questions. Because of space constraints, the spreadsheet is reproduced on three pages here. However, you should create one worksheet with all the accounts across the top.

Enter the opening (i.e., December 30, 1995) and ending (i.e., December 28, 1996 Actual Balance Sheet or Income Statement) balances into the accounts on your spreadsheet. Asset and expense accounts should have debit balances, liability, shareholders' equity, and sales accounts should have credit balances. The income statement accounts should have opening balances of $0. All figures are in thousands of dollars.

The row labeled "Unadjusted trial balance" should be defined so that each cell equals the sum of the opening balance and the transactions in that column. Each trial balance sum should be either a net debit or a net credit. Once you enter the data for transaction #19, your unadjusted trial balance row should equal the one on the sample spreadsheet.

The row labeled "Pre-closing balances" should be defined so that each cell equals the sum of the "Unadjusted trial balance" and the adjustments and reclassifications in that column.

The row labeled "Post-closing balances" should be defined so that each cell equals the "Pre-closing balance" plus the closing entry in that column.

The last row (i.e., December 28, 1996 Actual Balance Sheet or Income Statement) serves as a check that you get to the correct year-end balances. You can define another row that calculates the difference between the actual year-end balances and your calculated "Post-closing balances." A necessary (but not sufficient) condition for a correct spreadsheet is values of $0 in each cell of the "difference" row.

The last two columns serve as a check that each journal entry has been properly posted and that each row of the spreadsheet is in balance. The column labeled "Total debits" should be defined as the sum of each asset, liability, owners' equity, and income statement debit in that row. Define the column labeled "Total credits" in a similar fashion. In each row, the debits should equal the credits.

Some journal entries will affect only the balance sheet (e.g. journal entry #3), some will affect both the balance sheet and the income statement (e.g. journal entry #1). Post the entry to the individual accounts using the debit or credit columns as appropriate. How the account is affected by a debit or credit entry is indicated in each column heading in the sample spreadsheet, either (+) for an increase or (-) for a decrease.

The column labeled "Retained Earnings" should be used only for the dividend entry (#14), the large aggregate entry (#19) and the closing entry. All transaction and adjusting journal entries that affect Income Statement accounts should be posted to the Income Statement accounts and then closed to the column labeled "Retained Earnings" in part *i* of the case.

Concepts

a. Prior to examining the opening balance sheet, think about what a grocery chain does. What accounts do you expect to see on the balance sheet? Which are the major assets? Liabilities?

Process

b. Prepare journal entries, as needed, for each of the following fiscal 1996 "transactions." All figures are in thousands of dollars.

1. The company had $8,476,918 in cash sales to customers. The cost of these groceries was $6,661,516.
2. The company had $529,014 in credit sales to large institutional customers. The cost of these groceries was $410,409.
3. The company collected $505,846 of accounts receivable.
4. The company purchased $7,222,670 of groceries on account.
5. The company paid $7,115,247 of accounts payable.
6. The company paid cash for employees' wages and other operating expenses totaling $1,252,553.
7. The company decided to pay $12,258 to settle certain non-current liabilities relating to prior-year expenses.
8. Food Lion management signed a new labor agreement with its employees. The two-year agreement takes effect on January 1, 1997 and calls for total wage increases of $150,000 per year.
9. During fiscal 1996, the company paid bondholders $76,631 of interest.
10. On December 28, 1996, the company paid $33,660 for a one-year casualty and property insurance policy that covers calendar 1997.
11. The company received $250,010 when it issued a short-term note payable.
12. The company repaid debt amounting to $83,420. This debt was classified as long-term debt (non-current liabilities).
13. The company issued additional shares of Class A common stock and received $3,086 in cash.
14. The company declared and paid $52,310 of dividends.
15. The company repurchased its own stock for $44,345 cash.
16. The company purchased property and equipment for $283,564 in cash.
17. Food Lion disposed of property with a book value of $27,930 for cash proceeds of $27,464. The difference is considered an operating loss on the income statement.
18. The company acquired the Kash N Karry food chain for $121,578 in cash. The purchase included inventory of $49,229, property, plant and equipment of $103,078, goodwill (an intangible asset) of $269,348. As well, Food Lion assumed Kash N Karry's non-current liabilities of $300,077.
19. During the year the company had several other transactions. In particular, the company paid income tax and recorded deferred tax assets and liabilities, converted $927 worth of debt to stock, and entered into additional long-term leases. These transactions have already been entered into the spreadsheet in aggregate.

c. Post the journal entries for the transactions to the spreadsheet. Note that some of the spreadsheet headings for liability and shareholders' equity accounts are in summary form.

d. Prepare an unadjusted trial balance from the spreadsheet. *Hint*: the unadjusted balance for Retained Earnings is $773,626.

e. Based on the transactions you recorded in parts *b* and *c*, list at least three adjustments or reclassifications that need to be made prior to preparing the final financial statements.

f. Prepare journal entries for the following "adjustments and reclassifications."

20. Food Lion employees took a physical count of inventory on December 28, 1996. The cost of goods in the company's possession on that date was $1,065,743.

21. The last payday for the company was December 22, 1996. Employees had earned, but the company had not yet paid, $49,229 of additional wages and profit sharing through December 28, 1996.

22. On December 30, 1995, the casualty and property insurance premium of $23,344 (covering fiscal 1996) was paid and recorded as "prepaid expense" (on the balance sheet) by Food Lion. Adjust for this expired insurance premium at December 28, 1996.

23. Depreciation and amortization expense was $165,286 for the fiscal year.

24. A review of the company's long-term debt indicated that $3,889 of interest had accrued but had not yet been paid.

25. A review of the company's long-term debt also indicated that $7,911 of the long-term debt and long-term leases is due on or before the end of the next fiscal year (i.e. fiscal 1997).

26. In December 1996, a consulting firm hired by Food Lion issued a report stating that the "Food Lion" brand name is worth $500,000.

27. In December 1996, an independent appraiser determined that the value of certain of the company's assets (recorded as property, plant and equipment) were overstated by $9,587 and that this impairment of value is permanent.

g. Post the journal entries for the adjustments and reclassifications to the spreadsheet.

h. Construct an income statement for the year ended December 28, 1996. Use the headings from your spreadsheet columns as the account titles.

i. Close all the temporary accounts on the Income Statement to Retained Earnings.

j. Prepare the December 28, 1996 balance sheet. Use the headings from your spreadsheet columns as the account titles.

k. For each of the transactions that involve cash, indicate whether the transaction would appear in the "operating," "investing," or "financing" section of the statement of cash flows.

Food Lion, Inc. Asset accounts (in $000's)	**Cash & Cash Equivalents**		**Receivables**		**Inventories**		**Prepaid Expenses & Other Current Assets**		**Property, at Cost, Less Depreciation**		**Goodwill & Non-current Assets**	
	Debit (+)	Credit (-)	Debit (+)	Credit (-)	Debit (+)	Credit (-)	Debit (+)	Credit (-)	Debit (+)	Credit (-)	Debit (+)	Credit (-)
Balance Dec. 30, 1995	70,035		127,995		881,021		73,362		1,491,069		1,783	
Transactions:												
1.												
2.												
3.												
4.												
5.												
6.												
7.												
8.												
9.												
10.												
11.												
12.												
13.												
14.												
15.												
16.												
17.												
18.												
19. Leases, tax, debt & stock		155,422					25,789		97,595		16,214	
Unadjusted trial balance		85,387	127,995		881,021		99,151		1,588,664		17,997	
Adjustments:												
20.												
21.												
22.												
23.												
24.												
25.												
26.												
27.												
Pre-closing balances		85,387	127,995		881,021		99,151		1,588,664		17,997	
i) Closing entry												
Post-closing balances												
December 28, 1996 Actual Balance Sheet	102,371		151,163		1,065,743		109,467		1,772,503		287,345	

Food Lion, Inc. Liability and SH equity	**Current Liabilities**		**Non-current Liabilities**		**Contributed Capital**		**Retained Earnings**	
	Debit (-)	Credit (+)	Debit (-)	Credit (+)	Debit (-)	Credit (+)	Debit (-)	Credit (+)
Balance Dec. 30, 1995		698,695		844,060		237,568		864,942
Transactions:								
1.								
2.								
3.								
4.								
5.								
6.								
7.								
8.								
9.								
10.								
11.								
12.								
13.								
14.								
15.								
16.								
17.								
18.								
19. Leases, tax, debt & stock		37,078		77,871		39,933	39,006	
Unadjusted trial balance		735,773		921,931		277,501		825,936
Adjustments:								
20.								
21.								
22.								
23.								
24.								
25.								
26.								
27.								
Pre-closing balances		735,773		921,931		277,501		825,936
i) Closing entry								
Post-closing balances								
December 28, 1996 Actual Balance Sheet		1,154,235		1,118,419		236,242		979,696

Food Lion, Inc. Income Stmt accounts	**Net Sales**		**Cost of Goods Sold**		**S&A Expenses**		**Depreciation and Amortization**		**Asset Impairment**		**Interest expense**		**Income Tax Provision (expense)**		**Total Debits**	**Total Credits**
	Debit (-)	Credit (+)	Debit (+)	Credit (-)	Debit (+)	Credit (-)	Debit (+)	Credit (-)	Debit (+)	Credit (-)	Debit (+)	Credit (-)	Debit (+)	Debit (+)		
Balances Dec. 30, 1995		0	0		0		0		0		0		0		2,645,265	2,645,265
Transactions:																
1.																
2.																
3.																
4.																
5.																
6.																
7.																
8.																
9.																
10.																
11.																
12.																
13.																
14.																
15.																
16.																
17.																
18.																
19. Leases, tax, debt & stock													131,700		310,304	310,304
Unadjusted trial balance		0	0		0		0		0		0		131,700		2,846,528	2,846,528
Adjustments:																
20.																
21.																
22.																
23.																
24.																
25.																
26.																
27.																
Pre-closing balances																
i) Closing entry																
Post-closing balances		0	0		0		0		0		0		131,700		2,846,528	2,846,528
December 28, 1996 Actual Income Statement		9,005,932	7,087,177		1,325,592		165,286		9,587		80,520		131,700		3,488,592	3,488,592

Taiwan Semiconductor Manufacturing Company Limited —Transactions & Periodic Adjustments

Taiwan Semiconductor Manufacturing Company Limited (TSMC), a corporation in the Republic of China, is engaged in the manufacture, sale, packaging, testing, and design of integrated circuits and other semiconductor devices. The company also manufactures masks. The company's shares trade on the Taiwan Stock Exchange and, since October 1997, on the New York Stock Exchange as American Depository Receipts. TSMC was the first and remains the largest dedicated semiconductor foundry (contract manufacturer) in the world. TSMC makes chips for hundreds of manufacturers such as Philips and Motorola (which outsource to TSMC to boost capacity) and fabless chip companies such as Broadcom and NVIDIA (for whom TSMC makes whole product lines).

Learning Objectives

- Observe the differences between Taiwanese and U.S. GAAP.
- Use financial statement information to infer underlying transactions.
- Understand some common linkages between balance sheet and income statement accounts.
- Distinguish between transaction and adjusting journal entries.
- Prepare transaction and adjusting journal entries.

Refer to TSMC's 2001 financial statements and the excerpted notes. Each part of this case is independent. Restrict the account titles used in your answers to those used in the TSMC financial statements and notes.

Concepts

a. TSMC's financial statements are prepared in accordance with accounting principles generally accepted in the Republic of China.

   i. Refer to the consolidated balance sheet. How does TSMC's balance sheet differ from U.S. balance sheets?

   ii. Refer to the consolidated statement of income. How does TSMC's income statement differ from U.S. income statements?

b. To prepare accrual-based financial statements, a company must make periodic adjustments to its accounts. This is accomplished with adjusting journal entries.

   i. Consider the "Inventories" account. What types of transactions or events necessitate year-end adjustments to the various inventory accounts?

   ii. Consider the "Accounts receivable" account. What types of transactions or events necessitate year-end adjustments to this group of accounts?

   iii. Consider the "Accrued expenses and other current liabilities" account. What types of transactions or events necessitate year-end adjustments to this group of accounts?

   iv. What other accounts on TSMC's balance sheet may need adjusting journal entries? Explain.

Process

c. For each item in quotations, provide the year-end total disclosed in TSMC's 2001 consolidated income statement. Write a journal entry to record the activity in the account in 2001. Assume that the company recorded a single (summary) journal entry.

   i. "Gross Sales." Assume that all sales are on account. Refer to note 16 for information about sales made to related parties.

   ii. "Marketing" expenses. Assume that all these costs were paid in cash.

iii. "Royalty income." Assume that this income was received from unrelated parties in cash.

d. For each item in quotations, provide the amount and direction of the cash flow disclosed in TSMC's 2001 consolidated cash flow statement. Write a journal entry to record the cash inflow or outflow in 2001. Assume that the company recorded a single (summary) journal entry.

   i. "Proceeds from issuance of: Capital stock."

   ii. "Payments on: Long-term bank loans."

   iii. "Acquisitions of: Property, plant and equipment."

e. For each of the following items in quotations, assume the given amount comes from TSMC's *unadjusted* trial balance at December 31, 2001. Write an adjusting journal entry that reconciles the *unadjusted* trial balance to the final 'adjusted' amount on the balance sheet or income statement.

   i. The unadjusted trial balance for "Depreciation and amortization" expense was NT$0. Refer to the statement of cash flows to determine the amount of depreciation expense for 2001. Assume that TSMC includes this expense on two lines of its income statement: 5% is in "General and administrative" and 95% in "Cost of sales."

   ii. The unadjusted trial balance for "Allowance for losses" on inventory was NT$567,626. Refer to financial statement note 6, to determine the amount of the allowance at December 31, 2001. Why might this account have increased during the year. How might TSMC determine the appropriate account balance at year end? Refer to financial statement note 2 for a hint.

   iii. The unadjusted trial balance for "Research and Development" was NT$10,149,019. The difference between this and the final adjusted balance pertains to bonuses to certain production-design teams that exceeded performance goals during the fourth quarter of 2001. The bonuses will be paid in early 2002.

   iv. The unadjusted trial balance for "Allowance for doubtful receivables" was NT$741,225. Assume that TSMC includes bad debt expense in "General and administrative" on the income statement. How might TSMC determine the appropriate account balance at year end? How might the auditors assess the adequacy of the account balance at year end?

   v. The unadjusted trial balance for "Allowance for sales returns and others" was NT$2,355,001. How might TSMC determine the appropriate account balance at year end? How might the auditors assess the adequacy of the account balance at year end?

Analysis

f. TSMC's notes to the financial statements disclose considerable information about related party transactions. These notes detail TSMC's ownership structure as well as transactions with affiliates and other related parties. Apart from regulatory reasons, why might TSMC provide this sort of information? How might financial statement readers use this information?

English Translation of Financial Statements Originally Issued in Chinese

TAIWAN SEMICONDUCTOR MANUFACTURING COMPANY LTD. AND SUBSIDIARIES
CONSOLIDATED BALANCE SHEETS
December 31, 2001 and 2000
(In Thousand New Taiwan Dollars, Except Par Value)

	2001		2000	
ASSETS	Amount	%	Amount	%
CURRENT ASSETS				
Cash and cash equivalents (Notes 2 and 4)	$37,556,295	10	$38,840,217	11
Short-term investments (Notes 2, 5 and 10)	1,398,071	-	1,502,098	1
Receivable from related parties (Note 16)	494,732	-	948,726	-
Notes receivable	176,582	-	125,175	-
Accounts receivable	19,957,636	5	30,335,314	8
Allowance for doubtful receivables (Note 2)	(1,100,492)	-	(946,734)	-
Allowance for sales returns and others (Note 2)	(2,581,551)	(1)	(2,458,323)	(1)
Inventories - net (Notes 2 and 6)	9,828,328	3	12,785,723	3
Deferred income tax assets (Notes 2 and 15)	2,350,147	1	8,178,016	2
Prepaid expenses and other current assets (Notes 16, 17 and 19)	2,721,421	1	3,034,624	1
Total Current Assets	70,801,169	19	92,344,836	25
LONG-TERM INVESTMENTS (Notes 2, 7 and 20)	11,599,150	3	10,663,804	3
PROPERTY, PLANT AND EQUIPMENT (Notes 2, 8, 16 and 11)				
Cost				
Land and land improvements	877,371	-	829,239	-
Buildings	60,523,505	17	53,874,708	15
Machinery and equipment	280,023,690	76	241,995,862	65
Office equipment	6,062,496	2	4,865,610	1
Total cost	347,487,062	95	301,565,419	81
Accumulated depreciation	(155,948,960)	(42)	(103,884,879)	(28)
Advance payments and construction in progress	59,749,530	16	47,067,352	13
Net Property, Plant and Equipment	251,287,632	69	244,747,892	66
CONSOLIDATED DEBITS (Note 2)	11,437,572	3	11,530,973	3
OTHER ASSETS				
Deferred income tax assets (Notes 2 and 15)	16,245,828	5	6,629,805	2
Deferred charges - net (Notes 2 and 9)	3,769,750	1	3,335,665	1
Refundable deposits (Note 18)	784,089	-	979,067	-
Assets leased to others (Note 2)	555,053	-	625,647	-
Miscellaneous	37,452	-	28,290	-
Total Other Assets	21,392,172	6	11,598,474	3
TOTAL ASSETS	$366,517,695	100	$370,885,979	100

The accompanying notes are an integral part of the consolidated financial statements.

LIABILITIES AND SHAREHOLDERS' EQUITY	2001 Amount	2001 %	2000 Amount	2000 %
CURRENT LIABILITIES				
Short-term bank loans (Note 10)	$6,269,181	2	$3,833,841	1
Payable to related parties (Note 16)	1,048,273	-	2,606,339	1
Accounts payable	1,397,879	-	8,507,827	2
Payable to contractors and equipment suppliers (Note 20)	12,867,236	4	25,550,273	7
Income tax payable (Notes 2 and 15)	81,483	-	3,298	-
Current portion of bonds (Note 12)	5,000,000	1	-	-
Accrued expenses and other current liabilities (Note 19)	6,665,000	2	6,923,414	2
Total Current Liabilities	33,329,052	9	47,424,992	13
LONG-TERM LIABILITIES				
Long-term bank loans (Notes 11)	22,399,360	6	23,339,367	6
Bonds - net of current portion (Note 12)	24,000,000	7	29,000,000	8
Total Long-term Liabilities	46,399,360	13	52,339,367	14
OTHER LIABILITIES				
Guarantee deposits (Note 18)	7,212,688	2	7,086,379	2
Accrued pension cost (Notes 2 and 14)	1,856,617	-	1,511,277	-
Deferred gain on sale-leaseback (Note 2)	268,165	-	434,183	-
Miscellaneous	141,498	-	14,356	-
Total Other Liabilities	9,478,968	2	9,046,195	2
MINORITY INTEREST IN SUBSIDIARIES (Note 2)	120,240	-	321,726	-
Total Liabilities	89,327,620	24	109,132,280	29
SHAREHOLDERS' EQUITY (Notes 2 and 13)				
Capital stock - $10 par value				
Authorized: 24,600,000 thousand shares in 2001 and 17,800,000 thousand shares in 2000				
Issued: Preferred - 1,300,000 thousand shares	13,000,000	3	13,000,000	3
Common - 16,832,554 thousand shares in 2001 and 11,689,365 thousand shares in 2000	168,325,531	46	116,893,646	32
Capital surplus	57,128,433	16	55,285,821	15
Retained earnings:				
Appropriated as legal reserve	17,180,067	5	10,689,323	3
Appropriated as special reserve	349,941	-	1,091,003	-
Unappropriated earnings	19,977,402	6	65,143,847	18
Cumulative translation adjustments	1,228,701	-	(278,377)	-
Unrealized loss on long-term investments	-	-	(71,564)	-
Total Shareholders' Equity	277,190,075	76	261,753,699	71
TOTAL LIABILITIES AND SHAREHOLDERS' EQUITY	$366,517,695	100	$370,885,979	100

English Translation of Financial Statements Originally Issued in Chinese

TAIWAN SEMICONDUCTOR MANUFACTURING COMPANY LTD. AND SUBSIDIARIES
CONSOLIDATED STATEMENTS OF INCOME
For the Years Ended December 31, 2001 and 2000
(In Thousand New Taiwan Dollars, Except Consolidated Earnings Per Share)

	2001		2000	
	Amount	%	Amount	%
GROSS SALES (Notes 2, 16 and 20)	$128,560,708		$169,192,312	
SALES RETURNS AND ALLOWANCES (Note 2)	(2,675,816)		(2,994,708)	
NET SALES	125,884,892	100	166,197,604	100
COST OF SALES (Note 16)	92,228,098	73	87,609,670	53
GROSS PROFIT	33,656,794	27	78,587,934	47
OPERATING EXPENSES (Notes 16 and 20)				
Research and development	10,649,019	9	7,203,591	4
General and administrative	7,939,839	6	7,408,121	4
Marketing	2,290,139	2	2,681,534	2
Total Operating Expenses	20,878,997	17	17,293,246	10
INCOME FROM OPERATIONS	12,777,797	10	61,294,688	37
NON-OPERATING INCOME (Note 20)				
Gain on sales of short-term investments- net (Note 2)	1,619,062	1	1,060,919	1
Interest	1,486,656	1	1,679,736	1
Royalty income (Note 18)	1,301,606	1	524,194	-
Insurance compensation-net	860,835	1	1,623,832	1
Premium income-net (Notes 2 and 19)	234,732	-	8,115	-
Gain on sales of long-term investments - net	105,439	-	15,144	-
Technical service income (Notes 16 and 18)	55,077	-	138,514	-
Gain on sales of property, plant and equipment	52,376	-	62,921	-
Foreign exchange gain - net (Note 2)	-	-	828,025	-
Other	759,793	1	178,403	-
Total Non-Operating Income	6,475,576	5	6,119,803	3
NON-OPERATING EXPENSES (Note 20)				
Equity in net losses of investee companies - net (Notes 2 and 7)	3,959,020	3	187,179	-
Interest (Notes 2, 8, and 19)	3,144,042	3	2,717,035	2
Foreign exchange loss - net (Notes 2 and 19)	695,620	-	-	-
Loss on sales of and provision for loss on property, plant and equipment	235,629	-	114,768	-

(Forward)

Amortization of issuance costs of bonds (Note 2)	$12,504	-	$32,658	-
Other	420,053	-	461,327	-
Total Non-Operating Expenses	8,466,868	6	3,512,967	2
INCOME BEFORE INCOME TAX (Note 20)	10,786,505	9	63,901,524	38
INCOME TAX BENEFIT (Notes 2 and 15)	3,740,678	3	1,167,884	1
INCOME BEFORE MINORITY INTEREST	14,527,183	12	65,069,408	39
MINORITY INTEREST IN LOSS (INCOME) OF SUBSIDIARIES (Notes 2 and 20)	(44,009)	-	36,786	-
NET INCOME	$14,483,174	12	$65,106,194	39
CONSOLIDATED EARNINGS PER SHARE				
Based on weighted-average number of common shares outstanding - 16,832,554 thousand shares in 2001 and 11,400,882 thousand shares in 2000	$0.83		$5.71	
Based on 16,417,270 thousand shares			$3.96	

The accompanying notes are an integral part of the consolidated financial statements.

English Translation of Financial Statements Originally Issued in Chinese

TAIWAN SEMICONDUCTOR MANUFACTURING COMPANY LTD. AND SUBSIDIARIES
CONSOLIDATED STATEMENTS OF CHANGES IN SHAREHOLDERS' EQUITY
For the Years Ended December 31, 2001 and 2000

(In Thousand New Taiwan Dollars)

	CAPITAL STOCK ISSUED					CAPITAL SURPLUS (Note 2)							RETAINED EARNINGS (Note 13)				UNREALIZED LOSS ON LONG-TERM INVESTMENT (NOTE 2)	CUMULATIVE TRANSLATION ADJUSTMENTS (NOTE 2)	TOTAL SHAREHOLDERS EQUITY
	Preferred Stock		Common Stock																
	Shares (Thousand)	Amount	Shares (Thousand)	Amount	Subscribe Capital	From Consolidation	Additional Paid-In Capital	From Long-term Investment	Excess on Foreign Bond Investment	Gain on Disposal of Properties	Donation	Total	Legal Reserve	Special Reserve	Unappropriated Earnings	Total			
BALANCE, JANUARY 1, 2000	-	$-	8,520,882	$85,208,817	$13,118,025	$12,120,000	$-	$472,300	$11,289,998	$69,058	$55	$23,951,411	$8,258,359	$-	$23,124,011	$31,382,370	$-	($1,090,106)	$152,570,517
Appropriations of prior year's earnings																			
Legal reserve	-	-	-	-	-	-	-	-	-	-	-	-	2,430,964	-	(2,430,964)	-	-	-	-
Special reserve	-	-	-	-	-	-	-	-	-	-	-	-	-	1,091,003	(1,091,003)	-	-	-	-
Bonus to employees - stock	-	-	172,121	1,721,208	-		-	-		-	-	-	-	-	(1,721,208)	(1,721,208)	-	-	-
Stock dividends - 25.55%	-	-	1,959,910	19,599,103	-	-	-	-	-	-	-	-	-	-	(19,599,103)	(19,599,103)	-	-	-
Bonus to directors and supervisors	-	-	-	-	-	-	-	-	-	-	-	-	-	-	(215,151)	(215,151)	-	-	(215,151)
Capital Transferred from capital surplus - 2.45%	-	-	187,937	1,879,366	-	-	-	-	(1,879,366)	-	-	(1,879,366)	-	-	-	-	-	-	-
Issuance of shares January 28, 2000			300,000	3,000,000	(13,118,025)	12,000,000	-	-	-	-	-	12,000,000	-	-		-			1,881,975
Issuance of shares on June 8, 2000	-	-	115,000	1,150,000	-	-	23,172,550	-	-	-	-	23,172,550	-	-	-	-	-	-	24,322,550
Issuance of shares for the merge on June 30,2000	-	-	433,515	4,335,152	-	(1,790,871)	-	-	-	-	-	(1,790,871)	-	-	1,803,168	1,803,168	-	(897)	4,346,552
Issuance of preferred stocks on November 29, 2000	1,300,000	13,000,000	-	-	-	-	-	-	-	-	-	-	-	-	-	-	-	-	13,000,000
Net income in 2000	-	-	-	-	-	-	-	-	-	-	-	-	-	-	65,106,194	65,106,194	-	-	65,106,194
Gain on sales of property, plant and equipment	-	-	-	-	-	-	-	-	-	58,178	-	58,178	-	-	(58,178)	(58,178)	-	-	-
Gain on sales of property, plant and equipment from Investees	-	-	-	-	-	-	-	5,502	-	-	-	5,502	-	-	(5,502)	(5,502)	-	-	-
Adjustment arising from changes in shareholders' equity of investees	-	-	-	-	-	-	-	(231,583)	-	-	-	(231,583)	-	-	231,583	231,583	-	-	-
Unrealized loss on long-term investment	-	-	-	-	-	-	-	-	-	-	-	-	-	-	-	-	(71,564)	-	(71,564)
Translation adjustments	-	-	-	-	-	-	-	-	-	-	-	-	-	-	-	-	-	812,626	812,626
BALANCE, DECEMBER 31, 2000	1,300,000	13,000,000	11,689,365	116,893,646	-	22,329,129	23,172,550	246,219	9,410,632	127,236	55	55,285,821	10,689,323	1,091,003	65,143,847	76,924,173	(71,564)	(278,377)	261,753,699
Appropriations of prior year's earnings	-																		
Legal reserve	-	-	-	-	-	-	-	-	-	-	-	-	6,490,744	-	(6,490,744)	-	-	-	-
Special reserve	-	-	-	-	-	-	-	-	-	-	-	-	-	(741,062)	741,062	-	-	-	-
Bonus to employees - stock	-	-	467,443	4,674,426	-	-	-	-	-	-	-	-	-	-	(4,674,426)	(4,674,426)	-	-	-
Cash dividends paid for preferred stock	-	-	-	-	-	-	-	-	-	-	-	-	-	-	(41,137)	(41,137)	-	-	(41,137)
Stock dividends - 40%	-	-	4,675,746	46,757,459	-	-	-	-	-	-	-	-	-	-	(46,757,459)	(46,757,459)	-	-	-
Bonus to directors and supervisors	-	-	-	-	-	-	-	-	-	-	-	-	-	-	(584,303)	(584,303)	-	-	(584,303)
Net income in 2001	-	-	-	-	-	-	-	-	-	-	-	-	-	-	14,483,174	14,483,174	-	-	14,483,174
Reclassification of the accumulated deficits from the merged company	-	-	-	-	-	1,803,168	-	-	-	-	-	1,803,168	-	-	(1,803,168)	(1,803,168)	-	-	-
Gain on sales of property, plant and equipment	-	-	-	-	-	-	-	-	-	39,282	-	39,282	-	-	(39,282)	(39,282)	-	-	-
Gain on sales of property, plant and equipment from investees	-	-	-	-	-	-	-	162	-	-	-	162	-	-	(162)	(162)	-	-	-
Reversal of the unrealized loss on long-term investments	-	-	-	-	-	-	-	-	-	-	-	-	-	-	-	-	71,564	-	71,564
Translation adjustments	-	-	-	-	-	-	-	-	-	-	-	-	-	-	-	-	-	1,507,078	1,507,078
BALANCE, DECEMBER 31, 2001	1,300,000	$13,000,000	16,832,554	$168,325,531	$-	$24,132,297	$23,172,550	$246,381	$9,410,632	$166,518	$55	$57,128,433	$17,180,067	$349,941	$19,977,402	$37,507,410	$-	$1,228,701	$277,190,075

The accompanying notes are an integral part of the consolidated financial statements

English Translation of Financial Statements Originally Issued in Chinese

TAIWAN SEMICONDUCTOR MANUFACTURING COMPANY LTD. AND SUBSIDIARIES
CONSOLIDATED STATEMENTS OF CASH FLOWS
For the Years Ended December 31, 2001 and 2000
(In Thousand New Taiwan Dollars)

	2001	2000
CASH FLOWS FROM OPERATING ACTIVITIES		
Net income	$14,483,174	$65,106,194
Adjustments to reconcile net income to net cash provided by operating activities:		
Depreciation and amortization	55,323,040	41,446,137
Deferred income taxes	(3,788,154)	(956,118)
Equity in net losses of investee companies - net	3,959,020	187,179
Gain on sales of long-term investments - net	(105,439)	(15,144)
Loss on sales of and provision for loss on property, plant and equipment - net	183,253	51,847
Reversal of provision for losses on short-term investment	(13,146)	-
Accrued pension cost	345,340	370,276
Allowance for doubtful receivables	153,758	524,532
Allowance for sales returns and others	123,228	1,679,309
Minority interest in income (loss) of subsidiaries	44,009	(36,786)
Changes in operating assets and liabilities:		
Decrease (increase) in:		
Receivable from related parties	453,994	(737,105)
Notes receivable	(51,407)	38,959
Accounts receivable	10,377,678	(15,467,155)
Inventories - net	2,957,395	(4,033,836)
Prepaid expenses and other current assets	202,303	351,988
Forward exchange contract receivable	49,480	(113,730)
Increase (decrease) in:		
Payable to related parties	(1,558,066)	2,334,247
Notes payable	-	(4,303)
Accounts payable	(7,109,948)	3,174,958
Income tax payable	78,185	(151,828)
Forward exchange contract payable	218,165	(987,604)
Accrued expenses and other current liabilities	(508,150)	2,024,180
Net Cash Provided by Operating Activities	75,817,712	94,786,197

(Forward)

	2001	2000
CASH FLOWS FROM INVESTING ACTIVITIES		
Decrease (increase) in short-term investments	$117,173	($524,154)
Decrease in pledged time deposits	-	3,161,693
Acquisitions of:		
Property, plant and equipment	(70,201,205)	(103,761,905)
Long-term investments	(5,120,580)	(2,956,758)
Proceeds from sales of:		
Property, plant, and equipment	301,416	364,875
Long-term investments	559,137	49,376
Increase in deferred charges	(1,805,250)	(1,793,209)
Decrease (increase) in refundable deposits	194,978	(915,559)
Decrease (increase) in other assets	(9,162)	77,451
Decrease in minority interest in subsidiaries	(249,166)	(7,165,656)
Increase in consolidated debit	(1,019,227)	(8,221,266)
Cash inflow from the merged companies	-	736,594
Net Cash Used in Investing Activities	(77,231,886)	(120,948,518)
CASH FLOWS FROM FINANCING ACTIVITIES		
Proceeds from issuance of:		
Short-term bank loans	2,435,340	-
Long-term bonds	-	9,000,000
Capital stock	-	39,204,525
Payments on:		
Short-term bank loans	-	(8,592,790)
Commercial paper	-	(4,241,048)
Long-term bank loans	(940,007)	(2,648,853)
Increase in guarantee deposits	126,309	2,978,984
Decrease in lease obligation	(51,286)	(1,052)
Bonus paid to directors and supervisors and cash dividends paid on preferred stocks	(625,440)	(215,151)
Increase in issuance cost of financing	(47,689)	(118,335)
Net Cash Provided by (Used in) Financing Activities	897,227	35,366,280
NET INCREASE (DECREASE) CASH AND CASHEQUIVALENTS	(516,947)	9,203,959
EFFECT OF EXCHANGES IN FOREING EXCHANGE RATE	(766,975)	118,576
CASH AND CASH EQUIVALENTS, BEGINNING OF THE YEAR	38,840,217	29,517,682
CASH AND CASH EQUIVALENTS, END OF THE YEAR	$37,556,295	$38,840,217
SUPPLEMENTAL INFORMATION		
Interest paid (excluding the amounts capitalized of NT$507,094 thousand and NT$541,078 thousand in 2001 and 2000, respectively)	$3,468,112	$4,036,210
Income tax paid	$20,767	$96,523
Noncash investing and financing activities:		
Effect of exchanges in foreign exchange rate on cash and cash equivalents	$1,258,395	$1,009,264

(Forward)

	2001	2000
Current portion of long-term liabilities	$5,001,116	$51,055
Cash paid for acquisition of property, plant and equipment:		
Total acquisitions	$57,518,168	$113,996,068
Decrease (increase) in payables to contractors and equipment suppliers	12,683,037	(10,234,163)
	$70,201,205	$103,761,905

SUPPLEMENTAL INFORMATION OF THE MERGERS:

TSMC had merged with Worldwide Semiconductor Manufacturing Corp. (WSMC) and had acquired TSMC-Acer Semiconductor Manufacturing Corp. (TASMC) by issuing new shares. The balance sheets as of June 30, 2000 of WSMC and TASMC were as follows:

	TASMC (Fair Value)	WSMC (Book Value)	Total
Cash	$736,594	$675,810	$1,412,404
Inventories	1,647,845	1,805,243	3,453,088
Other current assets	2,308,391	3,150,257	5,458,648
Property, plant and equipment - net	19,846,708	40,512,706	60,359,414
Other assets	7,335,526	5,101,000	12,436,526
Current liabilities	(16,699,147)	(12,454,686)	(29,153,833)
Long-term liabilities	(2,000,000)	(4,950,000)	(6,950,000)
Other liabilities	(654,863)	(23,498)	(678,361)
Net assets acquired	12,521,054	33,816,832	46,337,886
Cancellation of stocks of the dissolved companies	(8,173,605)	-	(8,173,605)
Issuance of stocks from the surviving company	(4,335,152)	(11,500,000)	(15,835,152)
Capital surplus	$12,297	$22,316,832	$22,329,129

The accompanying notes are an integral part of the consolidated financial statements.

TAIWAN SEMICONDUCTOR MANUFACTURING COMPANY LTD. AND SUBSIDIARIES

NOTES TO CONSOLIDATED FINANCIAL STATEMENTS

(Amounts in Thousand New Taiwan Dollars, Unless Specified Otherwise)

1. GENERAL

Taiwan Semiconductor Manufacturing Company Limited (TSMC), a Republic of China corporation, is engaged mainly in the manufacture, sale, packaging, testing and design of integrated circuits and other semiconductor devices, and the manufacture masks. TSMC was incorporated as a venture among the Government of the ROC, acting through the Development Fund of the Executive Yuan; Philips Electronics N.V. and certain of its affiliates (Philips); and certain other private investors. In September 1994, its shares were listed on the Taiwan Stock Exchange. In October 1997, TSMC listed its shares of stock on the New York Stock Exchange in the form of American Depositary Shares.

TSMC has five direct wholly-owned subsidiaries, namely, TSMC-North America, Taiwan Semiconductor Manufacturing Company Europe B.V (TSMC-Europe), TSMC-Japan, TSMC International Investment, TSMC Partners, a 99.5% owned subsidiary, Emerging Alliance Fund and several 25% owned affiliates - Po Cherng Investment, Chi Hsin Investment, Kung Cherng Investment, Chi Cherng Investment, Hsin Ruey Investment and Cherng Huei Investment. TSMC International Investment has two wholly-owned subsidiaries - TSMC Development, Inc. and TSMC Technology Inc., and two 97%-owned subsidiaries - InveStar Semiconductor Development Fund, Inc. and InveStar Semiconductor Development Fund (II), Inc., (incorporated in 2000). TSMC Development Inc. has a subsidiary, WaferTech, LLC, which has been 57% owned since its formation, increased to 68% owned in 1998; TSMC Development Inc. acquired an additional 29% and 2% at a purchase price of US$474,640 thousand and US$19,530 thousand in December 2000, and June 2001, respectively, thereby increasing its proportionate interest to 99% as of December 31, 2001.

The following diagram presents information regarding the relationship and ownership percentages among TSMC and its subsidiaries as of December 31, 2001:

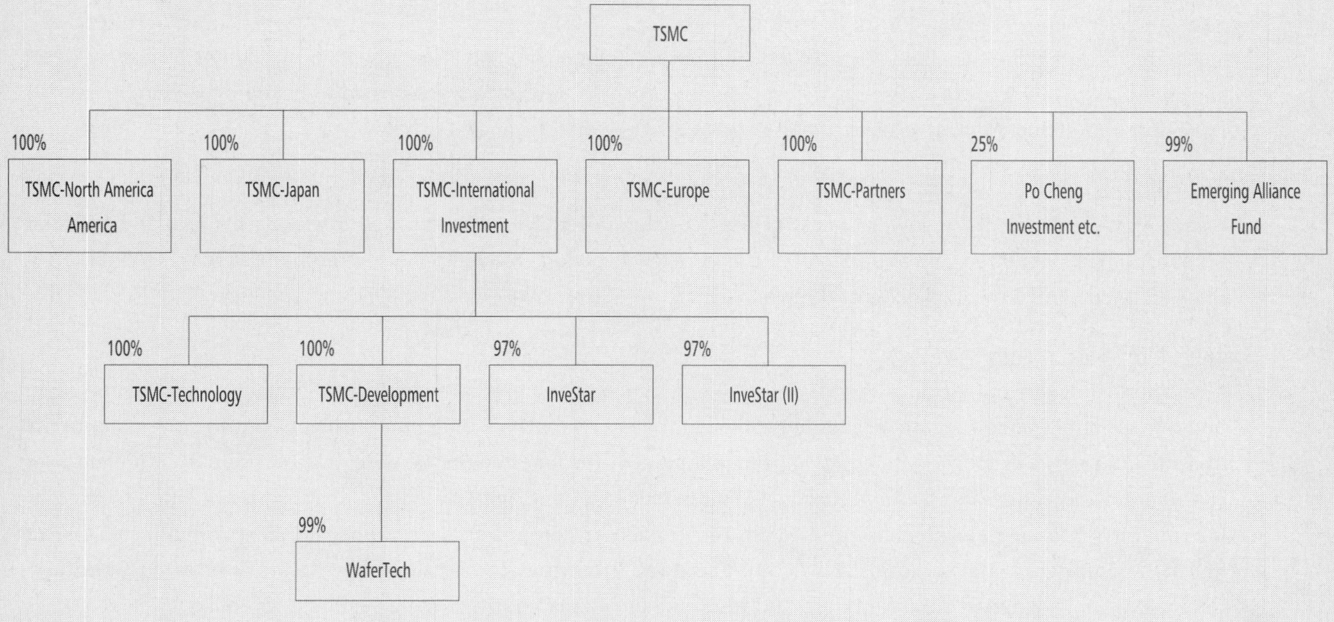

TSMC-North America, TSMC-Europe and TSMC-Japan are engaged mainly in marketing and engineering support activities. Emerging Alliance Fund, TSMC Partners and Po Cherng Investment etc. are engaged in investments. TSMC International Investment and its subsidiaries are engaged in investing in affairs focused on the design, manufacture, and other related business of semiconductors. WaferTech, LLC. is engaged in the foundry business.

2. SUMMARY OF SIGNIFICANT ACCOUNTING POLICIES

Consolidation

The Company consolidates the accounts of all majority (directly and indirectly) owned subsidiaries. The consolidated financial statements included, as of and for the year ended December 31, 2000 and 2001, the accounts of TSMC, TSMC-North America, TSMC-Europe, TSMC-Japan, TSMC Partners, Emerging Alliance Fund, Po Cherng Investment, Chi Hsin Investment, Kung Cherng Investment, Chi Cherng Investment, Hsin Ruey Investment, Cherng Huei Investment, TSMC International Investment and its subsidiaries, InveStar Semiconductor Development Fund, Inc. and InveStar Semiconductor Development Fund (II) Inc., TSMC Development Inc. (including WaferTech, LLC) and TSMC Technology Inc. All significant inter-company accounts and transactions have been eliminated.

Minority interests in Emerging Alliance Fund, InveStar, InveStar (II) and WaferTech are presented separately in the consolidated financial statements.

Cash and cash equivalents

Government bonds acquired under repurchase agreements that provide for their repurchase with less than three months from date of purchase are classified as cash equivalents.

Short-term investments

Short-term investments are carried at the lower of cost or market value. The costs of investments sold are determined using the specific identification method.

Allowance for doubtful receivable

Allowance for doubtful receivables is provided based on a review of the collectibility of accounts receivable.

Sales and Allowance for sales returns and others

Sales are recognized when titles of products and risks of ownerships are transferred to customers, primarily upon shipment. Allowance and related provisions for sales returns and others are provided based on experience; such provisions are deducted from sales and related costs are deducted from cost of sales.

Inventories

Inventories are stated at the lower of cost or market value. Inventories are recorded at standard costs, and adjusted to approximate weighted average cost at the end of each period. Market value represents net realizable value for finished goods and work in process and replacement value for raw materials, supplies and spare parts.

Long-term investments

Investments in shares of stock of companies wherein the Company exercises significant influence on their operating and financial policy decisions are accounted for using the equity method. The difference between the investment cost and the Company's proportionate equity in the net assets of the investee on the date of acquisition is amortized over five years using the straight-line method. Such amortization and the Company's proportionate share in the net income or net loss of investee companies are recognized as components of "Equity in net income or net loss in investee companies - net" account. When the Company subscribes to additional investee shares at a percentage different from its existing equity interest, the resulting carrying amount of the investment in equity investee differs from the amount of Company's proportionate share in the investee's net equity. The Company records such difference as an adjustment to "Capital surplus" and the "Long-term investments" accounts, respectively.

Abercrombie & Fitch Co.—Transactions and Financial Statements

Abercrombie & Fitch Co., a Delaware corporation, is principally engaged in the purchase, distribution and sale of men's, women's and kids' casual apparel. The Company's retail activities are conducted under the Abercrombie & Fitch and "Abercrombie" trade names through retail stores and a magazine/catalogue bearing the Company name. Merchandise is targeted to appeal to customers in specialty markets who have distinctive consumer characteristics.

Learning Objectives

- Record basic transactions, adjusting journal entries, and closing entries.
- Prepare a balance sheet and income statement.

Refer to the fiscal year 1999 financial statements of Abercrombie & Fitch Co. Note: "Fiscal year 1999" refers to the year that began on February 1, 1998 and ended on January 30, 1999.

 Process 

a. Open T-accounts for each balance sheet and income statement line item (i.e., for the permanent accounts: 9 asset T-accounts and 9 liability and owners' equity T-accounts; for the temporary accounts: 5 T-accounts). Enter the January 31, 1998 balance sheet amounts as the opening balance for fiscal 1999 and post the following fiscal 1999 transactions (figures in thousands of dollars):

1. Inventory costing $481,918 was purchased on account during the year.
2. Store Supplies costing $1,000 were purchased on account during the year.
3. Sales of $815,804 were made. Of these, $15,804 were on account.
4. The cost of merchandise sold was $465,000.
5. The company collected cash of $13,398 from its customers for sales previously recorded as accounts receivable.
6. Cash of $514,114 was used to pay suppliers for goods, supplies, and property and equipment previously purchased on account.
7. The company collected $23,785 from the Limited in satisfaction of amounts owed by the Limited to A&F.
8. Cash of $50,000 was used to repay principal on long-term debt.
9. Property and equipment were acquired on account (accounts payable) for $39,987.
10. The company paid $908 for shares of its own common stock. This is known as treasury stock. It is recorded at cost as a debit in the owners' equity section of the balance sheet.
11. The following represents a *single* composite journal entry for all remaining transactions during the year. Record the entry in the appropriate accounts:

	Account	Debit	Credit
Dr.	Other Current Assets	400	
Dr.	General, Admin., and Store Operating Expense	150,652	
Dr.	Provision for Income Taxes (Expense)	68,040	
Dr.	Deferred Income Taxes	6,978	
Dr.	Other assets	631	
Cr.	Cash		151,264
Cr.	Income Taxes Payable		17,736
Cr.	Other Long-Term Liabilities		3,327
Cr.	Interest Income		3,144
Cr.	Accrued Expenses		25,054
Cr.	Common Stock		6
Cr.	Paid-in Capital		26,170
	TOTAL	226,701	226,701

Explanation: to record all other activity for fiscal 1999

b. Prepare an unadjusted trial balance as at January 30, 1999 using the ending balances in the T-accounts obtained in part *a*.

c. Prepare 1999 adjusting journal entries for the following items and post them to the T-accounts prepared in part *a*.

12. Abercrombie & Fitch employees counted the company's merchandise inventory on January 30, 1999. The cost of inventory in stock on that day was $43,992.

13. Abercrombie & Fitch employees counted the company's store supplies on January 30, 1999. The cost of store supplies on that day was $5,887 (store supplies used are included in store operating expenses).

14. Assume that all of the activity in the "Other current assets" account is related to the company's insurance policies. The unadjusted amount in "Other current assets" (*Hint*: $1,696) represents the beginning balance for prepaid insurance premiums plus all cash payments for insurance during the year. At January 30, 1999, the amount of insurance that had not expired was $691.

15. The company recorded $20,946 of depreciation—part of general, administrative, and store operating expenses—on the property and equipment.

16. Abercrombie and Fitch employees' last payday was January 21st. At year-end there were 10 days of wages that had not been recorded. This amounted to $3,685 including all related payroll taxes.

d. Prepare an adjusted trial balance as at January 30, 1999 using the ending balances in the T-accounts obtained after recording the adjustments listed in part *c*.

e. Prepare the fiscal 1999 income statement.

f. Close the temporary T-accounts and provide the fiscal 1999 closing entry.

g. Prepare the January 30, 1999 balance sheet.

✧ Analysis ✧

h. Calculate the year-over-year percentage change in Net Sales for fiscal 1998 and 1999. Comment on this trend.

i. Comment on the level of inventory in 1999 compared to 1998 and 1997. (Inventory in 1997 was $34,943 and total assets were $105,761.) What conclusions do you draw from this trend?

j. What additional information might an investor in Abercrombie & Fitch seek in order to evaluate the company's future level of profitability?

ABERCROMBIE & FITCH CO.
CONSOLIDATED BALANCE SHEETS
(Thousands)

	January 30, 1999	January 31, 1998
ASSETS		
CURRENT ASSETS:		
Cash and Equivalents		$42,667
Accounts Receivable		1,695
Inventories		33,927
Store Supplies		5,592
Receivable from The Limited		23,785
Other current assets		1,296
TOTAL CURRENT ASSETS		108,962
PROPERTY AND EQUIPMENT, NET		70,517
DEFERRED INCOME TAXES		3,759
OTHER ASSETS		--
TOTAL ASSETS		$183,238
	?	
LIABILITIES AND SHAREHOLDERS' EQUITY		
CURRENT LIABILITIES:		
Accounts Payable		$15,968
Accrued Expenses		35,143
Income Taxes Payable		15,851
TOTAL CURRENT LIABILITIES		66,962
LONG-TERM DEBT		50,000
OTHER LONG-TERM LIABILITIES		7,501
SHAREHOLDERS' EQUITY:		
Common Stock		511
Paid-In Capital		117,972
Retained Earnings (Deficit)		(58,931)
		59,552
Less: Treasury Stock, at Average Cost		(777)
TOTAL SHAREHOLDERS' EQUITY		58,775
TOTAL LIABILITIES AND SHAREHOLDERS' EQUITY		$183,238

The accompanying Notes are an integral part of these Consolidated Financial Statements.

ABERCROMBIE & FITCH CO.
CONSOLIDATED STATEMENTS OF INCOME
(Thousands except per share amounts)

	1999	1998	1997
NET SALES		$521,617	$335,372
Costs of Goods Sold, Occupancy and Buying Costs		320,537	211,606
GROSS INCOME		201,080	123,766
General, Administrative and Store Operating Expenses		116,955	77,773
OPERATING INCOME		84,125	45,993
Interest (Income)/Expense, Net		3,583	4,919
INCOME BEFORE INCOME TAXES		80,542	41,074
Provision for Income Taxes		32,220	16,400
NET INCOME	?	$48,322	$24,674

The accompanying Notes are an integral part of these Consolidated Financial Statements.

Vodafone Group Plc—Time Value of Money

Vodafone Group Plc is the world's leading mobile telecommunications company, with a significant presence in Europe, the United States and the Asia Pacific region. The Group also has arrangements to market certain of its services, through its "Partner Networks" scheme, in additional territories, without the need for equity investment. The Group provides a wide range of mobile telecommunications services, including voice and data telecommunications. The Company's ordinary shares are listed on the London Stock Exchange and the Company's American Depositary Shares are listed on the New York Stock Exchange. The Company had a total market capitalization of approximately £92 billion at 24 May 2004, making it the second largest company in the Financial Times Stock Exchange (FTSE) 100 index and the eleventh largest company in the world based on market capitalization.

Learning Objectives

- Calculate the present value and the future value of a single payment.
- Calculate the present value of a stream of payments.
- Understand the effect of compounding on present and future values.
- Determine the effective interest rate underlying a series of cash flows.

Refer to the 2004 financial statements and Note 18—Creditors of the Vodafone Group, Plc. Focus on the Group (i.e., consolidated) data. Vodafone's fiscal year ends on March 31st.

 Concepts 

a. The following questions test your understanding of time value of money concepts.

   i. Would you rather receive \$100 today or \$100 in exactly one year? Explain your choice.

   ii. What is a lump sum payment?

   iii. What is an annuity? What is an ordinary annuity (annuity in arrears)? What is an annuity due?

   iv. How does compound interest differ from simple interest?

✧ Process 

b. Refer to Note 18—Creditors. Consider the 5.0% U.S. dollar bond due 2013. Assume that Vodafone issued this bond on March 31, 2004 and it matures in 9 years.

   i. How much did Vodafone receive when it issued the bonds? (ignore issuance costs and fees)

   ii. Where does this debt appear on Vodafone's balance sheet? Statement of cash flows? Where does the cost of this debt appear on Vodafone's income statement?

c. Because market conditions appeared favorable, Vodafone's Treasurer decided to raise funds through a debt issuance. Assume that on March 31, 2004, the company issued its 5.625% Sterling bonds due 2025. As the company had no immediate plans for the funds raised, the Treasurer placed the proceeds in an interest-bearing bank account.

   i. Assume that the account pays 3% interest per year. The interest is paid annually on the anniversary date of the deposit and is left in the account. What will the balance of the bank account be on March 31, 2005? March 31, 2006? March 31, 2007? Use the first row in the table on the following page to tabulate your answers.

   ii. Now assume that the account pays 5% per year. Complete the second row of the table.

   iii. Now assume that the interest of 5% per year is paid semi-annually (i.e., 2.5% every six months). Complete the third row of the table.

Interest rate	Balance March 31, 2005	Balance March 31, 2006	Balance March 31, 2007
3% annually			
5% annually			
2.5% semiannually			

d. Vodafone's Treasurer is considering issuing some additional debt denominated in Japanese yen. The company wants to issue zero-coupon bonds. These are bonds that make no periodic interest payments. Rather, they pay a single lump sum at maturity. Vodafone is contemplating the issuance of 5-year zero-coupon bonds with a value at maturity (i.e., a face value) of ¥100 billion.

   i. If the effective (i.e., market) interest rate on this type of debt is 3% per annum, how much would Vodafone receive when it sells the bonds? How much would they receive if the market rate is 6%? Use the first column in the table below to tabulate your answers.

   ii. If instead, the bonds matured in 10 years, how much would Vodafone receive? Complete the second column in the table.

Interest rate	Proceeds on issuance of 5-year zero-coupon bond	Proceeds on issuance of 10-year zero-coupon bond
3% annually		
6% annually		

e. In Note 18, Vodafone indicates that it has some "Finance leases" included in its long-term debt. Finance leases are leases that are accounted for as though the company purchased an asset and borrowed funds for the purchase.

   i. Assume that one of Vodafone's finance leases requires the company to make payments of £10 on March 31st of each of the next 5 years. What is the present value of those lease payments if the appropriate discount (i.e., interest) rate is 7%?

   ii. Assume that another of Vodafone's finance leases requires the company to make payments of £12 on March 31st each year. The 15-year lease is structured so that there will be 10 payments made where the first payment will be made at the end of the fifth year (and annually thereafter). What is the present value of those lease payments if the appropriate discount (i.e., interest) rate is 7%? Drawing a time line that lays out the cash flows will make this analysis easier.

f. Consider the 5.0% Euro bond due 2018. Assume that this bond was issued on March 31, 2004 and matures in 14 years. Assume that the face value of the bond is (in Pounds Sterling) £550.

   i. If Vodafone pays interest on this bond annually, how much interest will the company pay each year?

   ii. What proceeds did Vodafone receive when it issued this bond?

   iii. What annual effective interest rate will Vodafone pay on this bond over the 14 years to maturity? To answer this question, calculate the rate at which the proceeds received exactly equals the annual interest payments plus the repayment of the face value at maturity.

   iv. How would your answer to part *iii* differ if the Vodafone paid 2.5% interest semi-annually instead of 5% annually?

Consolidated Profit and Loss Accounts

For the years ended 31 March

	Note	2004 $m	2004 £m	2003 £m	2002 £m
Total Group turnover: Group and share of joint ventures and associated undertakings					
– Continuing operations		78,973	42,920	37,324	32,125
– Discontinued operations		1,505	818	1,828	1,416
		80,478	43,738	39,152	33,541
Less: Share of joint ventures		–	–	(8)	(3)
Share of associated undertakings		(18,729)	(10,179)	(8,769)	(10,693)
Group turnover	3	61,749	33,559	30,375	22,845
Group turnover	3				
– Continuing operations		60,244	32,741	28,547	21,767
– Discontinued operations		1,505	818	1,828	1,078
		61,749	33,559	30,375	22,845
Operating (loss)/profit	3, 4, 5				
– Continuing operations		(8,909)	(4,842)	(5,052)	(9,966)
– Discontinued operations		121	66	(243)	(411)
		(8,788)	(4,776)	(5,295)	(10,377)
Share of operating profit/(loss) in joint ventures and associated undertakings		1,005	546	(156)	(1,457)
Total Group operating loss					
Group and share of joint ventures and associated undertakings	3	(7,783)	(4,230)	(5,451)	(11,834)
Exceptional non-operating items	6	(190)	(103)	(5)	(860)
– Continuing operations		(81)	(44)	20	(860)
– Discontinued operations		(109)	(59)	(25)	–
Loss on ordinary activities before interest	3	(7,973)	(4,333)	(5,456)	(12,694)
Net interest payable and similar items	7	(1,314)	(714)	(752)	(845)
Group		(918)	(499)	(457)	(503)
Share of joint ventures and associated undertakings		(396)	(215)	(295)	(342)
Loss on ordinary activities before taxation		(9,287)	(5,047)	(6,208)	(13,539)
Tax on loss on ordinary activities	8	(5,803)	(3,154)	(2,956)	(2,140)
Group		(5,273)	(2,866)	(2,624)	(1,925)
Share of joint ventures and associated undertakings		(530)	(288)	(332)	(215)
Loss on ordinary activities after taxation		(15,090)	(8,201)	(9,164)	(15,679)
Equity minority interests		(1,386)	(753)	(593)	(415)
Non-equity minority interests		(112)	(61)	(62)	(61)
Loss for the financial year		(16,588)	(9,015)	(9,819)	(16,155)
Equity dividends	9	(2,535)	(1,378)	(1,154)	(1,025)
Retained loss for the Group and its share of joint ventures and associated undertakings	23	(19,123)	(10,393)	(10,973)	(17,180)
Basic and diluted loss per share	10	(24.36)¢	(13.24)p	(14.41)p	(23.77)p

The accompanying notes are an integral part of these Consolidated Financial Statements.

The unaudited US dollar amounts are prepared on the basis set out in note 1.

Balance Sheets

At 31 March

	Note	Group 2004 $m	Group 2004 £m	Group 2003 as restated £m	Company 2004 £m	Company 2003 £m
Fixed assets						
Intangible assets	11	172,264	93,622	108,085	–	–
Tangible assets	12	33,273	18,083	19,574	–	–
Investments		40,986	22,275	26,989	106,177	104,655
Investments in associated undertakings	13	39,056	21,226	25,825	–	–
Other investments	13	1,930	1,049	1,164	106,177	104,655
		246,523	133,980	154,648	106,177	104,655
Current assets						
Stocks	14	843	458	365	–	–
Debtors	15	12,698	6,901	7,460	65,627	44,699
Investments	16	8,061	4,381	291	–	287
Cash at bank and in hand		2,593	1,409	475	53	215
		24,195	13,149	8,591	65,680	45,201
Creditors: amounts falling due within one year	17	(27,648)	(15,026)	(14,293)	(95,679)	(76,087)
Net current liabilities		(3,453)	(1,877)	(5,702)	(29,999)	(30,886)
Total assets less current liabilities		243,070	132,103	148,946	76,178	73,769
Creditors: amounts falling due after more than one year	18	(23,874)	(12,975)	(13,757)	(9,271)	(8,171)
Provisions for liabilities and charges	21	(7,723)	(4,197)	(3,696)	–	–
		211,473	114,931	131,493	66,907	65,598
Capital and reserves						
Called up share capital	22	7,875	4,280	4,275	4,280	4,275
Share premium account	23	95,963	52,154	52,073	52,154	52,073
Merger reserve		182,026	98,927	98,927	–	–
Capital reserve		–	–	–	88	88
Own shares held	23	(2,090)	(1,136)	(41)	(1,088)	–
Other reserve	23	1,312	713	843	713	843
Profit and loss account	23	(79,146)	(43,014)	(27,447)	10,760	8,319
Total equity shareholders' funds		205,940	111,924	128,630	66,907	65,598
Equity minority interests		3,923	2,132	1,848	–	–
Non-equity minority interests	24	1,610	875	1,015	–	–
		211,473	114,931	131,493	66,907	65,598

The Consolidated Financial Statements were approved by the Board of directors on 25 May 2004 and were signed on its behalf by:

A SARIN Chief Executive

K J HYDON Financial Director

The accompanying notes are an integral part of these Consolidated Financial Statements.

The unaudited US dollar amounts are prepared on the basis set out in note 1.

Consolidated Cash Flows

For the years ended 31 March

	Note	2004 $m	2004 £m	2003 as restated £m	2002 as restated £m
Net cash inflow from operating activities	28	22,663	12,317	11,142	8,102
Dividends received from joint ventures and associated undertakings		3,314	1,801	742	139
Net cash outflow for returns on investments and servicing of finance	28	(81)	(44)	(551)	(936)
Taxation		(2,175)	(1,182)	(883)	(545)
Net cash outflow for capital expenditure and financial investment		(7,851)	(4,267)	(5,359)	(4,441)
Purchase of intangible fixed assets		(39)	(21)	(99)	(325)
Purchase of tangible fixed assets		(8,294)	(4,508)	(5,289)	(4,145)
Purchase of investments		(79)	(43)	(546)	(38)
Disposal of tangible fixed assets		291	158	109	75
Disposal of investments		226	123	575	319
Loans to joint ventures		–	–	(59)	(233)
Loans repaid by/(to) associated undertakings		44	24	–	(523)
Loans to businesses sold or acquired businesses held for sale		–	–	(50)	(116)
Loans repaid by acquired businesses held for sale		–	–	–	545
Net cash outflow from acquisitions and disposals		(2,414)	(1,312)	(4,880)	(7,691)
Purchase of interests in subsidiary undertakings		(3,797)	(2,064)	(3,519)	(3,078)
Net cash/(overdrafts) acquired with subsidiary undertakings		18	10	11	(2,514)
Purchase of interests in associated undertakings		–	–	(1,491)	(7,159)
Purchase of customer bases		–	–	(6)	(11)
Disposal of interests in subsidiary undertakings		1,831	995	125	–
Net cash disposed of with subsidiary undertakings		(475)	(258)	–	–
Disposal of interests in joint ventures and associated undertakings		9	5	–	–
Disposal of acquired businesses held for sale		–	–	–	5,071
Equity dividends paid		(2,315)	(1,258)	(1,052)	(978)
Cash inflow/(outflow) before management of liquid resources and financing		11,141	6,055	(841)	(6,350)
Management of liquid resources	29	(7,886)	(4,286)	1,384	7,042
Net cash outflow from financing	28	(1,288)	(700)	(150)	(681)
Issue of ordinary share capital		127	69	28	3,581
Increase/(decrease) in debt		515	280	(165)	(4,268)
Issue of shares to minorities		–	–	1	12
Purchase of treasury shares		(1,899)	(1,032)	–	–
Purchase of own shares in relation to employee share schemes		(31)	(17)	(14)	(6)
Increase in cash in the year		1,967	1,069	393	11
Reconciliation of net cash flow to movement in net debt					
Increase in cash in the year	29	1,967	1,069	393	11
Cash (inflow)/outflow from (increase)/decrease in debt	29	(515)	(280)	165	4,268
Cash outflow/(inflow) from increase/(decrease) in liquid resources	29	7,886	4,286	(1,384)	(7,042)
Decrease/(increase) in net debt resulting from cash flows	29	9,338	5,075	(826)	(2,763)
Net debt acquired on acquisition of subsidiary undertakings		(13)	(7)	–	(3,116)
Net debt disposed of on disposal of subsidiary undertakings		357	194	–	–
Translation difference		265	144	(826)	517
Premium on repayment of debt		(103)	(56)	(157)	–
Other movements		2	1	4	50
Decrease/(increase) in net debt in the year		9,846	5,351	(1,805)	(5,312)
Opening net debt		(25,464)	(13,839)	(12,034)	(6,722)
Closing net debt	29	(15,618)	(8,488)	(13,839)	(12,034)

The accompanying notes are an integral part of these Consolidated Financial Statements.
The unaudited US dollar amounts are prepared on the basis set out in note 1.

Consolidated Statements of Total Recognised Gains and Losses

For the years ended 31 March

	2004 $m	2004 £m	2003 £m	2002 £m
Loss for the financial year				
Group	(16,553)	(8,996)	(9,049)	(14,131)
Share of joint ventures	–	–	(62)	(211)
Share of associated undertakings	(35)	(19)	(708)	(1,813)
	(16,588)	(9,015)	(9,819)	(16,155)
Currency translation				
Group	(4,530)	(2,462)	10,484	(1,980)
Share of joint ventures	–	–	2	4
Share of associated undertakings	(5,207)	(2,830)	(1,447)	(287)
	(9,737)	(5,292)	9,039	(2,263)
Total recognised losses relating to the year	(26,325)	(14,307)	(780)	(18,418)

The accompanying notes are an integral part of these Consolidated Financial Statements.
The unaudited US dollar amounts are prepared on the basis set out in note 1.

Movements in Total Equity Shareholders' Funds

For the years ended 31 March

	2004 $m	2004 £m	2003 as restated £m	2002 as restated £m
Loss for the financial year	(16,588)	(9,015)	(9,819)	(16,155)
Equity dividends	(2,535)	(1,378)	(1,154)	(1,025)
	(19,123)	(10,393)	(10,973)	(17,180)
Currency translation	(9,737)	(5,292)	9,039	(2,263)
New share capital subscribed, net of issue costs	158	86	31	5,984
Goodwill transferred to the profit and loss account in respect of business disposals	–	–	–	3
Shares to be issued	–	–	–	(978)
Purchase of treasury shares	(2,002)	(1,088)	–	–
Purchase of shares in relation to employee share schemes	(31)	(17)	(14)	(6)
Own shares released on vesting of share awards	18	10	6	1
Other	(22)	(12)	1	–
Net movement in total equity shareholders' funds	(30,739)	(16,706)	(1,910)	(14,439)
Opening total equity shareholders' funds (originally £128,671 million before prior year adjustment of £41 million)	236,679	128,630	130,540	144,979
Closing total equity shareholders' funds	205,940	111,924	128,630	130,540

The accompanying notes are an integral part of these Consolidated Financial Statements.
The unaudited US dollar amounts are prepared on the basis set out in note 1.

16. Investments

	Group		Company	
	2004 £m	2003 £m	2004 £m	2003 £m
Liquid investments	4,381	291	–	287

Liquid investments principally comprise collateralised deposits and investments in commercial paper.

Included within liquid investments of the Group and Company, at 31 March 2003, was a restricted deposit account of £287 million for the deferred purchase of 48,935,625 shares in Vodafone Portugal. This was released for payment on 4 April 2003.

17. Creditors: amounts falling due within one year

	Group		Company	
	2004 £m	2003 £m	2004 £m	2003 £m
Bank overdrafts	42	–	–	–
Bank loans and other loans	2,000	1,078	956	351
Commercial paper	–	245	–	245
Finance leases	12	107	–	–
Trade creditors	2,842	2,497	–	–
Amounts owed to subsidiary undertakings	–	–	93,553	74,242
Amounts owed to associated undertakings	8	13	–	–
Taxation	4,275	4,137	–	–
Other taxes and social security costs	367	855	–	–
Other creditors	741	1,342	71	460
Accruals and deferred income	4,011	3,407	371	177
Proposed dividend	728	612	728	612
	15,026	14,293	95,679	76,087

18. Creditors: amounts falling due after more than one year

	Group		Company	
	2004 £m	2003 £m	2004 £m	2003 £m
Bank loans	1,504	1,803	23	–
Other loans	10,596	11,191	8,795	7,807
Finance leases	124	181	–	–
Other creditors	7	19	–	–
Accruals and deferred income	744	563	453	364
	12,975	13,757	9,271	8,171

Bank loans are repayable as follows:

	Group		Company	
	2004 £m	2003 £m	2004 £m	2003 £m
Repayable in more than one year but not more than two years	105	128	6	–
Repayable in more than two years but not more than five years	1,398	1,602	16	–
Repayable in more than five years	1	73	1	–
	1,504	1,803	23	–

Other loans are repayable as follows:

	Group		Company	
	2004 £m	2003 £m	2004 £m	2003 £m
Repayable in more than one year but not more than two years	303	1,994	–	–
Repayable in more than two years but not more than five years	3,108	2,878	2,549	3,072
Repayable in more than five years	7,185	6,319	6,246	4,735
	10,596	11,191	8,795	7,807

Notes to the Consolidated Financial Statements continued

18. Creditors: amounts falling due after more than one year continued

Other loans falling due after more than one year primarily comprise bond issues by the Company, or its subsidiaries, analysed as follows:

	Group		Company	
	2004 £m	2003 £m	2004 £m	2
4.875% Euro bond due 2004	–	859	–	
1.27% Japanese yen bond due 2005	134	139	–	
1.93% Japanese yen bond due 2005	135	140	–	
5.25% Euro bond due 2005	–	139	–	
6.35% US dollar bond due 2005	34	125	–	
7.625% US dollar bond due 2005	–	995	–	9
0.83% Japanese yen bond due 2006	16	16	16	
1.78% Japanese yen bond due 2006	135	139	–	
5.4% Euro bond due 2006	267	276	267	2
5.75% Euro bond due 2006	1,001	1,032	1,001	1,0
7.5% US dollar bond due 2006	121	258	–	
4.161% US dollar bond due 2007	81	95	81	
2.575% Japanese yen bond due 2008	136	140	–	
3.95% US dollar bond due 2008	271	315	271	3
4.625% Euro bond due 2008	504	344	504	3
5.5% Euro bond due 2008	32	146	–	
6.25% Sterling bond due 2008	249	248	249	2
6.25% Sterling bond due 2008	160	–	160	
6.65% US dollar bond due 2008	135	316	–	
4.25% Euro bond due 2009	1,266	1,306	1,266	1,3
4.75% Euro bond due 2009	548	567	–	
2.0% Japanese yen bond due 2010	135	139	–	
2.28% Japanese yen bond due 2010	133	136	–	
2.5% Japanese yen bond due 2010	137	141	–	
7.75% US dollar bond due 2010	1,473	1,711	1,487	1,7
5.0% US dollar bond due 2013	540	–	540	
5.125% Euro bond due 2015	333	–	333	
5.375% US dollar bond due 2015	495	251	495	2
5.0% Euro bond due 2018	499	–	499	
4.625% US dollar bond due 2018	270	–	270	
5.625% Sterling bond due 2025	246	–	246	
7.875% US dollar bond due 2030	400	465	400	4
5.9% Sterling bond due 2032	443	443	443	4
6.25% US dollar bond due 2032	267	310	267	3
	10,596	11,191	8,795	7,8

	Group 2004 £m	Group 2003 £m	Company 2004 £m	
Finance leases are repayable as follows:				
Repayable in more than one year but not more than two years	11	47	–	
Repayable in more than two years but not more than five years	30	39	–	
Repayable in more than five years	83	95	–	
	124	181	–	

Rhodia Group—Goodwill Impairment

Headquartered in Boulogne-Billancourt, France, Rhodia is one of the world's leading manufacturers of specialty chemicals, with 113 production sites, six research and development centers, and sales in over 130 countries. The company provides a wide range of products and services to the consumer care, food, industrial care, pharmaceuticals, agrochemicals, automotive, electronics and fibers markets, and has numerous worldwide market leading positions in products such as food phosphates, hydroquinone, vanillin, guar gum, aspirin, precipitated silica, and separated rare earths products. As of December 31, 2003, Rhodia had 23,059 employees. The company's shares are listed on the Paris and New York stock exchanges.

Learning Objectives

- Understand where financial statements use time value of money techniques.
- Understand the basic procedure for determining goodwill impairments.
- Appreciate the sensitivity of impairment charges to changes in valuation inputs.
- Assess the short-term solvency of a company in financial trouble.
- Use additional information to assess the impact of an accounting change.

Refer to the 2003 Consolidated Financial Statements of Rhodia Group.

Concepts

a. Review Rhodia's balance sheets and income statements. Where does the company apply time value of money techniques to measure assets, liabilities, revenues, and expenses?

b. Explain how using time value of money techniques to measure items in the financial statements affects the overall relevance and reliability of the financial reports.

Process

c. One of the biggest changes in Rhodia's performance from 2002 to 2003 is the substantial increase in "Amortisation of Goodwill." In Note 1—Accounting policies, Rhodia explains, "Goodwill represents the excess of the acquisition cost over the fair value of net identifiable assets of businesses acquired on the date of the transaction. [Under French GAAP,] Goodwill is amortised on a straight-line basis over a period of not more than forty years. [Under US GAAP and IFRS, annual amortization is not recorded.] ... For each Group activity corresponding to a reporting unit, Rhodia annually compares the net book value of the assets and liabilities that are associated with the enterprise, including goodwill, with the fair value of the activity. In the absence of an active market, this corresponds to the discounted cash flows of the activity. Rhodia updates this comparison whenever events or circumstances indicate that the net book value of goodwill may not be recoverable."

   i. Refer to Note 5—Goodwill. How much of the 2003 Amortisation of goodwill was due to asset impairments? Which business units were affected?

   ii. Consider the Pharma Solutions reporting unit referred to in Note 5. Perform a discounted cash flow analysis to determine whether the goodwill of this reporting unit is impaired. Follow the procedure outlined in Note 5 and use a spreadsheet to determine the present value of the cash flows at December 31, 2003 assuming all cash flows occur at year end and:

   - the starting (i.e., 2004) cash flow for the medium-term business plan is €60 million
   - the medium term growth rate in those cash flows is 2.5%. The long term growth rate, per Note 5, is 4.0%

- to arrive at a terminal value, you must capitalize the last cash flow of the plan by "the difference between WACC and the long-term growth rate." This is equivalent to multiplying that last cash flow by 1 / (WACC – long-term growth rate). This means that the numerator in your terminal value calculation is the cash flow expected for 2008.

The following is a summary of the assumptions for this question.

Starting cash flow	€60.0
Medium Term growth rate	2.5%
Long Term growth rate	4.0%
WACC	10.0%

Use the following table to organize your analysis.

	2004	2005	2006	2007	2008	Terminal value
Cash Flow	60.0					
Number of years out	1	2	3	4	5	
Present value	54.5					
Total Present value						

iii. If the fair value (without goodwill) of the Pharma Solutions business unit was €832, use your answer to part *ii* and information in Note 5, to determine the pre-impairment book value of the Pharma Solutions goodwill. Use the table below to organize your analysis.

Impairment Calculation	
PV of Cash Flows from analysis in part ii, above	
Fair Value of Non-Goodwill net assets	832
Implied Fair Value of Goodwill before impairment	
Book Value of Goodwill, from note 5	
Impairment, from note 5	

iv. What would the 2003 impairment charge for the Pharma Solutions unit have been if (holding the other assumptions constant):

- WACC was 9%? 11%?
- The long-term growth rate was 3.5%? 1.5%?
- The starting cash flows were €50? €80?

Fill in the following table and compare your findings under the various combinations of assumptions.

Impairment Calculation	**Original Assumptions**	**WACC 9%**	**WACC 11%**	**LT growth 3.5%**	**LT growth 1.5%**	**CF €50**	**CF €80**
PV Cash Flows							
FV of Non GW net assets							
Implied FV of Goodwill							
BV of Goodwill							
Impairment							

v. Goodwill impairments are sometimes referred to as non-cash charges. Often, in press releases and other corporate communications, the tone of the message is that readers should ignore these non-cash charges. Comment on whether and when that makes sense.

✧ Analysis ✧

d. Rhodia finds itself in financial difficulty. Indeed, an extensive note to its financial statements outlines a number of concerns and the company's belief that, despite the challenges, it is appropriate to prepare its financial statements assuming the company will remain a going concern (see Note 1—Accounting policies).

   i. The current ratio is defined as: $\frac{\text{Current Assets}}{\text{Current Liabilities}}$. Calculate the ratio at December 31, 2002 and 2003. What does this common balance sheet ratio suggest about the company's ability to pay its creditors in the short run?

   ii. What other ratios and financial indicators suggest the company is in financial difficulty?

e. An article entitled "Rhodia seeks to reassure investors in profit outlook" appeared in the *Financial Times* on January 20, 2005, before the company released its 2004 financial statements. The reporter refers to two changes that will arise as Rhodia (along with all listed European Union companies) begins to use International Financial Reporting Standards (IFRS) in 2005.

   > "Rhodia said the introduction this year of International Financial Reporting Standards would have a marked effect on its balance sheet but would not change its cash position or financial covenants for bank debt.
   >
   > The company said the inclusion of unfunded pension obligations on its balance sheet would reduce shareholder equity by €620m from this year. It added that the consolidation of securitisations programmes would increase net debt by €413m."

   You would like to estimate the effect of the accounting changes that IFRS compliance will bring.

   i. The total debt to equity ratio is defined as: $\frac{\text{Total Liabilities}}{\text{Total Owners' Equity}}$. Calculate the ratio at December 31, 2003. Include minority interest with Owners' Equity.

   ii. What would the ratio be if the company included its unfunded pension obligations on its balance sheet, as it will under IFRS? Assume the amounts in the article approximate the December 31, 2003 amounts.

   iii. What would the ratio be if the company included the debt from its asset "securitisation programmes" on its balance sheet, as it will under IFRS? Assume the amounts in the article approximate the December 31, 2003 amounts.

Consolidated balance sheets

ASSETS

(in millions of euros)	note	31/12/03	31/12/02	31/12/01
Goodwill	5	437	1,186	1,354
Other intangible assets	6	132	177	206
Tangible assets	7	2,526	2,743	3,561
Investments and other assets				
> Deposits and long-term receivables		170	120	98
> Investments accounted for under equity method	8	123	172	238
> Investments at cost	9	54	67	75
> Deferred charges and other assets	10	526	571	353
Total long-term assets		**3,968**	**5,036**	**5,885**
Inventories	11	726	835	1,044
Accounts receivable	12	311	378	524
Other current assets	13	758	917	916
Marketable securities	16	253	108	180
Cash and cash equivalents		513	143	233
Total current assets		**2,561**	**2,381**	**2,897**
TOTAL ASSETS		6,529	7,417	8,782

The accompanying notes are an integral part of the consolidated financial statements.

LIABILITIES AND SHAREHOLDERS' EQUITY

(in millions of euros)	note	31/12/03	31/12/02	31/12/01
Common stock		179	179	2,690
Additional paid-in capital		2,513	2,514	3
Retained earnings/(deficit)		(1,841)	(418)	(374)
Cumulative translation adjustment		(599)	(440)	(52)
Total shareholders' equity	*17*	**252**	**1,835**	**2,267**
Minority interests	*18*	23	23	84
Total shareholders' equity and minority interests		**275**	**1,858**	**2,351**
Reserves for pensions, deferred income taxes and other costs in excess of one year	*19*	**945**	**963**	**1,008**
Other long-term liabilities		**70**	**141**	**149**
Long-term debt	*20*	**1,886**	**1,739**	**1,949**
Short-term borrowings and current portion of long-term debt	*20*	1,447	645	1,036
Accounts payable		784	948	885
Short-term reserves for pensions, deferred income taxes and other costs	*19*	311	301	474
Other current liabilities	*21*	811	822	930
Total current liabilities		**3,353**	**2,716**	**3,325**
TOTAL LIABILITIES AND SHAREHOLDERS' EQUITY		6,529	7,417	8,782

Off-balance sheet commitments: cf. Note 25.

The accompanying notes are an integral part of the consolidated financial statements.

111

Consolidated statement of operations

(in millions of euros)	note	2003	2002	2001
Net sales		**5,453**	**6,617**	**7,279**
Production costs and expenses		(4,218)	(4,844)	(5,541)
Administrative and selling costs		(612)	(749)	(745)
Research and development expenses	*27*	(187)	(201)	(197)
Depreciation and amortisation		(524)	(447)	(542)
Restructuring and environmental costs		(71)	(25)	(163)
Operating income/(loss)		**(159)**	**351**	**91**
Financial expense - net	*22*	(250)	(123)	(186)
Other income/(expense) – net	*23*	(98)	(72)	(108)
Income/(loss) of consolidated subsidiaries before income taxes		**(507)**	**156**	**(203)**
Income taxes	*24*	(142)	(66)	86
Income/(loss) of consolidated subsidiaries		**(649)**	**90**	**(117)**
Equity in earnings/(losses) of affiliated companies		(95)	(38)	(16)
Amortisation of goodwill		(602)	(47)	(75)
Income/(loss) before minority interests		**(1,346)**	**5**	**(208)**
Minority interests		(5)	(9)	(5)
NET INCOME/(LOSS)		**(1,351)**	**(4)**	**(213)**

	2003	2002	2001
> Basic earnings/(loss) per share (in euros)	**(7.53)**	**(0.02)**	**(1.19)**
Average shares outstanding	*179,309,188*	*178,765,518*	*179,103,640*
> Diluted earnings/(loss) per share (in euros)	**(7.53)**	**(0.02)**	**(1.19)**
Average shares after dilution	*179,309,188*	*178,765 518*	*179,103,640*

The accompanying notes are an integral part of the consolidated financial statements.

112

Consolidated statements of stockholder's equity

(in millions of euros)	Common stock (Note 17a)	Additional paid-in capital (Note 17a)	Retained earnings/ (deficit) (Note 17c)	Net income/ (loss)	Cumulative translation adjustment (Note 17d)	Total (note 17)
Au 31/12/2000	**2,690**	**3**	**(290)**	**216**	**(26)**	**2,593**
Allocation to retained earnings			216	(216)		-
Dividends paid			(85)	(85)		
Net Loss				(213)		(213)
Translation			(2)		(26)	(28)
Balance at 31/12/2001	**2,690**	**3**	**(161)**	**(213)**	**(52)**	**2,267**
Allocation to retained earnings			(213)	213		-
Dividends paid			(21)			(21)
Net loss				(4)		(4)
Reclassification	(1)	1				
Treasury stock transactions			(10)			(10)
Translation			(9)		(388)	(397)
Reduction in par value of common stock from 15€ to 1€	(2,510)	2,510				
Balance at 31/12/2002	**179**	**2,514**	**(414)**	**(4)**	**(440)**	**1,835**
Allocation to retained earnings		(1)	(3)	4		-
Dividends paid			(22)			(22)
Net loss				(1,351)		(1,351)
Change in accounting principles (1)			(48)			(48)
Translation			(3)		(159)	(162)
Balance at 31/12/2003	**179**	**2,513**	**(490)**	**(1,351)**	**(599)**	**252**

The accompanying notes are an integral part of the consolidated financial statements.

(1) Additional provisions for long-term service payments benefits related to the change in accounting principles described in Note 1.

113

Consolidated statement of cash flows

(in millions of euros)	2003	2002	2001
Net income/(loss)	**(1,351)**	**(4)**	**(213)**
Adjustments to reconcile net income/(loss) to net cash provided by operating activities			
Minority interests	5	9	5
Depreciation and amortization of assets	1,126	494	617
Change in operating reserves	79	(79)	142
Change in financial reserves	92	5	8
Equity in earnings/ (losses) of affiliated companies	95	38	16
Dividends received from affiliated companies	2	3	29
Net (gains)/losses from disposals of assets	31	35	(15)
Deferred income taxes	102	7	(180)
Foreign exchange losses (gains)	(35)	28	(4)
Cash flow	**146**	**536**	**405**
Change in working capital:			
- (Increase)/decrease in inventories	63	14	123
- (Increase)/decrease in accounts receivable	33	(19)	219
- Increase/(decrease) in accounts payable	(144)	204	(185)
- Increase/(decrease) in other operating assets and liabilities	(125)	(229)	114
Net cash provided by/(used for) operating activities	**(27)**	**506**	**676**
Additions to property, plant and equipment	(233)	(374)	(483)
Other capital investments	(42)	(52)	(102)
Proceeds from disposals of assets	92	363	500
(Increase)/decrease in loans and short-term investments	(173)	3	(69)
Net cash used for investing activities	**(356)**	**(60)**	**(154)**
Capital increase	-	-	6
Dividends paid to Rhodia stockholders	(22)	(21)	(85)
Share (purchases)/sales	-	(15)	-
New long-term borrowings	2 370	3 156	1 927
Repayments of long-term borrowings	(1,348)	(3,424)	(1,770)
Increase/(decrease) in short-term borrowings	(240)	(194)	(535)
Net cash provided by/(used for) financing activities	**760**	**(498)**	**(457)**
Net effect of exchange rate changes on cash	**(7)**	**(38)**	**3**
Increase/(decrease) in cash and cash equivalents	**370**	**(90)**	**68**
Cash and cash equivalents at beginning of year	143	233	165
Cash and cash equivalents at end of year	513	143	233

The accompanying notes are an integral part of the consolidated financial statements.

1. Accounting policies

The consolidated financial statements of Rhodia are prepared in accordance with Regulation No. 99-02 issued by the *"Comité de la Réglementation Comptable"* (CRC) relating to the consolidated financial statements of commercial societies and public companies.

Regulation No. 00-06, which defines how companies account for liabilities and came into force on January 1, 2002, has been applied in anticipation by Rhodia since January 1, 2000.

A change of accounting principles came into effect as from January 1, 2003. This change, based on Recommendation R.01 of the *"Conseil National de la Comptabilité"*, issued on April 1, 2003, concerns the rules governing the accounting for and evaluation of the commitments for retirement and similar benefits. It stipulates that the benefits paid out during an employee's working life are excluded from the similar benefits granted to retired persons. As a result of this new interpretation, benefits paid with respect to long-term service benefits are no longer governed by the special accounting rules applying to retirement commitments, and now fall within the scope of Regulation No. 2000-06 on liabilities, thereby making their accrual compulsory.

Since this is a change of rule, the additional adjustment required at the opening was entered in the shareholders' equity for an amount of €48 million net of tax effect (cf. "Consolidated statements of stockholder's equity" table, page 113).

Going concern

Due to depressed market conditions characterised by persistently high raw material purchase prices, weak demand and the negative impact of the dollar's weakness against the euro, Rhodia introduced, in October 2003, a recovery plan built principally around the following actions:

- A refocusing of the business portfolio designed to increase the pace of debt reduction through the implementation of an asset disposal plan, and aiming to generate €700 million from the proceeds of sales in 2004.
- The introduction of an administrative and commercial cost-cutting plan designed to save €120 million in 2005 and €165 million in 2006 (Note 19e).
- The consolidation of the Group's short and medium-term financing, certain short and medium-term funds carrying financial restriction clauses which were very unlikely to be respected at the end of the financial year.

In this context, Rhodia signed a refinancing agreement on 23 December 2003 (Secured Coordination Agreement – SCA) with 23 lending banks (Note 20a). This agreement enables Rhodia to keep certain existing credit lines amounting to €968 million until May 15, 2004. In return, Rhodia has agreed:

- To carry through the asset disposal plan described above in order to release at least €700 million in net receipts over the year 2004, including €400 million before June 30, 2004 (of which €200 million collected and €200 million to be collected before December 31, 2004).
- To launch an increase in capital generating net income of at least €300 million before May 15, 2004.
- To subscribe before February 27, 2004 a new credit line of €758 million to take the place of the current lines of relevance to the SCA. This new credit line will expire on March 31, 2006 and its use is subject to the increase in capital.

In addition, Rhodia does not consider it will be in a position to respect the financial restriction clauses (covenant) concerning the US private investment (USPP) of $290 million, and has initiated negotiations with the bondholders, making provision for their anticipated repayment over the first half of 2004 and accompanied by repayment penalties of approximately $84 million (Note 20c).

Finaly, in view of the continuing unfavourable economic climate and the impact of the restructuring programme, Rhodia does not expect to generate a positive cash flow from its industrial and commercial operations in the year 2004. This is the context in which Rhodia will have to repay two tranches of European bonds (EMTM). The first tranche, in an amount of €500 million, matures in May 2005, and the second (€300 million) in March 2006. Rhodia's ability to repay these bonds will depend on its success in finding new sources of finance.

Notwithstanding these difficulties, Rhodia's Senior Management delieves that the preparation of the consolidated accounts of Rhodia as o f december 31, 2003 in accordance with the conventional accounting principles of a going concern is appropriate. Considering the amount of cash and marketable securities available at December 31, 2003, i.e. €766 million, the expected proceeds from disposals of assets and the capital increase, Rhodia believes that it will have source of liquidity to meet its financing requirements in 2004. However, this assessment remains subject to the following areas of uncertainty and could affect that assessment:

- The forecasts concerning funds from the Group's industrial and commercial operations depend on outside factors (raw material prices, exchange rates, level of demand). An unfavourable trend would have a significant impact on Rhodia's liquidity.
- The collection of receipts from the planned sales of assets and the capital increase in line with the commitments made with respect to the SCA: Rhodia's Senior Management believes that such operations are probable but there is no certainty as to the Group's ability to carry them through within the deadlines set and for the amounts indicated.

5. Goodwill

(in millions of euros)	2003 Gross value	2003 Amortisation	2003 Net book Value	2002 Net book Value
Balance, January 1	2,040	(854)	1,186	1,354
Additions/(reductions) to goodwill	(71)	31	(40)	13
Goodwill amortisation	-	(602)	(602)	(47)
Translation	(261)	154	(107)	(134)
Balance, December 31,	**1,708**	**(1,271)**	**437**	**1,186**

Goodwill amortisation for 2003 totalled €602 million, which includes accelerated amortisation from the asset impairment tests of €546 million (see Note 3), and €20 million recorded as accelerated amortisation resulting from the sale of the polyurethane flame-retardants business on July 24, 2003.

Net goodwill per company	2003	2002
A&W	105	503
Chirex	74	354
RTZ	46	53
Stauffer Chemicals	76	115
Kofran	31	33
Other	105	128
Total	**437**	**1,186**

In accordance with Notes 1f and 3, asset impairment tests were performed for each reporting unit of Rhodia.

The methodology used consists of the development of discounted cash flows, using the following principal assumptions:

- Development by management of medium-term plans for five years for each reporting unit.
- Discounting the net cash flows from these plans for each reporting unit based on Rhodia's weighted average cost of capital (WACC) for each reporting unit, which is 8.0%, net of tax, (10% for the Pharma Solutions, including Chirex, reporting unit). In both cases, this is a 1.5 percentage point increase on the rate used for the tests carried out in the preceding year. This increase is mainly a reflection of the Group's worsening credit risk over the 2003 financial year.
- Determination of a terminal value by capitalising the last cash flow of the plan by the difference between the WACC and the long-term growth rate estimated for each reporting unit. This terminal value is then discounted using the WACC of each reporting unit.

In addition, for certain reporting units, comparisons were made between the discounted cash flows and appropriate market multiples in order to access the fair value of these reporting units.

Pharma Solutions activities linked to the acquisition of ChiRex:

- Beginning in 2003, activities acquired in the Chirex acquisition were integrated with other pharmaceutical activities of Rhodia to form a new reporting unit named Pharma Solutions.
- The reporting unit prepared re-estimated discounted cash flows in the light of a) the failure to achieve a swift and definitive signature of a key contract for the development of the activity, and b) a reduction of the estimated growth rate for the reporting unit as compared with the last strategic business plan (itself reflecting a reduction in the estimated rebound in the market for the pharmaceutical industry).
- The long term growth rate was lowered from 5% to 4% compared to the test performed at the end of 2002 in order to allow for the new market analysis.
- The valuation obtained by the discounted cash flow method at a rate of 10% revealed a loss in value of €232 million of the ChiRex goodwill attached to this reporting unit.

Phosphorus and Performance Derivatives reporting unit (resulting from the A&W acquisition):

- A portion of this reporting unit (polyurethane flame-retardants) was sold by Rhodia in July 2003. Discounted cash flow projections prepared in 2003 considered the same basis assumptions made in 2002, adjusted for the consequences of this sale and the impact of higher raw material costs in China.
- The long term growth rate used was 3.5% reflecting Rhodia's expectation that its position as a leader in this reporting unit's markets as well as innovation will support this growth rate.
- The discounted cash flows valuation was compared with an approach based on an EBITDA multiple. Adopting a multiple corresponding to the sale price of the flame-retardants activity, the valuation is similar to that obtained by the discounted cash flow method.
- The goodwill impairment determined in this way and for this reporting unit amounts to €110 million.

Specialty Phosphates reporting unit (activities from the A&W and Stauffer acquisitions):

- A growth rate of 0% was retained for this reporting unit, reflecting the mature market conditions of the majority of its products, in particular the detergents and water treatment businesses and to a lesser extent the food ingredients business.
- In addition to the discounted cash flows methods, and in view of the ongoing studies on the appropriateness of withdrawing from this activity, Rhodia also carried out a valuation based on a range of appropriate market multiples.
- The goodwill impairment for this reporting unit is calculated by referring to the average of the values obtained according to the two valuation methods, and amounts to €204 million (including €12 million for the excipient phosphates business of the Pharma Solutions reporting unit).

Net goodwill per reporting unit	2003	2002
Pharma Solutions	91	385
Phosphorus and Performance Derivatives	119	325
Specialty Phosphates	42	259
Other	185	217
Total	**437**	**1,186**

123

6. Other intangible assets

	2003			2002
(in millions of euros)	Gross value	Amortisation	Net book Value	Net book Value (1)
Patents and trademarks	94	(66)	28	38
Software	262	(179)	83	95
Other	52	(31)	21	44
Total	**408**	**(276)**	**132**	**177**

(1) Accumulated amortisation at December 31, 2002 was €264 million.

Amortisation charges relating to other intangible assets are as follows:

(in millions of euros)	2003	2002	2001
Patents, trademarks and software	(38)	(30)	(34)
Other (1)	(20)	(3)	(5)
Total	**(58)**	**(33)**	**(39)**

(1) Amortisation for 2003 includes accelerated amortisation of 18 million relating to a long-term supply contact from the A&W acquisition recorded as a result of the asset impairment tests (cf. Note 3).

Maple Leaf Gardens—Measurement Concepts & Valuation

Maple Leaf Gardens, Ltd., is in the entertainment business in Canada through its ownership and operation of the Toronto Maple Leaf Hockey Club and the arena facilities at 60 Carlton Street, Toronto, Ontario. It derives all of its operating income from these assets. Its revenues are derived from four sources: (1) admission fees from Maple Leaf games, (2) broadcast, promotional and advertising rights, (3) building use fees for events other than Maple Leaf games and (4) merchandising and concession sales.

Learning Objectives

- Explain how important assumptions underlying GAAP are reflected in the financial statements.
- Understand the difference between net book value and fair market value.
- Perform and interpret basic balance sheet and income statement-based valuation analyses.

Refer to the 1992 financial statements of Maple Leaf Gardens, Ltd.

 Concepts 

a. The Financial Accounting Standards Board's (FASB) Statement of Concepts No. 1, *Objectives of Financial Reporting by Business Enterprises*, discusses users and uses of financial reports.

   i. Speculate on who uses the Maple Leaf Gardens financial statements and what those users would like to know.

   ii. For users interested in assessing the financial performance of an enterprise, which basis of accounting, accrual or cash-basis, generally provides a better measure of current period performance? Why? Does Maple Leaf Gardens use accrual-basis or cash-basis accounting?

   iii. Financial statements are normally prepared under the assumption that the entity is a going concern. Explain what is meant by a "going concern" and how that assumption affects figures on the Maple Leaf Gardens financial statements.

b. FASB Statement of Concepts No. 2, *Qualitative Characteristics of Accounting Information*, identifies attributes of financial reporting that enhance its usefulness. The primary qualities are that accounting information be relevant and reliable.

   Relevance is described as "the capacity of information to make a difference in a decision by helping users to form predictions about outcomes of past, present, and future events or to confirm or correct prior expectations." Reliability is described as "the quality of information that assures that information is reasonably free from error and bias and faithfully represents what it purports to represent."

   One way to enhance the relevance of financial reporting is to enhance its timeliness.

   i. How often do public companies, like Maple Leaf Gardens, typically report their financial performance, financial position, and cash flows?

   ii. Speculate as to why Maple Leaf Gardens has a May 31 year end.

   iii. How does increasing the frequency of reporting affect the reliability of financial reports?

   iv. Discuss some ways an enterprise can enhance the relevance and reliability of its financial reporting. What are the benefits to managers and shareholders of doing so?

c. FASB Statement of Concepts No. 6 (a replacement for SCON No. 3), *Elements of Financial Statements*, describes the building blocks with which financial statements are constructed.

   Define each of the following elements and provide examples from Maple Leaf Gardens' financial statements where possible.

   i. Assets
   ii. Liabilities
   iii. Owners' Equity
   iv. Investments by Owners
   v. Distributions to Owners
   vi. Revenues
   vii. Expenses
   viii. Gains
   ix. Losses
   x. Comprehensive Income

d. FASB Statement of Concepts No. 5, *Recognition and Measurement in Financial Statements of Business Enterprises*, provides guidance on what information should be included in the financial statements and when. SCON No. 5 identifies four fundamental criteria for an item to be recognized in the financials: (1) the item should meet the *definition* of an element of financial statements (i.e., SCON No. 6), (2) the item is *relevant* to decision making, (3) the information is *reliable* (i.e., representationally faithful, verifiable, and neutral), and (4) it can be *measured* with sufficient reliability. Alternative measurement bases include historical cost, replacement cost, current market value, net realizable value, and the present value of future cash flows.

   Explain how each of the following items are measured in Maple Leaf Gardens' financial statements.

   i. Cash
   ii. Accounts Receivable
   iii. Land
   iv. National Hockey League Franchise
   v. Accounts Payable

e. Why don't Maple Leaf Gardens' financial statements measure all elements at their market values?

f. A customer purchases a season ticket package for 40 Toronto Maple Leaf hockey games.

   i. From an economic perspective, at the time of purchase, are Maple Leaf Gardens' shareholders better off?
   ii. Should Maple Leaf Gardens treat the cash receipt as revenue? If so, why? If not, when should they do so? When does the company recognize revenue?

g. Maple Leaf Gardens signs a National Hockey League player to a five-year contract. The contract specifies that a signing bonus of $1 million be paid immediately. The player will receive an additional $1 million per year for each of the following five years.

   i. From an economic perspective, at the time of payment of the signing bonus, are Maple Leaf Gardens' shareholders better or worse off?
   ii. Should the company treat the cash payment as an expense? If so, why? If not, when should they do so? How does your answer relate to the notion of matching revenues and expenses?

✧ Analysis ✧

h. For this question, refer only to the May 31, 1992 financial statements of Maple Leaf Gardens.

   i. What is the net book value of Maple Leaf Gardens, Ltd. (the company, not the individual assets or liabilities) at May 31, 1992? What does this amount represent?

   ii. Which individual accounts most likely have fair market values that differ significantly from the book values recorded on the balance sheet? What accounting principles give rise to these differences?

   iii. Assume that the fair market value of the company's National Hockey League (NHL) franchise is equal to the amount charged new teams entering the League (see Note 3—assume that $1 Cdn = $.75 U.S.). In addition, as the land owned by the company is a prime parcel of real estate located in downtown Toronto, assume that the book value of the land is only 15% of its fair market value. Finally, assume that all other amounts recorded on the balance sheet approximate their fair market values. Based on your restated balance sheet, what is the net fair market value of Maple Leaf Gardens, Ltd. at May 31, 1992?

   iv. Compare your responses to parts *h i.* (net book value) and *h iii.* (fair market value of net assets). Why are these amounts so different? What does the difference represent?

i. One way that financial analysts approximate the value of a company is by applying a "multiple" to the company's net income. This multiple is commonly known as the Price-Earnings (or PE) multiple. It is a simple, but easily applied, valuation method. For example, if a company had net income per share of $5 and analysts considered the appropriate PE multiple to be 12, the share would be valued at $60. The fair market value of the company would be $60 times the number of outstanding shares.

   Conceptually, a PE multiple is akin to the factor for the present value of an annuity. When an annuity payment is expected to be perpetual (i.e., an infinite number of equal payments), the present value of an annuity factor converges to $(1 / r)$. Thus, a PE multiple of 12 is equivalent to 1 / .08333. Applying the multiple to a given level of earnings is equivalent to valuing the company as though it would provide an annuity of "earnings" every year, for an infinite number of years, using 8.333% as the discount rate.

   i. If Maple Leaf Gardens' shares are trading at a PE multiple (based on 1992 net income) of 15.38, what is the implied discount rate? (Assume, as above, an annuity paying for an infinite number of years.) Does this discount rate seem reasonable? Explain.

   ii. Based on a PE multiple of 15.38, use Net Income from Continuing Operations to estimate the fair market value of Maple Leaf Gardens' equity. In using Net Income from Continuing Operations, what are you implicitly assuming?

   iii. PE multiples can also accommodate earnings growth. If earnings are predicted to grow at a constant rate, g, then the PE multiple can be written as $(1 + g) / (r - g)$. Assume that Maple Leaf Gardens' shares have a PE multiple of 15.38 and that you believe that 15% is an appropriate discount rate for the company given its risk level. What is the implied growth rate embedded in the PE multiple of 15.38? Explain how you would assess whether the growth rate was reasonable.

   iv. Compare your responses to parts *h iii.* (fair market value of net assets) and *i ii.* (fair market value of the equity). Why are these amounts so different? What do the differences represent?

j. Refer to the *Wall Street Journal* article ("Ontario Pension Fund..." April 5, 1994) that appears after Maple Leaf Gardens, financial statements. Compute the fair market value of the company based on information provided in the article. Why is this value different than the value computed in part *i ii.* above?

MAPLE LEAF GARDENS, LIMITED

(Incorporated under the laws of Ontario)
BALANCE SHEETS
May 31, 1992 and 1991

Assets	1992	1991
Current assets:		
Cash and interest-bearing deposits	$ 4,622,115	$ 4,657,808
Accounts Receivable (note 7)	1,597,442	1,402,951
Prepaid expenses and other assets	456,254	232,877
	6,675,811	6,293,636
Fixed assets (note 2):		
Land, building and equipment	22,310,285	18,524,076
Less accumulated depreciation	(9,325,069)	(8,538,294)
	12,985,216	9,985,782
Deferred charges	1,400,428	363,052
Deferred income taxes	468,980	647,980
Franchises:		
National Hockey League	100,001	100,001
	$21,630,436	$17,390,451

AUDITORS' REPORT TO THE SHAREHOLDERS

We have audited the balance sheets of Maple Leaf Gardens, Limited as at May 31, 1992 and 1991 and the statements of income, retained earnings and changes in cash flow for the years then ended. These financial statements are the responsibility of the Corporation's management. Our responsibility is to express an opinion on these financial statements based on our audits.

We conducted our audits in accordance with generally accepted auditing standards. Those standards require that we plan and perform an audit to obtain reasonable assurance whether the financial statements are free of material misstatements. An audit includes examining, on a test basis, evidence supporting the amounts and disclosures in the financial statements. An audit also includes assessing the accounting principles used and significant estimates made by management, as well as evaluating the overall financial statement presentation.

In our opinion, these financial statements present fairly, in all material respects, the financial position of the Corporation as at May 31, 1992 and 1991 and the results of its operations and the changes in its financial position for the years then ended in accordance with generally accepted accounting principles.

Toronto, Canada
July 3, 1992

PEAT MARWICK THORNE
Chartered Accountants

MAPLE LEAF GARDENS, LIMITED

BALANCE SHEETS
May 31, 1992 and 1991

Liabilities and Shareholders' Equity	1992	1991
Current liabilities:		
Accounts payable and accrued liabilities	$ 3,766,694	$ 3,068,605
Income and other taxes payable	1,349,313	2,010,252
Deferred income	1,379,629	1,211,184
	6,495,636	6,290,041
Net liabilities of discontinued operations (note 4)	–	191,575
Shareholders' equity:		
Capital stock:		
Authorized: 5,000,000 common shares		
Issued: 3,677,900 common shares	36,779	36,779
Retained earnings	15,098,021	10,872,056
	15,134,800	10,908,835
Commitments and contingencies (note 5)		
	$21,630,436	$17,390,451

See accompanying notes to financial statements.

MAPLE LEAF GARDENS, LIMITED
STATEMENTS OF INCOME
Years ended May 31, 1992 and 1991

	1992	1991
Revenue from operations	$41,191,271	$36,263,051
Investment and other income	947,356	1,195,984
	42,138,627	37,459,035
Operating expenses other than the undernoted	32,901,247	26,417,459
Operating income before the following	9,237,380	11,041,576
Depreciation	786,774	603,297
Amortization	1,243,892	969,804
	7,206,714	9,468,475
N.H.L. expansion fees (note 3)	4,958,571	3,276,927
Income before income taxes	12,165,285	12,745,402
Income taxes (note 6)		
Current	4,818,000	5,263,000
Deferred	179,000	150,000
	4,997,000	5,413,000
Income before gain from discontinued operations	7,168,285	7,332,402
Gain from discontinued operations (note 4)	—	167,000
Net income	$ 7,168,285	$ 7,499,402
Earnings per share:		
Before discontinued operations	$1.95	$1.99
Net income	$1.95	$2.04

See accompanying notes to financial statements.

STATEMENTS OF RETAINED EARNINGS

Years ended May 31, 1992 and 1991	1992	1991
Retained earnings, beginning of year	$10,872,056	$15,693,619
Net income	7,168,285	7,499,402
	18,040,341	23,193,021
Dividends—$0.80 per share in 1992 and $3.35 per share in 1991, including a special dividend of $2.75 per share	2,942,320	12,320,965
Retained earnings, end of year	$15,098,021	$10,872,056

See accompanying notes to financial statements.

MAPLE LEAF GARDENS, LIMITED
STATEMENTS OF CHANGES IN CASH FLOW
Years ended May 31, 1992 and 1991

	1992	1991
Cash provided by (used for):		
(a) Operations	$ 8,974,103	$10,335,168
(b) Investments	(6,067,476)	(2,886,185)
Dividends	(2,942,320)	(12,320,965)
Decrease during the year	(35,693)	(4,871,982)
Cash and interest-bearing deposits, beginning of year	4,657,808	9,529,790
Cash and interest-bearing deposits, end of year	$ 4,622,115	$ 4,657,808
(a) Operating Activities:		
Net income	$ 7,168,285	$ 7,499,402
Items not involving cash from operations:		
Depreciation and amortization	2,030,666	1,573,101
Deferred income taxes	179,000	150,000
Gain from discontinued operations	–	(167,000)
	9,377,951	9,055,503
Other non-cash working capital items	(403,848)	1,279,665
	$ 8,974,103	$10,335,168
(b) Investment activities:		
Purchase of fixed assets	$(3,786,208)	$(2,005,197)
Increase in deferred charges	(2,281,268)	(720,608)
Advances to fund discontinued operations	–	(160,380)
	$(6,067,476)	$(2,886,185)
Other non-cash working capital items:		
Increase in accounts receivable	$(194,491)	$(65,176)
Decrease (increase) in prepaid expenses and other assets	(223,377)	40,185
Increase (decrease) in accounts payable and accrued liabilities	506,514	(593,114)
Increase (decrease) in income and other taxes payable	(660,939)	1,675,134
Increase in deferred income	168,445	222,636
	$ (403,848)	$ 1,279,665

See accompanying notes to financial statements.

MAPLE LEAF GARDENS, LIMITED

1. Significant Accounting Policies:

(a) Segmented reporting:

The Corporation's directors have determined that the dominant industry segment of the Corporation is its operations in the entertainment industry in Canada.

(b) Fixed assets:

Land, building and equipment are stated at cost. Depreciation is provided on a diminishing balance basis using rates of 5% per annum for buildings and 20% and 30% per annum for equipment.

(c) Deferred charges:

The Corporation has entered into employment contracts with certain of its employees which provide for substantial initial cash payments. These cash payments are reflected on the balance sheet as deferred charges and are being amortized over the life of the employment contracts. Any unamortized balance relating to a terminated contract is written off in the year of termination.

(d) Franchises:

The National Hockey League ("N.H.L.") franchise represents the costs of purchase of the predecessor hockey club which upon reorganization eventually became the Toronto Maple Leaf Hockey Club and a member of the N.H.L. The franchise rights are recorded as an intangible asset.

(e) Deferred income:

Deferred income represents payments received in advance for events and services which have not yet been performed. These amounts will be recorded in income as earned.

(f) Revenue:

Included in revenue from operations are:

(i) the gross revenues for those attractions for which the Corporation is the promoter;

(ii) the Corporation's share of the gross revenues for those attractions for which the Corporation is a co-promoter; and

(iii) a minimum rent or percentage of the gate (whichever is greater) in those cases where the Corporation offers its facility as a landlord.

2. Fixed Assets:

		1992		1991
	Cost	Accumulated depreciation	Net book value	Net book value
Land	$ 358,811	$ —	$ 358,811	$ 358,811
Building	16,618,730	5,583,670	11,035,060	7,842,780
Equipment	5,297,874	3,741,399	1,556,475	1,008,142
Construction-in-progress	34,870	—	34,870	776,049
	$22,310,285	$9,325,069	$12,985,216	$9,985,782

3. N.H.L. Expansion Fees:

In 1991, the N.H.L. granted expansion franchises to groups representing the cities of San Jose, California, Tampa Bay, Florida, and Ottawa, Ontario. These franchises were granted on a conditional basis as both the N.H.L. and the owners of the expansion franchises were obligated to meet certain conditions. Accordingly, the Corporation chose to record the fees as income only when both the cash was received and the conditions which the N.H.L. was obligated to meet had been met. The fee charged for these individual franchises was $50,000,000 (U.S.), including a deposit (non-refundable) of $5,000,000 (U.S.) upon the granting of the franchise, and the fee was allocated equally to the then existing 21 N.H.L. member clubs. The initial expansion fees from the Tampa Bay and Ottawa franchises and the entire expansion fee of the San Jose franchise were received by the N.H.L. in 1991 and were distributed to its member clubs. The Corporation's share of these fees amounted to $3,276,927 (Cdn.) which was recorded as income in 1991.

In 1992, the Corporation received its share of the remaining expansion fees due from the groups representing the cities of Tampa Bay and Ottawa, aggregating $4,958,571 (Cdn.) which has been recorded as income.

4. Loss (Gain) from Discontinued Operations:

Effective May 31, 1990, the Board of Directors approved formal plans to sell or otherwise dispose of the Davis Printing Division. The operations were closed on October 15, 1990 and its assets, excluding accounts receivable were sold to a third party on October 27, 1990 for cash proceeds in the amount of $470,000. The gain from discontinued operations represented the result of recording a provision for loss in excess of the required amount which excess, net of income tax, was recorded as income in 1991. The net liabilities of discontinued operations was principally a provision for future rental payments, the net liability for which has been included in accounts payable in 1992.

5. Commitments and Contingencies:

(a) There are a number of actions in Canada against the Corporation for unpaid amounts and breach of contract, among other things. While these actions are being defended, it is not possible, in the opinion of the Corporation's solicitors, to predict the outcome or the extent of any liability should any of the actions ultimately be successful.

There are a number of actions in the United States against the N.H.L. and its member clubs for damages and costs allegedly sustained by plaintiff by reason of, amongst other items, alleged violations of United States anti-trust laws.

In addition to the above described litigation, certain retired N.H.L. players have commenced actions, both in the United States and Canada, seeking to set aside an amendment to the N.H.L. Club Pension Plan and Trust Agreement. The players are seeking the reallocation of approximately $32 million plus interest to the Pension Plan. Should this application be successful in whole or in part, individual N.H.L. member clubs will have to pay into the Pension Society those amounts which would otherwise have been payable. The total exposure is not shared equally by all N.H.L. member clubs because of their respective date of entry into the league. The Corporation is not able to determine its share of any potential liability in this matter at this time.

While the actions described in the preceding two paragraphs are being defended, it is not possible, in the opinion of the N.H.L's solicitors, to predict the outcome or the extent of any liability should any of the actions ultimately be successful.

No provision has been made in the accounts for any legal awards which may be incurred as a result of the above described actions. Any amounts awarded against the Corporation as a result of the actions will be recorded as a prior period adjustment in the year of such award.

(b) In discussions with another N.H.L. member club, Revenue Canada has indicated they intend to challenge the tax filing position adopted by the corporation and fellow Canadian member clubs on expansion receipts received in 1991 and 1992. The Corporation intends to oppose this proposed reassessment and believes they have very strong defenses on this matter. Should Revenue Canada reassess in the manner they are proposing and should this reassessment be upheld, the exposure to the Corporation at present, including interest, would be approximately $750,000. Any amounts awarded against the Corporation as a result of this proposed reassessment will be recorded as a prior period adjustment in the year of such award.

(c) At May 31, 1992, the Corporation has planned capital expenditures for the 1993 fiscal year of approximately $2,000,000.

(d) The Corporation has an employment contract with its chief operating officer. This agreement has a remaining term of four years and provides for salary continuation of $625,000 on expiration which is being amortized over the initial five-year term of the employment contract. This agreement provides the employee with the right to terminate this contract if a change in control as defined occurs and his responsibilities are altered in a meaningful fashion. The agreement also provides for severance arrangements if the employee is terminated without cause. The compensation payable to this executive, should the contract be terminated as described above, is approximately $1.5 million.

6. Income Taxes:

Income tax expense differs from the amount which would be obtained by applying the combined Federal/Provincial statutory income tax rate to the respective year's income before income taxes. The difference results from the following items:

	1992	1991
Statutory income tax rate	44.3%	44.3%
Increase (decrease) in tax rate resulting from:		
Non-taxable portion of N.H.L. expansion fees	(3.3)	(2.2)
Non-deductible expenses	0.1	0.4
Effective income tax rate	41.1%	42.5%

7. Related Party Transactions:

(a) The Corporation earned revenue on the sale of television and radio rights to N.H.L. hockey, promotional and other advertising activities in the amount of approximately $8,108,000 (1991 $7,100,000) from the Molson Companies Limited which beneficially owns approximately 19.9% of the common shares of the Corporation. These shares were acquired under an option agreement, are held in trust and are subject to cross-ownership rules of the N.H.L. These cross-ownership rules may require the Molson Companies Limited to dispose of these shares.

Included in accounts receivable is an amount of $458,061 (1991—$499,544) due from this party.

(b) During 1992, the Corporation licensed arena space for a number of entertainment events to BCL Entertainment Corp., a corporation partially owned by a related party. This party owned a significant interest in a holding corporation until November, 1991. This holding corporation in turn owns a majority interest in the Corporation. Subsequent to November, 1991, BCL Entertainment Corp. is no longer considered to be a related party. Total license revenue from this corporation amounted to approximately $116,000 in 1992 (1991—$220,000).

B5 THE WALL STREET JOURNAL TUESDAY, APRIL 5, 1994

Ontario Pension Fund To Buy 49% of Owner Of NHL Maple Leafs

By a WALL STREET JOURNAL *Staff Reporter*

TORONTO—An Ontario teachers pension fund agreed to pay about 61 million Canadian dollars (US $44 million) for a 49% stake in **Maple Leaf Gardens** Ltd., the owner of the Toronto Maple Leafs hockey team.

The purchase will be made under a takeover offer, valued at about C$125 million, for Maple Leaf Gardens by its chairman and chief executive officer, Steve Stavro. Mr. Stavro agreed to acquire the 19.9% stake in Maple Leaf Gardens held by Molson Cos., and the 60.3% stake held by the estate of former Maple leaf Gardens owner Harold Ballard. Mr. Stavro also plans to bid for the remaining public shares of Maple Leaf Gardens. All shareholders will receive C$34 per share.

After the acquisition, Mr. Stavro will sell the 49% stake to the **Ontario Teachers Pension Plan Board**, which invests the C$34 billion of pension funds held by Ontario's 200,000 teachers. Toronto Dominion Bank also will purchase a small stake, but control of Maple Leaf Gardens will rest with Mr. Stavro.

Several pension fund managers and consultants to professional sports teams said they didn't know of any pension funds owning stakes in a pro team.

"We didn't really look at it as a pro team," said George Engman, vice president of investment research and development for the pension fund. Maple Leaf Gardens is a well-run business with good cash flow, he said. Two fund officials will be named to the board of Maple Leaf Gardens, but the fund isn't interested in influencing the day-to-day operations of the hockey club, Mr. Engman said.

Maple Leaf Gardens jumped C$4, or 14%, to C$32.50 in light trading on the Toronto Stock Exchange yesterday.

The deal is subject to regulatory and National Hockey League approval.

Pharmacia Corporation—Persistence of Earnings

Pharmacia Corporation is a leading global pharmaceutical enterprise with a $2 billion research engine that drives new product flow. The roots of Pharmacia Corporation date back to 1853 when Italian pharmacist, Carlo Erba, started Farmitalia Carlo Erba. This company, along with Kabi Pharmacia and Pharmacia Aktiebolag, form the main points of origin for Pharmacia AB, a Swedish-based company. In the USA, The Upjohn Pill and Granule Company began in 1886.In 1888, G.D. Searle & Co., developed many "firsts" including the first bulk laxative, the first motion sickness drug, sugar substitute aspartame, and others. In 1985, G.D. Searle & Co. became the pharmaceutical unit of Monsanto. In 1995, Pharmacia & Upjohn was formed through the merger of Pharmacia AB and The Upjohn Company. In April 2000, Pharmacia & Upjohn completed a merger with Monsanto and Searle. On July 15, 2002, Pfizer announced its intention to acquire Pharmacia in a stock-for-stock transaction expected to close in 2003.

Learning Objectives

- Explain why income statements are "classified."
- Understand the concept of earnings persistence.
- Use the income statement to value a company.

Refer to the 2002 financial statements of Pharmacia Corporation.

 **Concepts** 

a. What are the major classifications on an income statement?

b. Explain why, under GAAP, companies are required to provide "classified" income statements. Consider, in particular, whether items on Pharmacia's income statement are equally persistent. That is, are all the elements on Pharmacia's 2002 income statement expected to recur in future years? *Hint*: refer to information in the excerpts from Management's Discussion and Analysis.

 **Analysis** 

c. Net income from continuing operations can be used to approximate the average annual cash flow from an entity over an extended period of time. As Pharmacia's earnings include a number of unusual items, how would you use the income statement to value the company? Keep your answers to parts *a* and *b* in mind as you answer this question.

d. Using a 12% annual discount rate, a 40-year time horizon, and information in the 2002 income statement, estimate the current value of Pharmacia's common equity.

e. Estimate Pharmacia's market capitalization (i.e. the market value of the company) by multiplying the number of common shares outstanding by the closing common stock market price at December 31, 2002 ($41.80). Compare this estimate to your answer to part *d*. What factors might cause these two estimates to differ? (*Note*: the number of common shares *outstanding* equals the number of issued shares less the number of shares in treasury.)

f. Refine the equity valuation you performed in *d.* by assuming that net income from continuing operations is expected to grow by 15% until 2007. Thereafter, you expect it to grow at the more moderate rate of 3% (roughly the long term rate of growth of the economy). Assume a 12% cost of equity capital (i.e., discount rate) and an infinite time horizon. How does your valuation compare with the ones you derived in *d* and *e*? How does it compare with the $60 billion that Pfizer offered for Pharmacia shares in July 2002 (based on a price per share of $45.08)?

PHARMACIA CORPORATION
CONSOLIDATED STATEMENTS OF EARNINGS

DOLLAR AMOUNTS IN MILLIONS, EXCEPT PER-SHARE DATA FOR THE YEARS ENDED DECEMBER 31,	2002	2001	2000
NET SALES	$13,993	$13,835	$12,651
COST OF PRODUCTS SOLD	3,077	2,978	2,882
RESEARCH AND DEVELOPMENT	2,359	2,361	2,165
SELLING, GENERAL AND ADMINISTRATIVE	6,179	5,902	5,486
AMORTIZATION OF GOODWILL	--	103	115
MERGER AND RESTRUCTURING	68	673	975
INTEREST EXPENSE	154	255	182
INTEREST INCOME	(65)	(110)	(124)
ALL OTHER, NET	(1,085)	82	(74)
EARNINGS FROM CONTINUING OPERATIONS BEFORE INCOME TAXES	3,306	1,591	1,044
PROVISION FOR INCOME TAXES	869	298	238
EARNINGS FROM CONTINUING OPERATIONS	2,437	1,293	806
INCOME FROM DISCONTINUED OPERATIONS, NET OF TAX	--	227	178
LOSS ON DISPOSAL OF DISCONTINUED OPERATIONS, NET OF TAX	(952)	(8)	(37)
EARNINGS BEFORE EXTRAORDINARY ITEMS AND CUMULATIVE EFFECT OF ACCOUNTING CHANGE	1,485	1,512	947
EXTRAORDINARY ITEMS, NET OF TAX	653	(12)	(32)
CUMULATIVE EFFECT OF ACCOUNTING CHANGE, NET OF TAX	(1,541)	1	(198)
NET EARNINGS	$ 597	$ 1,501	$ 717
NET EARNINGS PER COMMON SHARE:			
BASIC			
EARNINGS FROM CONTINUING OPERATIONS	$ 1.88	$ .98	$ .62
NET EARNINGS	.45	1.14	.55
DILUTED			
EARNINGS FROM CONTINUING OPERATIONS	1.84	.97	.61
NET EARNINGS	.44	1.12	.54

The accompanying notes are an integral part of the consolidated financial statements.

PHARMACIA CORPORATION

CONSOLIDATED BALANCE SHEETS

Dollar amounts in millions December 31,	2002	2001
Current Assets:		
Cash and cash equivalents	$ 2,241	$ 1,276
Short-term investments	469	119
Short-term notes receivable-Monsanto	--	254
Trade accounts receivable, less allowance of $136 (2001: $132)	2,457	2,433
Inventories	2,177	1,683
Deferred income taxes	717	932
Receivables from Monsanto	44	87
Other	1,175	879
Total Current Assets	9,280	7,663
Long-term investments	287	288
Properties, net	5,683	4,856
Goodwill, net of accumulated amortization of $682 (2001: $620)	1,150	1,059
Other intangible assets, net of accumulated amortization of $641 (2001: $561)	393	416
Deferred income taxes	1,331	1,038
Other noncurrent assets	393	709
Net assets of discontinued operations	--	6,348
Total Assets	$18,517	$22,377
Current Liabilities:		
Short-term debt	$ 854	$ 470
Short-term notes payable-Monsanto	--	30
Trade accounts payable	780	1,048
Payables to Monsanto	--	44
Compensation and compensated absences	576	501
Dividends payable	179	180
Income taxes payable	740	685
Other accrued liabilities	1,851	2,031
Total Current Liabilities	4,980	4,989
Long-term debt	2,585	2,612
Guarantee of ESOP debt	64	119
Postretirement benefit obligation	1,213	996
Deferred income taxes	299	143
Other noncurrent liabilities	1,393	1,128
Total Liabilities	10,534	9,987
Commitments and Contingent Liabilities - Note 16		
Shareholders' Equity:		
Preferred stock, one cent par value; at stated value; authorized 10 million shares, issued 6,130 (2001: 6,401 shares)	247	258
Common stock, two dollar par value; authorized 3 billion shares, issued 1.485 billion shares (2001: 1.485 billion shares)	2,970	2,970
Capital in excess of par value	3,656	3,499
Retained earnings	6,950	11,586
ESOP-related accounts	(216)	(294)
Treasury stock, at cost	(3,257)	(2,789)
Accumulated other comprehensive income (loss):		
Currency translation adjustments	(1,897)	(2,892)
Unrealized investment gains, net	33	142
Minimum pension liability adjustment	(497)	(96)
Unrealized hedging instrument (losses) gains	(6)	6
Total Shareholders' Equity	7,983	12,390
Total Liabilities And Shareholders' Equity	$18,517	$22,377

The accompanying notes are an integral part of the consolidated financial statements.

PHARMACIA CORPORATION

CONSOLIDATED STATEMENTS OF SHAREHOLDERS' EQUITY AND COMPREHENSIVE INCOME

Dollar amounts in millions For The Years Ended December 31,	2002	2001	2000
Preferred Stock:			
Balance at beginning of year	$ 258	$ 263	$ 270
Redemptions and conversions	(11)	(5)	(7)
Balance at end of year	247	258	263
Common Stock:			
Balance at beginning of year	2,970	2,937	2,931
Issuance of shares	--	33	6
Balance at end of year	2,970	2,970	2,937
Capital In Excess Of Par Value:			
Balance at beginning of year	3,499	2,730	1,827
Agricultural subsidiary stock offering	--	--	(380)
Issuance of shares	--	667	--
Stock option, incentive, dividend reinvestment plans and other	157	102	1,283
Balance at end of year	3,656	3,499	2,730
Retained Earnings:			
Balance at beginning of year	11,586	10,781	10,696
Spin-off of Monsanto	(4,523)	--	--
Net earnings	597	1,501	717
Dividends declared	(697)	(683)	(619)
Dividends on preferred stock (net of tax)	(13)	(13)	(13)
Balance at end of year	6,950	11,586	10,781
ESOP-Related Accounts:			
Balance at beginning of year	(294)	(307)	(330)
Third-party debt repayment	45	41	39
Spin-off of Monsanto	25	--	--
Other	8	(28)	(16)
Balance at end of year	(216)	(294)	(307)
Treasury Stock:			
Balance at beginning of year	(2,789)	(2,003)	(2,432)
Stock options, incentive plans and other	152	78	429
Purchases of treasury stock	(620)	(864)	--
Balance at end of year	(3,257)	(2,789)	(2,003)
Accumulated Other Comprehensive Loss:			
Balance at beginning of year	(2,840)	(2,480)	(2,051)
Spin-off of Monsanto	1,020	--	--
Other comprehensive loss	(547)	(360)	(429)
Balance at end of year	(2,367)	(2,840)	(2,480)
Total Shareholders' Equity	$ 7,983	$12,390	$11,921
Comprehensive Income (Loss) (Net of Tax):			
Currency translation adjustments	$ 123	$ (368)	$ (509)
Unrealized investment (losses) gains	(105)	41	71
Minimum pension liability adjustments	(540)	(39)	9
Unrealized hedging instrument (losses) gains	(25)	6	--
Other comprehensive loss	(547)	(360)	(429)
Net earnings	597	1,501	717
Total Comprehensive Income	$ 50	$ 1,141	$ 288

The accompanying notes are an integral part of the consolidated financial statements.

Excerpt from Note 17:

Treasury Stock

The balances at December 31, 2002 and 2001 were $3,257 and $2,789, respectively, carried at cost. The corresponding shares associated with these balances were 191,510,000 in 2002 and 186,354,000 in 2001. The 5,156,000 increase in shares in 2002 reflects purchases under the share repurchase program announced in 2001 and is net of the conversion of Sugen debt to common stock. The share repurchase program was suspended in mid-2002 due to the merger negotiations with Pfizer.

PHARMACIA CORPORATION

CONSOLIDATED STATEMENTS OF CASH FLOWS

Dollar amounts in millions For The Years Ended December 31,	2002	2001	2000
Cash Flows From Operations:			
Net Earnings	$ 597	$ 1,501	$ 717
Adjustments to net earnings:			
Income from discontinued operations, net	--	(227)	(178)
Disposal of discontinued operations, net	952	8	37
Extraordinary items	(653)	12	32
Cumulative effect of accounting change	1,541	(1)	198
Depreciation and amortization	587	610	632
Deferred income taxes	329	(424)	(376)
Acquired in-process R&D expenses	--	67	--
Stock option revaluations	--	--	232
Gain on return of AMBIEN rights	(661)	--	--
Other	(148)	182	53
Changes in:			
Accounts receivable	86	(37)	(419)
Inventories	(364)	(247)	(74)
Accounts payable	(307)	235	106
Other liabilities	(41)	(31)	(211)
Other operating items	(604)	154	370
Net cash provided by continuing operations	1,314	1,802	1,119
Net cash provided (required) by discontinued operations	39	99	(112)
Net Cash Provided By Operations	1,353	1,901	1,007
Cash Flows (Required) Provided By Investment Activities:			
Purchases of property, plant and equipment	(1,142)	(1,020)	(773)
Other acquisitions and investments	(434)	(262)	(138)
Investment and property disposal proceeds	121	169	249
Proceeds from sale of subsidiaries	1,671	46	76
Proceeds from discontinued operations, net	--	--	1,669
Discontinued operations receivable/payable, net	224	206	(293)
Investment in employee benefits trust	(225)	--	--
Other investment activities	--	--	(67)
Net Cash Provided (Required) By Investment Activities	215	(861)	723
Cash Flows (Required) Provided By Financing Activities:			
Repayment of long-term debt	(47)	(768)	(1,773)
Net increase (decrease) in short-term borrowings	416	(248)	(6)
Issuance of stock	188	872	1,268
Treasury stock purchases	(620)	(864)	--
Dividend payments	(711)	(651)	(622)
Other financing activities	(53)	(62)	(29)
Net Cash Required By Financing Activities	(827)	(1,721)	(1,162)
Effect of exchange rate changes on cash and cash equivalents	224	(78)	(107)
Increase (decrease) in cash and cash equivalents	965	(759)	461
Cash and cash equivalents, beginning of year	1,276	2,035	1,574
Cash and cash equivalents, end of year	$ 2,241	$ 1,276	$ 2,035
Cash paid during the year for:			
Interest (net of amounts capitalized)	$ 175	$ 247	$ 358
Income taxes	$ 660	$ 428	$ 716

The accompanying notes are an integral part of the consolidated financial statements.

PHARMACIA CORPORATION

Excerpts from Management's Discussion and Analysis

Merger and Restructuring Charges

Dollars in millions	2002	2001	2000
Merger costs:			
Merger integration costs	$ 16	$340	$599
Other merger-related costs	--	79	--
Pfizer merger costs	44	--	--
Total merger costs	60	419	599
Restructuring costs:			
Employee termination costs	8	177	278
Asset write-downs	--	58	88
Other	18	44	25
Reversals	(18)	(25)	(15)
Total restructuring costs	8	254	376
Total merger and restructuring	$ 68	$673	$975

The Company recorded merger and restructuring charges of $68 million, $673 million and $975 million during 2002, 2001 and 2000, respectively. All of these charges were recorded on the "Merger and restructuring" line of the consolidated statements of earnings. In 2002, 2001 and 2000, merger and restructuring charges comprised $60 million of merger expense and $8 million of net restructuring expense, $419 million of merger expense and $254 million of net restructuring expense and $599 million of merger expense and $376 million of net restructuring expense, respectively.

During 2000, former Monsanto and P&U merged to form Pharmacia Corporation. As a result of that merger, there were many duplicate functions and locations, particularly in the prescription pharmaceutical segment and corporate functions. The Company began a restructuring in order to integrate the two companies, eliminate duplicate positions and facilities and create a consolidated headquarters in New Jersey.

The board of directors approved a comprehensive integration and restructuring plan in the spring of 2000. Due to the comprehensive nature of this restructuring, the timelines for the various plans were expected to occur over multiple years and the related restructuring charges also were intended to be taken over three or four years. As of December 31, 2002, merger charges relating to this plan are essentially complete.

On July 13, 2002, the Company entered into a definitive merger agreement with Pfizer. Pharmacia incurred certain costs in 2002 necessary to facilitate the completion of the merger.

Merger Costs

The $60 million of merger costs recorded in 2002 is comprised of the following:

- $16 million to integrate the former Monsanto and P&U organizations; comprised largely of costs relating to information technology integration projects.
- $44 million to facilitate the completion of the merger with Pfizer; comprised of $10 million relating to legal fees; $12 million relating to travel, benefits consulting, contract terminations and other merger related costs and a non-cash charge of $22 million for the accelerated vesting of certain restricted stock awards as a result of the shareholder approval of the merger agreement with Pfizer.

The $419 million of merger costs recorded in 2001 is comprised of the following:

- $340 million to integrate the former Monsanto and P&U organizations; comprised of $139 million of consulting fees for system and process integration, $52 million relating to information technology integration projects, $26 million of contract termination fees and employee relocation costs, $123 million relating to other out-of-pocket merger costs such as travel, temporary payroll, incentives and other costs necessary to complete the merger.
- $79 million relating to the formation and partial sale of Biovitrum. The $79 million is comprised of a noncash charge of $63 million relating to asset write-downs and $16 million of other related cash expenses. Biovitrum was established during the second quarter of 2001 as the result of the Company's plan to exit its Sweden-based metabolic disease research activities, its biopharmaceutical development unit and the Company's plasma business. The Company has partially divested of its ownership in Biovitrum and currently owns less than 20 percent.

The $599 million of merger costs recorded in 2000 is comprised of the following:

- $100 million relating to investment bankers, $42 million in connection with legal and SEC fees, $48 million relating to consultant expense, $11 million relating to employee moving and relocation costs, $166 million of other merger costs necessary to integrate the two companies and a noncash charge of $232 million. This noncash charge related to certain former Monsanto employee stock options that contained a contractual reset provision that was triggered upon change-of-control so that, upon consummation of the merger, the original above-market exercise price was reduced to equal the fair market value on the date of grant.

Restructuring Costs

The $8 million of net restructuring charges recorded in 2002 is comprised of the following:

- $21 million associated with restructuring Prescription Pharmaceuticals. This was necessitated by the combination of G.D. Searle, the pharmaceutical business of former Monsanto, and P&U operations worldwide. The merger resulted in duplicate facilities, computer systems and positions around the world. The charges consist of $5 million relating to the separation of approximately 45 employees worldwide in R&D, manufacturing, marketing and administrative functions; $9 million relating to contract and lease termination fees and $7 million of other exit costs.

- $5 million relating to the consolidation of corporate and administrative functions and other areas of former Monsanto and P&U and eliminating duplicative positions. This charge is comprised entirely of costs relating to the separation of approximately 35 employees.

- $18 million of total reversals. This is comprised of a reversal of $5 million relating to restructuring liabilities established in 1999 and 2000 under the Monsanto restructuring plan that were reversed as a result of lower actual severance costs than originally estimated and $13 million relating to a change in a previous restructuring plan for a facility. As the result of a subsequent restructuring plan, sale of the building resulted in a gain.

The $254 million of restructuring charges recorded in 2001 is comprised of the following:

- $225 million associated with restructuring Prescription Pharmaceuticals. This was necessitated by the combination of G.D. Searle and P&U operations worldwide. The merger resulted in duplicate facilities, computer systems and positions around the world. The charges consist of $144 million relating to the separation of approximately 1,050 employees worldwide in R&D, manufacturing, marketing and administrative functions; $41 million relating to asset write-downs resulting from duplicate computer equipment and facilities; $33 million relating to contract and lease termination fees and $7 million of other exit costs.

- $29 million, net, relating to the consolidation of corporate and administrative functions in the Company's New Jersey headquarters and the elimination of duplicate administrative positions and a reversal of $25 million of prior accruals relating to the previous P&U restructuring plans due to lower separation payments than initially anticipated. This charge is comprised of $33 million relating to the separation of approximately 240 employees primarily in corporate and administrative functions, $17 million relating to asset write-downs of duplicate computer systems and leasehold improvements in duplicate facilities and $4 million of contract and lease termination costs.

The $376 million of restructuring charges recorded in 2000 is comprised of the following:

- $241 million associated with restructuring Prescription Pharmaceuticals. This was necessitated by the combination of G.D. Searle and P&U operations worldwide. The merger resulted in duplicate facilities, computer systems and positions around the world. The charges consist of $165 million relating to the separation of approximately 1,360 employees worldwide in R&D, manufacturing, marketing and administrative functions; $51 million relating to asset write-downs resulting from duplicate computer systems and facilities; $22 million relating to contract and lease terminations and $3 million of other exit costs.

- $150 million relating to the consolidation of corporate and administrative functions in New Jersey and the elimination of duplicate administrative positions. This charge is comprised of $113 million relating to the separation of approximately 210 employees in corporate and administrative functions and $37 million relating to asset write-downs (duplicate computer systems and leasehold improvements in duplicate facilities), lease termination fees and other exit costs.

- $15 million relating to the reversals of prior P&U restructuring reserves that resulted from higher than anticipated proceeds on asset sales and lower than anticipated separation payments.

Restructuring charges and spending associated with the current restructuring plans relating to the integration of the former Monsanto and P&U companies follow. The table below does not include activity incurred under previous P&U restructuring plans, which began in 1995 and 1997. All activities relating to these plans have been completed.

Dollars in millions	Workforce Reductions	Other Exit Costs	Total
Balance January 1, 2000	$ --	$ --	$ --
Additions	278	25	303
Deductions	(119)	(15)	(134)
Balance December 31, 2000	159	10	169
Additions	177	37	214
Deductions	(221)	(37)	(258)
Balance December 31, 2001	$ 115	$ 10	$ 125
Additions	10	16	26
Deductions	(113)	(9)	(122)
Reversals	(5)	--	(5)
Balance December 31, 2002	$ 7	$ 17	$ 24

As of December 31, 2002, cash payments totaling $453 relating to the separation of approximately 2,740 employees have been paid and charged against the liability.

As of December 31, 2002, all activities relating to the restructuring plans associated with former Monsanto have been substantially completed.

All Other, Net

All other, net consists of income and expense items that are dissimilar to the other line captions on the consolidated statements of earnings. All other, net for 2002 was $1,085 million of net gains. "All other, net" for 2001 was $82 million of net expense versus $74 million of net gains in 2000. The change between 2002, 2001 and 2000 is attributable in large part to transactions with Sanofi related to AMBIEN. 2002 includes a $661 million gain relating to the return of U.S. product rights of AMBIEN to Sanofi and $73 million in income received in the first quarter for the Company's share to AMBIEN earnings. Prior to January 1, 2002, the Company recorded the sales and expenses of AMBIEN. Related payments made to Sanofi were included as part of All other, net. 2002 also includes a net $100 million gain resulting from a settlement of an intellectual property legal suit in the ophthalmology field, $60 million royalty income, a $28 million gain relating to the sale of clinical study data to Boehringer Ingelheim, a $45 million gain on the sale and license of non-strategic product rights and a $71 million gain on the sale of non-strategic equity investments. The 2001 net expense of $82 million was comprised of approximately $220 million net costs related to AMBIEN, partly offset by $70 million royalty income and $56 million realized gains on sales of investments. The 2000 net income of $74 million was comprised of $70 million royalty income, $48 million gains on sales of assets, $41 million gains on investments and $81 million net gain from other miscellaneous items offset by $166 million AMBIEN related costs. In addition, the Company periodically makes certain equity investments and loans in companies with which it has a collaborative agreement. In 2002 and 2001, certain of these investments were considered impaired on an other-than-temporary basis. The Company reduced the capitalized value of these investments and recognized losses of $28 million in 2002 and $40 million in 2001 to bring them to current market value.

Kohl's Corporation—Statement of Cash Flows

Kohl's operates family-oriented, specialty department stores that feature quality, national brand merchandise primarily moderately priced apparel, shoes, accessories and home products targeted to middle-income customers. Kohl's stores have fewer departments than traditional, full-line department stores but offer merchandise in complete selections of styles, colors, and sizes. As of January 31, 2004, the company operated 542 stores. In March 2004, Kohl's opened 21 additional stores and operated 563 stores in 37 states.

Learning Objectives

- Contrast and compare the information contained in the Statement of Cash Flows to the Statement of Operations (Income Statement).
- Identify the three components of the Statement of Cash Flows.
- Understand the operations section of the Statement of Cash Flows and how it ties into line items on the balance sheet and the income statement.
- Analyze year over year changes in certain balance sheet accounts.

Refer to the 2004 financial statements of Kohl's Corporation.

Concepts

a. What information does the statement of cash flows provide? How is this different from the information contained in the statement of operations (income statement?)

b. What are the two different methods for preparing the statement of cash flows? Which method does Kohl's use? How do you know?

c. What are the three sections of the statement of cash flows?

d. How do each of the three sections of the statement of cash flows relate to the balance sheet?

e. The balance sheet includes an item called "Cash and cash equivalents." What are "cash equivalents"?

f. Net income is determined on an accrual basis. Yet, net income is the first item on the statement of cash flows. Explain this apparent inconsistency.

Process

Using information from the balance sheet, the income statement, and the footnotes only, determine the following components of Kohl's cash flow statement for the year ended January 31, 2004:

g. Net income.

h. Depreciation and amortization.

   i. Using information from the income statement, provide the journal entry that Kohl's made to record depreciation and amortization during the year. How much of this expense involved the use of cash? How much of this expense was included in net income?

   ii. What amount did Kohl's report on the statement of cash flows for depreciation and amortization? Speculate why this amount differs from the income statement amount. (*Hint*: there are many possible answers and you do not have enough information in the financial statement excerpts to know for sure. Make some informed guesses.)

   iii. Explain in your own words, why in general, "Depreciation and amortization" is included on the statement of cash flows when depreciation expense involves no cash.

i. Current asset and liability account balances changed during the year. For each of the following accounts, calculate the change in the account. Is the change added to or subtracted from net income to determine cash from operations? Explain.

   i. Accounts receivable trade, net.

   ii. Merchandise inventories.

   iii. Other current assets.

   iv. Accounts payable.

   v. Accrued liabilities.

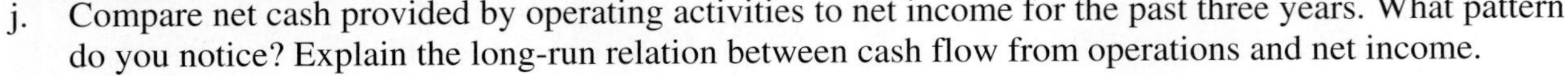

j. Compare net cash provided by operating activities to net income for the past three years. What pattern do you notice? Explain the long-run relation between cash flow from operations and net income.

KOHL'S CORPORATION

CONSOLIDATED BALANCE SHEETS
(In Thousands, Except Per Share Data)

	January 31, 2004	February 1, 2003
ASSETS		
Current assets:		
Cash and cash equivalents	**$ 112,748**	$ 90,085
Short–term investments	**34,285**	475,991
Accounts receivable trade, net of allowance for doubtful accounts of $22,521 and $20,880, respectively	**1,150,157**	990,810
Merchandise inventories	**1,606,990**	1,626,996
Deferred income taxes	**49,822**	56,693
Other	**70,837**	43,714
Total current assets	**3,024,839**	3,284,289
Property and equipment, net	**3,324,243**	2,739,290
Favorable lease rights, net	**235,491**	180,420
Goodwill	**9,338**	9,338
Other assets	**104,539**	102,361
Total assets	**$ 6,698,450**	$ 6,315,698
LIABILITIES AND SHAREHOLDERS' EQUITY		
Current liabilities:		
Accounts payable	**$ 532,599**	$ 650,731
Accrued liabilities	**441,902**	359,842
Income taxes payable	**135,327**	142,150
Current portion of long–term debt and capital leases	**12,529**	355,464
Total current liabilities	**1,122,357**	1,508,187
Long–term debt and capital leases	**1,075,973**	1,058,784
Deferred income taxes	**236,712**	171,951
Other long–term liabilities	**72,069**	64,859
Shareholders' equity:		
Common stock–$.01 par value, 800,000 shares authorized, 340,141 and 337,322 shares issued, respectively	**3,401**	3,373
Paid–in capital	**1,170,519**	1,082,277
Retained earnings	**3,017,419**	2,426,267
Total shareholders' equity	**4,191,339**	3,511,917
Total liabilities and shareholders' equity	**$ 6,698,450**	$ 6,315,698

See accompanying notes

KOHL'S CORPORATION

CONSOLIDATED STATEMENTS OF INCOME
(In Thousands, Except Per Share Data)

	Fiscal Year Ended		
	January 31, 2004	**February 1, 2003**	**February 2, 2002**
Net sales	**$ 10,282,094**	$ 9,120,287	$ 7,488,654
Cost of merchandise sold	**6,887,033**	5,981,219	4,923,527
Gross margin	**3,395,061**	3,139,068	2,565,127
Operating expenses:			
Selling, general and administrative	**2,091,374**	1,817,968	1,527,478
Depreciation and amortization	**236,864**	191,439	151,965
Goodwill amortization	**—**	—	5,200
Preopening expenses	**43,519**	39,278	30,509
Total operating expenses	**2,371,757**	2,048,685	1,715,152
Operating income	**1,023,304**	1,090,383	849,975
Other expense (income):			
Interest expense	**75,240**	59,449	57,351
Interest income	**(2,309)**	(3,440)	(7,240)
Income before income taxes	**950,373**	1,034,374	799,864
Provision for income taxes	**359,221**	390,993	304,188
Net income	**$ 591,152**	$ 643,381	$ 495,676
Net income per share:			
Basic	**$ 1.74**	$ 1.91	$ 1.48
Diluted	**$ 1.72**	$ 1.87	$ 1.45

See accompanying notes

KOHL'S CORPORATION

CONSOLIDATED STATEMENT OF CHANGES IN SHAREHOLDERS' EQUITY
(In Thousands)

	Common Stock		Paid–In	Retained	Total Shareholders'
	Shares	Amount	Capital	Earnings	Equity
Balance at February 3, 2001	332,167	$ 3,322	$ 912,107	$ 1,287,210	$ 2,202,639
Exercise of stock options	2,971	29	36,099	—	36,128
Income tax benefit from exercise of stock options	—	—	56,963	—	56,963
Net income	—	—	—	495,676	495,676
Balance at February 2, 2002	335,138	3,351	1,005,169	1,782,886	2,791,406
Exercise of stock options	2,184	22	31,277	—	31,299
Income tax benefit from exercise of stock options	—	—	45,831	—	45,831
Net income	—	—	—	643,381	643,381
Balance at February 1, 2003	337,322	3,373	1,082,277	2,426,267	3,511,917
Exercise of stock options	**2,819**	**28**	**46,229**	—	**46,257**
Income tax benefit from exercise of stock options	—	—	**42,013**	—	**42,013**
Net income	—	—	—	**591,152**	**591,152**
Balance at January 31, 2004	**340,141**	**$ 3,401**	**$ 1,170,519**	**$ 3,017,419**	**$ 4,191,339**

See accompanying notes

KOHL'S CORPORATION

CONSOLIDATED STATEMENTS OF CASH FLOWS
(In Thousands)

	Fiscal Year Ended		
	January 31, 2004	**February 1, 2003**	**February 2, 2002**
Operating activities			
Net income	**$ 591,152**	$ 643,381	$ 495,676
Adjustments to reconcile net income to net cash provided by operating activities:			
Depreciation and amortization	**243,900**	192,410	157,939
Deferred income taxes	**71,632**	53,322	17,211
Amortization of debt discount	**3,576**	9,381	9,110
Changes in operating assets and liabilities:			
Accounts receivable trade, net	**(159,347)**	(154,864)	(154,690)
Merchandise inventories	**20,006**	(428,689)	(195,017)
Other current assets	**(27,123)**	(2,314)	(15,801)
Accounts payable	**(118,132)**	171,861	78,931
Accrued and other long–term liabilities	**93,607**	122,200	79,337
Income taxes	**35,190**	62,896	69,121
Net cash provided by operating activities	**754,461**	669,584	541,817
Investing activities			
Acquisition of property and equipment and favorable lease rights	**(831,599)**	(715,968)	(662,011)
Net sales (purchases) of short–term investments	**441,706**	(246,614)	(180,777)
Acquisition of software and other	**(25,624)**	(32,473)	(28,520)
Net cash used in investing activities	**(415,517)**	(995,055)	(871,308)
Financing activities			
Net repayments of short–term debt	**—**	—	(5,000)
Proceeds from public debt offering, net	—	297,759	299,503
Payments of convertible and other long–term debt	**(362,353)**	(16,772)	(16,424)
Payments of financing fees on debt	**(185)**	(3,452)	(1,615)
Net proceeds from issuance of common shares	**46,257**	31,299	36,128
Net cash (used in) provided by financing activities	**(316,281)**	308,834	312,592
Net increase (decrease) in cash and cash equivalents	**22,663**	(16,637)	(16,899)
Cash and cash equivalents at beginning of year	**90,085**	106,722	123,621
Cash and cash equivalents at end of year	**$ 112,748**	$ 90,085	$ 106,722

See accompanying notes

Mayor's Jewelers, Inc.—Statement of Cash Flows

Mayor's is an upscale retailer of fine quality guild jewelry, watches, and giftware. As a guild jeweler, the company does not sell costume or gold filled jewelry; rather, all of its jewelry is constructed of 18 karat gold, platinum, or sterling silver, with or without precious gemstones. Mayor's distinguishes itself from most of its competitors by offering a larger selection of distinctive and higher quality merchandise at many different price points, and by placing substantial emphasis on professionalism and training in its sales force.

Learning Objectives

- Prepare a direct-method statement of cash flows from basic transactions.
- Understand how to recast certain operating cash flows from the direct method to the indirect method.
- Explain why most companies choose to use the indirect method.
- Interpret information from the statement of cash flows.

Refer to the 2002 financial statements of Mayor's Jewelers, Inc.

 Concepts 

a. Which method—the direct method or the indirect method—does Mayor's Jewelers use to prepare its statement of cash flows? How do you know? Describe the differences between the method used by the company and the other, more commonly used, method.

b. Why do most companies prepare their statement of cash flows on an indirect basis?

c. By how much does Mayor's cash balance change during fiscal 2002? By how much do Mayor's other, non-cash asset, liability, and equity accounts change during the year? In general, does this relation hold? Why or why not?

 Process 

d. Prepare journal entries for each of the following transactions for the year ended February 2, 2002. All figures are in thousands of dollars. Use Mayor's 2001 and 2002 financial statements to determine account names.

1. The company purchased $76,069 of merchandise on account.
2. The company had sales of $166,735. Of this, $92,565 was received in cash and the balance was on account.
3. The cost of sales for the year was $103,027.
4. The company collected $74,264 of accounts receivable.
5. The company paid cash for general and administrative expenses totaling $14,632.
6. The company paid cash for advertising and marketing expenses totaling $8,810.
7. The company paid cash for wages to employees and for other operating and selling expenses totaling $53,794.
8. The company received cash of $184,607 from lines of credit during the year. As well, the company repaid $175,533 on the lines of credit. These lines of credit are included in 'Current portion of long-term debt' on the balance sheet.
9. The company paid $79,339 of accounts payable.
10. The company paid bondholders $3,788 of interest.
11. The company received $174 in interest from customer accounts.

12. The company received $706 from employees' exercise of stock options and issued 298,817 shares. Because the par value of the company's stock is $0.0001, the offsetting entry to common stock was rounded down to $0 (in thousands) and a credit of $706 was made to additional paid-in capital.
13. The company purchased long-lived assets (property) for $6,400 in cash.
14. The company paid $2,186 to settle certain liabilities that related to financing arrangements the company made during the previous year. These liabilities were included in 'Accrued expenses' at February 3, 2001.
15. The company recorded depreciation on property of $7,832 and amortization on 'Excess of cost over fair value of net assets acquired' (i.e. goodwill) of $1,939.
16. The company paid income taxes of $662 in cash.
17. The company determined that $3,035 of accounts receivable is probably not collectible. The company established an allowance for doubtful accounts (a contra-asset account to accounts receivable) on the balance sheet and offset 'Net sales' on the income statement for $3,035.
18. The company initiated a major restructuring during fiscal 2002 and aggregated the following events in an expense account labeled 'Restructuring, asset impairment and other charges.'
    a. The company paid severance of $810 to certain employees and forgave loans to these employees totaling $2,633. These loans were included in 'Other current assets' at February 3, 2001.
    b. The company closed a number of stores and disposed of certain store property with a net book value of $11,300. The company received no proceeds for these transactions.
    c. The company decided that the value of certain remaining restructured assets was permanently impaired. Thus, the company wrote-down 'Property, net' by $4,464 and 'Other assets' by $433.
    d. The company anticipates making additional restructuring payments of $8,574 during the next fiscal year. Because these future payments relate to the Company's current restructuring plan, they are accrued (i.e. set up as a liability) and recorded as expenses in fiscal 2002.
19. The company paid $4,839 to settle certain assets and liabilities ('Net liabilities') on discontinued operations. These net liabilities related to operating assets and liabilities of closed stores. Thus, the cash flow is an operating cash flow.
20. The company removed certain deferred tax assets and liabilities from their balance sheet. These related to assets and liabilities of the closed properties and thus, were no longer appropriately recorded on the company's balance sheet. The company made the following journal entry to write-off deferred tax accounts:

Dr Accrued expenses	1,870	
Dr Other liabilities	1,794	
Dr Tax expense	2,769	
Cr Other current assets		5,676
Cr Other assets		757

21. The company hired an appraiser who determined that the company's goodwill had no market value and that the impairment was permanent.

e. Open T-accounts for all balance sheet accounts as February 3, 2001. Post the journal entries from part *d* above, to T-accounts. Open temporary accounts for revenues and expenses as needed. For each entry in the *cash* T-account, determine whether the transaction is operating, investing or financing.

f. From the cash T-account, prepare Mayor's statement of cash flows using the direct method. Make your statement of cash flow as detailed as you like. You can check your work against the statement of cash flows provided. Note that Mayor's combines some cash payments on its statement of cash flows. For example, cash for purchases and cash paid for wages and other operating expenses are aggregated. As well, certain balance sheet changes are aggregated on the statement of cash flows. Also, you may discover some rounding differences between Mayor's SCF and yours. Ignore them.

g. Prepare Mayor's income statement for the year using the income statement (temporary) T-accounts.

h. From the income statement, determine "Net sales" for the year ended February 2, 2002. Where does the cash-based equivalent of "Net sales" appear on the statement of cash flows and how much is it for the year ended February 2, 2002? Quantify the difference between the two numbers. Why are they different? Mayor's provides a reconciliation of accrual-based net loss with cash from operations. Identify the two items that reconcile accrual-basis and cash-basis sales.

i. From the income statement, determine "Cost of sales" for the year ended February 2, 2002. Where does the cash-based equivalent of "Cost of sales" appear on the statement of cash flows and how much is it for the year ended February 2, 2002? *Hint:* refer to your cash T-account. Quantify the difference between the two numbers. Why are they different? Mayor's provides a reconciliation of accrual-based net income with cash from operations. Find the two items that reconcile accrual-basis and cash-basis cost of sales.

j. Mayor's reconciles net loss to net cash provided by operating activities at the bottom of the statement of cash flows. The reconciliation begins with the following:

"Depreciation and amortization $ 9,771"

Explain why depreciation is added to the net loss on the income statement to arrive at cash flow from operations. Where does depreciation appear on the statement of cash flows under the direct method? Explain.

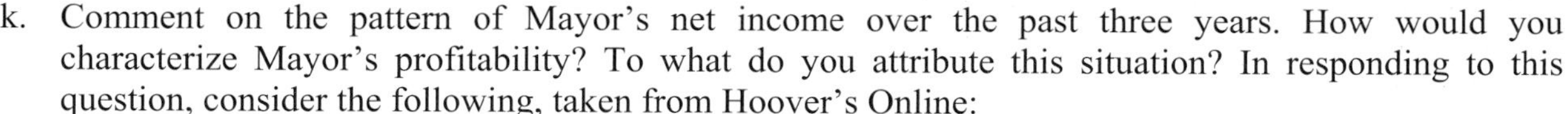

Analysis

k. Comment on the pattern of Mayor's net income over the past three years. How would you characterize Mayor's profitability? To what do you attribute this situation? In responding to this question, consider the following, taken from Hoover's Online:

"Sam's Club may have broken off the engagement, but Mayor's Jewelers found itself a new suitor. Mayor's (nee Jan Bell Marketing) operates nearly 30 upscale jewelry stores in Florida and Georgia. Its stores, where the average price is about $1,800 per item, focus on designer jewelry in 18-karat gold, platinum, and sterling silver. Mayor's also sells giftware and watches (Rolex accounts for 37% of sales). Mayor's deal to run the jewelry departments at Sam's Club warehouse stores, which represented 55% of sales, was terminated in early 2001. Mayor's later put itself up for sale, and said "Yes" in 2002 to a proposal from Canadian jeweler Henry Birks & Sons; Birks now owns more than 75% of Mayor's."

l. Comment on the pattern of Mayor's operating cash flows over the past three years. How would you characterize Mayor's cash flow situation? To what do you attribute this situation?

m. To assess a firm's liquidity, financial statement users typically assess working capital level (current assets minus current liabilities) as well as the firm's current ratio (current assets divided by current liabilities) and quick ratio (cash plus marketable securities plus net accounts receivable all divided by current liabilities). Calculate these metrics for Mayor's for fiscal 2001 and 2002. Based on these ratios, how would you assess Mayor's liquidity?

MAYOR'S JEWELERS, INC. AND SUBSIDIARIES

CONSOLIDATED BALANCE SHEETS
(Amounts shown in thousands except share and per share data)

	February 2, 2002	February 3, 2001
ASSETS		
Current Assets:		
Cash and cash equivalents	$ 2,886	$ 1,363
Accounts receivable (net of allowance for doubtful accounts of $1,487 and $1,403, respectively)	31,845	34,974
Inventories	80,716	107,674
Other current assets	2,604	10,913
Total current assets	118,051	154,924
Property, net	25,455	42,651
Excess of cost over fair value of net assets acquired	—	24,204
Other assets	1,083	2,273
Total non-current assets	26,538	69,128
Total assets	$ 144,589	$ 224,052
LIABILITIES AND STOCKHOLDERS' EQUITY		
Current Liabilities:		
Accounts payable	$ 10,769	$ 14,039
Accrued expenses	7,318	11,374
Accrued restructuring	8,574	—
Current portion of long term debt	53,464	—
Net liabilities of discontinued operations	—	4,839
Total current liabilities	80,125	30,252
Long term debt	—	44,390
Other long term liabilities	3,357	5,151
Total long term liabilities	3,357	49,541
Commitments and contingencies (Notes H, J and K)	—	—
Stockholders' Equity:		
Common stock, $.0001 par value, 50,000,000 shares authorized, 29,509,703 and 29,210,886 shares issued, respectively	3	3
Additional paid-in capital	194,527	193,821
Accumulated deficit	(104,023)	(20,165)
Less: 9,983,954 shares of treasury stock, at cost	(29,400)	(29,400)
Total stockholders' equity	61,107	144,259
Total liabilities and stockholders' equity	$ 144,589	$ 224,052

See notes to consolidated financial statements.

MAYOR'S JEWELERS, INC. AND SUBSIDIARIES

CONSOLIDATED STATEMENTS OF OPERATIONS
(Amounts shown in thousands except share and per share data)

	Year Ended February 2, 2002	Year Ended February 3, 2001	Year Ended January 29, 2000
Net sales	$ 163,700	$ 181,256	$ 157,629
Cost of sales	103,027	102,463	95,155
Gross profit	60,673	78,793	62,474
Store operating and selling expenses	53,794	45,284	43,185
Store contribution	6,879	33,509	19,289
General and administrative expenses	14,632	16,186	16,505
Advertising and marketing expenses	8,810	8,595	3,538
Subtotal	(16,563)	8,728	(754)
Restructuring, asset impairments and other charges	28,214	—	—
Depreciation and amortization	9,771	8,046	7,648
Goodwill impairment writedown	22,265	—	—
	60,250	8,046	7,648
Operating (loss) income	(76,813)	682	(8,402)
Interest and other income	174	213	90
Interest expense	(3,788)	(3,450)	(2,619)
Loss from continuing operations before cumulative effect of a change in accounting principle and income taxes	(80,427)	(2,555)	(10,931)
Income taxes	3,431	—	—
Cumulative effect of a change in accounting principle	—	—	(2,173)
Loss from continuing operations	(83,858)	(2,555)	(13,104)
Income from discontinued operations, net of income tax liability of $531	—	—	8,019
Gain from disposition of discontinued operations, net of income tax liability of $393	—	13,552	—
Net (loss) income	$ (83,858)	$ 10,997	$ (5,085)
Weighted average shares outstanding, basic and diluted	19,416,398	19,587,322	25,535,852
(Loss) earnings per share, basic and diluted:			
Continuing operations before cumulative effect of a change in accounting principle	$ (4.32)	$ (0.13)	$ (0.43)
Cumulative effect of a change in accounting principle	—	—	(0.09)
Discontinued operations	—	0.69	0.32
	$ (4.32)	$ 0.56	$ (0.20)

See notes to consolidated financial statements.

MAYOR'S JEWELERS, INC. AND SUBSIDIARIES

CONSOLIDATED STATEMENTS OF STOCKHOLDERS' EQUITY
(Amounts in thousands except share data)

	Common Shares Outstanding	Common Stock	Additional Paid-In Capital	Accumulated Deficit	Comprehensive Income (Loss)	Accumulated Other Comprehensive Income (Loss)	Treasury Stock	Total
BALANCE AT JANUARY 30, 1999	28,358,475	$ 3	$ 191,538	$ (26,077)		$ (1,778)	$ 0	$ 163,686
Comprehensive income (loss):								
Net loss	—	—	—	(5,085)	$ (5,085)	—	—	(5,085)
Foreign currency translation adjustment	—	—	—	—	1,778	1,778	—	1,778
					$ (3,307)			
Purchase plan exercise	76,261	—	216	—		—	—	216
Issuance of common stock	22,898	—	56	—		—	—	56
Treasury stock	(8,078,798)	—	—	—		—	(24,096)	(24,096)
BALANCE AT JANUARY 29, 2000	20,378,836	3	191,810	(31,162)		0	(24,096)	136,555
Comprehensive income:								
Net income	—	—	—	10,997	$ 10,997	—	—	10,997
Purchase plan exercise	87,796	—	182	—		—	—	182
Issuance of common stock	665,456	—	1,829	—		—	—	1,829
Treasury stock	(1,905,156)	—	—	—		—	(5,304)	(5,304)
BALANCE AT FEBRUARY 3, 2001	19,226,932	3	193,821	(20,165)		0	(29,400)	144,259
Comprehensive income (loss):								
Net loss	—	—	—	(83,858)	$ (83,858)	—	—	(83,858)
Purchase plan exercise	71,503	—	136	—		—	—	136
Issuance of common stock	227,314	—	570	—		—	—	570
BALANCE AT FEBRUARY 2, 2002	19,525,749	$ 3	$ 194,527	$ (104,023)		$ 0	$ (29,400)	$ 61,107

See notes to consolidated financial statements.

MAYOR'S JEWELERS, INC. AND SUBSIDIARIES

CONSOLIDATED STATEMENTS OF CASH FLOWS
(Amounts shown in thousands)

	Year Ended February 2, 2002	Year Ended February 3, 2001	Year Ended January 29, 2000
Cash flows from operating activities:			
Cash received from customers	$ 166,829	$ 172,164	$ 157,130
Cash paid to suppliers and employees	(157,384)	(222,239)	(170,806)
Interest and other income received	174	213	91
Interest paid	(3,788)	(3,450)	(2,619)
Income taxes paid	(662)	(58)	(262)
Net cash provided by (used in) continuing operations	5,169	(53,370)	(16,466)
Net cash (used in) provided by discontinued operations	(4,839)	58,563	51,543
Net cash provided by operating activities	330	5,193	35,077
Cash flows from investing activities:			
Investment in Mayor's, net of cash acquired	—	423	(2,686)
Capital expenditures	(6,400)	(20,214)	(8,373)
Net cash used in investing activities	(6,400)	(19,791)	(11,059)
Cash flows from financing activities:			
Borrowings under line of credit	184,607	461,950	501,703
Line of credit repayments	(175,533)	(441,984)	(503,689)
Purchase of treasury stock	—	(5,304)	(24,096)
Proceeds from sale of employee stock plans	705	2,011	272
Cash paid from due to Mayor's prior shareholders	—	(5,095)	(1,050)
Payment of commitment fee	—	—	(75)
Other	(2,186)	3,334	436
Net cash provided by (used in) financing activities	7,593	14,912	(26,499)
Net increase (decrease) in cash and cash equivalents	1,523	314	(2,481)
Cash and cash equivalents at beginning of year	1,363	1,049	3,530
Cash and cash equivalents at end of year	$ 2,886	$ 1,363	$ 1,049
Reconciliation of net (loss) income to net cash provided by operating activities:			
Net (loss) income	$ (83,858)	$ 10,997	$ (5,085)
Deduct gain/income from discontinued operations	—	(13,552)	(8,019)
Loss from continuing operations	(83,858)	(2,555)	(13,104)
Adjustments to reconcile net income (loss) to net cash provided by operating activities:			
Depreciation and amortization	9,771	8,046	7,648
Deferred tax asset write-off	2,769	—	—
Provision for doubtful accounts	3,035	1,403	1,274
Goodwill impairment writedown	22,265	—	—
Closing stores asset writedown	11,300	—	—
Building and related assets writedown	4,897	—	—
Cumulative effect of change in accounting principle	—	—	2,173
(Increase) decrease in assets:			
Accounts receivable	95	(10,493)	(1,773)
Inventories	26,958	(29,034)	(10,665)
Other assets	3,958	(8,702)	(492)
Increase (decrease) in liabilities:			
Accounts payable	(3,270)	(10,348)	(1,359)
Accrued expenses	(1,325)	(1,687)	(168)
Accrued restructuring	8,574	—	—
Net cash provided by (used in) continuing operations	5,169	(53,370)	(16,466)
Net cash (used in) provided by discontinued operations	(4,839)	58,563	51,543
Net cash provided by operating activities	$ 330	$ 5,193	$ 35,077

See notes to consolidated financial statements.

Weis Markets, Inc.—Statement of Cash Flows

Weis Markets, Inc. is a Pennsylvania business corporation formed in 1924. The Company is engaged principally in the retail sale of food. The business of the Company is highly competitive and the Company competes based on price and service with national retail food chains, local chains and independent food stores. Weis Markets continues to expand operations in its primary marketing areas: Pennsylvania and Maryland. The Company operates 151 supermarkets under the names Weis Markets, Mr. Z's, Scot's, and King's, and 35 SuperPetz pet supply stores.

Learning Objectives

- Analyze the changes in balance sheet accounts by inferring transactions.
- Construct a complete statement of cash flows on the indirect basis.
- Interpret the statement of cash flows, comparing key figures to net income.
- Evaluate a company's ROE in light of its operations and asset base.

Refer to the 1995 financial statements of Weis Markets, Inc.

a. Construct the 1995 statement of cash flows using the indirect method. The following items provide information to help you. All figures are in thousands.

   Recall that the change in cash (i.e., the cash flow statement) is algebraically related to the balance sheet as follows:

   Δ Cash = Δ Liabilities + Δ Owners' Equity – Δ All Other Assets

   Thus, if you can "explain" the changes in all the non-cash balance sheet accounts (and only those accounts), you will have generated a statement of cash flows. Use a spreadsheet or set of T-accounts to help you organize your efforts.

1. Note 4 to the 1995 financial statements reveals the following:

(4) Property and Equipment

Property and equipment, as of December 30, 1995 and December 31, 1994, consisted of:

(dollars in thousands)	Useful Life (in years)	**1995**	1994
Land		**$42,940**	$32,557
Buildings & Improvements	10-60	**197,277**	177,025
Equipment	3-12	**326,689**	293,043
Leasehold Improvements	5-20	**46,195**	39,811
Total, at cost		**613,101**	542,436
Less accumulated depreciation and amortization		**327,108**	297,173
Property and equipment, net		**$285,993**	$245,263

In 1995, depreciation and amortization on property and equipment was $31,504. During 1995, the company purchased $72,759 of new property, plant, and equipment. Property and equipment that originally cost $2,094 was sold for $1,107 in 1995. No other property and equipment was sold in 1995.

Activities in the fixed asset accounts affect the statement of cash flows in four ways. Determine each of the following four items (*i* through *iv* below). To do this, create two T-accounts, one for property and equipment at cost and another for accumulated depreciation and amortization. Use the information from Weis' Note 4 to analyze the activity in both accounts during the year.

i. Depreciation and amortization expense is included in the operating section of the statement of cash flows. Explain why. Does depreciation expense actually 'generate' cash for Weis?

ii. Capital expenditures (i.e. cash used to purchase new property and equipment) are included in the investing section of the statement of cash flows.

iii. Cash proceeds on the disposal of property and equipment are included in the investing section as a source of cash.

iv. Gains on disposals of fixed assets are included in the operating section of the statement of cash flows. *Hint*: To determine the gain on disposal, you will need to determine the cost of the disposed property (the credit that balances the gross property and equipment T-account) and the related depreciation on the disposed property (the debit that balances the accumulated depreciation account). The difference between the cost of the disposed property and the related depreciation is the net book value of the disposed property. Compare the net book value to the cash proceeds to determine the gain.

2. In 1995, the company purchased \$3,284 of new intangible assets with cash. During the year, amortization of intangible assets was \$1,664. Create a T-account to analyze the activity in Intangible assets during 1995.

3. Create a T-account to analyze the activity in Marketable Securities during the year. The company sold \$37,428 of marketable securities in 1995. There was no gain or loss recorded on the sale. No additional marketable securities were purchased.

   At year-end, Weis Markets adjusts its Marketable Securities to market value. Unrealized gains and losses are added to or subtracted from a separate component of owners' equity. These unrealized gains and losses affect neither net income nor cash. Therefore, they are not a reconciling item on the statement of cash flows. At the end of fiscal 1995, the company recorded the following journal entry to reflect the unrealized gain on marketable securities for 1995. Use this journal entry to analyze the activity in Marketable Securities (and in Deferred Income Taxes—see item 4 for more on deferred taxes).

Dr.	Marketable Securities (B/S)	16,585	
Cr.	Net Unrealized Gain on Marketable Securities (B/S)		9,815
Cr.	Deferred Income Taxes (B/S)		6,770

4. The Weis balance sheet reports three Deferred Income Tax accounts (one asset and two liabilities) but the statement of cash flows does not distinguish among the three. Combine them to create one T-account to analyze the Deferred Income Tax activities for the year. This account will be a net deferred tax liability.

   According to Note 2—Income Taxes, Weis recorded a deferred income tax benefit of \$136, in 1995. The company recorded the following journal entry to reflect the benefit:

Dr.	Deferred Income Taxes (B/S)	136	
Cr.	Provision for Income Taxes (I/S)		136

   Use this journal entry and the one in item 3 to analyze the Deferred Income Tax net liability.

5. The Minority Interest account on the income statement represents the minority shareholders' share of the losses incurred by affiliated companies (i.e., those not owned 100% by Weis) during 1995. It is similar to a non-cash revenue or expense and therefore is a reconciling item in the operating section of the statement of cash flows. During the year, the company recorded the following journal entry to reflect the minority shareholders' share of the losses from Weis' affiliates:

Dr.	Minority Interest (B/S)	178	
Cr.	Minority Interest (I/S)		178

✧ Analysis ✧

b. Using the 1995 Statement of Cash Flows you constructed and those reported for 1993 and 1994, evaluate Weis Markets' financial performance from a net income perspective and from a cash generating perspective.

c. Which data, the income or the cash flow data provide a clearer picture of Weis' long-term performance? Which appears to be more predictable? Why?

d. Calculate Weis Markets' overall return on equity for 1994 and 1995. Does the figure appear to be reasonable? Evaluate that return in relation to what you consider a reasonable return to Weis' shareholders to be (consider the nature of the business in relation to 'risk free' investments and other 'risky' investments).

e. What adjustments could you make to the numbers in your ROE calculations to better gauge Weis Markets' performance as a supermarket? (*Hint*: consider whether there are items on the balance sheet that could be removed and still allow Weis to generate about the same net income from supermarket operations.)

WEIS MARKETS, INC. AND SUBSIDIARIES

CONSOLIDATED BALANCE SHEETS

(dollars in thousands) December 30, 1995 and December 31, 1994	1995	1994
Assets		
Current:		
Cash	$ 3,285	$ 4,011
Marketable securities	432,174	453,017
Accounts receivable, net	31,517	24,132
Inventories	131,727	130,019
Prepaid expenses	7,764	4,229
Deferred income taxes	–	2,344
Total current assets	606,467	617,752
Property and equipment, net	285,993	245,263
Intangible and other assets, net	30,698	29,078
	$923,158	$892,093
Liabilities		
Current:		
Accounts payable	$ 72,262	$ 82,529
Accrued expenses	12,997	8,266
Accrued self-insurance	13,285	10,462
Payable to employee benefit plans	7,453	7,957
Income taxes payable	4,077	3,089
Deferred income taxes	5,258	–
Total current liabilities	115,332	112,303
Deferred income taxes	16,527	17,495
Minority Interest	(263)	(85)
Shareholders' equity:		
Common stock, no par value, 100,800,000 shares authorized, 47,445,929 and 47,445,929 shares issued, respectively	7,380	7,380
Retained earnings	879,916	834,995
Net unrealized gain on marketable securities	14,748	4,933
	902,044	847,308
Treasury stock at cost 4,912,312 and 3,962,388 shares, respectively	(110,482)	(84,928)
Total shareholders' equity	791,562	762,380
	$923,158	$892,093

See accompanying notes to consolidated financial statements

WEIS MARKETS, INC. AND SUBSIDIARIES
CONSOLIDATED STATEMENTS OF INCOME

(dollars in thousands, except per share amounts)
For the Fiscal Years Ended December 30, 1995,
December 31, 1994, and December 25, 1993

	1995	1994	1993
Net sales	$1,646,435	$1,556,663	$1,441,090
Cost of sales, including warehousing and distribution expenses	1,224,339	1,162,068	1,073,140
Gross profit on sales	422,096	394,595	367,950
Operating, general and administrative expenses	335,899	314,593	288,280
Income from operations	86,197	80,002	79,670
Interest and dividend income	21,383	21,607	21,528
Other income	13,959	15,499	12,456
Minority Interest	178	85	–
Income before income taxes	121,717	117,193	113,654
Provision for income taxes	42,297	40,944	40,701
Net income	$ 79,420	$ 76,249	$ 72,953
Per share of common stock:			
Net income	$ 1.84	$ 1.75	$ 1.66
Cash dividends	$ .80	$ .74	$ .70
Weighted average shares outstanding	43,083,449	43,662,031	43,827,168

See accompanying notes to consolidated financial statements

WEIS MARKETS, INC. AND SUBSIDIARIES

STATEMENTS OF CONSOLIDATED STOCKHOLDERS' EQUITY
For the Fiscal Years Ended December 30, 1995
December 31, 1994 and December 25, 1993

	Common Stock	Retained Earnings	Net Unrealized Gain (Loss) on Marketable Securities	Minimum Pension Liability	Treasury Stock	Total Shareholders' Equity
Balance-December 26, 1992	$7,147	$748,796	$ —	$ —	$ (75,678)	$680,265
Shares issued for options	108	—	—	—	—	108
Treasury stock purchased (41,790 shares)	—	—	—	—	(1,149)	(1,149)
Dividends paid	—	(30,677)	—	—	—	(30,677)
Change in accounting for marketable securities	—	—	16,740	—	—	16,740
Minimum pension liability	—	—	—	(125)	—	(125)
Net income	—	72,953	—	—	—	72,953
Balance-December 25, 1993	7,255	791,072	16,740	(125)	(76,827)	738,115
Shares issued for options	125	—	—	—	—	125
Treasury stock purchased (320,542 shares)	—	—	—	—	(8,101)	(8,101)
Dividends paid	—	(32,326)	—	—	—	(32,326)
Net unrealized loss on marketable securities	—	—	(11,807)	—	—	(11,807)
Minimum pension liability	—	—	—	125	—	125
Net income	—	76,249	—	—	—	76,249
Balance-December 31, 1994	7,380	834,995	4,933	—	(84,928)	762,380
Treasury stock purchased (949,924 shares)	—	—	—	—	(25,554)	(25,554)
Dividends paid	—	(34,499)	—	—	—	(34,499)
Net unrealized gain on marketable securities	—	—	9,815	—	—	9,815
Net income	—	79,420	—	—	—	79,420
Balance-December 30, 1995	$7,380	$879,916	$14,748	$ —	$(110,482)	$791,562

See accompanying notes to consolidated financial statements.

WEIS MARKETS, INC. AND SUBSIDIARIES

CONSOLIDATED STATEMENTS OF CASH FLOWS
(dollars in thousands)

For the Fiscal Years Ended December 30, 1995, December 31, 1994, and December 25, 1993	1995	1994	1993
Cash flows from operating activities:			
Net income		$76,249	$72,953
Adjustments to reconcile net income to net cash provided by operating activities:			
Depreciation and amortization		30,607	28,959
(Gain) loss on sale of fixed assets		(298)	(798)
Changes in operating assets and liabilities:			
(Increase) decrease in accounts receivable		(3,754)	1,896
(Increase) in inventories		(18,172)	(14,188)
(Increase) decrease in prepaid expenses		2,151	1,825
Increase (decrease) in accounts payable		25,849	7,444
Increase in accrued expenses		1,366	656
Increase in accrued self-insurance		2,576	155
Increase (decrease) in payable to employee benefit plans		(1,037)	3,397
Increase in income taxes payable		1,151	1,938
Decrease in minority interest		(85)	--
Increase (decrease) in deferred income taxes		2,769	(134)
	?		
Net cash provided by operating activities		119,372	104,103
Cash flows from investing activities:			
Purchase of property and equipment		(49,421)	(49,188)
Proceeds from the sale of property and equipment		985	1,928
(Increase) decrease in marketable securities		(15,631)	(9,448)
(Increase) in intangible and other assets		(20,058)	(7,909)
Net cash used by investing activities		(84,125)	(64,617)
Cash flows from financing activities:			
Proceeds from issuance of common stock		125	108
Dividends paid		(32,326)	(30,677)
Purchase of treasury stock		(8,101)	(1,149)
Net cash used by financing activities		(40,302)	(31,718)
Net increase (decrease) in cash		(5,055)	7,768
Cash at beginning of year		9,066	1,298
Cash at end of year	$	$ 4,011	$ 9,066

See accompanying notes to consolidated financial statements.

Lucent Technologies, Inc.—Revenue Recognition

Lucent Technologies designs and delivers networks for the world's largest communications service providers. Backed by Bell Labs research and development, Lucent relies on its strengths in mobility, optical, data and voice networking technologies as well as software and services to develop next-generation networks. The company's systems, services and software are designed to help customers quickly deploy and better manage their networks and create new, revenue-generating services that help businesses and consumers. As of December 31, 2002, Lucent employed approximately 40,000 people worldwide (two years prior, the figure was close to 123,000). Lucent is listed on the New York Stock Exchange under the symbol LU.

Learning Objectives

- Define revenues and gains. Explain the difference between the two.
- Critically assess the revenue recognition policies of a particular company.
- Consider the tradeoffs between rules-based and principles-based accounting standards.
- Understand the role of audit committees in corporate governance and financial reporting.
- Explain how financial statement users can evaluate the quality of a company's reported revenue.

Refer to the 2002 financial statements of Lucent Technologies, Inc.

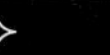

Concepts

a. In your own words, define "revenues." Explain how revenues are different from "gains."

b. Describe what it means for a business to "recognize" revenues. What specific accounts and financial statements are affected by the process of revenue recognition?

c. When does Lucent recognize revenues?

d. In general, what incentives do company managers have to make self-serving revenue recognition choices?

Process

e. Assume that all of Lucent's sales revenue is "on account." Prepare a journal entry that summarizes the sales activity for fiscal 2002.

f. Consider the following hypothetical revenue recognition scenarios and answer the associated questions. Note that there may be more than one acceptable answer. Support your answers with reasoned argumentation. Indicate where more information is required.

   i. In September 2002, Lucent contracted to provide services to a regional Bell operating company (RBOC) for a four-year period beginning November 1, 2002. The $50 million contract calls for annual payments of $12 million in monthly installments of $1 million. At the signing of the contract in September 2002, Lucent received $2 million. How much revenue will Lucent recognize in fiscal 2002? Provide a journal entry that records the receipt of the initial payment.

   ii. On June 30, 2002, Lucent sold telecom equipment to a small start-up company. The contract states that the sales price is $15 million. The equipment has been installed, tested, and accepted by the customer. Because the customer is short of cash, Lucent's sales team agreed to provide vendor financing for the sale. The customer is scheduled to make the $15 million payment in full on June 30, 2004. Assume that Lucent's cost of borrowing is 10% and the customer's is 15%. Provide the journal entries recorded by Lucent on June 30 and September 30, 2002 as well as June 30, 2004. Assume that Lucent prepares formal financial statements quarterly.

iii. On December 31, 2002, Lucent learned that the customer in part *ii* failed to achieve success in the marketplace with its main product. The start-up company remains short of cash and is having trouble negotiating with its lenders. Provide the journal entry Lucent would make if they learned that the customer's borrowing cost had risen to 17%.

iv. At the end of September 2002, Lucent signed a $200 million contract to provide equipment, software, and services to an RBOC. By September 30, 2002, some of the equipment had been delivered and installed at the RBOC. Other equipment had been manufactured and shipped, but not yet received by the customer. Still other products are to be delivered over the following two fiscal years. All products contain a two-year warranty. Lucent has promised to maintain the products and provide software upgrades and a dedicated customer support team for a three-year period. How should Lucent recognize revenue on this contract?

v. For the contract in part *iv*, how would your answer change if you learned that there was a side agreement allowing the RBOC to return the products, no questions asked, through January 31, 2003? What if Lucent promised significant discounts on future purchases in return for signing the initial $200 million contract?

vi. How could Lucent manage its reported earnings through strategic revenue recognition choices for the contract in part *iv*?

✧ Analysis ✧

g. Evaluate the three-year trend in Lucent's sales and margins. Conduct an internet search to establish reasons for the change. Good starting points include the company's website www.lucent.com, the Securities and Exchange Commission's EDGAR service (where Lucent is required to file financial reports) at www.sec.gov, and online investing sites.

h. Refer to the accompanying article, Disparities in How U.K. Companies Report Sales Make Investors Wary, from the April 1, 2002 issue of *The Wall Street Journal*.

i. Why do markets 'punish' firms that use unconventional or aggressive revenue recognition methods?

ii. What can companies do to avoid such outcomes?

iii. Nick Gomer, the Ernst and Young partner quoted in the article, suggests that the best practice is to follow detailed U.S. guidance. Why might he suggest that? How does his argument hold up against the call for accounting standards to be more principles-based and less rules-based?

i. Assume that you are a member of Lucent's audit committee. Your role, in part, is to evaluate the appropriateness of the company's financial reporting policies and choices. Each quarter, you meet with Lucent's external auditors and discuss financial reporting matters with them.

i. What questions would you ask Lucent's external auditors to assure yourself that the company's revenue recognition policy was reasonable?

ii. What signs might indicate that a company aggressively recognizes revenue? By those standards, does Lucent recognize revenue aggressively?

WSJ.com THE WALL STREET JOURNAL. ONLINE

April 1, 2002

WORLD STOCK MARKETS

Disparities in How U.K. Companies Report Sales Make Investors Wary

By Gren Manuel

LONDON—When is a "sale" a sale?

Don't ask United Kingdom companies. The way in which these concerns report sales varies widely, according to a survey of 588 recent annual reports released last month by Company Reporting, a research house based in Edinburgh, Scotland. The disparities in the U.K. come as accounting has become a hot-button issue in the U.S., making global investors wary of companies that seem to bend the rules.

To get a sense of how critical this issue can be, look at British Airways. Although normally conservative about its financial reporting—it books sales only when a passenger has paid and is belted into the seat—it is a different story when it comes to reporting revenue from frequent-flier programs. British Airways books revenue as fliers rack up air miles, whereas U.S. accounting rules call for revenue to be recognized when air miles are exchanged for seats.

The result: In the year ended March 31, 2001, British Airways reported GBP 15 million ($21.4 million) of revenue that it couldn't have booked in the U.S. In a year when pretax profit was GBP 150 million, that is significant.

British Airways wasn't available to comment.

Company Reporting's study found that even U.K. companies in similar businesses report sales differently. For instance, of 100 companies in the consumer-goods sector, 26 reported revenue on delivery of service, 26 when an invoice is issued, 11 over the life of a contract, three on acceptance of a contract, and one on the completion of a contract. The rest of the companies surveyed didn't disclose a policy.

In particular, wide variations were found in the building industry, with some companies booking sales on the exchange of contracts, some when buildings are substantially complete and contracts are exchanged, and others only when a sale is complete and legal title is passed over. With sales in this sector often bracketed in the GBP 1 million range, even a small number of sales booked in a different year can make a big difference.

High-technology companies tended to disclose more information about how they book revenue than other sectors. Many of these tech companies were nudged along by the fact that they have U.S. investors or prepare accounts according to U.S. standards.

The sector includes Cable & Wireless PLC, a company that demonstrated how critical this issue can be after being panned by analysts for booking revenue upfront on long-term sales of network capacity even if the contracts span decades. Sales of such long-term network capacity have been cited as a factor in the downfall of Global Crossing Ltd., now in Chapter 11 bankruptcy proceedings. In Cable & Wireless's case, however, the company did disclose its policy in its annual report.

In terms of active disclosure, no company matches ARM Holdings PLC, a company whose core business is long-term licensing of chip technology. Its 20 paragraphs of explanation in its annual report seem designed to broadcast a message of conservatism and stability.

Nick Gomer, a partner for Ernst & Young in the U.K., says the real problem is companies that don't explain policy. "Having different policies is not in itself a problem, if it's very clearly explained how the numbers are arrived at," he said. "It does make it much more difficult to compare the performance of businesses."

He said that for simple businesses, there isn't much leeway in how revenue is recognized, but for other sectors, such as software, there are many options. The best practice is to follow the increasingly detailed guidance coming out of the U.S.

The clear risk to investors from this issue was demonstrated March 19, when Amey PLC, a services company heavily involved in long-term government contracts, was punished by the market when it switched its accounting, including its policy on revenue recognition. Analysts expecting a profit were instead shocked with an GBP 18.3 million loss due to more-conservative accounting. The stock fell 17% and caused widespread fallout in the sector. This was despite management protests that operating results were better than expected.

LUCENT TECHNOLOGIES INC. AND SUBSIDIARIES

CONSOLIDATED STATEMENTS OF OPERATIONS

(Amounts in Millions, Except Per Share Amounts)	*Years ended September 30,*		
	2002	**2001**	**2000**
Revenues:			
Products	$ 9,632	$ 17,132	$23,978
Services	2,689	4,162	4,926
Total revenues	12,321	21,294	28,904
Costs:			
Products	8,452	15,596	13,265
Services	2,317	3,640	3,925
Total costs	10,769	19,236	17,190
Gross margin	1,552	2,058	11,714
Operating expenses:			
Selling, general and administrative	3,969	7,410	5,610
Research and development	2,310	3,520	3,179
Purchased in-process research and development	–	–	559
Business restructuring charges and asset impairments, net	2,252	10,157	–
Total operating expenses	8,531	21,087	9,348
Operating income (loss)	(6,979)	(19,029)	2,366
Other income (expense), net	292	(357)	333
Interest expense	382	518	342
Income (loss) from continuing operations before income taxes	(7,069)	(19,904)	2,357
Provision (benefit) for income taxes	4,757	(5,734)	924
Income (loss) from continuing operations	**(11,826)**	**(14,170)**	**1,433**
Income (loss) from discontinued operations, net	73	(3,172)	(214)
Income (loss) before extraordinary item and cumulative effect of accounting changes	(11,753)	(17,342)	1,219
Extraordinary gain, net	–	1,182	–
Cumulative effect of accounting changes, net	–	(38)	–
Net income (loss)	(11,753)	(16,198)	1,219
Conversion cost – 8% redeemable convertible preferred stock	(29)	–	–
Preferred stock dividends and accretion	(167)	(28)	–
Net income (loss) applicable to common shareowners	**$(11,949)**	**$(16,226)**	**$ 1,219**
EARNINGS (LOSS) PER COMMON SHARE – BASIC			
Income (loss) from continuing operations	$ (3.51)	$ (4.18)	$ 0.44
Net income (loss) applicable to common shareowners	$ (3.49)	$ (4.77)	$ 0.38
EARNINGS (LOSS) PER COMMON SHARE – DILUTED			
Income (loss) from continuing operations	$ (3.51)	$ (4.18)	$ 0.43
Net income (loss) applicable to common shareowners	$ (3.49)	$ (4.77)	$ 0.37
Weighted average number of common shares outstanding – basic	3,426.7	3,400.7	3,232.3
Weighted average number of common shares outstanding – diluted	3,426.7	3,400.7	3,325.9

See Notes to Consolidated Financial Statements.

LUCENT TECHNOLOGIES INC. AND SUBSIDIARIES

CONSOLIDATED BALANCE SHEETS

(Dollars in Millions, Except Per Share Amounts)	*September 30,*	
	2002	**2001**
ASSETS		
Cash and cash equivalents	$ 2,894	$ 2,390
Short-term investments	1,526	–
Receivables, less allowance of $325 in 2002 and $634 in 2001	1,647	4,594
Inventories	1,363	3,646
Contracts in process, net	10	1,027
Deferred income taxes, net	–	2,658
Other current assets	1,715	1,788
Total current assets	9,155	16,103
Property, plant and equipment, net	1,977	4,416
Prepaid pension costs	4,355	4,958
Deferred income taxes, net	–	2,695
Goodwill and other acquired intangibles, net of accumulated amortization of $910 in 2002 and $832 in 2001	224	1,466
Other assets	2,080	2,724
Net long-term assets of discontinued operations	–	1,302
Total assets	**$17,791**	**$33,664**
LIABILITIES		
Accounts payable	$ 1,298	$ 1,844
Payroll and benefit-related liabilities	1,094	1,500
Debt maturing within one year	120	1,135
Other current liabilities	3,814	5,285
Net current liabilities of discontinued operations	–	405
Total current liabilities	**6,326**	**10,169**
Postretirement and postemployment benefit liabilities	5,230	5,481
Pension liability	2,752	80
Long-term debt	3,236	3,274
Company-obligated 7.75% mandatorily redeemable convertible preferred securities of subsidiary trust	1,750	–
Deferred income taxes, net	–	152
Other liabilities	1,551	1,651
Total liabilities	**20,845**	**20,807**
Commitments and contingencies		
8.00% redeemable convertible preferred stock	**1,680**	**1,834**
SHAREOWNERS' (DEFICIT) EQUITY		
Preferred Stock – par value $1.00 per share; authorized shares: 250,000,000; issued and outstanding none	–	–
Common stock – par value $.01 per share; Authorized shares: 10,000,000,000; 3,491,585,126 issued and 3,490,310,034 outstanding shares at September 30, 2002 and 3,414,815,908 issued and 3,414,167,155 outstanding shares at September 30, 2001	35	34
Additional paid-in capital	20,606	21,702
Accumulated deficit	(22,025)	(10,272)
Accumulated other comprehensive loss	(3,350)	(441)
Total shareowners' (deficit) equity	**(4,734)**	**11,023**
Total liabilities, redeemable convertible preferred stock and shareowners' (deficit) equity	**$17,791**	**$33,664**

See Notes to Consolidated Financial Statements.

LUCENT TECHNOLOGIES INC. AND SUBSIDIARIES

CONSOLIDATED STATEMENTS OF CASH FLOWS

(Dollars in Millions)	*Years ended September 30,*		
	2002	**2001**	**2000**
OPERATING ACTIVITIES			
Net income (loss)	$(11,753)	$(16,198)	$1,219
Less: Income (loss) from discontinued operations	73	(3,172)	(214)
Extraordinary gain	–	1,182	–
Cumulative effect of accounting changes	–	(38)	–
Income (loss) from continuing operations	(11,826)	(14,170)	1,433
Adjustments to reconcile income (loss) from continuing operations to net cash used in operating activities, net of effects of acquisitions and dispositions of businesses and manufacturing operations:			
Non-cash portion of business restructuring charges, net	827	9,322	–
Asset impairment charges	975	–	–
Depreciation and amortization	1,470	2,536	1,667
Provision for bad debts and customer financings	1,253	2,249	505
Tax benefit from employee stock options	–	18	1,064
Deferred income taxes	5,268	(5,935)	491
Purchased in-process research and development	–	–	559
Net pension and postretirement benefit credit	(972)	(1,083)	(802)
Gains on sales of businesses	(725)	(56)	(30)
Other adjustments for non-cash items	843	551	(222)
Changes in operating assets and liabilities:			
Decrease (increase) in receivables	2,493	3,627	(1,626)
Decrease (increase) in inventories and contracts in process	2,552	881	(2,242)
(Decrease) increase in accounts payable	(539)	(759)	263
Changes in other operating assets and liabilities	(2,375)	(602)	(1,763)
Net cash used in operating activities from continuing operations	**(756)**	**(3,421)**	**(703)**
INVESTING ACTIVITIES			
Capital expenditures	(449)	(1,390)	(1,915)
Dispositions of businesses and manufacturing operations, net of cash disposed	2,576	3,187	250
Sales or maturity of investments	31	57	820
Purchases of non-consolidated investments	(30)	(101)	(680)
Purchases of short-term investments	(1,518)	–	–
Proceeds from the sale or disposal of property, plant and equipment	194	177	26
Other investing activities	(47)	21	(60)
Net cash provided by (used in) investing activities from continuing operations	**757**	**1,951**	**(1,559)**
FINANCING ACTIVITIES			
Issuance of company-obligated 7.75% mandatorily redeemable convertible preferred securities of subsidiary trust	1,750	–	–
(Repayments of)proceeds from credit facilities	(1,000)	3,500	–
Net (repayments of) proceeds from other short-term borrowings	(104)	(2,147)	1,355
Issuance of long-term debt	–	302	72
Repayments of long-term debt	(47)	(754)	(387)
Issuance of 8% redeemable convertible preferred stock	–	1,831	–
Issuance of common stock	64	222	1,444
Dividends paid on preferred and common stock	(149)	(204)	(255)
Other financing activities	(46)	(125)	–
Net cash provided by financing activities from continuing operations	**468**	**2,625**	**2,229**
Effect of exchange rate changes on cash and cash equivalents	35	4	10
Net cash provided by (used in) continuing operations	504	1,159	(23)
Net cash used in discontinued operations	–	(236)	(196)
Net increase (decrease) in cash and cash equivalents	504	923	(219)
Cash and cash equivalents at beginning of year	2,390	1,467	1,686
Cash and cash equivalents at end of year	**$ 2,894**	**$ 2,390**	**$1,467**

See Notes to Consolidated Financial Statements.

1. SUMMARY OF SIGNIFICANT ACCOUNTING POLICIES

Basis of Consolidation

The consolidated financial statements include all majority-owned subsidiaries in which Lucent Technologies Inc. ("Lucent" or "the Company") exercises control. Investments in which Lucent exercises significant influence, but which it does not control (generally a 20% to 50% ownership interest), are accounted for under the equity method of accounting. All material intercompany transactions and balances have been eliminated. Except as otherwise noted, all amounts and disclosures reflect only Lucent's continuing operations.

Use of Estimates

The consolidated financial statements are prepared in conformity with generally accepted accounting principles. Management is required to make estimates and assumptions that affect the amounts reported in the consolidated financial statements and accompanying disclosures. Actual results could differ from those estimates. Among other things, estimates are used in accounting for long-term contracts, allowances for bad debts and customer financings, inventory obsolescence, restructuring reserves, product warranty, amortization and impairment of intangibles, goodwill, and capitalized software, depreciation and impairment of property, plant and equipment, employee benefits, income taxes, contingencies, and loss reserves for discontinued operations. Estimates and assumptions are periodically reviewed and the effects of any material revisions are reflected in the consolidated financial statements in the period that they are determined to be necessary.

Foreign Currency Translation

For operations outside the U.S. that prepare financial statements in currencies other than the U.S. dollar, results of operations and cash flows are translated at average exchange rates during the period, and assets and liabilities are translated at end-of-period exchange rates. Translation adjustments are included as a separate component of accumulated other comprehensive loss in shareowners' (deficit) equity.

Revenue Recognition

Revenue is recognized when persuasive evidence of an agreement exists, delivery has occurred, the fee is fixed and determinable, and collection of the resulting receivable, including receivables of customers to which Lucent has provided customer financing, is probable. For sales generated from long-term contracts, primarily those related to customized network solutions and network build-outs, Lucent generally uses the percentage of completion method of accounting. In doing so, Lucent makes important judgments in estimating revenue and costs and in measuring progress toward completion. These judgments underlie the determinations regarding overall contract value, contract profitability and timing of revenue recognition. Revenue and cost estimates are revised periodically based on changes in circumstances; any losses on contracts are recognized immediately. Lucent also sells products through multiple distribution channels, including resellers and distributors. For products sold through these channels, revenue is generally recognized when the reseller or distributor sells the product to the end user.

Most sales are generated from complex contractual arrangements that require significant revenue recognition judgments, particularly in the areas of multiple element arrangements and collectibility. Revenues from contracts with multiple element arrangements, such as those including installation and integration services, are recognized as each element is earned based on the relative fair value of each element and when there are no undelivered elements that are essential to the functionality of the delivered elements. Lucent has determined that most equipment is generally installed by Lucent within 90 days, but can be installed by the customer or a third party, and as a result, revenue is recognized when title passes to the customer, which usually is upon delivery of the equipment, provided all other revenue recognition criteria are met. Services revenues are generally recognized at time of performance. The assessment of collectibility is particularly critical in determining whether revenue should be recognized in the current market environment. As part of the revenue recognition process, Lucent determines whether trade and notes receivables are reasonably assured of collection based on various factors, including the ability to sell those receivables and whether there has been deterioration in the credit quality of customers that could result in the inability to collect or sell the receivables. In situations where Lucent has the ability to sell the receivables, revenue is recognized to the extent of the value Lucent could reasonably expect to realize from the sale. Lucent defers revenue and related costs when it is uncertain as to whether it will be able to collect or sell the receivable. Lucent defers revenue but recognizes costs when it determines that the collection or sale of the receivables is unlikely.

Research and Development and Software Development Costs

Research and development costs are charged to expense as incurred. However, the costs incurred for the development of computer software that will be sold, leased or otherwise marketed are capitalized when technological feasibility has been established, generally when all of the planning, designing, coding and testing activities that are necessary in order to establish that the product can be produced to meet its design specifications including functions, features and technical performance requirements are completed. These capitalized costs are subject to an ongoing assessment of recoverability based on anticipated future revenues and changes in hardware and software technologies. Costs that are capitalized include direct labor and related overhead.

Amortization of capitalized software development costs begins when the product is available for general release. Amortization is provided on a product-by-product basis on the straight-line method over periods not exceeding 18 months. Unamortized capitalized software development costs determined to be in excess of the net realizable value of the product are expensed immediately.

Alcatel—Accounts Receivable

Headquartered in Paris, France, Alcatel provides end-to-end communications solutions, enabling carriers, service providers and enterprises to deliver contents to any type of user, anywhere in the world. Leveraging its long-term leadership in telecommunications networks equipment as well as its expertise in innovative applications and network services, Alcatel enables its customers to focus on optimizing their service offerings and revenue streams. With sales of € 16.5 billion in 2002, Alcatel operates in more than 130 countries. Its shares trade in Paris and New York.

Learning Objectives

- Understand accounts receivable terminology.
- Calculate annual and quarterly ratios for accounts receivable.
- Compare calculated ratios to those included in a press article and explore the differences.
- Learn about factoring and securitization of receivables.

Refer to the Alcatel financial statements released as part of a press release reporting fourth quarter and full year 2002 results. All figures are in millions of euros (€).

✧ Concepts ✧

a. What is an account receivable? What other names does this asset go by?

b. How do accounts receivable differ from notes receivable?

c. Alcatel's balance sheet reports a balance for trade receivables and related accounts, net. What are the trade receivables net of?

d. If Alcatel anticipates that some accounts are uncollectible, why did the company extend credit to those customers in the first place? Discuss the risks that must be managed with respect to accounts receivable and vendor financing.

✧ Process ✧

e. The balance in Alcatel's allowance for doubtful accounts (for trade receivables) was €1,092 at December 31, 2002 and €928 at December 31, 2001. Assume that Alcatel wrote off €115 of trade receivables as uncollectible during 2002. Create two T-accounts, one for gross trade receivables (that is, trade receivables before deducting the allowance) and another for the allowance for doubtful accounts. Analyze the change in both T-accounts between December 31, 2001 and 2002. Four journal entries are required to reconcile the two T-accounts: one to record sales, one to record the collection of trade receivables, one to record the write-off of trade receivables, and one to record bad debt expense.

✧ Analysis ✧

f. Refer to the accompanying *Wall Street Journal* article (Alcatel Allays Some Anxiety, Though Perils for Firm Persist). Chief Financial Officer Jean-Pascal Beaufret indicated that Alcatel collected its trade receivables in 104 days in 2002 (117 in 2001). The average collection period for accounts receivable (called trade receivables at Alcatel) can be estimated using the following formula (the denominator is referred to as the accounts receivable turnover ratio):

$$\text{Average Collection Period} = \frac{365 \text{ days}}{\left[\dfrac{\text{Credit Sales (annual)}}{\text{Accounts Receivable}}\right]}$$

Confirm the figures reported by Alcatel's CFO using data for trade receivables from the accompanying financial statements. Assume that all sales are on account. That is, they are all 'credit sales.' Comment on the trend. Provide possible reasons for the change.

g. What was the average collection period for the fourth quarter of 2002? For the same period in 2001? You will have to adjust the average collection period formula so that it appropriately considers quarterly data. Comment on the trend and the relation to the annual data.

h. In the *Wall Street Journal* article, the reporter refers to the practice of 'factoring' receivables. Explain what factoring is and why some companies do it.

i. Data reported in Alcatel's 2002 financial statements (but not in the press release) indicate that the company effectively factored a portion of its trade receivables through a secured vendor financing agreement. In essence, under this agreement, Alcatel 'sells' receivables to a trust that 'buys' them by issuing bonds or other securities to investors. The trust's bonds are repaid using the cash flows from the receivables. According to note 29 of Alcatel's 2002 financial statements, \$428 million and \$700 million were outstanding under the securitization program at the end of 2002 and 2001, respectively (at December 31, 2002, \$1 = €0.954, at December 31, 2001, \$1 = €1.123).

   i. Explain in general terms how securitization of receivables affects the average collection period.

   ii. Assume that Alcatel had not securitized its receivables. Estimate the average collection period for 2002 and 2001 and compare it to the results you obtained in part *f.*

j. Under French GAAP, Alcatel treated the securitization of its receivables as a sale of receivables. Under U.S. GAAP, Alcatel's securitization would be considered secured borrowing (i.e. a loan secured by the receivables). How would Alcatel's balance sheet differ if the company had followed U.S. GAAP for its receivables securitization?

Consolidated income statements

in millions of euros except per share information

	Q4 2002 (unaudited)	Q4 2001* (unaudited)	2002	2001*	2000
Net sales	4,508	6,766	16,547	25,353	31,408
Cost of sales	(3,279)	(5,528)	(12,186)	(19,074)	(22,193)
Gross profit	**1,229**	**1,238**	**4,361**	**6,279**	**9,215**
Admini strative and selling expenses	(647)	(893)	(2,862)	(3,773)	(4,136)
R&D costs	(562)	(713)	(2,226)	(2,867)	(2,828)
Income (loss) from operations	**20**	**(368)**	**(727)**	**(361)**	**2,251**
Interest expense on notes mandatorily redeemable for shares	(1)	-	(1)	-	-
Financial loss	(136)	(248)	(1,018)	(1,568)	(435)
Restructuring costs	(500)	(598)	(1,474)	(2,124)	(143)
Other revenue (expense)	(292)	(456)	(830)	(213)	623
Income (loss) before amortization of goodwill and taxes	**(909)**	**(1,670)**	**(4,050)**	**(4,266)**	**2,296**
Income tax	(62)	396	19	1,261	(497)
Share in net income of equity affiliates and discontinued operations	24	(16)	(107)	(16)	125
Consolidated net income (loss) before amortization of goodwill and purchased R&D	**(947)**	**(1,290)**	**(4,138)**	**(3,021)**	**1,924**
Amortization of goodwill	(147)	(185)	(589)	(1,933)	(576)
Purchased R&D	-	-	-	(4)	(21)
Minority interests	(25)	(23)	(18)	(5)	(3)
Net income (loss)	**(1,119)**	**(1,498)**	**(4,745)**	**(4,963)**	**1,324**
Ordinary Shares (A)**					
Basic earnings per share	*(0.93,*	*(1.28,*	*(3.99)*	*(4.33)*	*1.25*
Diluted earnings per share	*(0.93,*	*(1.28,*	*(3.99)*	*(4.33)*	*1.20*
*Alcatel tracking stock (O) (Optronics division)****					
Basic earnings per share	*(1.06,*	*(1.52,*	*(3.86)*	*(1.47)*	*0.14*
Diluted earnings per share	*(1.06,*	*(1.52,*	*(3.86)*	*(1.47)*	*0.14*

* In order to make comparisons easier, restated income statements are presented to take into account significant changes in consolidated companies during the second half of 2001 and the first half 2002.

** Net income per class A share for 2000 was restated to take into account the split by 5 of the nominal value of the class A shares approved by the shareholders' meeting of May 16, 2000.

*** For 2000net income has been taken into account from October 20, 2000, issuance date of the class O shares.

Consolidated balance sheets at December 31

in millions of euros

ASSETS	2002	2001	2000
Goodwill, net	4,597	5,257	7,043
Other intangible assets, net	312	472	504
Intangible assets, net	**4,909**	**5,729**	**7,547**
Property, plant and equipment	8,236	9,698	11,941
Depreciation	(5,737)	(5,496)	(7,283)
Property, plant and equipment, net	**2,499**	**4,202**	**4,658**
Share in net assets of equity affiliates and net assets and liabilities of discontinued operations	306	799	1,152
Other investments and miscellaneous, net	975	1,169	3,327
Investments and other financial assets	**1,281**	**1,968**	**4,479**
TOTAL FIXED ASSETS	**8,689**	**11,899**	**16,684**
Inventories and work in progress	**2,329**	**4,681**	**7,415**
Trade receivables and related accounts net	4,716	8,105	10,659
Other accounts receivable net	4,037	6,851	5,160
Accounts receivable	**8,753**	**14,956**	**15,819**
Marketable securities, net*	716	490	443
Cash (net)	5,393	4,523	2,617
Cash and cash equivalents*	**6,109**	**5,013**	**3,060**
TOTAL CURRENT ASSETS	**17,191**	**24,650**	**26,294**
TOTAL ASSETS	**25,880**	**36,549**	**42,978**

* Cash and cash equivalent as of December 31, 2002 includes in the marketable securities net line item, listed securities amounting to €44 million. Without listed securities, cash and cash equivalent amounts to €6,065 million as indicated in the consolidated statements of cash flows.

in millions of euros

LIABILITIES AND SHAREHOLDERS' EQUITY	2002		2001	2000*
	Before	After	After	After
	Appropriation		Appropriation	Appropriation
Capital stock (Euro 2 nominal value : 1,239,193,498 class A shares and 25,515,000 class O shares issued at December 31, 2002 ; 1,215,254,797 class A shares and 25,515,000 class O shares issued at December 31, 2001 and 1,212,210,685 class A shares and 16,500,000 class O shares at December 31, 2000)	2,529	2,529	2,481	2,457
Additional paid-in capital	9,573	9,573	9,565	9,558
Retained earnings	(333)	(5,078)	(389)	4,719
Cumulative translation adjustments	(283)	(283)	(185)	(350)
Net income	(4,745)	-	-	-
Less treasury stock at cost	(1,734)	(1,734)	(1,842)	(2,023)
SHAREHOLDERS' EQUITY	**5,007**	**5,007**	**9,630**	**14,361**
MINORITY INTERESTS	**343**	**343**	**219**	**435**
OTHER EQUITY				
Notes mandatorily redeemable for shares	**645**	**645**	**-**	**-**
Accrued pension and retirement obligations	1,016	1,016	1,120	1,292
Other reserves (a)	3,301	3,301	4,154	3,005
TOTAL RESERVES FOR LIABILITIES AND CHARGES	**4,317**	**4,317**	**5,274**	**4,297**
Bonds and notes issued	5,325	5,325	5,969	4,972
Other borrowings	458	458	1,706	2,418
TOTAL FINANCIAL DEBT	**5,783**	**5,783**	**7,675**	**7,390**
(of which medium and long-term portion)	*4,687*	*4,687*	*5,879*	*5,577*
Customers' deposits and advances	1,482	1,482	1,693	1,560
Trade payables and related accounts (a)	4,162	4,162	5,080	6,393
Debts linked to bank activity	246	246	660	932
Other payables	3,895	3,895	6,318	7,610
TOTAL OTHER LIABILITIES	**9,785**	**9,785**	**13,751**	**16,495**
TOTAL LIABILITIES AND SHAREHOLDERS' EQUITY	**25,880**	**25,880**	**36,549**	**42,978**

(a) Accrued contract costs previously under the line "accrued contracts costs and other reserves" have been reclassified under the line "trade payables"(€650 million at December 31, 2000).

Consolidated statements of cash flows

in millions of euros

	Nine months 2002 (unaudited)	Q4 2002 (unaudited)	2002	2001	2000
Cash flows from operating activities					
Net income (loss)	(3,626)	(1,119)	(4,745)	(4,963)	1,324
Minority interests	(7)	25	18	5	3
Adjustments to reconcile income before minority interests to net cash provided by operating activities:					
- Depreciation and amortization, net	739	271	1,010	1,279	1,189
- Amortization and depreciation of goodwill and purchased R&D	442	147	589	1,937	597
- Net allowances in reserves for pension obligations	8	(11)	(3)	41	24
- Changes in valuation allowances and other reserves, net	1,374	(16)	1,358	2,001	(32)
- Net (gain) loss on disposal of non-current assets	(413)	126	(287)	(943)	(915)
- Share in net income of equity affiliates (net of dividends received)	214	(26)	188	88	(47)
Working capital provided (used) by operations	**(1,269)**	**(603)**	**(1,872)**	**(555)**	**2,143**
Net change in current assets and liabilities:					
- Decrease (increase) in inventories	1,244	756	2,000	1,186	(3,330)
- Decrease (increase) in accounts receivable	3,103	333	3,436	1,407	(1,192)
- Decrease (increase) in advances and progress payments	3	107	110	(99)	74
- Increase (decrease) in accounts payable and accrued expenses	(1,038)	(46)	(1,084)	(925)	898
- Increase (decrease) in customers deposits and advances	(279)	106	(173)	153	424
- Increase (decrease) in other receivables and debts	136	170	306	(622)	(262)
Net cash provided (used) by operating activities (a)	**1,900**	**823**	**2,723**	**545**	**(1,245)**
Cash flows from investing activities					
Proceeds from disposal of fixed assets	236	44	280	182	107
Capital expenditures	(399)	(91)	(490)	(1,748)	(1,834)
Decrease (increase) in loans (b)	(720)	(119)	(839)	299	(962)
Cash expenditures for acquisition of consolidated companies, net of cash acquired, and for acquisition of unconsolidated companies	(206)	13	(193)	(743)	(834)
Cash proceeds from sale of previously consolidated companies, net of cash sold, and from sale of unconsolidated companies	797	16	813	3,627	1,579
Net cash provided (used) by investing activities	**(292)**	**(137)**	**(429)**	**1,617**	**(1,944)**
Net cash flows after investment	**1,608**	**686**	**2,294**	**2,162**	**(3,189)**
Cash flows from financing activities					
Increase (decrease) in short-term debt	(1,192)	(277)	(1,469)	(1,401)	(889)
Proceeds from issuance of long-term debt	-	645	645	1,744	2,565
Proceeds from issuance of shares	8	-	8	8	1,490
Dividends paid	(269)	(7)	(276)	(567)	(508)
Net cash provided (used) by financing activities	**(1,453)**	**361**	**(1,092)**	**(216)**	**2,658**
Net effect of exchange rate changes	(67)	(83)	(150)	7	(4)
Net increase (decrease) in cash and cash equivalents	**88**	**964**	**1,052**	**1,953**	**(535)**
Cash and cash equivalents at beginning of year	**5,013**	**5,101**	**5,013**	**3,060**	**3,595**
Cash and cash equivalents at end of year without listed securities	**5,101**	**6,065**	**6,065**	**5,013**	**3,060**

Operational cash flows (a) + (b) = Net cash provided (used) by operating activities + Decrease (increase) in loans (b)	**1,180**	**704**	**1,884**	**844**	**(2,207)**

February 5, 2003

HEARD IN EUROPE

Alcatel Allays Some Anxiety, Though Perils for Firm Persist

By DAVID REILLY
Staff Reporter of THE WALL STREET JOURNAL

Alcatel SA is finally managing to squeeze some lemonade from this lemon of a market. Whether it's a beverage that's ready to be drunk, though, is an open question.

Europe's largest telecom-equipment maker did a surprisingly good job of reducing inventories and getting customers to pay their bills faster in the fourth quarter. As a result, Paris-based Alcatel said it generated €704 million ($759 million) in operating cash flow during the fourth quarter and moved to a small net cash position on its balance sheet by the end of 2002, although this was helped in part by a convertible-bond issue in December. The company also managed to eke out €20 million in operating profit in the fourth quarter even though sales were down 33% from a year earlier.

The good news didn't stop there. Alcatel reiterated its expectation of being able to break even on costs of €3 billion a quarter by the end of 2003, while Chairman and Chief Executive Serge Tchuruk said Alcatel expects to show a net profit by year-end.

Taken together, this is proof to some investors that the company is now turning the corner in its restructuring program. It should also finally put an end to worries the company could go belly up because it wouldn't be able to cut costs as quickly as sales are falling.

"Is this company going bankrupt? No," says Richard Windsor, an analyst at Nomura. He adds that Alcatel appears to be in a better position than rivals such as **Lucent Technologies** Inc., **Nortel Networks** Ltd. and **Telefon AB L.M. Ericsson**. "It's got more revenues, is much stronger financially, its sales are more geographically split, it has a more diverse product portfolio and its revenue stream should be stronger in the future."

That's not to say that the results were all sweetness and light. Mr. Tchuruk said sales could drop 25% to 30% in the first quarter compared with the same period of 2002, while the global market for telecommunications equipment could drop 15% in 2003.

So until there are signs that revenue can stabilize, the stock will remain volatile and is best avoided, Mustapha Omar, head of research at U.K. broker Collins Stewart, said in a note to clients.

Investors focused on this danger and shaved 7.7% off Alcatel's stock, which closed at €6.20 in Paris Tuesday.

RECENT HEARDS

- Sogecable Deal May Surprise 1/29
- Hurry Up and Wait 1/27
- Deutsche Boerse Again Courts LSE 1/24

COMPANIES

Dow Jones, Reuters

Alcatel S.A. ADS (ALA)	
PRICE	6.94
CHANGE	0.16
U.S. dollars	2/5
Lucent Technologies Inc. (LU)	
PRICE	1.59
CHANGE	-0.06
U.S. dollars	2/5
Nortel Networks Corp. (NT)	
PRICE	2.29
CHANGE	0.00
U.S. dollars	2/5
L.M. Ericsson Telephone Co. ADS (ERICY)	
PRICE	6.72
CHANGE	0.07
U.S. dollars	2/5

* At Market Close

Adding to the gloom, some analysts fretted about Alcatel's improvement in working capital, the money it needs to finance sales through inventory, outstanding customer bills and amounts due to suppliers. Alcatel said working capital as a portion of sales had fallen to just 9.4% of revenue at the end of the year, compared with 14.4% at the end of September and 24.6% at the end of 2001.

First, there were concerns about the contribution to cash flow from the sale of outstanding customer bills, a practice known as factoring receivables. Alcatel doesn't disclose how much money it raises through such sales. During a conference call with analysts, Mr. Tchuruk said there was "nothing new" on this front and that there was no change in the level of factoring from the third quarter. An Alcatel spokeswoman later said this meant that the level of factoring hadn't changed in absolute euro terms, although it would have increased as a percentage of the amount of overall receivables.

Second, it wasn't clear how much the reduction of inventory to €2.3 billion at the end of the year, compared with €3.2 billion at the end of September or €4.6 billion at the end of 2001, was helped by write-downs. The company said it wrote off €873 million in assets during 2002. While Chief Financial Officer Jean-Pascal Beaufret said the lion's share of this amount related to asset write-offs at the company's optronics division, he didn't give an exact figure. That led some analysts to worry that the write-downs could have flattered the figures that show how many times Alcatel turned over its inventory during the year, an efficiency measure.

The spokeswoman said the company didn't provide details about how much of the drop in inventories resulted from write-downs.

Finally, analysts questioned whether Alcatel could keep releasing cash by squeezing working capital, especially if sales start to rise. (A company generally needs more working capital to finance growth.)

Messrs. Tchuruk and Beaufret tried to allay these fears by saying the company still wasn't being run as efficiently as they would like or as well as some of its North American peers. Mr. Beaufret said during the conference call that at the end of 2002 the company was collecting on bills within 104 days. This was an improvement from 117 days at the end of 2001, but he said the company could still improve greatly on this level.

As for inventory turns, the spokeswoman said Alcatel has room to improve there: It had an inventory turn ratio of 5.2 times in 2002, compared with about 7.9 times for Nortel and about 8.2 times for Lucent.

Finally, the company has about €8 billion in liquid resources to draw on if it needs to finance a rise in sales.

All that is reassuring. But until sales stop falling, investors are to be forgiven for finding Alcatel's shares a bit too tart at this point.

Write to David Reilly at david.reilly@wsj.com;

Caterpillar, Inc., Deere & Company, and CNH Global N.V.—Inventory

Caterpillar operates in three principal lines of business: machinery (design, manufacture and marketing of construction, mining, agricultural and forestry machinery), engines (for Caterpillar machinery as well as free-standing electric power generation systems and on and off-highway vehicles and locomotives), and financial products (providing loans and insurance products to customers and dealers). Caterpillar's products and support services are sold worldwide in a variety of highly competitive markets.

Deere & Company, founded in 1837, is a worldwide corporation doing business in more than 160 countries and employing over 40,000 people. Deere & Company consists of three equipment operations (agriculture, construction & forestry, and commercial & consumer), credit operations (with over 1.8 million accounts), and four support operations (parts, power systems, technology services, and health care).

CNH is the power behind leading agricultural and construction equipment brands of the Case and New Holland brand families. Supported by more than 12,000 dealers in approximately 160 countries, CNH brings together the knowledge and heritage of its brands with the strength and resources of its worldwide commercial, industrial, product support and finance organizations.

Learning Objectives

- Explain how cost flow assumptions affect inventory balances and cost of goods sold.
- Explain the financial statement effects of using different cost flow assumptions.
- Analyze the activity in inventory and related accounts.
- Restate a company's inventory balances and cost of sales to reflect alternative cost flow assumptions.
- Calculate inventory turnover and holding period under different cost flow assumptions.
- Understand the risks and benefits of holding inventory.

Refer to the fiscal 2003 financial statements of Caterpillar, Inc.

✧ Concepts ✧

a. Explain the risks and benefits associated with holding inventory.

b. Note 3 reveals that the balance sheet inventory amount consists of four types of inventory. What types of costs do you expect to be in the raw materials inventory? In the work-in-process inventory? In the finished goods inventory? In the supplies inventory?

c. In general, why must companies use cost-flow assumptions to cost their inventories? What cost flow assumption does Caterpillar use to cost its inventories?

d. Assume that the prices Caterpillar pays for inventory typically increase over time. Explain in general terms, how the Caterpillar balance sheet would have been different had the company used the first-in, first-out (FIFO) method of inventory costing instead of the last-in, first-out (LIFO) method. How would the income statement have differed? The statement of cash flows? What if prices typically *de*crease over time?

✧ Process ✧

e. Set up *one* T-account for Caterpillar's total Inventories (that is, combine the four inventory accounts for this analysis). Enter the 2002 and 2003 ending balances in the T-account. Use information from the financial statements to recreate the activity that took place in the account during fiscal 2003 and answer the following questions. Caterpillar credits the total inventory account for the entire cost of goods sold. Note that the income statement line item Cost of goods sold includes the labor and overhead needed to manufacture the equipment. Assume that the raw material costs represent half of the total cost of manufacturing the inventory.

i. How much raw material inventory did Caterpillar purchase in fiscal 2003? Assume that raw material inventory was acquired in a single purchase. Provide the journal entry Caterpillar made to record that purchase.

ii. Now set up a T-account for Accounts payable. Enter the 2002 and 2003 ending balances in the T-account. Assume that Accounts payable includes only inventory-related transactions and that all raw material is purchased on account. How much did Caterpillar pay its suppliers for inventory in fiscal 2003? Assume that Caterpillar made a single payment to all its suppliers in fiscal 2003. Provide the journal entry Caterpillar made to record that payment.

Analysis

f. You want to compare Caterpillar's operations for fiscal 2003 to those of two of its close competitors, Deere & Co. and CNH Global. In particular you want to compare five inventory-related metrics: net income, growth in net income, and common-sized cost of sales, net income, and inventory.

However, the three companies do not use the same inventory costing methods: Caterpillar and Deere use LIFO whereas CNH Global uses FIFO. To compare the three companies, you first must restate Caterpillar's and Deere's relevant balance sheet and income statement numbers assuming that the companies had always used the FIFO method of inventory costing. To assist you, part of the analysis for Deere & Co. is completed in the table below.

Calculate the five inventory-related metrics for all three companies first using their reported numbers and then assuming they use FIFO to cost their inventories. Then, complete the table on the following page and comment on the results.

From Deere & Co. Financial Statements:	2003	2002	2001
Sales	13,349.1	11,702.8	
LIFO Cost of goods sold (COGS)	10,752.7	9,593.4	
LIFO net income	643.1	319.2	
LIFO Inventory from the balance sheet	1,366.1	1,371.8	1,505.7
LIFO reserve from financial statement notes	950.0	948.0	1,004.0
Total assets from the balance sheet	26,258.0	23,768.0	
Calculations to convert LIFO to FIFO:			
FIFO Inventory = LIFO inventory + LIFO reserve	2,316.1	2,319.8	2,509.7
FIFO Assets = LIFO Assets + LIFO reserve	27,208.0	24,716.0	
Increase in LIFO reserve during the year	2.0	(56.0)	
FIFO COGS = LIFO COGS - increase in LIFO reserve	10,750.7	9,649.4	
Average tax rate = Tax expense / Pretax income	34.7%	42.9%	
After tax effect of LIFO assumption = (1-average tax rate) × increase in LIFO reserve	1.3	(32.0)	
FIFO Net income = LIFO net income – after tax effect of LIFO assumption	641.8	351.2	

Fiscal 2003	*Caterpillar*	*Deere*	*CNH*
Sales		13,349	
COGS as reported		10,753	
COGS FIFO		10,751	
Common-size COGS as reported[1]		80.6%	
Common-size COGS FIFO		80.5%	
Net income (loss) as reported		643	
Net income (loss) FIFO		642	
Growth in net income (loss) as reported		101.5%	
Growth in net income (loss) FIFO		82.7%	
Common-size Net income as reported		4.8%	
Common-size Net income FIFO		4.8%	
Total assets as reported		26,258	
Total assets FIFO		27,208	
Inventory as reported		1,366	
Inventory FIFO		2,316	
Common-size inventory as reported[2]		5.2%	
Common-size inventory FIFO		8.5%	

Notes:
[1] To common size items from the income statement, divide by Net sales.
[2] To common size items from the balance sheet, divide by Total assets.

g. The average inventory holding period is estimated using the following formula (the denominator is referred to as the inventory turnover ratio):

$$\text{Average Inventory Holding Period} = \frac{365 \text{ days}}{\left[\dfrac{\text{Cost of Sales}}{\text{Average Inventory}}\right]}$$

Use data in the financial statements to estimate the average inventory holding period for Caterpillar, Deere and CNH Global for fiscal 2002 and 2003. Calculate the ratios with FIFO based numbers. Evaluate how well Caterpillar manages its inventory relative to its competitors. Additional information: CNH's inventory balance for fiscal 2001 was $2,204. Now recalculate the numbers for Deere and Caterpillar using their as-reported (LIFO) numbers. Do you come to a different conclusion about their inventory turnover?

h. Assume that Caterpillar's inventory balances for accounting and for tax purposes are the same. Estimate the cumulative tax savings through September 30, 2003 that Caterpillar has realized by choosing the LIFO method of inventory costing instead of the FIFO method.

i. Explain what is meant by the term "channel stuffing." Is channel stuffing likely to be a concern at a company like Caterpillar? Explain.

CATERPILLAR

Consolidated Results of Operations for the Years Ended December 31
Dollars in millions except per share data

	2003	2002	2001
Sales and revenues:			
Sales of Machinery and Engines	$ 21,048	$ 18,648	$ 19,027
Revenues of Financial Products	1,715	1,504	1,423
Total sales and revenues	22,763	20,152	20,450
Operating costs:			
Cost of goods sold	16,945	15,146	15,179
Selling general and admin expenses	2,470	2,094	2,140
Research and development expenses	669	656	696
Interest expense of Financial Products	470	521	657
Other operating expenses	521	411	467
Total operating costs	21,075	18,828	19,139
Operating profit	1,688	1,324	1,311
Interest expense excluding Financial Products	246	279	285
Other income (expense)	35	69	143
Consolidated profit before taxes	1,477	1,114	1,169
Provision for income taxes	398	312	367
Profit of consolidated companies	1,079	802	802
Equity in profit (loss) of unconsolidated affiliates	20	(4)	3
Profit	$ 1,099	$ 798	$ 805

CATERPILLAR
Consolidated Financial Position at December 31
Dollars in millions

	2003	2002	2001
Assets			
Current assets:			
Cash and short-term investments	$ 342	$ 309	$ 400
Receivables-trade and other	3,666	2,838	2,592
Receivables-finance	7,605	6,748	5,849
Deferred and refundable income taxes	707	781	434
Prepaid expenses	1,424	1,224	1,139
Inventories	3,047	2,763	2,925
Total current assets	16,791	14,663	13,339
Property, plant and equipment-net	7,290	7,046	6,603
Long-term receivables-trade and other	82	66	55
Long-term receivables-finance	7,822	6,714	6,267
Investments in unconsolidated affiliates	800	747	787
Deferred income taxes	616	711	927
Intangible assets	239	281	274
Goodwill	1,398	1,402	1,397
Other assets	1,427	1,117	936
Total assets	$ 36,465	$ 32,747	$ 30,585
Liabilities			
Current liabilities:			
Short-term borrowings:			
-Machinery and Engines	$ 72	$ 64	$ 219
-Financial Products	2,685	2,111	1,961
Accounts payable	3,100	2,269	2,123
Accrued expenses	1,638	1,620	1,419
Accrued wages, salaries and benefits	1,802	1,779	1,403
Dividends payable	127	120	120
Deferred and current taxes payable	216	70	11
Long-term debt due within one year:			
-Machinery and Engines	32	258	73
-Financial Products	2,949	3,654	3,058
Total current liabilities	12,621	11,945	10,387
Long-term debt due after one year:			
-Machinery and Engines	3,367	3,403	3,492
-Financial Products	10,711	8,193	7,799
Liability for postemployment benefits	3,172	3,333	2,920
Deferred taxes and other liabilities	516	401	376
Total liabilities	30,387	27,275	24,974
Contingencies (Note 21)			
Stockholders' equity			
Common stock, $1.00 par, Authorized 900,000,000, Issued 407,447,312	1,059	1,034	1,043
Treasury stock (63,685,272; 63,192,245; and 64,070,868 shares)	(2,914)	(2,669)	(2,696)
Profit employed in the business	8,450	7,849	7,533
Accumulated other comprehensive income	(517)	(742)	(269)
Total stockholders' equity	6,078	5,472	5,611
Total liabilities and equity	$ 36,465	$ 32,747	$ 30,585

CATERPILLAR

Notes to Consolidated Financial Statements (excerpts only)
Dollars in millions except per share data

1. Operations and summary of significant accounting policies

D. Inventories

Inventories are stated at the lower of cost or market. Cost is principally determined using the last-in, first-out (LIFO) method. The value of inventories on the LIFO basis represented about 80% of total inventories at December 31, 2003, 2002 and 2001.

If the FIFO (first-in, first-out) method had been in use, inventories would have been $1,863 million, $1,977 million and $1,923 million higher than reported at December 31, 2003, 2002 and 2001, respectively.

6. Inventories

	December 31,		
	2003	2002	2001
	(Millions of dollars)		
Raw materials	$ 1,105	$ 900	$ 954
Work-in-process	377	311	214
Finished goods	1,381	1,365	1,575
Supplies	184	187	182
	$ 3,047	$ 2,763	$ 2,925

We had long-term material purchase obligations of approximately $857 million at December 31, 2003.

Consolidated Statements of Operations

FOR THE YEARS ENDED DECEMBER 31, 2003, 2002 AND 2001 (AND SUPPLEMENTAL INFORMATION)
(IN MILLIONS, EXCEPT PER SHARE DATA)

	CONSOLIDATED			SUPPLEMENTAL INFORMATION: EQUIPMENT OPERATIONS			SUPPLEMENTAL INFORMATION: FINANCIAL SERVICES		
	2003	2002	2001	**2003**	2002	2001	**2003**	2002	2001
Revenues:									
Net sales	**$ 10,069**	$ 9,331	$ 9,030	**$ 10,069**	$ 9,331	$ 9,030	**$ —**	$ —	$ —
Finance and interest income	**597**	609	685	**83**	100	149	**621**	641	739
	10,666	9,940	9,715	**10,152**	9,431	9,179	**621**	641	739
Costs and Expenses:									
Cost of goods sold	**8,590**	7,902	7,586	**8,590**	7,902	7,586	**—**	—	—
Selling, general and administrative	**1,042**	1,094	1,224	**839**	884	915	**203**	210	314
Research, development and engineering	**259**	283	306	**259**	283	306	**—**	—	—
Restructuring and other merger-related costs	**271**	51	104	**268**	50	97	**3**	1	7
Interest expense — Fiat affiliates	**113**	236	358	**85**	198	308	**28**	38	50
Interest expense — other	**368**	318	368	**236**	192	178	**182**	204	289
Interest compensation to Financial Services	**—**	—	—	**79**	76	99	**—**	—	—
Other, net	**241**	182	193	**149**	62	112	**71**	98	81
	10,884	10,066	10,139	**10,505**	9,647	9,601	**487**	551	741
Equity in Income (Loss) of Unconsolidated Subsidiaries and Affiliates:									
Financial Services	**6**	4	6	**93**	60	4	**6**	4	6
Equipment Operations	**13**	15	(14)	**13**	15	(14)	**—**	—	—
Income (loss) before taxes, minority interest and cumulative effect of change in accounting principle	**(199)**	(107)	(432)	**(247)**	(141)	(432)	**140**	94	4
Income tax provision (benefit)	**(49)**	(14)	(105)	**(97)**	(48)	(105)	**47**	34	—
Minority interest	**7**	8	5	**7**	8	5	**—**	—	—
Net income (loss) before cumulative effect of change in accounting principle	**(157)**	(101)	(332)	**(157)**	(101)	(332)	**93**	60	4
Cumulative effect of change in accounting principle, net of tax	**—**	(325)	—	**—**	(325)	—	**—**	—	—
Net income (loss)	**$ (157)**	$ (426)	$ (332)	**$ (157)**	$ (426)	$ (332)	**$ 93**	$ 60	$ 4
Per share data:									
Basic earnings (loss) per share before cumulative effect of change in accounting principle	**$ (1.19)**	$ (1.05)	$ (6.00)						
Cumulative effect of change in accounting principle, net of tax	**—**	(3.35)	—						
Basic earnings (loss) per share	**$ (1.19)**	$ (4.40)	$ (6.00)						
Diluted earnings (loss) per share before cumulative effect of change in accounting principle	**$ (1.19)**	$ (1.05)	$ (6.00)						
Cumulative effect of change in accounting principle, net of tax	**—**	(3.35)	—						
Diluted earnings (loss) per share	**$ (1.19)**	$ (4.40)	$ (6.00)						

The "Consolidated" data in this statement include CNH Global N.V. and its consolidated subsidiaries and conform to the requirements of SFAS No. 94. The supplemental "Equipment Operations" (with "Financial Services" on the equity basis) data in this statement include primarily CNH Global N.V.'s agricultural and construction equipment operations. The supplemental "Financial Services" data in this statement include primarily CNH Global N.V.'s financial services business. Transactions between "Equipment Operations" and "Financial Services" have been eliminated to arrive at the "Consolidated" data. The accompanying notes to consolidated financial statements are an integral part of these Statements of Operations.

Consolidated Balance Sheets

AS OF DECEMBER 31, 2003 AND 2002 (AND SUPPLEMENTAL INFORMATION)
(IN MILLIONS, EXCEPT SHARE DATA)

	CONSOLIDATED		SUPPLEMENTAL INFORMATION: EQUIPMENT OPERATIONS		SUPPLEMENTAL INFORMATION: FINANCIAL SERVICES	
	2003	2002	2003	2002	2003	2002
ASSETS						
Current Assets:						
Cash and cash equivalents — Fiat	$ 1,325	$ 544	$ 1,315	$ 336	$ 10	$ 208
Cash and cash equivalents — other	619	231	486	133	133	98
Total cash and cash equivalents	1,944	775	1,801	469	143	306
Accounts and notes receivable	3,797	3,612	2,077	1,791	2,074	2,147
Intersegment notes receivable	—	—	312	1,083	—	354
Inventories	2,478	2,054	2,478	2,054	—	—
Deferred income taxes	498	505	406	393	92	112
Prepayments and other	80	108	76	102	4	6
Total current assets	8,797	7,054	7,150	5,892	2,313	2,925
Long-Term Receivables	2,199	2,099	270	230	1,929	1,869
Intersegment Long-Term Notes Receivable	—	—	700	700	—	—
Property, Plant and Equipment, net	1,528	1,449	1,518	1,437	10	12
Other Assets:						
Investments in unconsolidated subsidiaries and affiliates	429	375	364	328	65	47
Investment in Financial Services	—	—	1,241	1,019	—	—
Equipment on operating leases, net	353	544	—	—	353	544
Goodwill	2,554	2,533	2,409	2,395	145	138
Intangible assets	839	852	839	850	—	2
Other	1,962	1,854	1,659	1,516	303	338
Total other assets	6,137	6,158	6,512	6,108	866	1,069
Total	$ 18,661	$ 16,760	$ 16,150	$ 14,367	$ 5,118	$ 5,875
LIABILITIES AND SHAREHOLDERS' EQUITY						
Current Liabilities:						
Current maturities of long-term debt — Fiat affiliates	$ 62	$ 514	$ 17	$ 514	$ 45	$ —
Current maturities of long-term debt — other	781	604	71	310	710	294
Short-term debt — Fiat affiliates	698	1,086	403	817	295	269
Short-term debt — other	1,412	1,663	1,119	1,067	293	596
Intersegment short-term debt	—	—	—	354	312	1,083
Accounts payable	1,635	1,436	1,836	1,555	139	183
Restructuring liability	72	50	71	50	1	—
Other accrued liabilities	1,795	1,712	1,608	1,567	201	169
Total current liabilities	6,455	7,065	5,125	6,234	1,996	2,594
Long-Term Debt — Fiat Affiliates	1,669	2,285	1,363	1,918	306	367
Long-Term Debt — Other	2,374	1,712	1,742	796	632	916
Intersegment Long-Term Debt	—	—	—	—	700	700
Other Liabilities:						
Pension, postretirement and postemployment benefits	2,040	1,759	2,021	1,739	19	20
Other	1,174	1,105	951	847	223	258
Total other liabilities	3,214	2,864	2,972	2,586	242	278
Commitments and Contingencies (Note 16)						
Minority Interest	75	73	74	72	1	1
Shareholders' Equity:						
Preference Shares, €2.25 par value; authorized 200,000,000 shares in 2003 and 60,000,000 shares in 2002; issued 8,000,000 shares in 2003 and 0 shares in 2002	19	—	19	—	—	—
Common Shares, €2.25 par value; authorized 400,000,000 shares in 2003 and 140,000,000 shares in 2002, issued 132,913,714 shares in 2003 and 131,238,200 shares in 2002	309	305	309	305	135	118
Paid-in capital	6,310	4,327	6,310	4,327	947	910
Treasury stock, 116,706 shares in 2003 and 2002, at cost	(7)	(7)	(7)	(7)	—	—
Retained earnings (deficit)	(1,217)	(1,027)	(1,217)	(1,027)	120	49
Accumulated other comprehensive income (loss)	(539)	(835)	(539)	(835)	39	(58)
Unearned compensation on restricted shares and options	(1)	(2)	(1)	(2)	—	—
Total shareholders' equity	4,874	2,761	4,874	2,761	1,241	1,019
Total	$ 18,661	$ 16,760	$ 16,150	$ 14,367	$ 5,118	$ 5,875

The "Consolidated" data in this statement include CNH Global N.V. and its consolidated subsidiaries and conform to the requirements of SFAS No. 94. The supplemental "Equipment Operations" (with "Financial Services" on the equity basis) data in this statement include primarily CNH Global N.V.'s agricultural and construction equipment operations. The supplemental "Financial Services" data in this statement include primarily CNH Global N.V.'s financial services business. Transactions between "Equipment Operations" and "Financial Services" have been eliminated to arrive at the "Consolidated" data. The accompanying notes to consolidated financial statements are an integral part of these Balance Sheets.

Notes to Consolidated Financial Statements

Note 5: Inventories

Inventories as of December 31, 2003 and 2002 consist of the following:

(IN MILLIONS)	2003	2002
Raw materials	$ 416	$ 295
Work-in-process	243	267
Finished goods	1,819	1,492
Total inventories	$ 2,478	$ 2,054

Note 6: Property, Plant and Equipment

A summary of property, plant and equipment as of December 31, 2003 and 2002 is as follows:

(IN MILLIONS)	2003	2002
Land, buildings and improvements	$ 802	$ 606
Plant and machinery	1,977	1,875
Other equipment	458	282
Construction in progress	89	169
	3,326	2,932
Accumulated depreciation	(1,798)	(1,483)
Net property, plant and equipment	$ 1,528	$ 1,449

Depreciation expense totaled $213 million, $202 million and $207 million for the years ended December 31, 2003, 2002 and 2001, respectively.

Note 7: Investments in Unconsolidated Subsidiaries and Affiliates

A summary of investments in unconsolidated subsidiaries and affiliates as of December 31, 2003 and 2002 is as follows:

METHOD OF ACCOUNTING (IN MILLIONS)	2003	2002
Equity method	$ 422	$ 370
Cost method	7	5
Total	$ 429	$ 375

During 2002, investments in unconsolidated subsidiaries and affiliates increased as a result of CNH's investment in Kobelco Japan and CNH Capital Europe. At December 31, 2003, investments accounted for using the equity method primarily include interests CNH has in various ventures in the United States, Europe, Turkey, Mexico, Japan, India and Pakistan.

Note 8: Equipment on Operating Leases

A summary of Financial Services' equipment on operating leases as of December 31, 2003 and 2002 is as follows:

(IN MILLIONS)	2003	2002
Equipment on operating leases	$ 525	$ 716
Accumulated depreciation	(172)	(172)
Net equipment on operating leases	$ 353	$ 544

Depreciation expense totaled $96 million, $114 million and $92 million for the years ended December 31, 2003, 2002 and 2001, respectively.

Callaway Golf Company—Manufacturing Inventory

Callaway Golf Company is a California corporation formed in 1982. The Company designs, develops, manufactures and markets high-quality, innovative golf clubs. Callaway Golf's primary products include Big Bertha® metal woods with the War Bird® soleplate, Great Big Bertha® titanium metal woods, Biggest Big Bertha® titanium drivers, Big Bertha® Steelhead™ metal woods, Big Bertha® irons, Great Big Bertha® Tungsten® Titanium™ irons, Big Bertha® X-12™ irons, Odyssey® putters and wedges and various other putters. Callaway launched its Rule 35™ Firmfeel™ and Softfeel™ golf balls on February 4, 2000.

Learning Objectives

- Disaggregate manufacturing inventory and understand its underlying components.
- Interpret the allowance for obsolete inventory.
- Trace product cost flows from raw materials through to finished goods inventory.
- Infer raw material purchases and calculate cash disbursements related to inventory.
- Calculate and analyze financial statement ratios related to inventory.

Refer to the 1999 financial statements of Callaway Golf Company.

Concepts

a. Note 3 reveals that the balance sheet inventory amount consists of three types of inventory. What types of costs do you expect to be in the raw materials inventory? In the work-in-process inventory? In the finished goods inventory?

b. The balance sheet inventory line item is called "Inventories, net." What are inventories *net* of? What is the *gross* amount of inventory at the end of 1998? 1999?

c. What portion of the reserve for obsolescence do you think is attributable to each of the three types of inventory held by Callaway?

Process

d. Recreate the journal entry Callaway prepared to adjust the reserve for obsolescence in 1999.

Analysis

e. Make the following simplifying assumptions. The only activity in the "accounts payable" account (see Note 3) is for raw materials purchases and payments for those purchases. During 1999, a total of $50,000,000 of manufacturing salaries and overhead was debited to the work-in-process account. All other activity in the work-in-process account is from raw materials transfers and transfers of completed products to finished goods. The allowance for obsolescence is included in the finished goods balance presented in Note 3. Determine the following amounts. (*Hint*: Set up separate T-accounts for all three inventory accounts as well as for "cost of goods sold" and "accounts payable and accrued expenses.")

   i. The cost of finished goods sold in 1999.

   ii. The cost of finished goods transferred from work-in-process in 1999 (i.e., the cost of goods manufactured).

   iii. The cost of raw materials transferred to work-in-process in 1999.

   iv. The cost of raw materials purchased during 1999.

v. The amount of cash disbursed for raw material purchases during 1999.

f. The inventory turnover rat6io measures how efficiently management uses its assets. It is defined as:

$$\frac{\text{Cost of Goods Sold}}{\text{Inventory}}$$

How many times did Callaway Golf's inventory turn over in 1999 and 1998?

g. The inventory turnover ratio can be reframed as the average time it takes to sell inventory. The inventory holding period is defined as:

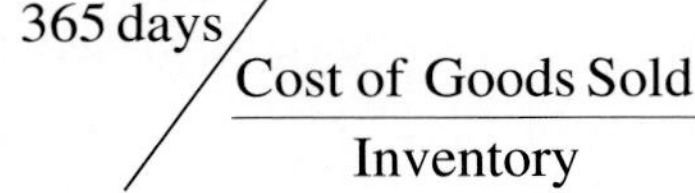

On average, how many days did it take for Callaway to manufacture and sell its inventory in 1999 and 1998? That is, what is the inventory holding period for 1999 and 1998?

h. Assume that the obsolete inventory was entirely finished goods. What percent of finished goods was estimated to be obsolete in 1999 and 1998? What could explain the change?

(Note: the inventory turnover ratios can be calculated using average balances for inventory. We use the ending balances here in order to obtain data for the trend analysis.)

Consolidated Balance Sheet

(in thousands, except share and per share data)	December 31, 1999	1998
ASSETS		
Current assets:		
Cash and cash equivalents	$ 112,602	$ 45,618
Accounts receivable, net	54,252	73,466
Inventories, net	97,938	149,192
Deferred taxes	32,558	51,029
Other current assets	13,122	4,301
Total current assets	310,472	323,606
Property, plant and equipment, net	142,214	172,794
Intangible assets, net	120,143	127,779
Other assets	43,954	31,648
	$ 616,783	$ 655,827
LIABILITIES AND SHAREHOLDERS' EQUITY		
Current liabilities:		
Accounts payable and accrued expenses	$ 46,664	$ 35,928
Accrued employee compensation and benefits	21,126	11,083
Accrued warranty expense	36,105	35,815
Line of credit		70,919
Note payable		12,971
Accrued restructuring costs	1,379	7,389
Income taxes payable		9,903
Total current liabilities	105,274	184,008
Long-term liabilities:		
Deferred compensation	11,575	7,606
Accrued restructuring costs		11,117
Commitments and contingencies (Note 11)		
Shareholders' equity:		
Preferred Stock, $.01 par value, 3,000,000 shares authorized, none issued and outstanding at December 31, 1999 and 1998		
Common Stock, $.01 par value, 240,000,000 shares authorized, 76,302,196 and 75,095,087 issued and outstanding at December 31, 1999 and 1998	763	751
Paid-in capital	307,329	258,015
Unearned compensation	(2,784)	(5,653)
Retained earnings	288,090	252,528
Accumulated other comprehensive income	280	1,780
Less: Grantor Stock Trust (5,300,000 shares at December 31, 1999 and 1998) at market (Note 6)	(93,744)	(54,325)
Total shareholders' equity	499,934	453,096
	$ 616,783	$ 655,827

See accompanying notes to consolidated financial statements.

Consolidated Statement of Operations

(in thousands, except per share data)	Year ended December 31, 1999		1998		1997	
Net sales	$714,471	100%	$697,621	100%	$842,927	100%
Cost of goods sold	376,405	53%	401,607	58%	400,127	47%
Gross profit	338,066	47%	296,014	42%	442,800	53%
Selling expenses	131,858	18%	147,022	21%	120,589	14%
General and administrative expenses	92,478	13%	98,048	14%	70,724	8%
Research and development costs	34,002	5%	36,848	5%	30,298	4%
Restructuring costs (Note 12)	(5,894)	(1%)	54,235	8%		
Sumitomo transition costs (Note 15)	5,713	1%				
Litigation settlement					12,000	1%
Income (loss) from operations	79,909	11%	(40,139)	(6%)	209,189	25%
Interest and other income, net (Note 9)	9,182		3,911		4,586	
Interest expense	(3,594)		(2,671)		(10)	
Income (loss) before income taxes	85,497	12%	(38,899)	(6%)	213,765	25%
Income tax provision (benefit)	30,175		(12,335)		81,061	
Net income (loss)	$ 55,322	8%	($ 26,564)	(4%)	$132,704	16%
Earnings (loss) per common share:						
Basic	$0.79		($0.38)		$1.94	
Diluted	$0.78		($0.38)		$1.85	
Common equivalent shares:						
Basic	70,397		69,463		68,407	
Diluted	71,214		69,463		71,698	

See accompanying notes to consolidated financial statements.

Consolidated Statement of Cash Flows

(in thousands)	Year ended December 31, 1999	1998	1997
Cash flows from operating activities:			
Net income (loss)	$ 55,322	($ 26,564)	$ 132,704
Adjustments to reconcile net income (loss) to net cash provided by operating activities:			
Depreciation and amortization	39,877	35,885	19,408
Non-cash compensation	1,390	2,887	2,041
Tax benefit from exercise of stock options	2,377	3,068	29,786
Deferred taxes	9,971	(36,235)	1,030
Non-cash restructuring costs	(8,609)	25,497	
Loss on disposal of assets	315	1,298	2
Changes in assets and liabilities, net of effects from acquisitions:			
Accounts receivable, net	19,690	51,575	(36,936)
Inventories, net	51,092	(42,665)	6,271
Other assets	(12,966)	(12,149)	(6,818)
Accounts payable and accrued expenses	12,225	(4,357)	13,529
Accrued employee compensation and benefits	9,875	(3,411)	(2,437)
Accrued warranty expense	286	7,760	756
Income taxes payable	(10,001)	9,652	(2,636)
Accrued restructuring costs	(3,476)	7,389	
Deferred compensation	3,969	(299)	2,796
Accrued restructuring costs - long-term	(5,041)	11,117	
Net cash provided by operating activities	166,296	30,448	159,496
Cash flows from investing activities:			
Capital expenditures	(56,244)	(67,859)	(67,938)
Acquisitions, net of cash acquired	(2,389)	(10,672)	(129,256)
Proceeds from sale of assets	5,095	3,417	72
Net cash used in investing activities	(53,538)	(75,114)	(197,122)
Cash flows from financing activities:			
Net (payments on) proceeds from line of credit	(70,919)	70,919	
Proceeds from note payable	35,761	12,971	
Short-term debt retirement		(10,373)	
Issuance of Common Stock	9,009	10,343	27,530
Retirement of Common Stock		(917)	(52,985)
Dividends paid, net	(19,760)	(19,485)	(19,123)
Net cash (used in) provided by financing activities	(45,909)	63,458	(44,578)
Effect of exchange rate changes on cash	135	622	(49)
Net increase (decrease) in cash and cash equivalents	66,984	19,414	(82,253)
Cash and cash equivalents at beginning of year	45,618	26,204	108,457
Cash and cash equivalents at end of year	$ 112,602	$ 45,618	$ 26,204
Supplemental disclosures:			
Non-cash financing (Note 4)	$ 48,732		
Cash paid for interest and fees	$ 3,637	$ 2,162	$ 10
Cash paid for income taxes	$ 30,670	$ 8,165	$ 54,358

See accompanying notes to consolidated financial statements.

NOTE 3

SELECTED FINANCIAL STATEMENT INFORMATION

(in thousands)	December 31, 1999	1998
Cash and cash equivalents:		
Cash, interest bearing	$110,157	$ 41,689
Cash, non-interest bearing	2,445	3,929
	$112,602	$ 45,618
Accounts receivable, net:		
Trade accounts receivable	$ 59,543	$ 83,405
Allowance for doubtful accounts	(5,291)	(9,939)
	$ 54,252	$ 73,466
Inventories, net:		
Raw materials	$ 45,868	$102,352
Work-in-process	1,403	1,820
Finished goods	65,661	81,868
	112,932	186,040
Reserve for obsolescence	(14,994)	(36,848)
	$ 97,938	$149,192
Property, plant and equipment, net:		
Land	$ 12,358	$ 13,375
Buildings and improvements	87,910	55,307
Machinery and equipment	50,942	57,334
Furniture, computers and equipment	64,334	55,629
Production molds	22,714	17,472
Construction-in-process	5,032	52,920
	243,290	252,037
Accumulated depreciation	(101,076)	(79,243)
	$142,214	$172,794
Intangible assets:		
Trade name	$ 69,629	$ 69,629
Trademark and trade dress	29,841	29,841
Patents, goodwill and other	34,911	35,765
	134,381	135,235
Accumulated amortization	(14,238)	(7,456)
	$120,143	$127,779
Accounts payable and accrued expenses:		
Accounts payable	$ 11,297	$ 10,341
Note to related party (Note 16)		6,766
Accrued expenses	35,367	18,821
	$ 46,664	$ 35,928
Accrued employee compensation and benefits:		
Accrued payroll and taxes	$ 15,303	$ 6,178
Accrued vacation and sick pay	4,571	4,423
Accrued commissions	1,252	482
	$ 21,126	$ 11,083

NOTE 4

BANK LINE OF CREDIT AND NOTE PAYABLE

On February 12, 1999, the Company consummated the amendment of its credit facility to increase the facility to up to $120,000,000 (the "Amended Credit Agreement"). The Amended Credit Agreement has a five-year term and is secured by substantially all of the assets of the Company. The Amended Credit Agreement bears interest at the Company's election at the London Interbank Offering Rate ("LIBOR") plus a margin or the higher of the base rate on corporate loans at large U.S. money center commercial banks (prime rate) or the Federal Funds Rate plus 50 basis points. The line of credit requires the Company to maintain certain minimum financial ratios, including a fixed charge coverage ratio, as well as other restrictive covenants. As of December 31, 1999, up to $115,739,000 of the credit facility remained available for borrowings (including a reduction of $4,261,000 for outstanding letters of credit), subject to meeting certain availability requirements under a borrowing base formula and other limitations.

On December 30, 1998, Callaway Golf Ball Company, a wholly-owned subsidiary of the Company, entered into a master lease agreement for the acquisition and lease of up to $56,000,000 of machinery and equipment. As of December 31, 1999, the Company had finalized its lease program and leased $50,000,000 of equipment pursuant to the master lease agreement. This lease program includes an interim finance agreement (the "Finance Agreement"). The Finance Agreement provides pre-lease financing advances for the acquisition and installation costs of the aforementioned machinery and equipment. The Finance Agreement bears interest at LIBOR plus a margin and is secured by the underlying machinery and equipment and a corporate guarantee from the Company. During the third and fourth quarters of 1999, the Company converted the balance of this note payable to the operating lease discussed above. As of December 31, 1999, no amount was outstanding under this facility.

Tasty Baking Company—Property, Plant, & Equipment

Incorporated in Pennsylvania in 1914, Tasty BakingCompany manufactures and sells approximately 100 varieties of premium single portion cakes, pies, cookies, pretzels, brownies, pastries, donuts, and snack bars under the well established trademark, TASTYKAKE. The products with the widest sales acceptance are various sponge cakes marketed under the trademarks JUNIORS and KRIMPETS, and chocolate enrobed cakes under KANDY KAKES. The company's principal competitor in the premium snack cake market is Interstate Bakeries Corporation which owns three major brands - Hostess, Dolly Madison, and Drakes.

Learning Objectives

- Use information from the financial statements to analyze fixed asset and depreciation transactions.
- Prepare journal entries related to fixed asset transactions.
- Understand why and how certain costs are capitalized.
- Compute depreciation expenses using common accounting methods.
- Calculate gains and losses on fixed asset disposals.
- Calculate and interpret the fixed asset turnover ratio.

Refer to the 2003 financial statements of Tasty Baking Company.

✧ Concepts ✧

a. Based on the above description of Tasty Baking, what sort of property and equipment do you think the company has?

b. Does Tasty Baking *own* all the property, plant and equipment it reports on the balance sheet?

c. The 2003 balance sheet shows accumulated depreciation of $136,156. How much of this is attributable to the land account?

d. How does Tasty Baking depreciate property and equipment? Does this policy seem reasonable? Explain the tradeoffs management makes in choosing a depreciation policy.

e. According to note 1, Tasty Baking "capitalized" a number of costs during the year. Explain in your own words, what it means to capitalize a cost. What is the alternative to capitalizing a cost? What specific types of costs did Tasty Baking capitalize?

✧ Process ✧

f. Use two T-accounts to reconstruct the activity in the gross "Property, plant and equipment" and "Accumulated depreciation and amortization" accounts for the period December 29, 2002 to December 27, 2003. Begin by entering the opening and ending balances in both accounts. Then, determine the appropriate increases and decreases in the account due to the following activities (*Hint*: what journal entry did the company record for each of the following events?):

   i. The purchase of new property, plant and equipment in fiscal 2003 for cash.

   ii. The addition of new property under capital lease in fiscal 2003. (*Hint*: the Statement of Cash Flows reports supplemental information related to new capital leases during the year.)

   iii. Depreciation expense for fiscal 2003.

   iv. The sale of property and equipment in fiscal 2003.

g. According to the statement of cash flows, Tasty Baking received proceeds on the sale of fixed assets amounting to $147 in fiscal 2003. Calculate the gain or loss that Tasty Baking incurred on this transaction. Prepare the journal entry to record the transaction. Where is this gain or loss included on the income statement? On the statement of cash flows?

h. Assume that $1,276 of the fixed assets purchased during fiscal 2003 have an expected useful life of five years and a salvage value of $176. Prepare a table showing the depreciation expense and net book value of this equipment over its expected life assuming that a full year of depreciation is taken in fiscal 2003 and the company uses:

    i. Straight-line depreciation.

    ii. Double declining balance depreciation.

i. Assume that the equipment from part *h.* was sold on the first day of fiscal 2004 for proceeds of $900. Assume that Tasty Baking's accounting policy states that no depreciation is taken in the year of sale.

    i. Calculate any gain or loss on this transaction assuming that the company used straight-line depreciation. Prepare the journal entry to record the transaction. What is the total income statement impact of these assets over their lives? Consider both the gain or loss on disposal as well as the total depreciation recorded on these assets (i.e. the amount from part *h. i.*).

    ii. Now, calculate any gain or loss on this transaction assuming the company used double declining balance depreciation. Prepare the journal entry. What is the total income statement impact of these assets over their lives? Consider both the gain or loss on disposal as well as the total depreciation recorded on these assets (i.e. the amount from part *h. ii.*).

    iii. Compare the total income statement impact of the assets under the two depreciation policies. Comment on the difference.

j. According to note 13, Tasty Baking capitalized interest costs during the year. Prepare the journal entry that Tasty Baking made during the year to capitalize interest. Where is this capitalized interest included on the income statement? On the statement of cash flows?

✧ Analysis ✧

k. You want to compare Tasty Baking to its competitor, Interstate Bakeries. To compare the companies, you calculate common-sized numbers. To common-size balance sheet numbers, divide by total assets and to common-size income statement numbers, divide by net sales. Calculate common-size property plant and equipment and depreciation expense for fiscal 2002 and 2003. The Interstate Bakeries data are in the table that follows. Comment on the trends over time and levels across companies.

l. A ratio analysts use to gauge the efficiency with which management is using its invested capital is the fixed asset turnover ratio. The ratio is defined as:

$$\text{Fixed Asset Turnover} = \frac{\text{Net Sales}}{\text{Fixed Assets}}.$$

Determine Tasty Baking's fixed asset turnover ratio for fiscal 2002 and 2003. Explain what this ratio measures. Comment on the trends over time and levels across companies.

	Interstate Bakeries		Tasty Baking	
	FY 2003	*FY 2002*	*FY 2003*	*FY 2002*
Net PPE	$853,473,000	$845,005,000		
Total Assets	$1,645,691,000	$1,602,942,000		
Common-size	51.9%	52.7%		
Depreciation	$95,177,000	$95,343,000		
Net Sales	$3,525,780,000	$3,531,623,000		
Common-size	2.7%	2.7%		
Fixed Asset Turnover	4.131	4.179		

CONSOLIDATED FINANCIAL STATEMENTS
Tasty Baking Company and Subsidiaries

Consolidated Statements of Operations and Retained Earnings
(000's, except per share amounts)

	52 Weeks Ended Dec. 27, 2003	52 Weeks Ended Dec. 28, 2002	52 Weeks Ended Dec. 29, 2001
Operations			
Gross sales	$ 250,648	$ 255,504	$ 255,336
Less discounts and allowances	(91,519)	(93,241)	(89,091)
Net sales	159,129	162,263	166,245
Costs and expenses:			
Cost of sales	108,444	111,187	103,297
Depreciation	7,148	6,807	7,204
Selling, general and administrative	48,394	45,941	44,008
Restructure charge net of reversals	(71)	6,341	1,728
Interest expense	909	1,066	1,103
Gain on sale of routes	(1,077)	–	–
Other income, net	(873)	(1,165)	(1,190)
	162,874	170,177	156,150
Income (loss) before provision for income taxes	(3,745)	(7,914)	10,095
Provision for (benefit from) income taxes:			
Federal	(3,089)	(11)	3,286
State	709	(316)	(90)
Deferred	997	(3,246)	579
	(1,383)	(3,573)	3,775
Net income (loss)	(2,362)	(4,341)	6,320
Retained Earnings			
Balance, beginning of year	26,622	34,839	32,352
Cash dividends paid on common shares ($.20 per share in 2003 and $.48 per share in 2002 and 2001)	(1,619)	(3,876)	(3,833)
Balance, end of year	$ 22,641	$ 26,622	$ 34,839
Per share of common stock:			
Net income (loss):			
Basic	$ (.29)	$ (.54)	$ .79
Diluted	$ (.29)	$ (.54)	$ .78

See Notes to Consolidated Financial Statements.

Consolidated Statements of Cash Flows
(000's)

	52 Weeks Ended Dec. 27, 2003	52 Weeks Ended Dec. 28, 2002	52 Weeks Ended Dec. 29, 2001
Cash flows from (used for) operating activities			
Net income (loss)	$ (2,362)	$ (4,341)	$ 6,320
Adjustments to reconcile net income to net cash provided by operating activities:			
Depreciation	7,148	6,807	7,204
Gain on sale of routes	(1,077)	–	–
Restructure charges net of reversals	(71)	6,341	1,728
Conditional stock grant	–	–	805
Pension expense	1,700	5,456	(217)
Pension contributions	–	(1,000)	–
Deferred taxes	997	(3,246)	579
Restructure payments	(3,209)	(1,207)	(877)
Other	1,222	(455)	352
Changes in assets and liabilities:			
Decrease (increase) in receivables	320	393	(2,234)
Decrease (increase) in inventories	1,047	1,635	(2,481)
Increase in prepayments and other	(331)	(1,840)	(198)
Increase (decrease) in accounts payable, accrued payroll and other accrued liabilities	4,019	1,572	(77)
Net cash from operating activities	9,403	10,115	10,904
Cash flows from (used for) investing activities			
Proceeds from independent sales distributor loan repayments	3,540	3,987	3,495
Proceeds from sale of property, plant and equipment	147	–	–
Purchase of property, plant and equipment	(6,676)	(5,359)	(7,314)
Loans to independent sales distributors	(3,628)	(3,881)	(4,043)
Other	(414)	(46)	46
Net cash used for investing activities	(7,031)	(5,299)	(7,816)
Cash flows from (used for) financing activities			
Dividends paid	(1,619)	(3,876)	(3,833)
Payment of long-term debt	(1,402)	(2,117)	(3,217)
Net increase in short-term debt	400	600	1,700
Additional long-term debt	–	–	1,000
Net proceeds from sale of common stock	–	492	1,318
Net cash used for financing activities	(2,621)	(4,901)	(3,032)
Net increase (decrease) in cash	(249)	(85)	56
Cash, beginning of year	282	367	311
Cash, end of year	$ 33	$ 282	$ 367
Supplemental cash flow information			
Cash paid during the year for:			
Interest	$ 841	$ 1,084	$ 1,232
Income Taxes	$ 98	$ 1,012	$ 3,065
Noncash investing and financing activities			
Capital leases	$ 2,079	$ –	$ –
Loans to independent sales distributors	$ (1,076)	$ –	$ –

See Notes to Consolidated Financial Statements.

Consolidated Balance Sheets
(000's)

	Dec. 27, 2003	Dec. 28, 2002
Assets		
Current Assets:		
Cash	$ 33	$ 282
Receivables, less allowance of $3,648 and $3,606, respectively	19,503	20,881
Inventories	5,730	6,777
Deferred income taxes	3,902	5,214
Prepayments and other	3,271	2,941
Total current assets	32,439	36,095
Property, plant and equipment:		
Land	1,098	1,098
Buildings and improvements	40,288	37,832
Machinery and equipment	158,286	152,689
	199,672	191,619
Less accumulated depreciation and amortization	136,156	129,529
	63,516	62,090
Other assets:		
Long-term receivables from independent sales distributors	11,253	10,095
Deferred income taxes	9,267	8,230
Miscellaneous	768	50
	21,288	18,375
	$ 117,243	$ 116,560

See Notes to Consolidated Financial Statements.

	Dec. 27, 2003	Dec. 28, 2002
Liabilities		
Current liabilities:		
Current obligations under capital leases	$ 634	$ 176
Notes payable, banks	4,900	4,500
Accounts payable	9,261	6,074
Accrued payroll and employee benefits	6,013	6,480
Reserve for restructure	1,331	2,417
Other accrued liabilities	2,280	981
Total current liabilities	24,419	20,628
Long-term debt	8,000	9,000
Long-term obligations under capital leases, less current portion	4,705	3,486
Reserve for restructures, less current portion	1,044	3,568
Accrued pensions and other liabilities	19,938	15,669
Postretirement benefits other than pensions	16,718	16,684
Total liabilities	74,824	69,035
Shareholders' Equity		
Common stock, par value $.50 per share, and entitled to one vote per share:		
Authorized 15,000 shares, issued 9,116 shares	4,558	4,558
Capital in excess of par value of stock	29,393	29,433
Retained earnings	22,641	26,622
	56,592	60,613
Less:		
Accumulated other comprehensive loss	1,236	–
Treasury stock, at cost:		
1,020 shares and 1,013 shares, respectively	12,545	12,539
Management Stock Purchase Plan receivables and deferrals	392	549
	42,419	47,525
	$ 117,243	$ 116,560

See Notes to Consolidated Financial Statements.

Notes to Consolidated Financial Statements

(000's, except share and per share amounts)
All disclosures are pre-tax, unless otherwise noted.

1. Summary of Significant Accounting Policies

Nature of the Business
Tasty Baking Company is a leading producer of sweet baked goods and one of the nation's oldest and largest independent baking companies, in operation since 1914. It has two manufacturing facilities, one at Hunting Park Avenue in Philadelphia, PA, and a second facility at Oxford, PA.

Fiscal Year
The company and its subsidiaries operate on a 52-53 week fiscal year, ending on the last Saturday of December.

Basis of Consolidation
The consolidated financial statements include the accounts of the company and its subsidiaries. Inter-company transactions are eliminated.

Use of Estimates
Certain amounts included in the accompanying consolidated financial statements and related footnotes reflect the use of estimates based on assumptions made by management. These estimates are made using all information available to management, and management believes that these estimates are as accurate as possible as of the dates and for the periods that the financial statements are presented. Actual amounts could differ from these estimates.

Concentration of Credit
The company encounters, in the normal course of business, exposure to concentrations of credit risk with respect to trade receivables. Ongoing credit evaluations of customers' financial condition are performed and, generally, no collateral is required. The company maintains reserves for potential credit losses and such losses have not exceeded management's expectations. The company's top twenty customers represent 57.9% of its 2003 net sales dollars, relatively consistent with 2002 and 2001. Of these customers, the company's largest customer, Wal-Mart, represents 15.2% of the net sales in 2003. The company's largest customer, Wal-Mart, represented 13.3% of the 2002 net sales, relatively consistent with 2001.

Revenue Recognition
Revenue is recognized when title and risk of loss pass, which is generally upon receipt of goods by the customer. Provisions for estimated discounts, product returns and other adjustments are provided in the same period that the related sales are recorded.

Cash and Cash Equivalents
The company considers all investments with an original maturity of three months or less on their acquisition date to be cash equivalents.

Inventory Valuation
Inventories are stated at the lower of cost or market, cost being determined using the first-in, first-out (FIFO) method.

Property and Depreciation
Property, plant and equipment are carried at cost. Depreciation is computed by the straight-line method over the estimated useful lives of the assets. Buildings and improvements are depreciated over thirty-nine years. The principal manufacturing plant is leased from the company's pension plan and is amortized over twenty years. Leasehold improvements are generally depreciated over five years. Machinery and equipment are depreciated over a range of seven to fifteen years. Spare parts are capitalized as part of machinery and equipment and are expensed as utilized.

Costs of major additions, replacements and betterments are capitalized, while maintenance and repairs, which do not improve or extend the life of the respective assets are charged to income as incurred.

The company capitalizes interest and labor costs associated with the construction and installation of plant and equipment.

Long-lived assets are reviewed for impairment whenever events or changes in circumstances indicate that the carrying amount may not be recoverable. If this review indicates that the expected future undiscounted net cash flows of the related asset is less than the asset's carrying value, an impairment loss is recognized.

Marketing costs
The company expenses marketing costs, which include advertising and consumer promotions, as incurred. Marketing costs are included as a part of selling, general and administrative expense. Marketing expenses totaled $5,708, $2,105 and $1,640, for the years ended December 27, 2003, December 28, 2002, and December 29, 2001, respectively.

Shipping and Handling Costs
Shipping and handling costs are included as a part of selling, general and administrative expense.

12. Stock Option Plans (continued)

Under the terms of the 1997 Long Term Incentive Plan, options to purchase a total of 375,000 common shares may be granted to key executives of the company. Options become exercisable in five equal installments beginning on the date of grant until fully exercisable after four years. The option price is determined by the Board and, in the case of incentive stock options, will be no less than the fair market value of the shares on the date of grant. Options lapse at the earlier of the expiration of the option term specified by the Long-Term Incentive Plan Committee of the Board (not more than ten years in the case of incentive stock options) or three months following the date on which employment with the company terminates. The company also has options outstanding under the 1994 Long Term Incentive Plan, the terms and conditions of which are similar to the 1997 Long Term Incentive Plan.

In addition, effective December 17, 1999, the Board of Directors approved a resolution to distribute 79,304 shares to executives and managers of the company as a conditional stock grant expiring December 17, 2002. The shares were to be distributed to the executives and managers in one-third increments upon reaching the targeted stock prices of $12, $14 and $16. Compensation expense was required to be recognized for the number of shares granted at the time the targeted stock price levels were reached. Compensation expense was recognized for 2000 in the amount of $319 upon reaching the targeted stock price of $12. In the first quarter of 2001 the final two targets of $14 and $16 were reached which resulted in compensation expense of $805 in the first quarter of 2001. All shares related to the plan were distributed by the end of the first quarter of 2001.

13. Capitalization of Interest Costs

The company capitalizes interest as a component of the cost of significant construction projects. The following table sets forth data relative to capitalized interest:

	2003	2002	2001
Total interest	$ 911	$ 1,096	$ 1,265
Less capitalized interest	2	30	162
Interest expense	$ 909	$ 1,066	$ 1,103

14. Other Income, Net

Other income, net consists of the following:

	2003	2002	2001
Interest income	$ 817	$ 957	$ 996
Other, net	56	208	194
	$ 873	$ 1,165	$ 1,190

15. Income Taxes

The effective tax rates were a benefit of 36.9% and 45.2% in 2003 and 2002, respectively, and a provision of 37.4% in 2001. The rates differ from the amounts derived from applying the statutory U.S. federal income tax rate of 34% to income before provision (benefit) for income taxes as follows:

	2003	2002	2001
Statutory tax provision	$ (1,273)	$ (2,691)	$ 3,433
State income taxes, net of federal income tax benefit	(300)	(816)	70
Addition to (release of) tax reserves	(163)	(128)	182
Valuation allowance	286	–	–
Non-deductible expenses and other	67	62	90
Provision (benefit) for income taxes	$ (1,383)	$ (3,573)	$ 3,775

In 2001, additional tax reserves were established for tax exposure that was determined to be unnecessary and released in 2002. During 2003, the company released $163 of its tax reserves due to enacted state tax law changes.

WorldCom, Inc.—Capitalized Costs and Earnings Quality

Organized in 1983, WorldCom, Inc. provides a broad range of communications services to both U.S. and non-U.S. based businesses and consumers. The company's strategy is to provide service through their own facilities throughout the world instead of being restricted to a particular geographic location. The company's core business is communications services, which include voice, data, Internet and international services. During the second quarter of 2002, WorldCom announced that costs totaling $3.9 billion had been improperly capitalized in five preceding quarters which overstated pre-tax earnings by the same amount. Subsequently, the magnitude of the fraudulent accounting entries has increased and WorldCom filed for Chapter 11 bankruptcy protection.

Learning Objectives

- Distinguish between costs and expenses.
- Distinguish between costs that should be capitalized and costs that should be expensed.
- Restate earnings to reflect generally accepted accounting principles.
- Understand management's incentives to engage in "aggressive accounting."

Refer to the 2001 financial statements and notes for WorldCom, Inc. and to the *Wall Street Journal* article dated June 27, 2002.

 **Concepts** 

a. FASB Statement of Concepts No. 6 (a replacement for SCON No. 3), *Elements of Financial Statements*, describes the building blocks with which financial statements are constructed.

   i. Explain, in your own words, how SCON 6 defines 'asset' and 'expense'

   ii. In general, when should costs be expensed and when should they be capitalized as assets?

b. What becomes of 'costs' after their initial capitalization? Describe, in general terms, how the balance sheet and the income statement are affected by a decision to capitalize a given cost.

 **Process** 

c. Refer to WorldCom's statement of operations. What did the company report as line costs for the year ended December 31, 2001? Prepare the journal entry to record these transactions for the year. Explain in your own words, what these "line costs" are.

d. Refer to the *Wall Street Journal* article. Describe the types of costs that were improperly capitalized at WorldCom. Explain, in your own words, what transactions give rise to these costs. Do these costs meet your definition of 'asset' in part *a* above?

e. Prepare a single journal entry to record the improperly capitalized line costs of $3.055 billion for the year. Where did these costs appear on the balance sheet? Where on the statement of cash flows?

✧ **Analysis** 

f. In a sworn statement to the Securities and Exchange Commission, WorldCom revealed details of the improperly capitalized amounts in 2001: $771 in the first quarter, $610 in the second quarter, $743 in the third quarter, and $931 in the fourth quarter. Assume that WorldCom planned to depreciate these capitalized costs over the midpoint of the range for transmission equipment as disclosed in note 1. Further assume that depreciation begins in the quarter that assets are acquired (or costs capitalized). Calculate the related depreciation expense for 2001. Prepare the journal entry to record this depreciation.

g. Use your answers to parts e and f above, to determine what WorldCom's net income would have been in 2001 had line-costs not been improperly capitalized. Use WorldCom's 2001 income tax rate as reported, in your calculations. State any other assumptions you make. Is the difference in net income material?

h. "*... former employees and people familiar with WorldCom's operations, reveal a grow-at-any-cost culture that made it possible for employees and managers to game the system internally and to deceive investors about the health of the business.*" (Washington Post, August 29, 2002). Why would WorldCom's management engage in such deception (i.e., capitalizing costs that are normally immediately expensed)? That is, what incentives did WorldCom management have to defer costs?

i. In your opinion, what rules and internal controls might have been put in place at WorldCom to detect this sort of improper accounting?

j. What economic consequences arise when a publicly-traded company's financial reports are revealed as fraudulent?

June 27, 2002 1:33 p.m. EDT

PAGE ONE

Accounting Spot-Check Unearthed A Scandal in WorldCom's Books

By JARED SANDBERG, DEBORAH SOLOMON and REBECCA BLUMENSTEIN
Staff Reporters of THE WALL STREET JOURNAL

NEW YORK -- It all started a few weeks ago with a check of the books by Cynthia Cooper, an internal auditor for **WorldCom** Inc. The telecom giant's newly installed chief executive had asked for a financial review, and her job was to spot-check records of capital expenditures.

According to people familiar with the matter, Ms. Cooper soon found something that caught her eye. In quarter after quarter, starting in 2001, WorldCom's chief financial officer, Scott Sullivan, had been using an unorthodox technique to account for one of the long-distance company's biggest expenses: charges paid to local telephone networks to complete calls.

Instead of marking them as operating expenses, he moved a significant portion into the category of capital expenditures. The maneuver was worth hundreds of millions of dollars to WorldCom's bottom line, effectively turning a loss for all of 2001 and the first quarter of 2002 into a profit.

Ms. Cooper contacted Max Bobbitt, the head of WorldCom's auditing committee, setting in motion a chain of events that resulted in Mr. Sullivan's firing late Tuesday. The company said that it had turned up $3.8 billion of expenses that were improperly booked and will now be restated.

Even in a season when one giant company after another has been laid low by accounting scandals, WorldCom's disclosure stands out. The coming financial restatement will almost certainly be one of the largest in corporate history -- more than six times that of Enron Corp. More important, it offers the clearest warning sign yet of the ease with which telecom companies, operating on the frontiers of accounting amidst a huge speculative excess, could manipulate their books to inflate their earnings.

President Bush himself called for a full investigation into the spiraling scandal, calling the accounting irregularities "outrageous."

The loss of trust by investors, customers and financial institutions has been profound. Shareholders have lost more than $2 trillion, and more than 500,000 telecom workers have lost their jobs.

"There was so much pressure on companies to continue to grow and support those share prices," says Charles H. Noski, who is a vice chairman of **AT&T** Corp. and its former chief financial officer. AT&T hasn't come under fire for its accounting, although its stock has tumbled amid the general industry malaise. "People are going to try to figure out how do you know enough to trust what corporations are telling investors. There is an overhang on the market now."

Stock markets around the world reacted swiftly Wednesday to a growing sense of unease that, like WorldCom itself, much of the explosive, double-digit growth of the stock market boom may have been a mirage. The Dow Jones Industrial Average fell 6.7 points. **Qwest Communications International** Inc., a big Denver telecom company under investigation by the Securities and Exchange Commission for alleged accounting irregularities, saw its stock fall nearly 60% Wednesday, to $1.79 a share. The company has denied wrongdoing.

For WorldCom, the development could well spell the end of the nation's No. 2 long-distance company, which sells to consumers under the MCI brand name. WorldCom's banks said they wouldn't immediately act on debt covenants that could allow them to call their loans. But people familiar with the matter said a bankruptcy-court filing remains an option. Nasdaq halted trading in WorldCom's stock all day Wednesday. It currently stands at 83 cents, far from its high of $64.50 in 1999.

The SEC Wednesday filed civil fraud charges[7] against WorldCom, saying the company "falsely portrayed itself as a profitable business." The U.S. Justice Department has launched a probe that could result in criminal charges, according to people familiar with the situation. These people said WorldCom and Mr. Sullivan could potentially face charges including securities fraud, bank fraud and mail fraud.

Scott Sullivan

Andrew J. Graham, Mr. Sullivan's attorney, said he wouldn't comment. But people familiar with Mr. Sullivan say he firmly believes he didn't do anything wrong.

Brad Burns, a spokesman for WorldCom, declined to comment on the SEC charges but said the company is "very focused on serving our customers, working with our bank lenders and ensuring our employees that we'll get through these difficult times."

WorldCom had already been reeling under a heavy debt load and declining revenues. In April, the board ousted the long-time chief executive, Bernard J. Ebbers, in part because of a controversy surrounding a $408 million loan WorldCom extended to him to cover margin calls on loans secured by company stock. Since then, its new chief executive, John Sidgmore, has been trying to hold off a financial crisis and restore investor confidence.

Internal Investigation

At this point, it's unclear whether anyone else at WorldCom knew what Mr. Sullivan was doing. The company has launched an internal investigation and is trying to determine who knew what and when. WorldCom has hired William McLucas, an SEC former enforcement chief who assisted in an internal probe of Enron's accounting, to help in the WorldCom investigation. One of the people under scrutiny is Mr. Ebbers, a close confidant of Mr. Sullivan. The two men shared an adjoining office at their Clinton, Miss., headquarters.

Mr. Ebbers couldn't be reached for comment, and his attorney didn't have any immediate comment.

What is clear is that over the past five quarters as the market softened, Mr. Sullivan undertook an aggressive approach to the company's way of accounting for one of its biggest expenses.

This happened just as WorldCom's acquisition machine was grinding to a halt. Mr. Ebbers had cobbled together his empire from modest roots as a long-distance reseller and motel owner in Mississippi. Mr. Sullivan became a trusted ally after Mr. Ebbers acquired his company, Advanced Telecommunications Corp., in 1992. The two executives worked in tandem as WorldCom, then known as LDDS, acquired dozens of companies, seemingly springing out of nowhere to snag MCI Communications Corp. in 1998. WorldCom's double-digit growth rates helped it win a takeover battle for MCI, trumping a bid by GTE Corp.

But by early 2001, the growth had started to slow. The booming telecommunications market was beginning to falter from a glut of capacity after a frenzied investment in fiber-optic networks. Suddenly, it found it had too much capacity. It had signed multibillion-dollar contracts with third-party telecommunications firms such as Baby Bells to insure it would be able to complete calls for its customers. An appraisal commissioned by WorldCom showed that roughly 15% of these costs weren't producing revenue, according to a WorldCom insider.

Mr. Sullivan made an important decision, says a person familiar with his thinking. Instead of reducing profits by those costs whenever WorldCom issued results in 2001, Mr. Sullivan would spread those costs to a future time when the anticipated revenue might arrive.

He was in a murky area. One of accounting's most basic rules is that capital costs have to be connected to long-term investments, not ongoing activities.

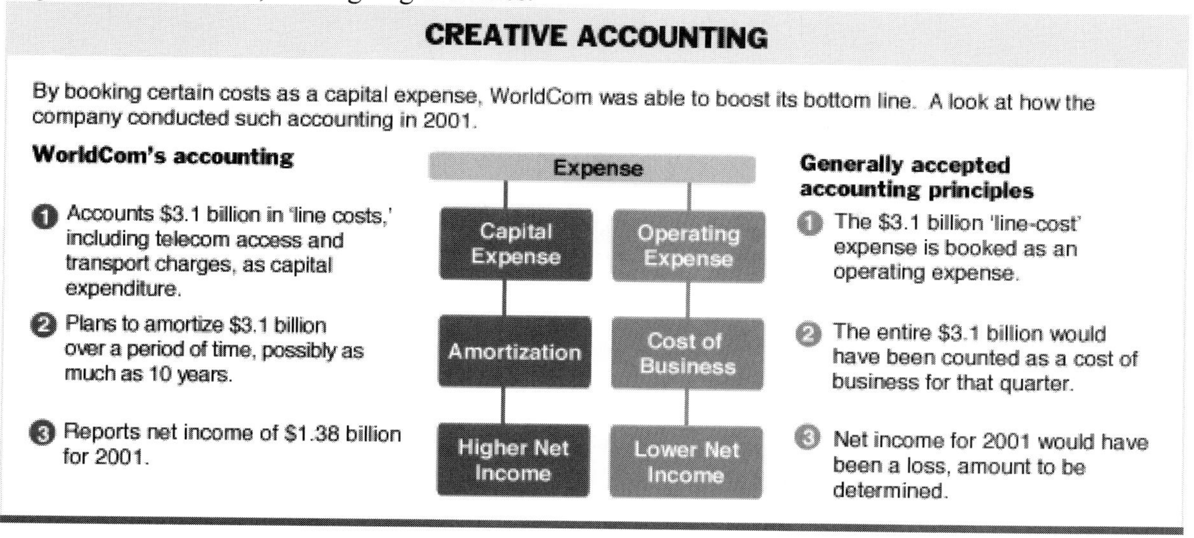

According to WorldCom, the company transferred more than $3.8 billion in "line cost" expenses to its capital accounts. WorldCom hasn't provided more detail about what those costs included, or what portions of their line costs were improperly capitalized. But line costs, according to the company's most recent annual report filed with the SEC, consist principally of access charges and transport charges. WorldCom's "line costs" totaled $8.12 billion in 2001, according to the company's income statement.

While companies can capitalize some costs like installation and labor, the magnitude of WorldCom's capitalization appears to be far beyond its industry peers.

A person familiar with the matter says Mr. Sullivan didn't appear to have realized any personal financial gain from his strategy. At WorldCom's peak in 1999, his shares were worth more than $150 million, and he currently owns about 3.2 million shares. But he hasn't sold any WorldCom stock in nearly two years, according to Thomson Financial/Lancer Analytics, a data service.

Mr. Sullivan never attempted to cover up the aggressive accounting method, the person familiar with the matter says. Details are spelled out clearly enough in internal company documents, this person says, that "other people had to see it unless they were blind." Still, Arthur Andersen, WorldCom's auditor at the time, said it wasn't consulted or notified about the capitalized expenses.

The CFO capitalized costs in amounts ranging from $540 million to $797 million each quarter. When April results came out this year, though, he began to doubt whether some of his revenue projections related to the line costs would be realized. In May, according to people familiar with his thinking, Mr. Sullivan was contemplating taking a charge. On May 23, the board was notified that a charge would include the line costs, but didn't signal how much it would be, a person familiar with the matter said.

Then in early June, Ms. Cooper called Mr. Bobbitt, chairman of the board's audit committee, notifying him that she had found suspect entries in the books.

Mr. Bobbitt had been under fire for months for his controversial role in extending Mr. Ebbers the $408 million personal loan from WorldCom. He quickly notified the newly hired accountants, KPMG LLP, of the discrepancy. The firm set to work.

Two weeks ago, KPMG came to WorldCom's offices in Washington and told the committee there was a problem. The investigation continued through the week and last Thursday the audit committee met at KPMG's Washington offices to ask Mr. Sullivan and company controller David Myers to justify their accounting treatment. Mr. Sullivan, according to people familiar with the situation, gave an impassioned defense of his decision, saying that since WorldCom wasn't receiving revenue, he could defer the costs of leasing the lines until they produced revenue. But KPMG officials weren't satisfied, citing accounting rules that clearly dictate that the costs of operating leases can't be delayed. The KPMG partner in charge of the WorldCom account, told Mr. Sullivan that he couldn't "get past the theory" but gave him the weekend to produce a so-called white paper that would set out his justification, a person close to the matter said.

Accounting experts say the rules are clear on what costs can be capitalized and what has to be expensed. "If the amounts being paid out are going to have created a long-lasting asset, then the costs depreciate and can be amortized over several years," says Carr Conway, a former SEC official and senior forensic accountant with Dickerson Financial Group in Denver. Unless the asset is going to generate value in future years, the cost for it can't be capitalized, he adds.

Weekend Huddle

Mr. Sullivan spent the weekend huddled with his team in Clinton, Miss., reviewing documents and constructing the white paper. But it wasn't going well. "He was becoming increasingly pessimistic" that he would have enough time to satisfy KPMG, said one person familiar with the matter.

At a board meeting Monday night at WorldCom's offices, Mr. Sullivan again made his case. A national practice specialist at KPMG said, however, that the issue was "an open-and-shut case," said one person who attended. "The KPMG people left no door open." After asking Mr. Sullivan to leave the room, board members concluded at the meeting that they would have to restate earnings. The meeting ended without a vote, which was postponed until Tuesday when Mr. Sullivan was fired and Mr. Myers was asked to resign.

Through it all, Mr. Sullivan was "very calm and articulate," says one person who attended the meetings. "He handled himself very well, though you could tell he was pained." As far as the board members, added another person, "most people were absolutely flabbergasted."

In a speech Wednesday, Mr. Sidgmore tried to make the most out of a bad situation. "We want to make clear that WorldCom reported itself in this matter and moved swiftly to do so," he said. "We turned ourselves in, in other words."

Write to Jared Sandberg at jared.sandberg@wsj.com, Deborah Solomon at deborah.solomon@wsj.com and Rebecca Blumenstein at rebecca.blumenstein@wsj.com

URL for this article:
http://online.wsj.com/article/0,,SB1025129017210305 20,00.html

WORLDCOM, INC. AND SUBSIDIARIES
CONSOLIDATED BALANCE SHEETS
(In Millions, Except Share Data)

	December 31, 2000	December 31, 2001
ASSETS		
Current assets:		
Cash and cash equivalents	$ 761	$ 1,416
Accounts receivable, net of allowance for bad debts of $1,532 in 2000 and $1,086 in 2001	6,815	5,308
Deferred tax asset	172	251
Other current assets	2,007	2,230
Total current assets	9,755	9,205
Property and equipment:		
Transmission equipment	20,288	23,814
Communications equipment	8,100	7,878
Furniture, fixtures and other	9,342	11,263
Construction in progress	6,897	5,706
	44,627	48,661
Accumulated depreciation	(7,204)	(9,852)
	37,423	38,809
Goodwill and other intangible assets	46,594	50,537
Other assets	5,131	5,363
	$ 98,903	$ 103,914
LIABILITIES AND SHAREHOLDERS' INVESTMENT		
Current liabilities:		
Short-term debt and current maturities of long-term debt	$ 7,200	$ 172
Accrued interest	446	618
Accounts payable and accrued line costs	6,022	4,844
Other current liabilities	4,005	3,576
Total current liabilities	17,673	9,210
Long-term liabilities, less current portion:		
Long-term debt	17,696	30,038
Deferred tax liability	3,611	4,066
Other liabilities	1,124	576
Total long-term liabilities	22,431	34,680
Commitments and contingencies		
Minority interests	2,592	101
Company obligated mandatorily redeemable and other preferred securities	798	1,993
Shareholders' investment:		
Series B preferred stock, par value $.01 per share; authorized, issued and outstanding: 10,693,437 shares in 2000 and none in 2001 (liquidation preference of $1.00 per share plus unpaid dividends)	—	—
Preferred stock, par value $.01 per share; authorized: 31,155,008 shares in 2000 and 30,967,637 shares in 2001; none issued	—	—
Common stock:		
WorldCom, Inc. common stock, par value $.01 per share; authorized: 5,000,000,000 shares in 2000 and none in 2001; issued and outstanding: 2,887,960,378 shares in 2000 and none in 2001	29	—
WorldCom group common stock, par value $.01 per share; authorized: none in 2000 and 4,850,000,000 shares in 2001; issued and outstanding: none in 2000 and 2,967,436,680 shares in 2001	—	30
MCI group common stock, par value $.01 per share; authorized: none in 2000 and 150,000,000 shares in 2001; issued and outstanding: none in 2000 and 118,595,711 in 2001	—	1
Additional paid-in capital	52,877	54,297
Retained earnings	3,160	4,400
Unrealized holding gain (loss) on marketable equity securities	345	(51)
Cumulative foreign currency translation adjustment	(817)	(562)
Treasury stock, at cost, 6,765,316 shares of WorldCom, Inc. in 2000, 6,765,316 shares of WorldCom group stock and 270,613 shares of MCI group stock in 2001	(185)	(185)
Total shareholders' investment	55,409	57,930
	$ 98,903	$ 103,914

The accompanying notes are an integral part of these statements.

WORLDCOM, INC. AND SUBSIDIARIES
CONSOLIDATED STATEMENTS OF OPERATIONS
(In Millions, Except Per Share Data)

	For the Years Ended December 31,		
	1999	2000	2001
Revenues	$35,908	$39,090	$35,179
Operating expenses:			
Line costs	14,739	15,462	14,739
Selling, general and administrative	8,935	10,597	11,046
Depreciation and amortization	4,354	4,878	5,880
Other charges	(8)	—	—
Total	28,020	30,937	31,665
Operating income	7,888	8,153	3,514
Other income (expense):			
Interest expense	(966)	(970)	(1,533)
Miscellaneous	242	385	412
Income before income taxes, minority interests and cumulative effect of accounting change	7,164	7,568	2,393
Provision for income taxes	2,965	3,025	927
Income before minority interests and cumulative effect of accounting change	4,199	4,543	1,466
Minority interests	(186)	(305)	35
Income before cumulative effect of accounting change	4,013	4,238	1,501
Cumulative effect of accounting change (net of income tax of $50 in 2000)	—	(85)	—
Net income	4,013	4,153	1,501
Distributions on mandatorily redeemable preferred securities and other preferred dividend requirements	72	65	117
Net income applicable to common shareholders	$ 3,941	$ 4,088	$ 1,384
Net income attributed to WorldCom group before cumulative effect of accounting change	$ 2,294	$ 2,608	$ 1,407
Cumulative effect of accounting change	$ —	$ (75)	$ —
Net income attributed to WorldCom group	$ 2,294	$ 2,533	$ 1,407
Net income (loss) attributed to MCI group before cumulative effect of accounting change	$ 1,647	$ 1,565	$ (23)
Cumulative effect of accounting change	$ —	$ (10)	$ —
Net income (loss) attributed to MCI group	$ 1,647	$ 1,555	$ (23)

Earnings (loss) per common share:	Pro Forma		
WorldCom group:			
Net income attributed to WorldCom group before cumulative effect of accounting change:			
Basic	$ 0.81	$ 0.91	$ 0.48
Diluted	$ 0.78	$ 0.90	$ 0.48
Cumulative effect of accounting change	$ —	$ (0.03)	$ —
Net income attributed to WorldCom group:			
Basic	$ 0.81	$ 0.88	$ 0.48
Diluted	$ 0.78	$ 0.87	$ 0.48
MCI group:			
Net income (loss) attributed to MCI group before cumulative effect of accounting change:			
Basic	$ 14.32	$ 13.61	$ (0.20)
Diluted	$ 14.32	$ 13.61	$ (0.20)
Cumulative effect of accounting change	$ —	$ (0.09)	$ —
Net income (loss) attributed to MCI group:			
Basic	$ 14.32	$ 13.52	$ (0.20)
Diluted	$ 14.32	$ 13.52	$ (0.20)

The accompanying notes are an integral part of these statements.

WORLDCOM, INC. AND SUBSIDIARIES
CONSOLIDATED STATEMENTS OF CASH FLOWS
(In Millions)

	For the Years Ended December 31,		
	1999	2000	2001
Cash flows from operating activities:			
Net income	$ 4,013	$ 4,153	$ 1,501
Adjustments to reconcile net income to net cash provided by operating activities:			
Cumulative effect of accounting change	—	85	—
Minority interests	186	305	(35)
Other charges	(8)	—	—
Depreciation and amortization	4,354	4,878	5,880
Provision for deferred income taxes	2,903	1,649	1,104
Change in assets and liabilities, net of effect of business combinations:			
Accounts receivable, net	(875)	(1,126)	281
Other current assets	143	(797)	164
Accounts payable and other current liabilities	692	(1,050)	(1,154)
All other operating activities	(403)	(431)	253
Net cash provided by operating activities	11,005	7,666	7,994
Cash flows from investing activities:			
Capital expenditures	(8,716)	(11,484)	(7,886)
Acquisitions and related costs	(1,078)	(14)	(206)
Increase in intangible assets	(743)	(938)	(694)
Decrease in other liabilities	(650)	(839)	(480)
All other investing activities	1,632	(1,110)	(424)
Net cash used in investing activities	(9,555)	(14,385)	(9,690)
Cash flows from financing activities:			
Principal borrowings (repayments) on debt, net	(2,894)	6,377	3,031
Common stock issuance	886	585	124
Distributions on mandatorily redeemable and other preferred securities and dividends paid on other equity securities	(72)	(65)	(154)
Redemptions of preferred stock	—	(190)	(200)
All other financing activities	—	(84)	(272)
Net cash provided by (used in) financing activities	(2,080)	6,623	2,529
Effect of exchange rate changes on cash	(221)	(19)	38
Net increase (decrease) in cash and cash equivalents	(851)	(115)	871
Cash and cash equivalents at beginning of period	1,727	876	761
Deconsolidation of Embratel	—	—	(216)
Cash and cash equivalents at end of period	$ 876	$ 761	$ 1,416

The accompanying notes are an integral part of these statements.

WORLDCOM, INC. AND SUBSIDIARIES

NOTES TO CONSOLIDATED FINANCIAL STATEMENTS (Continued)

DECEMBER 31, 2001

(1) The Company and Significant Accounting Policies— (Continued)

Our equity in Embratel's loss for 2001 is included in miscellaneous income/(expense) in the accompanying consolidated financial statements.

Fair Value of Financial Instruments:

The fair value of long-term debt and company obligated mandatorily redeemable and other preferred securities is determined based on quoted market rates or the cash flows from such financial instruments discounted at our estimated current interest rate to enter into similar financial instruments. The carrying amounts and fair values of these financial instruments were $25.7 billion and $25.3 billion, respectively, at December 31, 2000 and $32.2 billion and $32.9 billion, respectively, at December 31, 2001. The carrying values for all our other financial instruments approximate their respective fair values.

Cash and Cash Equivalents:

We consider cash in banks and short-term investments with original maturities of three months or less as cash and cash equivalents.

Property and Equipment:

Property and equipment are stated at cost. Depreciation is provided for financial reporting purposes using the straight-line method over the following estimated useful lives:

Transmission equipment (including conduit)	4 to 40 years
Communications equipment	5 to 10 years
Furniture, fixtures, buildings and other	4 to 39 years

We evaluate the recoverability of property and equipment when events and circumstances indicate that such assets might be impaired. We determine impairment by comparing the undiscounted future cash flows estimated to be generated by these assets to their respective carrying amounts. In the event an impairment exists, a loss is recognized based on the amount by which the carrying value exceeds the fair value of the asset. If quoted market prices for an asset are not available, fair market value is determined primarily using the anticipated cash flows discounted at a rate commensurate with the risk involved. Losses on property and equipment to be disposed of are determined in a similar manner, except that fair market values are reduced for the cost to dispose.

Maintenance and repairs are expensed as incurred. Replacements and betterments are capitalized. The cost and related reserves of assets sold or retired are removed from the accounts, and any resulting gain or loss is reflected in results of operations.

We construct certain of our own transmission systems and related facilities. Internal costs directly related to the construction of such facilities, including interest and salaries of certain employees, are capitalized. Such internal costs were $625 million ($339 million in interest), $842 million ($495 million in interest) and $858 million ($498 million in interest) in 1999, 2000 and 2001, respectively.

Dr. Reddy's Laboratories Limited— Research & Development Costs

Dr. Reddy's Laboratories Limited together with its subsidiaries is a leading India-based pharmaceutical company headquartered in Hyderabad, India. The Company's principal areas of operation are formulations, active pharmaceutical ingredients and intermediates, generics, critical care and biotechnology, and drug discovery. The Company's principal research and development and manufacturing facilities are located in Andhra Pradesh, India with marketing facilities in India, Russia, the United States, the United Kingdom and Brazil. The Company's shares trade on several stock exchanges in India and, since April 11, 2001, on the New York Stock Exchange.

Learning Objectives

- Use management's discussion and analysis and other public information to interpret economic events.
- Consider the cost components that underlie research and development expense.
- Compare and evaluate alternative accounting treatments of research and development costs.
- Understand how capitalizing previously expensed costs affects the balance sheet, the income statement, and the statement of cash flows.
- Adjust net income and balance sheet amounts to quantify the accounting effect of capitalizing previously expensed development costs.

Refer to the 2004 financial statements of Dr. Reddy's Laboratories and to the excerpt from Dr. Reddy's Annual Report on Form 20-F, which contains information about the company's research and development (R&D) program. Dr. Reddy's prepares financial statements under Indian GAAP as well as U.S. GAAP. The U.S. GAAP statements follow SFAS No. 2 that requires R&D costs be expensed as they are incurred.

✧ Concepts ✧

a. The 2004 statement of operations shows research and development expenses of Rs 1,991,629 (thousands of Rupees). What types of costs are likely included in these amounts?

b. If Dr. Reddy's followed international GAAP, its R&D accounting would be different. International GAAP is set by the International Accounting Standards Board (IASB) and promulgated through a series of International Accounting Standards (IAS) and International Financial Reporting Standards (IFRS). An excerpt from IAS 38—*Intangible Assets*, pertaining to R&D accounting, is provided.

   In your opinion, which accounting principles provide a better matching of costs and benefits, those of FASB's SFAS No. 2 or the IASB's IAS 38? Explain with particular reference to Dr. Reddy's research program.

✧ Process ✧

c. Provide the journal entry Dr. Reddy's Laboratories made to record 2004 R&D expense. Consider your answer to part *a* in determining which accounts are affected. (*Hint*: you will not be able to allocate specific amounts for each of the credited accounts, but you should be able to identify the accounts that are likely to be credited.)

✧ Analysis ✧

d. Assume that you are a financial analyst. You would like to compare Dr. Reddy's Laboratories to a company that follows IAS 38. As such, you decide to prepare pro-forma (i.e., "as if") information for Dr. Reddy's assuming they follow international GAAP (IAS 38).

   To create the pro-forma information assume the following.

- Consistent with the company's prior drug development strategy, all R&D costs incurred prior to fiscal 2002 were considered "research" costs under IAS 38.
- Beginning in fiscal 2002, 25% of the total R&D expenditures could be considered "development" costs and would be eligible for capitalization under IAS 38.
- Internal forecasts predict that capitalized development costs have an estimated useful life of five years. Had Dr. Reddy's followed IAS 38, they would have amortized the development costs on a straight line basis over five years, beginning the year subsequent to their capitalization.

i. What would Dr. Reddy's Laboratories have reported as Operating Income in 2004, 2003, and 2002 under international GAAP? Comment on the trend. Are there other costs that might benefit from the same sort of pro-forma analysis?

ii. What gross asset amount for deferred development costs would be shown on the balance sheet at the end of each of the three years under international GAAP? What would the accumulated amortization be in each of the three years? What would the net asset be at the end of each year?

iii. How would cash be affected for fiscal 2004 if Dr. Reddy's Laboratories followed international GAAP? Would the cash flow statement be different?

e. Refer to the accompanying article, "Dr. Reddy's loses US patent court challenge." The article appeared in the March 2, 2004 issue of *The Financial Times*. If Dr. Reddy's Laboratories had followed IAS 38, what effect would the U.S. court decision have had on the fiscal 2004 financial statements?

f. Of late, the accounting for intangibles such as research and development has come under fire. Some people claim that current U.S. GAAP is deficient in measuring what they argue to be the United States' most important asset: knowledge. Comment on that position in light of the analyses you just completed.

DR. REDDY'S LABORATORIES LIMITED

EXCERPT FROM ANNUAL REPORT ON FORM 20-F
Year Ended March 31, 2004

Strategy

Our vision is to build a discovery-led global pharmaceutical company, with a strong pipeline of generics as well as innovative products. Our core businesses of active pharmaceutical ingredients and intermediates and formulations are well established with a track record of growth and profitability. In our generics business, we have built a pipeline of products that will help us drive growth in the medium-term. In addition, we are focusing our investments on innovation led businesses, including specialty pharmaceuticals and drug discovery. These businesses, while being investment intensive and with long lead times, have the potential to provide significant growth as well as sustained revenues and profitability for much longer periods due to patent protected franchises. As a result, we believe that, over the next few years, our fully established core businesses will fund the growth of our generics business and the establishment of our innovation businesses.

Research and Development

Our research and development activities can be classified into several categories, which rum (sic) parallel to the activities in our principal areas of operations:

- Formulations, where our research and development activities are directed at the development of product formulations, process validation, bioequivalency testing and other data needed to prepare a growing list of drugs that are equivalent to numerous brand name products for sale in the emerging markets.
- Active pharmaceutical ingredients and intermediates, where our research and development activities concentrate on development of chemical processes for the synthesis of active pharmaceutical ingredients for use in our generics and formulations segments and for sales in the emerging and developed markets to third parties.
- Generics, where our research and development activities are directed at the development of product formulations, process validation, bioequivalency testing and other data needed to prepare a growing list of drugs that are equivalent to numerous brand name products whose patents and regulatory exclusivity periods have expired or are nearing expiration in the regulated markets of the United States and Europe.

  During fiscal 2004, we integrated the product development capabilities in our API, generics and formulations segments to increase our focus on productivity and product delivery, by combining technical excellence with process excellence. We also strengthened our technical, intellectual property and legal skills to enhance our new product development process. This will help us leverage our core technology strengths in chemistry and formulation development with legal, regulatory and intellectual property management expertise to expand our product pipeline.
- Critical care and biotechnology, where research and development activities are directed at the development of oncology and biotechnology products for the emerging as well as regulated markets.
- Custom pharmaceuticals, where we intend to leverage the strength of our process chemistry skills to cater to the niche segment of the specialty chemical industry targeting innovator pharmaceutical companies. The research and development is directed toward supporting the business to focus on marketing of process development and manufacturing services to emerging and established pharmaceutical companies.
- Drug discovery, where we are actively pursuing discovery and development of NCEs. Our research programs focus on the following therapeutic areas:
  - Metabolic disorders
  - Cardiovascular disorders
  - Cancer
  - Bacterial infections

We are pursuing an integrated research strategy with our laboratories in the U.S. focusing on discovery of new molecular targets and designing of screening assays to screen for promising lead molecules. Discovery is followed by selection and optimization of lead molecules and further clinical development of those optimized leads at our laboratories in India.

FT FINANCIAL TIMES
World business newspaper

2 March 2004 20

COMPANIES INTERNATIONAL PHARMACEUTICALS

Dr Reddy's loses US patent court challenge

By DAVID FIRN and KHOZEM MERCHANT

Dr Reddy's, the Indian drugs manufacturer, yesterday saw a fifth of its market value wiped out after a significant setback on a patent challenge in a US court.

The company's share price finished 18 per cent weaker at a two-year low and its capitalisation lighter by about $400m as India's leading patent-challenger said it would develop more speciality drugs despite the blow to its version of Pfizer's blockbuster drug Norvasc.

On Friday a US court overturned a lower-court judgment allowing Dr Reddy's to sell AmVaz, its version of Norvasc, a hypertension treatment that generates global revenues in excess of $2bn a year for Pfizer.

Dr Reddy's, India's second-largest drugs manufacturer, with sales of $380m in the year to March 2003, said it was "very disappointed" with the majority verdict that effectively brings to a halt its most ambitious drugs project. It had spent $10m developing AmVaz.

Dr Reddy's wants to develop value-added medicines to ease its dependency on generics, the bedrock of India's $6bn drugs industry.

AmVaz was the company's first foray into what Dr Reddy's calls speciality drugs but the strategy depended on persuading a US court that it was a genuinely new drug, not simply a slightly altered version of Norvasc.

Dr Reddy's has filed a second application on a new drug with US regulators, which should be decided in a year's time. But the company says future development will be based on drugs innovation rather than exploiting regulatory loopholes.

"This was a risky option but one we hope to mitigate by building our portfolio of speciality drugs," the company said.

A ruling in favour of Dr Reddy's would have had industry-wide implications.

"By using Pfizer's early experimental data, Dr Reddy's has been able to show bio-equivalence with a different salt of amlodipine (a chemical compound used for treating hypertension)," said Morgan Stanley in a report published before the court judgment.

"This could set a precedent for future new drug filings for alternative 'salt' versions of drugs."

Additional reporting by David Firn in London

Internally Generated Intangible Assets (excerpt from IAS 38—*Intangible Assets*)

39. It is sometimes difficult to assess whether an internally generated intangible asset qualifies for recognition. It is often difficult to:
    (a) identify whether, and the point of time when, there is an identifiable asset that will generate probable future economic benefits; and
    (b) determine the cost of the asset reliably. In some cases, the cost of generating an intangible asset internally cannot be distinguished from the cost of maintaining or enhancing the enterprise's internally generated goodwill or of running day-to-day operations.

    Therefore, in addition to complying with the general requirements for the recognition and initial measurement of an intangible asset, an enterprise applies the requirements and guidance in paragraphs 40-55 below to all internally generated intangible assets.

40. To assess whether an internally generated intangible asset meets the criteria for recognition, an enterprise classifies the generation of the asset into:
    (a) a research phase; and
    (b) a development phase.

    Although the terms 'research' and 'development' are defined, the terms 'research phase' and 'development phase' have a broader meaning for the purpose of this Standard.

41. If an enterprise cannot distinguish the research phase from the development phase of an internal project to create an intangible asset, the enterprise treats the expenditure on that project as if it were incurred in the research phase only.

Research Phase

42. No intangible asset arising from research (or from the research phase of an internal project) should be recognized. Expenditure on research (or on the research phase of an internal project) should be recognized as an expense when it is incurred.

43. This Standard takes the view that, in the research phase of a project, an enterprise cannot demonstrate that an intangible asset exists that will generate probable future economic benefits. Therefore, this expenditure is always recognized as an expense when it is incurred.

44. Examples of research activities are:
    (a) activities aimed at obtaining new knowledge;
    (b) the search for, evaluation and final selection of, applications of research findings or other knowledge;
    (c) the search for alternatives for materials, devices, products, processes, systems or services; and
    (d) the formulation, design, evaluation and final selection of possible alternatives for new or improved materials, devices, products, processes, systems or services.

Development Phase

45. An intangible asset arising from development (or from the development phase of an internal project) should be recognized if, and only if, an enterprise can demonstrate all of the following:
    (a) the technical feasibility of completing the intangible asset so that it will be available for use or sale;
    (b) its intention to complete the intangible asset and use or sell it;
    (c) its ability to use or sell the intangible asset;
    (d) how the intangible asset will generate probable future economic benefits. Among other things, the enterprise should demonstrate the existence of a market for the output of the intangible asset or the intangible asset itself or, if it is to be used internally, the usefulness of the intangible asset;
    (e) the availability of adequate technical, financial and other resources to complete the development and to use or sell the intangible asset; and
    (f) its ability to measure the expenditure the expenditure attributable to the intangible asset during its development reliably.

46. In the development phase of a project, an enterprise can, in some instances, identify an intangible asset and demonstrate that the asset will generate probable future economic benefits. This is because the development phase of a project is further advanced than the research phase.

47. Examples of development activities are:
    (a) the design, construction and testing or pre-production or pre-use prototypes and models;
    (b) the design of tools, jigs, moulds and dies involving new technology;
    (c) the design, construction and operation of a pilot plant that is not of a scale economically feasible for commercial production; and
    (d) the design, construction and testing of a chosen alternative for new or improved materials, devices, products, processes, systems or services.

Report of Independent Registered Public Accounting Firm

The Board of Directors and Stockholders
Dr. Reddy's Laboratories Limited

We have audited the accompanying consolidated balance sheets of Dr. Reddy's Laboratories Limited and subsidiaries as at March 31, 2004 and 2003, and the related consolidated statements of operations, stockholders' equity and comprehensive income, and cash flows for each of the years in the three-year period ended March 31, 2004. These consolidated financial statements are the responsibility of the Company's management. Our responsibility is to express an opinion on these consolidated financial statements based on our audits.

We conducted our audits in accordance with the standards of the Public Company Accounting Oversight Board (United States). Those standards require that we plan and perform the audit to obtain reasonable assurance about whether the financial statements are free of material misstatement. An audit includes examining, on a test basis, evidence supporting the amounts and disclosures in the financial statements. An audit also includes assessing the accounting principles used and significant estimates made by management, as well as evaluating the overall financial statement presentation. We believe that our audits provide a reasonable basis for our opinion.

In our opinion, the consolidated financial statements referred to above present fairly, in all material respects, the financial position of Dr. Reddy's Laboratories Limited and subsidiaries as at March 31, 2004 and 2003, and the results of their operations and their cash flows for each of the years in the three-year period ended March 31, 2004, in conformity with U.S. generally accepted accounting principles.

As discussed in Note 4 to the consolidated financial statements, effective April 1, 2002, the Company adopted the provisions of Statement of Financial Accounting Standards (SFAS) No. 142, Goodwill and Other Intangible Assets. As discussed in Note 2(q) to the consolidated financial statements, effective April 1, 2003, the Company changed its method of accounting for stock-based employee compensation.

KPMG LLP
Manchester, United Kingdom
May 28, 2004

DR. REDDY'S LABORATORIES LIMITED AND SUBSIDIARIES
CONSOLIDATED BALANCE SHEETS
(in thousands, except share data)

	As of March 31,		
	2003	2004	2004 Convenience translation into U.S.$ (unaudited)
ASSETS			
Current assets:			
Cash and cash equivalents	Rs.7,273,398	Rs.4,376,235	U.S.$100,835
Investment securities	-	2,536,223	58,438
Restricted cash	26,709	107,170	2,469
Accounts receivable, net of allowances	3,620,020	3,730,139	85,948
Inventories	2,781,384	3,031,651	69,854
Deferred income taxes	166,510	152,220	3,507
Due from related parties	22,863	22,437	517
Other current assets	1,235,999	1,712,864	39,467
Total current assets	15,126,883	15,668,939	361,035
Property, plant and equipment, net	4,830,480	6,331,135	145,879
Due from related parties	44,047	21,019	484
Investment securities	8,715	1,563,875	36,034
Investment in affiliates	170,184	279,182	6,433
Goodwill and intangible assets	2,867,567	2,665,620	61,420
Other assets	43,791	89,533	2,063
Total assets	Rs.23,091,667	Rs.26,619,303	U.S.$613,348
LIABILITIES AND STOCKHOLDERS' EQUITY			
Current liabilities:			
Borrowings from banks	Rs.146,340	Rs.320,582	U.S.$ 7,387
Current portion of long-term debt	143,801	152,658	3,517
Trade accounts payable	1,685,382	2,174,295	50,099
Due to related parties	4,388	201,170	4,635
Accrued expenses	769,895	1,244,082	28,665
Other current liabilities	353,606	472,888	10,896
Total current liabilities	3,103,412	4,565,675	105,200
Long-term debt, excluding current portion	40,909	31,065	716
Deferred revenue	288,382	288,382	6,645
Deferred income taxes	700,274	571,558	13,170
Other liabilities	126,849	123,265	2,840
Total liabilities	Rs.4,259,826	Rs.5,579,945	U.S.$128,570
Stockholders' equity:			
Equity shares at Rs.5 par value; 100,000,000 shares authorized; Issued and outstanding; 76,515,948 shares and 76,518,949 shares as of March 31, 2003 and 2004 respectively	Rs.382,580	Rs.382,595	U.S.$8,816
Additional paid-in capital	10,085,004	10,089,152	232,469
Equity-options outstanding	135,694	256,748	5,916
Retained earnings	8,187,117	10,229,672	235,707
Equity shares held by a controlled trust: 41,400 shares	(4,882)	(4,882)	(112)
Accumulated other comprehensive income	46,328	86,073	1,983
Total stockholders' equity	18,831,841	21,039,358	484,778
Total liabilities and stockholders' equity	Rs.23,091,667	Rs.26,619,303	U.S.$613,348

See accompanying notes to the consolidated financial statements.

DR. REDDY'S LABORATORIES LIMITED AND SUBSIDIARIES
CONSOLIDATED STATEMENTS OF OPERATION
(in thousands, except share data)

	Year ended March 31,			
	2002	**2003**	**2004**	**2004** Convenience translation into U.S.$ **(unaudited)**
Revenues:				
Product sales, net of allowances for sales returns (includes excise duties of Rs.789,718, Rs.817,135 and Rs.870,079 for the years ended March 31, 2002, 2003 and 2004, respectively)	Rs.16,408,797	Rs.18,069,812	Rs.20,081,249	U.S.$462,702
License fees	124,757	-	-	-
Services	89,128	-	-	-
	16,622,682	18,069,812	20,081,249	462,702
Cost of revenues	6,868,958	7,847,573	9,346,117	215,348
Gross profit	9,753,724	10,222,239	10,735,132	247,353
Operating expenses:				
Selling, general and administrative expenses	3,674,058	5,103,213	6,562,856	151,218
Research and development expenses	742,384	1,411,838	1,991,629	45,890
Amortization expenses	487,715	419,439	382,857	8,822
Foreign exchange (gain)/loss	(208,965)	70,108	(282,419)	(6,507)
Total operating expenses	4,695,192	7,004,598	8,654,923	199,422
Operating income	5,058,532	3,217,641	2,080,209	47,931
Equity in loss of affiliates	(130,534)	(92,094)	(44,362)	(1,022)
Other (expense)/income, net	154,480	683,124	504,191	11,617
Income before income taxes and minority interest	5,082,478	3,808,671	2,540,038	58,526
Income taxes	(153,844)	(398,062)	(69,249)	(1,596)
Minority interest	(14,803)	(6,734)	3,364	78
Net income	Rs.4,913,831	Rs.3,403,875	Rs.2,474,153	U.S.$57,008
Earnings per equity share				
Basic	64.63	44.49	32.34	0.75
Diluted	64.53	44.49	32.32	0.75
Weighted average number of equity shares used in computing earnings per equity share				
Basic	76,027,565	76,515,948	76,513,764	76,513,764
Diluted	76,149,568	76,515,948	76,549,598	76,549,598

See accompanying notes to the consolidated financial statements.

DR. REDDY'S LABORATORIES LIMITED AND SUBSIDIARIES
CONSOLIDATED STATEMENT OF STOCKHOLDERS' EQUITY AND COMPREHENSIVE INCOME
(in thousands, except share data)

	Equity Shares				Equity Shares held by a Controlled Trust					
	No. of shares	Amount	Additional Paid In Capital	Comprehensive Income	No. of Shares	Amount	Accumulated Other Comprehensive Income	Equity – Options Outstanding	Retained Earnings/ (Accumulated Deficit)	Total Stockholders' Equity
Balance as of March 31, 2001	63,177,560	315,889	4,296,154		41,400	(4,882)	6,166		627,137	5,240,464
Dividends	-	-	-	-	-	-	-	-	(561,676)	(561,676)
Common stock issued for ADS listing	13,225,000	66,125	5,716,600	-	-	-	-	-	-	5,782,725
Common stock issued for acquisition of minority interest	113,388	566	72,250	-	-	-	-	-	-	72,816
Comprehensive income	-	-	-		-	-	-	-	-	-
Net income	-	-	-	Rs.4,913,831	-	-	-	-	4,913,831	4,913,831
Translation adjustment	-	-	-	2,337	-	-	2,337	-	-	2,337
Unrealized gain on investments, net	-	-	-	(276)	-	-	(276)	-	-	(276)
Comprehensive income	-	-	-	Rs.4,915,892	-	-	-	-	-	-
Application of SFAS 123	-	-	-		-	-	-	7,211	-	7,211
Balance as of March 31, 2002	76,515,948	Rs.382,580	Rs.10,085,004		41,400	Rs.(4,882)	Rs.8,227	Rs.7,211	Rs.4,979,292	Rs.15,457,432
Dividends	-	-	-	-	-	-	-		(191,290)	(191,290)
Net loss for the quarter ended March 31, 2003 for the change in the fiscal year end of a consolidated subsidiary	-	-	-	-	-	-	-	-	(4,760)	(4,760)
Comprehensive income	-	-	-	-	-	-	-	-	-	
Net income	-	-	-	Rs.3,403,875	-	-	-	-	3,403,875	3,403,875
Translation adjustment	-	-	-	38,073	-	-	38,073	-	-	38,073
Unrealized gain on investments, net	-	-	-	28	-	-	28	-	-	28
Comprehensive income	-	-	-	Rs.3,441,976	-	-	-	-	-	-
Application of SFAS 123	-	-	-		-	-	-	128,483	-	128,483
Balance as of March 31, 2003	76,515,948	Rs.382,580	Rs.10,085,004	-	41,400	Rs.(4,882)	Rs.46,328	Rs.135,694	Rs.8,187,117	Rs.18,831,841
Issuance of equity shares on exercise of options	3,001	15	4,148	-				(1,123)		3,040
Dividends	-	-	-	-	-	-	-	-	(431,598)	(431,598)
Comprehensive income	-	-	-	-	-	-	-	-		
Net income	-	-	-	Rs.2,474,153	-	-	-	-	2,474,153	2,474,153
Translation adjustment	-	-	-	24,725	-	-	24,725	-		24,725
Unrealized gain on investments, net	-	-	-	15,020	-	-	15,020	-	-	15,020
Comprehensive income	-	-	-	Rs.2,513,898	-	-	-	-	-	-
Application of SFAS 123	-	-	-		-	-	-	122,177	-	122,177
Balance as of March 31,2004	76,518,949	Rs.382,595	Rs.10,089,152		41,400	Rs.(4,882)	Rs.86,073	Rs.256,748	Rs.10,229,672	Rs.21,039,358
Convenience translation into U.S.$		U.S.$ 8,816	U.S.$ 232,469			U.S.$ (112)	U.S.$ 1,983	U.S.$ 5,916	U.S.$ 235,707	U.S.$ 484,778

See accompanying notes to the consolidated financial statements.

DR. REDDY'S LABORATORIES LIMITED AND SUBSIDIARIES
CONSOLIDATED STATEMENTS OF CASH FLOWS
(in thousands, except share data)

	Year ended March 31,			
	2002	2003	2004	2004 Convenience translation into U.S.$ (unaudited)
Cash flows from operating activities:				
Net income	Rs.4,913,831	Rs.3,403,875	Rs.2,474,153	U.S.$ 57,008
Adjustments to reconcile net income to net cash from operating activities:				
Deferred tax expense/(benefit)	(268,589)	547	(134,867)	(3,108)
Gain on sale of investments	(19,420)	(6,284)	(24,786)	(571)
Depreciation and amortization	946,280	1,017,813	1,128,453	26,001
Loss on sale of property, plant and equipment	27,050	248	29,319	676
Provision for doubtful accounts receivable	78,700	93,883	19,871	458
Allowance for sales returns	92,130	193,229	169,511	3,906
Inventory write-downs.	103,141	34,239	31,898	735
Equity in loss of affiliates.	130,534	92,094	44,362	1,022
Write-down of investment.	8,209	1,679	-	-
Unrealised exchange (gain)/loss	(81,926)	79,947	(109,602)	(2,525)
Employees stock based compensation	7,211	128,483	147,730	3,404
Loss on sale of subsidiary interest	-	-	58,473	1,347
Minority interest	14,803	6,734	(3,364)	(78)
Changes in operating assets and liabilities:				
Accounts receivable	(1,451,643)	159,697	(379,413)	(8,742)
Inventories	(365,088)	(440,856)	(335,092)	(7,721)
Other assets	(180,960)	(665,278)	(276,467)	(6,370)
Due to / from related parties,net	(11,791)	5,997	148,576	3,423
Trade accounts payable	364,260	584,958	690,182	15,903
Accrued expenses	310,669	66,357	485,215	11,180
Deferred revenue	218,569	-	-	-
Taxes payable	(64,445)	(113,903)	(115,375)	(2,658)
Other liabilities	(118,740)	(276,727)	(49,547)	(1,142)
Net cash provided by operating activities	4,652,785	4,366,732	3,999,230	92,148
Cash flows from investing activities:				
Restricted cash	(6,515)	(1,524)	(67,221)	(1,549)
Expenditure on property, plant and equipment	(1,090,321)	(1,515,721)	(2,415,638)	(55,660)
Proceeds from sale of property, plant and equipment	49,301	4,311	33,558	773
Purchase of investment securities	(2,450,648)	(2,933,474)	(13,241,973)	(305,115)
Proceeds from sale of investment securities	2,363,680	2,939,603	9,167,150	211,225
Expenditure on intangible assets	(398,440)	(96,999)	(53,942)	(1,243)
Acquisition of minority interest	-	(3,208)	-	-
Proceeds from sale of subsidiary, net	-	-	81,464	1,877
Cash paid for acquisition, net of cash acquired	-	(347,684)	(9,453)	(218)
Net cash used in investing activities	(1,532,943)	(1,954,696)	(6,506,055)	(149,909)
Cash flows from financing activities:				
Proceeds from issuance of equity, net of expenses	5,782,725	-	3,040	70
Proceeds from issuance of equity, in subsidiary	-	-	2,435	56
Purchase of treasury stock	-	-	(115,990)	(2,673)
Proceeds from/(repayments of) borrowing from banks, net	(2,469,761)	43,700	184,519	4,252
Proceeds from issuance of long-term debt	6,141	1,009	-	-
Repayment of long-term debt	(1,335,546)	(6,440)	(11,072)	(255)
Principal payments under capital lease obligations	(109)	-	-	-
Dividends	(561,676)	(191,290)	(431,598)	(9,945)
Principal payments of short term loan	-	-	(7,448)	(172)
Net cash provided by/(used in) financing activities	1,421,774	(153,021)	(376,114)	(8,666)
Effect of exchange rate changes on cash	88,779	(94,991)	(14,224)	(328)
Net increase / (decrease) in cash and cash equivalents during the year	4,630,395	2,164,024	(2,897,163)	(66,755)
Cash and cash equivalents at the beginning of the year	478,979	5,109,374	7,273,398	167,590
Cash and cash equivalents at the end of the year	Rs.5,109,374	Rs.7,273,398	Rs.4,376,235	U.S.$ 100,835

BASF Group—Contingencies and Provisions

BASF is a world leader in the chemical industry. Its product line comprises high-value-added chemicals, plastics, colorants and pigments, dispersions, automotive and industrial coatings, crop-protection agents, fine chemicals, oil and gas. BASF's 93,000 employees operate production facilities in 38 countries and maintain contact with customers in more than 170 nations. The integrated network principle, the "Verbund," is instrumental in BASF's success. At Verbund sites, plants are integrated with each other. This translates into a more efficient and resource-saving utilization of raw materials and energy in all chemical processes. The synergistic effects in the Verbund are designed to help save the environment and save money as well. The BASF Group encompasses BASF Aktiengesellschaft with its parent plant in Ludwigshafen, Germany as well as 164 wholly-owned subsidiaries and six joint ventures. The consolidated financial statements also include 28 affiliated and associated companies whose equity capital is consolidated on a proportional basis. (BASF stands for Badische Anilin & Soda Fabrik.)

Learning Objectives

- Gain familiarity with environmental matters and accounting for contingencies.
- Read and interpret footnotes and management's discussion and analysis pertaining to environmental matters.
- Analyze environmental liability accounts and evaluate compliance with generally accepted accounting principles for contingencies.

Refer to the 2002 BASF financial statements and selected footnotes.

✧ Concepts ✧

a. In your own words, define "contingent liability."

b. Under U.S. GAAP and International Accounting Standards, when are contingent liabilities recorded?

c. Consider the balance sheet item "Other Provisions."

   i. What proportion of BASF's 2002 balance sheet is comprised of "Other Provisions"?

   ii. What do these "Other provisions" comprise?

✧ Process ✧

d. Consider the component of "Other Provisions" labeled "Environmental protection and remediation costs" (see note 24). According to note 1-c, Summary of significant accounting policies:

   Environmental expenditures that relate to an existing condition caused by past operations and prescribed by current legal requirements that do not have future economic benefit are expensed. Liabilities for these expenditures are recorded on an undiscounted basis when environmental assessments or clean-ups are probable, the costs can be reasonably estimated and no future economic benefit is expected. Provisions for required recultivation associated with oil and gas operations, especially the filling of wells and clearance of oilfields, or the operation of landfill sites are built up in installments over their expected service lives.

   i. Assume that at December 31, 2001, BASF was completely accurate in its estimate of environmental provisions that would be paid in 2002. Provide the journal entry the company would have made for these payments. Assume there was a single cash payment.

   ii. Again assuming complete accuracy at December 31, 2001, provide the adjusting journal entry necessary to arrive at the December 31, 2002 balance for Environmental protection and remediation costs.

iii. If BASF paid €100 million for environmental liabilities in 2002, what adjusting journal entry is required to arrive at the December 31, 2002 balance for Environmental protection and remediation costs?

iv. Discuss the challenges management faces in estimating such provisions.

e. Consider the component of "Other Provisions" labeled "Legal, damage claims, guarantees and related commitments."

i. Using the information in note 24, what expense did BASF record in 2002 for violations of antitrust laws and other litigation in the company's vitamin business?

ii. Using the information in note 24, estimate the amount BASF paid in 2002 for legal, damage claims, guarantees and related commitments.

✧ Analysis ✧

f. Consider the component of "Other Provisions" labeled "Maintenance and repair costs." According to note 1-c, Summary of significant accounting policies:

Other provisions are recorded for the expected amounts of contingent liabilities and probable losses from pending transactions. Maintenance provisions are established to cover omitted maintenance procedures as of the end of the year, expected to be incurred within the first three months of the following year. The amount provided is based on reasonable commercial judgment.

In addition, provisions are accrued in installments for regular shutdowns within prescribed intervals of certain large-scale plants as required by technical surveillance authorities. Provisions are accrued in the amount of the expected costs of the measures without costs for shutdown and lost earnings until the next scheduled shutdown.

i. The International Accounting Standards Board defines a liability as "a present obligation of the enterprise arising from past events, the settlement of which is expected to result in an outflow from the enterprise of resources embodying economic benefits." Do BASF's maintenance provisions meet this definition? Do the shutdown costs associated with activities mandated by the technical surveillance authorities meet this definition? Why or why not?

ii. If BASF management was compensated, in part, based on reported financial performance, what incentives would they have to strategically manage the "Maintenance and repair costs" provision? What forces exist to keep management from acting on those incentives?

BASF Group Consolidated Financial Statements and Notes

Consolidated Statements of Income
Year ended December 31

Million €	Explanations in Note	2002	2001
Sales		32,519.0	32,768.0
– Natural gas taxes		303.5	268.4
Sales, net of natural gas taxes	(5)	**32,215.5**	**32,499.6**
Cost of sales		21,815.5	22,187.8
Gross profit on sales		**10,400.0**	**10,311.8**
Selling expenses		4,763.9	5,143.6
General and administrative expenses		700.4	659.3
Research and development expenses		1,135.3	1,247.1
Other operating income	(6)	716.0	881.5
Other operating expenses	(7)	1,875.7	2,926.4
Income from operations		**2,640.7**	**1,216.9**
Expense/income from financial assets		123.8	(209.3)
Write-downs of, and losses from, retirement of financial assets as well as securities held as current assets		31.2	22.7
Interest result		(92.4)	(376.2)
Financial result	(8)	**0.2**	**(608.2)**
Income from ordinary activities		**2,640.9**	**608.7**
Extraordinary income	(9)	–	6,120.8
Income before taxes and minority interests		**2,640.9**	**6,729.5**
Effect of the change in accounting principles for deferred taxes	(2)	–	50.6
Income taxes	(10)	1,042.2	954.5
Income before minority interests		**1,598.7**	**5,825.6**
Minority interests	(11)	94.3	(32.6)
Net income		**1,504.4**	**5,858.2**
Earnings per share (€)		**2.60**	**9.72**

Consolidated Balance Sheets at December 31

Assets Million €	Explanations in Note	2002	2001
Intangible assets	(13)	3,464.6	3,942.7
Property, plant and equipment	(14)	13,744.7	14,189.8
Financial assets	(15)	3,248.9	3,360.7
Fixed assets		**20,458.2**	**21,493.2**
Inventories	(16)	4,798.4	5,006.8
Accounts receivable, trade		5,316.0	5,875.5
Receivables from affiliated companies		544.4	631.9
Miscellaneous receivables and other assets		1,786.9	1,531.7
Receivables and other assets	(17)	**7,647.3**	**8,039.1**
Marketable securities	(18)	131.8	382.9
Cash and cash equivalents		230.6	359.9
Liquid funds		**362.4**	**742.8**
Current assets		**12,808.1**	**13,788.7**
Deferred taxes	(10)	**1,204.2**	**1,372.5**
Prepaid expenses	(19)	**615.3**	**220.6**
Total assets		**35,085.8**	**36,875.0**

Stockholders' equity and liabilities Million €	Explanations in Note	2002	2001
Subscribed capital	(20)	1,460.0	1,493.5
Capital surplus	(20)	2,947.4	2,913.9
Retained earnings	(21)	12,468.2	12,222.4
Currency translation adjustment		(329.7)	532.3
Minority interests	(22)	396.3	359.7
Stockholders' equity		**16,942.2**	**17,521.8**
Provisions for pensions and similar obligations	(23)	3,910.0	3,952.7
Provisions for taxes		976.0	618.7
Other provisions	(24)	4,111.3	5,569.6
Provisions		**8,997.3**	**10,141.0**
Bonds and other liabilities to capital market	(25)	2,181.7	1,592.5
Liabilities to credit institutions	(25)	1,428.7	1,242.5
Accounts payable, trade		2,344.0	2,467.0
Liabilities to affiliated companies		547.8	572.6
Miscellaneous liabilities	(25)	2,274.3	2,986.2
Liabilities		**8,776.5**	**8,860.8**
Deferred income		**369.8**	**351.4**
Total stockholders' equity and liabilities		**35,085.8**	**36,875.0**

Consolidated Statements of Changes in Stockholders' Equity Year Ended December 31

Million €	Number of subscribed shares outstanding	Subscribed capital	Capital surplus	Retained earnings	Currency translation adjustment	Minority interests	Total stockholders' equity
January 1, 2002	**583,401,370**	**1,493.5**	**2,913.9**	**12,222.4**	**532.3**	**359.7**	**17,521.8**
Share buy-back and cancellation of own shares including own shares intended to be cancelled	(13,085,000)	(33.5)	33.5	(499.8)			(499.8)
Issuance of new stock as conditional capital through the exercise of conversion rights of former Wintershall stockholders	40						
Dividends paid				(758.4)		(85.0)*	(843.4)
Net income				1,504.4		94.3	1,598.7
(Decrease)/increase of foreign currency translation adjustments					(862.0)	(10.6)	(872.6)
Capital injection by minority interests						38.3	38.3
Changes in scope of consolidation and other changes				(0.4)		(0.4)	(0.8)
December 31, 2002	**570,316,410**	**1,460.0**	**2,947.4**	**12,468.2**	**(329.7)**	**396.3**	**16,942.2**
January 1, 2001	**607,399,370**	**1,554.9**	**2,745.7**	**8,851.1**	**661.8**	**481.3**	**14,294.8**
Issuance of new shares from conditional capital through the exercise of warrants attached to the 1986/2001 3% U.S. Dollar Option Bond of BASF Finance Europe N.V.	6,777,000	17.4	89.4				106.8
Share buy-back and cancellation of own shares including own shares intended to be cancelled	(30,775,000)	(78.8)	78.8	(1,299.5)			(1,299.5)
Dividends paid				(1,214.1)		(52.2)*	(1,266.3)
Net income				5,858.2		(32.6)	5,825.6
(Decrease)/increase of foreign currency translation adjustments					(129.5)		(129.5)
Capital injection by minority interests						68.8	68.8
Changes in scope of consolidation and other changes				26.7		(105.6)	(78.9)
December 31, 2001	**583,401,370**	**1,493.5**	**2,913.9**	**12,222.4**	**532.3**	**359.7**	**17,521.8**

* Profit and loss transfers to minority interests

Consolidated Statements of Cash Flows* Year Ended December 31

Million €		2002	2001
Net income (excluding extraordinary income)		1,504.4	(117.6)
Depreciation and amortization of fixed assets		2,501.6	2,933.1
Changes in pension provisions, prepaid pension assets and other non-cash items		(334.0)	260.1
(Gains) losses from disposal of fixed assets		(326.2)	(74.0)
Changes in inventories		(207.4)	100.3
Changes in receivables		(10.8)	(216.8)
Changes in other operating liabilities and provisions		(814.6)	(566.4)
Cash provided by operating activities	(12)	**2,313.0**	**2,318.7**
Additions to tangible and intangible fixed assets		(2,410.4)	(2,810.6)
Additions to financial assets and securities		(391.5)	(740.5)
Payments related to acquisitions		(267.2)	(461.3)
Proceeds from divestitures		5.4	7,503.4
Proceeds from the disposal of fixed assets and securities		899.8	628.6
Cash provided by (used in) investing activities		**(2,163.9)**	**4,119.6**
Proceeds from capital increases		38.3	175.5
Share repurchase		(499.8)	(1,299.4)
Proceeds from the addition of financial indebtedness		3,127.8	1,779.5
Repayment of financial indebtedness		(2,088.0)	(6,071.9)
Dividends paid			
To shareholders of BASF Aktiengesellschaft		(758.4)	(1,214.1)
To minority shareholders		(85.0)	(52.2)
Cash provided by (used in) financing activities		**(265.1)**	**(6,682.6)**
Net change in cash and cash equivalents		**(116.0)**	**(244.3)**
Effects on cash and cash equivalents			
From foreign exchange rates		(13.6)	3.7
From changes in scope of consolidation		0.3	95.0
Cash and cash equivalents as of beginning of year		**359.9**	**505.5**
Cash and cash equivalents as of end of year		**230.6**	**359.9**
Marketable securities		131.8	382.9
Liquid funds as shown on the balance sheet		**362.4**	**742.8**

* The statements of cash flows are discussed in detail in Management's Analysis "Liquidity and Capital Resources" on page 52 ff.

For other information regarding Consolidated Statements of Cash Flows see explanations in Note 12.

24. Other provisions

Million €	2002	Thereof current	2001	Thereof current
Oil and gas production	478.8	–	368.3	–
Environmental protection and remediation costs	264.0	30.2	309.1	44.3
Personnel costs	1,284.2	818.9	1,247.0	836.2
Sales and purchase risks	651.3	647.8	841.1	833.9
Integration, shutdown and restructuring costs	245.3	210.3	421.4	359.4
Legal, damage claims, guarantees and related commitments	679.4	115.2	1,873.0	426.2
Maintenance and repair costs	148.8	93.4	91.0	26.8
Outstanding billings from suppliers	76.4	76.4	87.1	87.1
Other	283.1	204.3	331.6	242.5
	4,111.3	**2,196.5**	**5,569.6**	**2,856.4**

Oil and gas production: Accrued costs for filling of wells and the removal of production equipment after the end of production are accumulated by installments during the expected production period.

Environmental protection and remediation costs: Expected costs for rehabilitating contaminated sites, water protection, recultivating landfills, removal of environmental contamination at existing production or warehouse equipment and other measures.

Personnel costs: The personnel cost provision includes obligations to grant long-time service bonuses and anniversary payments, remaining vacation pay, variable compensation including related social security contributions and other accruals as well as provisions for early retirement and short-working programs for employees nearing retirement. German BASF companies have various programs that entitle employees who are at least 55 years old to reduce their working hours to 50 % for up to six years. Under such arrangements, employees generally work full time during the first half of the transition period and leave the Company at the start of the second period. Employees receive a minimum 85 % of their net salary throughout the transition period.

Sales and purchase risks: The sales and purchase risks provision includes warranties, product liability, customer rebates, payment discounts and other price reductions, sales commissions and provisions for expected losses on committed purchases or similar obligations.

Integration, shutdown and restructuring costs: Such provisions include severance payments to employees as well as specific site shutdown or restructuring costs, including the costs for demolition and similar measures.

The movement in shutdown and restructuring provisions is as follows:

2002 Million €	Amount accrued as of January 1, 2002	Amount paid in 2002	Other changes 2002	Amount accrued as of December 31, 2002
Severance	237.3	105.4	28.5	160.4
Plant closure and demolition	121.0	58.6	15.2	77.6
Other	63.1	24.0	(31.8)	7.3
	421.4	**188.0**	**11.9**	**245.3**

2001 Million €	Amount accrued as of January 1, 2001	Amount paid in 2001	Other changes 2001	Amount accrued as of December 31, 2001
Severance	193.3	49.6	93.6	237.3
Plant closure and demolition	61.3	50.4	110.1	121.0
Other	30.4	9.6	42.3	63.1
	285.0	**109.6**	**246.0**	**421.4**

Additions in 2002 consisted primarily of personnel measures at the Ludwigshafen site, as well as restructuring measures in the Agricultural Products division.

Amounts paid in 2002 are related to the realization of restructuring measures initiated in 2001.

In 2001, provisions for severance payments had to be set up for the planned shutdown of numerous plants and production sites located predominantly in North America (NAFTA), South America, the United Kingdom, the Netherlands and Italy. Further charges arose from the restructuring of the Company's sales and marketing organization.

Legal, damage claims, guarantees and related commitments: Provisions are recorded for the expected cost of outstanding litigation and claims of third parties, including regulatory authorities, other guarantees and for antitrust proceedings. The significant proceedings are described in Note 26.

Payments were made in 2002 for compensation claims of vitamin customers in the U.S. after finalization of a settlement and for a fine of €296.2 million imposed by the E.U. Commission for violations of antitrust laws in the vitamin business, which occurred some years ago. An additional €100 million was added to the provision for the settlement of vitamin litigation due to the ongoing settlement of indirect vitamin customers' claims in the U.S. and the unsettled litigation in some other countries.

Additions in 2001 relate to guarantees granted and risks retained in connection with the sale of the pharmaceuticals business. An additional €200 million resulted from the fine imposed by the E.U. Commission for violations of antitrust laws relating to the sale of vitamin products. The provisions set up hitherto were insufficient due to the unexpectedly high fine. In addition, claims for damages by customers for vitamins from a class action lawsuit settled in 2000 that were previously reported as liabilities have been switched to provisions because numerous large customers have elected to opt out of the settlement.

Maintenance and repair costs: Provisions for maintenance and repair costs cover anticipated charges due to unperformed maintenance measures as well as for legally mandated inspection of large-scale plants within prescribed intervals.

Maytag Corporation—Contingencies and Deferred Taxes

Maytag Corporation is a leading appliance enterprise headquartered in Newton, Iowa. The company operates in three business segments: home appliances, commercial appliances, and international appliances. Maytag's appliance brands include Maytag, Amana, Hoover, Jenn-Air, Magic Chef, Dixie-Narco, Jade, and Dynasty.

Learning Objectives

- Understand the accounting implications of contingent liabilities.
- Account for multi-period warranties on products sold.
- Understand how differences in the accounting and income tax treatment of contingencies lead to deferred income tax balances.

For many years Maytag has been associated with the lonely repairman, waiting in his shop for a Maytag product to break and need servicing. Inspection of the notes to Maytag's financial statements shows that there must be some work for this lonely soul. Indeed, Maytag has accrued nearly $115 million of warranty obligations at the end of fiscal 2004.

Concepts

a. What is a contingent liability? Explain, in your own words, when a company would record a contingent liability (i.e. a contingent loss) on its books. List some types of contingent liabilities. Do companies ever record contingent assets (i.e. contingent gains)?

b. Product warranties are a common contingent liability. From the perspective of a Maytag customer, what is a product warranty? From an accrual accounting perspective, what is a warranty?

c. What judgments does management need to make to account for contingent liabilities in general and accrued warranty costs in particular?

d. In general, for income tax purposes, contingent liabilities including accrued warranty costs are deductible only when paid. Under this general assumption, do contingent liabilities give rise to a deferred tax asset or liability? Why?

✧ Process ✧

Parts *e* and *f* are hypothetical. Do not use information in the accompanying notes to Maytag's financial statements for these parts.

e. Assume that in 2004 Maytag began selling a new washing machine on which it provided a three-year warranty. A total of 500,000 units were sold in 2004. Each machine sold for $500 and cost Maytag $350 to manufacture. Maytag's engineers estimate that 5% of the machines will require service over the warranty period. The average cost of servicing a unit is (correctly) projected to be $150.

   i. Prepare all journal entries related to the new washers sold in 2004.

   ii. In 2004, 12,000 units were serviced under the warranty plan. Prepare the journal entry related to the warranty claims on washers sold and serviced in 2004.

   iii. Assume that 6,000 and 7,500 units were serviced under the warranty plan in 2005 and 2006, respectively. Prepare the 2005 and 2006 journal entries related to the warranty claims on washers sold in 2004.

f. Assume that for income tax purposes, Maytag deducts warranty costs as they are paid. Assuming an income tax rate of 36%, provide the journal entry to record deferred taxes with respect to the warranties in each of 2004, 2005, and 2006.

g. Refer to Maytag's balance sheet for the year ending January 1, 2005 and to the notes to the financial statements (pages 41 and 42 of Maytag's financial statements). What is the total warranty reserve at the end of fiscal 2004? Where is this reserve on Maytag's balance sheet?

h. Refer to Maytag's Warranty Reserve note (page 42 of Maytag's financial statements).

  i. Prepare the journal entry to record Maytag's warranty expense for 2004.

  ii. Prepare the journal entry to record Maytag's actual warranty payments for 2004.

i. Maytag's Neptune front-loading washing machine has had mechanical and technical problems since its introduction in 1996. A group of Neptune owners brought a class-action suit against Maytag in 2001. The following appeared on Consumer Reports' website, on September 10, 2004 (http://www.maytagfrontloadsettlement.com):

> What is this lawsuit about?
>
> This lawsuit alleges that owners of Maytag® Neptune® Front-Load Washing Machines have claims concerning the door latch, wax motor, motor control and related circuit board failures, causing the machines to function improperly and users to experience odor, mold and mildew. They are asking the Court for repayment of the money spent to purchase and/or repair their Neptune® washers or damages equal to the diminished value of their appliances. Maytag has responded that it's (sic) product is not defective, denies that it did anything wrong, and contends that it attempted to fix or repair all concerns raised by its customers.
>
> What does the Settlement provide?
>
> In addition to free repairs, the Settlement Agreement makes available three categories of benefits to Class Members. The first is Repair Reimbursement; the second is Replacement Cost; and the third is Purchase Certificates.

  i. Refer to Maytag's income statement for fiscal 2004. What journal entry did Maytag record to account for the front-load washer settlement during 2004?

  ii. The third-quarter report that Maytag filed with the Securities and Exchange Commission (10Q) in 2004 report reveals $18,500 was recorded as front-load washer litigation settlement in June 2004 despite the fact that the settlement was not official until September 2004. Why might Maytag have recorded the settlement in the third quarter (i.e. by July 3, 2004)?

  iii. Refer to Maytag's statement of cash flows. How much did Maytag pay in cash on this settlement during 2004? Prepare the journal entry to record these payments.

✧ Analysis ✧

j. Refer to the Income Taxes note to the financial statements (page 39 of Maytag's financial statements).

  i. What deferred tax asset did Maytag report pertaining to product warranty/liability accruals?

  ii. What specific types accruals are likely included in this amount?

  iii. Is the size of the deferred tax asset consistent with the size of Maytag's warranty reserve and product settlement accruals from parts *h* and *i* above? How might you reconcile the difference?

MAYTAG CORPORATION
CONSOLIDATED STATEMENTS OF OPERATIONS

	Year Ended		
	January 1 2005	January 3 2004	December 28 2002
	In thousands, except per share data		
Net sales	$ 4,721,538	$ 4,791,866	$ 4,666,031
Cost of sales	4,061,319	3,932,335	3,661,429
Gross profit	660,219	859,531	1,004,602
Selling, general and administrative expenses	507,013	555,092	577,995
Restructuring and related charges	69,758	64,929	67,112
Asset impairment	—	11,217	—
Goodwill impairment—Commercial Products	9,600	—	—
Front-load washer litigation	33,500	—	—
Operating income	40,348	228,293	359,495
Interest expense	(56,274)	(52,763)	(62,390)
Loss on investments	—	(7,185)	—
Adverse judgment on pre-acquisition distributor lawsuit	(10,505)	—	—
Other income (loss)	5,113	4,415	(1,449)
Income (loss) from continuing operations before income taxes and minority interests	(21,318)	172,760	295,656
Income tax expense (benefit)	(11,973)	58,382	100,523
Income (loss) from continuing operations before minority interests	(9,345)	114,378	195,133
Minority interests	—	—	(3,732)
Income (loss) from continuing operations	(9,345)	114,378	191,401
Discontinued operations, net of tax:			
Income (loss) from discontinued operations	339	(659)	(2,607)
Provision for impairment of China joint venture	—	(3,313)	—
Gain on sale of Blodgett	—	9,727	—
Gain (loss) from discontinued operations	339	5,755	(2,607)
Net income (loss)	$ (9,006)	$ 120,133	$ 188,794
Basic earnings (loss) per common share:			
Income (loss) from continuing operations	$ (0.12)	$ 1.46	$ 2.46
Discontinued operations	—	0.07	(0.03)
Net income (loss)	$ (0.11)	$ 1.53	$ 2.43
Diluted earnings (loss) per common share:			
Income (loss) from continuing operations	$ (0.12)	$ 1.45	$ 2.44
Discontinued operations	—	0.07	(0.03)
Net income (loss)	$ (0.11)	$ 1.53	$ 2.40
Cash dividends paid per share	$ 0.72	$ 0.72	$ 0.72

See notes to consolidated financial statements

CONSOLIDATED BALANCE SHEETS

	January 1 2005	January 3 2004
	In thousands, except share data	
ASSETS		
Current assets		
Cash and cash equivalents	$ 164,276	$ 6,756
Accounts receivable, less allowance for doubtful accounts (2004—$9,678; 2003—$15,752)	629,901	596,832
Inventories	515,321	468,345
Deferred income taxes	55,862	63,185
Prepaids and other current assets	80,137	94,030
Discontinued current assets	—	75,175
Total current assets	1,445,497	1,304,323
Noncurrent assets		
Deferred income taxes	253,428	183,685
Prepaid pension cost	1,492	1,666
Intangible pension asset	49,051	66,615
Goodwill	259,413	269,013
Other intangibles, less allowance for amortization (2004—$6,256; 2003—$4,679)	36,016	37,498
Other noncurrent assets	53,965	54,069
Discontinued noncurrent assets	—	60,336
Total noncurrent assets	653,365	672,882
Property, plant and equipment		
Land	15,489	23,365
Buildings and improvements	343,321	395,660
Machinery and equipment	1,866,485	2,100,608
Construction in progress	19,874	109,352
	2,245,169	2,628,985
Less accumulated depreciation	1,324,007	1,582,050
Total property, plant and equipment	921,162	1,046,935
Total assets	$ 3,020,024	$ 3,024,140

See notes to consolidated financial statements.

26

CONSOLIDATED BALANCE SHEETS

	January 1 2005	January 3 2004
	In thousands, except share data	
LIABILITIES AND SHAREOWNERS' EQUITY (DEFICIT)		
Current liabilities		
Notes payable	$ —	$ 71,491
Accounts payable	545,901	466,734
Compensation to employees	50,195	69,388
Accrued liabilities	307,924	245,935
Current portion of long-term debt	6,043	24,503
Discontinued current liability	—	105,739
Total current liabilities	910,063	983,790
Noncurrent liabilities		
Long-term debt, less current portion	972,568	874,832
Postretirement benefit liability	531,995	538,105
Accrued pension cost	496,480	398,495
Other noncurrent liabilities	183,942	144,341
Discontinued noncurrent liability	—	18,766
Total noncurrent liabilities	2,184,985	1,974,539
Shareowners' equity (deficit)		
Preferred stock:		
Authorized—24,000,000 shares (par value $1.00)		
Issued—none		
Common stock:		
Authorized—200,000,000 shares (par value $1.25)		
Issued—117,150,593 shares, including shares in treasury	146,438	146,438
Additional paid-in capital	428,889	435,409
Retained earnings	1,294,412	1,360,361
Cost of common stock in treasury (2004—37,737,263 shares; 2003—38,410,885 shares)	(1,430,176)	(1,455,706)
Employee stock plans	(3,913)	(3,530)
Accumulated other comprehensive loss	(510,674)	(417,161)
Total shareowners' equity (deficit)	(75,024)	65,811
Total liabilities and shareowners' equity (deficit)	$ 3,020,024	$ 3,024,140

See notes to consolidated financial statements.

CONSOLIDATED STATEMENTS OF CASH FLOWS

	Year Ended		
	January 1 2005	January 3 2004	December 28 2002
	In thousands		
Operating activities			
Net income (loss)	$ (9,006)	$ 120,133	$ 188,794
Adjustments to reconcile net income (loss) to net cash provided by continuing operating activities:			
Net (income) loss from discontinued operations	(339)	(5,755)	2,607
Minority interests	—	—	3,732
Depreciation	168,205	164,680	162,600
Amortization	1,577	1,105	1,108
Deferred income taxes	2,636	56,660	88,643
Restructuring and related charges, net of cash paid	36,859	45,939	62,483
Asset impairment	—	11,217	—
Loss on investment	—	7,185	—
Goodwill impairment-Commercial Products	9,600	—	—
Front-load washer litigation, net of cash paid	23,092	—	—
Gain on sale, property disposition	(9,711)		
Adverse judgment on pre-acquisition distributor lawsuit	10,505	—	—
Changes in working capital items			
Accounts receivable	(29,207)	1,403	35,211
Inventories	(46,836)	5,801	(21,985)
Other current assets	14,444	27,422	(74,905)
Trade payables	75,095	103,095	47,589
Other current liabilities	15,711	(10,804)	(792)
Pension expense	63,024	64,779	52,561
Pension contributions	(94,324)	(268,119)	(193,108)
Postretirement benefit liability	(6,110)	20,595	12,255
Other liabilities	29,167	12,817	(8,560)
Other assets	6,736	(11,654)	(5,050)
Other	9,837	7,883	11,534
Net cash provided by continuing operating activities	$ 270,955	$ 354,382	$ 364,717
Investing activities			
Capital expenditures-continuing operations	$ (94,420)	$ (199,300)	$ (229,764)
Settlement of Amana purchase contract	—	11,939	—
Proceeds from business disposition, net of transaction costs	11,248	16,168	—
Proceeds from property disposition, net of transaction costs	14,251	—	—
Investing activities-continuing operations	$ (68,921)	$ (171,193)	$ (229,764)
Financing activities			
Net proceeds (reduction) of notes payable	$ (71,491)	$ (107,068)	$ 30,312
Proceeds from issuance of long-term debt	100,000	200,000	—
Repayment of long-term debt	(21,521)	(220,524)	(129,881)
Stock repurchases	—	(1,021)	—
Stock options and employee stock	5,478	1,600	26,049
Dividends on common stock	(56,899)	(56,524)	(56,010)
Dividends on minority interests	—	—	(5,577)
Purchase of Anvil LLC member interest	—	—	(99,884)
Cash from (to) discontinued operations	(280)	(1,122)	(1,952)
Financing activities-continuing operations	$ (44,713)	$ (184,659)	$ (236,943)
Effect of exchange rates on cash	199	120	726
Increase (decrease) in cash and cash equivalents	157,520	(1,350)	(101,264)
Cash and cash equivalents at beginning of year	6,756	8,106	109,370
Cash and cash equivalents at end of year	$ 164,276	$ 6,756	$ 8,106
Cash flows from discontinued operations			
Net cash provided by (used in) discontinued operating activities	$ (4,666)	$ 4,050	$ (5,487)
Investing activities-discontinued operations	(733)	(2,213)	(1,198)
Financing activities-discontinued operations	281	1,177	1,958
Increase (decrease) in cash-discontinued operations	$ (5,118)	$ 3,014	$ (4,727)

See notes to consolidated financial statements.

MAYTAG CORPORATION
Notes to Consolidated Financial Statements (excerpts)

Income Taxes

Deferred income taxes reflect the expected future tax consequences of temporary differences between the book carrying amounts and the tax basis of assets and liabilities. Deferred tax assets and liabilities consisted of the following:

	January 1 2005	January 3 2004
	In thousands	
Deferred tax assets (liabilities):		
Property, plant and equipment	$ (126,633)	$ (132,696)
Postretirement benefit liability	204,610	200,427
Product warranty/liability accruals	75,829	56,451
Pensions and other employee benefits	155,605	124,410
Advertising and sales promotion accruals	8,219	7,836
Capital losses	38,574	32,650
Other — net	8,102	1,888
	364,306	290,966
Less valuation allowance for deferred tax assets	55,016	44,096
Net deferred tax assets	$ 309,290	$ 246,870
Recognized in Consolidated Balance Sheets:		
Deferred tax assets — current	$ 55,862	$ 63,185
Deferred tax assets — noncurrent	253,428	183,685
Net deferred tax assets	$ 309,290	$ 246,870

The Company has both recognized and unrecognized capital loss carryforwards for tax purposes. These capital losses can only be offset against capital gains and expire five years after they are realized. The Company has $102.2 million of capital loss carryforwards at January 1, 2005 that will begin to expire at December 31, 2006. The change in the valuation allowance in 2004 compared to 2003 shown in the table above resulted primarily from the generation of capital losses in 2004 with no tax benefit as well as U.S. losses with no tax benefit.

Components of the provision for income taxes consisted of the following:

	Year Ended		
	January 1 2005	January 3 2004	December 28 2002
		In thousands	
Current provision (benefit):			
Federal	$ (16,627)	$ (4,702)	$ 26,719
State	(979)	(1,586)	2,654
Foreign	2,997	8,010	(490)
	(14,609)	1,722	28,883
Deferred provision (benefit):			
Federal	5,629	50,524	64,714
State	(1,936)	6,781	6,926
Foreign	(1,057)	(645)	—
	2,636	56,660	71,640
Income tax expense (benefit)	$ (11,973)	$ 58,382	$ 100,523

Accrued Liabilities

Accrued liabilities consisted of the following:

	January 1 2005	January 3 2004
	In thousands	
Warranties	$ 80,632	$ 74,873
Advertising and sales promotion	87,359	70,797
Other	139,933	100,265
Accrued liabilities	$ 307,924	$ 245,935

Other accrued liabilities primarily contain accruals for restructuring reserves, litigation, extended service plans, taxes, interest payable and insurance.

Warranty Reserve

Maytag provides a basic limited warranty for all of its major appliance, floor care and commercial products. Changes in warranty liability during fiscal 2004, 2003 and 2002 are as follows:

	Year ended		
Warranty reserve (in thousands)	**January 1, 2005**	**January 3, 2004**	**December 28, 2002**
Balance at beginning of period	$ 103,226	$ 100,489	$ 111,725
Warranties accrued during the period	126,908	115,032	108,416
Settlements made during the period	(121,162)	(121,109)	(112,884)
Changes in liability for adjustments during the period, including expirations	5,933	8,814	(6,768)
Balance at end of period	$ 114,905	$ 103,226	$ 100,489
Warranty reserve-current portion	$ 80,632	$ 74,873	$ 74,284
Warranty reserve-noncurrent portion	34,273	28,353	26,205
Total warranty reserve at January 1, 2005	$ 114,905	$ 103,226	$ 100,489

In addition to the basic limited warranty, an optional extended warranty is offered to retail purchasers of the Company's major appliances. Sales of extended warranties are recorded as deferred revenue within accrued and noncurrent liabilities on the Consolidated Balance Sheet. Certain costs directly associated with sales of extended warranties are deferred within other current and noncurrent assets on the Consolidated Balance Sheet. The deferred revenue and associated costs are amortized into income on a straight-line basis over the length of the extended warranty contracts. Payments on extended warranty contracts are expensed as incurred.

Rite Aid Corporation—Long-Term Debt

With 3,382 stores in 28 states, Rite Aid is the third largest retail pharmacy in the U.S. The company has a first or second market position in approximately 60% of the markets where it operates. In fiscal 2004, Rite Aid pharmacists filled more than 200 million prescriptions, which accounted for 63.6% of total sales. In addition, Rite Aid stores sell a wide assortment of other merchandise including over-the-counter medications, health and beauty aids, household items, beverages, convenience foods, greeting cards, as well as photo processing. The company also offers 2,100 products under the Rite Aid private brand.

Learning Objectives

- Read and understand long-term debt footnote terminology.
- Understand discounts and premiums associated with long-term debt.
- Infer effective interest rates from footnote disclosures.
- Calculate and interpret common debt-related ratios.

Refer to the 2004 Rite Aid Corporation financial statements.

 **Concepts** 

a. Consider the various types of debt the company describes in footnote 10.

   i. Explain the difference between Rite Aid's secured and unsecured debt. Why would Rite Aid distinguish between these two types of debt?

   ii. What is meant by the terms "senior," "fixed-rate," and "convertible"?

   iii. Speculate as to why Rite Aid has many different types of debt with a range of interest rates?

 **Process** 

b. Consider Note 10, Indebtedness. How much total debt does Rite Aid have at February 28, 2004? How much of this is due within the coming fiscal year? Reconcile the total debt reported in Note 10 with what Rite Aid reports on its balance sheet.

c. Consider the 9.5% senior secured notes due February 2011.

   i. What is the face value (i.e. the principal) of these notes? How do you know?

   ii. Prepare the journal entry that Rite Aid must have made when these notes were issued.

   iii. Prepare the annual interest expense journal entry. Note that the interest paid on a note during the year equals the face value of the note times the stated rate (i.e., coupon rate) of the note.

   iv. Prepare the journal entry that Rite Aid will make when these notes mature in 2011.

d. Consider the 4.75% convertible notes due December 2006. Assume that interest is paid annually.

   i. What is the face value (or principal) of these notes? What is the carrying value (net book value) of these notes? Why do the two values differ?

   ii. How much interest did Rite Aid pay on these notes during the fiscal 2004?

   iii. Determine interest expense on these notes for the year ended February 28, 2004. Note that there are cash and non-cash portion to interest expense on these notes because they were issued at a discount. The non-cash portion of interest expense is the amortization of the discount during the year (that is, the amount by which the discount decreased during the year).

iv. Prepare the journal entry to record interest expense on these notes for 2004. Consider both the cash and discount (non-cash) portions of the interest expense from part *iii* above.

e. Consider the 8.125% notes due 2010. Assume that Rite Aid issued these notes on May 1, 2003 and that the company pays interest on the last day of April each year.

i. According to a press release issued by Rite Aid at the time of the issuance, the proceeds of the notes issue were 98.688% of the face value of the notes. Prepare the journal entry that Rite Aid must have made when these notes were issued.

ii. At what effective annual rate of interest were these notes issued?

iii. Assume that Rite Aid uses the effective interest rate method to account for this debt. Use the guidance for the table that follows to prepare an amortization schedule for these notes. Use the last column to verify that each year's interest expense uses the same interest *rate* even though the *expense* changes.

Date	*Interest Payment*	*Interest Expense*	*Bond Discount Amortization*	*Net Book Value of Debt*	*Effective Interest Rate*
May 1, 2003				$ 355,276.80	
May 1, 2004	$ 29,250				
May 1, 2005					
May 1, 2006					
May 1, 2007					
May 1, 2008					
May 1, 2009					
May 1, 2010					

- May 1, 2003 Net Book Value is the initial proceeds of the bond issuance, net of costs. The face value of this debt is $360,000; the discount is $4,723.20; the coupon rate is 8.125% and the effective rate (including fees) is 8.3803%.
- Interest Payment is the face value of the bond times the coupon rate of the bond.
- Interest Expense equals opening book value of the debt times the effective interest rate.
    - The difference between the interest payment and interest expense is the amortization of the bond discount. This is equivalent to saying that interest expense equals the interest paid plus the amortization of the bond discount.
    - Amortizing the discount increases the net book value of the bond.

iv. Prepare the journal entry that Rite Aid must have recorded February 28, 2004 to accrue interest expense on these notes.

v. Based on your answer to part *iv.* what is the book value of the notes at February 28, 2004?

vi. Your answer to part *v.* will be different from the amount that Rite Aid reported because the company used the straight line method to amortize the discount on these notes instead of the effective interest rate method. Use the guidance that follows to complete the following table using the straight line method to amortize the bond discount. Use the last column in the table to record the interest rate each year. Under this method, does Rite Aid report the same interest *rate* on these notes each year?

Date	*Interest Payment*	*Interest Expense*	*Bond Discount Amortization*	*Net Book Value of Debt*	*Straight Line Interest Rate*
May 1, 2003				$ 355,276.80	
May 1, 2004	$ 29,250				
May 1, 2005					
May 1, 2006					
May 1, 2007					
May 1, 2008					
May 1, 2009					
May 1, 2010					

- May 1, 2003 Net Book Value is the initial proceeds of the bond issuance, net of costs. The face value of this debt is $360,000; the discount is $4,723.20; the coupon rate is 8.125% and the effective rate (including fees) is 8.3803%.
- Interest Payment is the face value of the bond times the coupon rate of the bond.
- Interest Expense equals interest payment plus the amortization of the bond discount.
    - Under the straight line method the bond discount is amortized on a straight line basis over the life of the bond. That is, amortization is the same amount each year.
    - Amortizing the discount increases the net book value of the bond.

vii. Compare the year by year difference in interest expense derived from each method. What pattern do you observe? Is the difference material in any year?

f. Note 10 reports that Rite Aid engaged in some open-market debt transactions during year ended February 28, 2004 (see the part of note 10 marked "Debt Repurchased").

i. Prepare the journal entry required to record the repurchase of these notes.

ii. Why did Rite Aid not have to pay the face value to repurchase these notes on the open market?

iii. Explain why Rite Aid recorded a gain on all of the repurchased notes except on the 12.5% note on which it recorded a loss?

g. Consider the 4.75% Convertible notes. How would Rite Aid's balance sheet be affected if these notes were converted? Why do firms issue convertible notes? Why do investors buy such notes?

h. Refer to Note 20, Financial Instruments.

i. What is the fair-value of Rite Aid's fixed-rate debt at February 28, 2004? Why does it differ from the carrying amount?

ii. What is the fair-value of the variable-rate debt at February 28, 2004? Why does it *not* differ from its carrying amount?

iii. Why would financial statement users want to know the fair-value of Rite Aid's debt?

Analysis

i. You want to compare Rite Aid's leverage to other firms in the Retail Pharmaceutical industry. To assist you, the table below reports the industry averages for several common debt ratios. Calculate each of the ratios in the table for Rite Aid for the years ending February 28, 2004 and March 1, 2003. How does Rite Aid compare to the industry? What conclusion would you reach as a credit analyst?

Ratio	*Definition*	*Industry average*	*Rite Aid FY2004*	*Rite Aid FY2003*
Common-size debt	Total liabilities / Total assets	51.91%		
Common-size interest expense	Interest expense / Net sales	0.65%		
Debt to equity	Total liabilities / Total shareholders' equity	1.59		
Long-term debt to equity	Long-term debt / Total shareholders' equity	0.58		
Proportion of long-term debt due in one year	Long-term debt due in one year / Total long-term debt	13.00%		
Times-interest-earned (interest coverage)	(Pre-tax income + interest expense) / Interest expense	9.98×		

RITE AID CORPORATION AND SUBSIDIARIES
CONSOLIDATED BALANCE SHEETS

(In thousands, except per share amounts)

	February 28, 2004	March 1, 2003
ASSETS		
Current assets:		
Cash and cash equivalents	$ 334,755	$ 365,321
Accounts receivable, net	670,004	575,518
Inventories, net	2,223,171	2,195,030
Prepaid expenses and other current assets	150,067	108,018
Total current assets	3,377,997	3,243,887
Property, plant and equipment, net	1,883,808	1,868,579
Goodwill	684,535	684,535
Other intangibles, net	176,672	199,768
Other assets	123,667	136,746
Total assets	$ 6,246,679	$ 6,133,515
LIABILITIES AND STOCKHOLDERS' EQUITY (DEFICIT)		
Current liabilities:		
Short-term debt and current maturities of convertible notes, long-term debt and lease financing obligations	$ 23,976	$ 103,715
Accounts payable	758,290	755,284
Accrued salaries, wages and other current liabilities	701,484	707,999
Total current liabilities	1,483,750	1,566,998
Convertible notes	246,000	244,500
Long-term debt, less current maturities	3,451,352	3,345,365
Lease financing obligations, less current maturities	170,338	169,048
Other noncurrent liabilities	885,975	900,270
Total liabilities	6,237,415	6,226,181
Commitments and contingencies	—	—
Redeemable preferred stock	—	19,663
Stockholders' equity (deficit):		
Preferred stock, par value $1 per share; liquidation value $100 per share; 20,000 shares authorized; shares issued — 4,178 and 3,937	417,803	393,705
Common stock, par value $1 per share; 1,000,000 shares authorized; shares issued and outstanding 516,496 and 515,115	516,496	515,115
Additional paid-in capital	3,133,277	3,119,619
Accumulated deficit	(4,035,433)	(4,118,119)
Stock based and deferred compensation	—	5,369
Accumulated other comprehensive loss	(22,879)	(28,018)
Total stockholders' equity (deficit)	9,264	(112,329)
Total liabilities and stockholders' equity (deficit)	$ 6,246,679	$ 6,133,515

The accompanying notes are an integral part of these consolidated financial statements.

RITE AID CORPORATION AND SUBSIDIARIES
CONSOLIDATED STATEMENTS OF OPERATIONS

(In thousands, except per share amounts)

	Year Ended		
	February 28, 2004	March 1, 2003	March 2, 2002
Revenues	$16,600,449	$15,791,278	$15,166,170
Costs and expenses:			
Cost of goods sold, including occupancy costs	12,568,405	12,035,537	11,697,912
Selling, general and administrative expenses	3,594,405	3,471,573	3,422,383
Stock-based compensation expense (benefit)	29,821	4,806	(15,891)
Goodwill amortization	—	—	21,007
Store closing and impairment charges	22,466	135,328	251,617
Interest expense	313,498	330,020	396,064
Interest rate swap contracts	—	278	41,894
Loss (gain) on debt modifications and retirements, net	35,315	(13,628)	221,054
Share of loss from equity investments	—	—	12,092
Loss (gain) on sale of assets and investments, net	2,023	(18,620)	(42,536)
	16,565,933	15,945,294	16,005,596
Income (loss) before income taxes	34,516	(154,016)	(839,426)
Income tax benefit	(48,795)	(41,940)	(11,745)
Net income (loss)	$ 83,311	$ (112,076)	$ (827,681)
Computation of income (loss) applicable to common stockholders:			
Net income (loss)	$ 83,311	$ (112,076)	$ (827,681)
Accretion of redeemable preferred stock	(102)	(102)	(104)
Preferred stock beneficial conversion	(625)	—	(6,406)
Cumulative preferred stock dividends	(24,098)	(32,201)	(27,530)
Net income (loss) applicable to common stockholders	$ 58,486	$ (144,379)	$ (861,721)
Basic and diluted income (loss) per share:			
Net income (loss) per share	$ 0.11	$ (0.28)	$ (1.82)

The accompanying notes are an integral part of these consolidated financial statements.

RITE AID CORPORATION AND SUBSIDIARIES
CONSOLIDATED STATEMENTS OF CASH FLOWS

(In thousands)

	Year Ended		
	February 28, 2004	March 1, 2003	March 2, 2002
Operating Activities:			
Net income (loss)	$ 83,311	$(112,076)	$ (827,681)
Adjustments to reconcile to net cash provided by operations:			
Depreciation and amortization	264,288	285,334	349,840
Store closings and impairment loss	22,466	135,328	251,617
Interest rate swap contracts	—	278	41,894
Loss (gain) on sale of assets and investments, net	2,023	(18,620)	(42,536)
Stock-based compensation expense (benefit)	29,821	4,806	(15,891)
Loss (gain) on debt modifications and retirements, net	35,315	(13,628)	221,054
Changes in operating assets and liabilities:			
Accounts receivable	(94,486)	14,803	(69,004)
Inventories	(48,014)	40,555	112,649
Income taxes receivable/payable	(61,209)	24,018	(14,635)
Accounts payable	(17,162)	(62,314)	(5,004)
Other assets and liabilities, net	11,162	6,899	14,040
Net cash provided by operating activities	227,515	305,383	16,343
Investing Activities:			
Expenditures for property, plant and equipment	(250,668)	(104,507)	(175,183)
Intangible assets acquired	(16,705)	(11,647)	(12,200)
Proceeds from the sale of AdvancePCS securities and notes	—	—	484,214
Proceeds from dispositions	25,223	43,940	45,700
Net cash (used in) provided by investing activities	(242,150)	(72,214)	342,531
Financing activities:			
Net proceeds from the issuance of long-term debt	—	—	1,378,462
Net change in bank credit facilities	(222,500)	(5,962)	—
Proceeds from the issuance of bonds	502,950	300,000	392,500
Principal payments on long-term debt	(264,324)	(477,466)	(2,277,431)
Change in zero balance cash account	(4,613)	(12,936)	(48,131)
Net proceeds from the issuance of common stock	3,541	279	530,589
Deferred financing costs paid	(30,985)	(15,818)	(83,098)
Net cash used in financing activities	(15,931)	(211,903)	(107,109)
Increase (decrease) in cash and cash equivalents	(30,566)	21,266	251,765
Cash and cash equivalents, beginning of year	365,321	344,055	92,290
Cash and cash equivalents, end of year	$ 334,755	$ 365,321	$ 344,055

The accompanying notes are an integral part of these consolidated financial statements.

RITE AID CORPORATION AND SUBSIDIARIES
NOTES TO CONSOLIDATED FINANCIAL STATEMENTS (continued)
For the Years Ended February 28, 2004, March 1, 2003 and March 2, 2002

(In thousands, except per share amounts)

10. Indebtedness and Credit Agreements

Following is a summary of indebtedness and lease financing obligations at February 28, 2004 and March 1, 2003:

	February 28, 2004	March 1, 2003
Secured Debt:		
Senior secured credit facility due April 2008	$1,150,000	$ —
Senior secured credit facility due March 2005	—	1,372,500
12.5% senior secured notes due September 2006 ($142,025 and $152,025 face value less unamortized discount of $4,158 and 6,143)	137,867	145,882
8.125% senior secured notes due May 2010 ($360,000 face value less unamortized discount of $4,168)	355,832	—
9.5% senior secured notes due February 2011	300,000	300,000
Other	5,125	6,540
	1,948,824	1,824,922
Lease Financing Obligations	183,169	176,186
Unsecured Debt:		
6.0% dealer remarketable securities due October 2003	—	58,125
7.625% senior notes due April 2005	198,000	198,000
6.0% fixed-rate senior notes due December 2005	38,047	75,895
4.75% convertible notes due December 2006 ($250,000 face value less unamortized discount of $4,000 and $5,500)	246,000	244,500
7.125% notes due January 2007	210,074	335,000
11.25% senior notes due July 2008	150,000	150,000
6.125% fixed-rate senior notes due December 2008	150,000	150,000
9.25% senior notes due June 2013 ($150,000 face value less unamortized discount of $2,221)	147,779	—
6.875% senior debentures due August 2013	184,773	200,000
7.7% notes due February 2027	295,000	300,000
6.875% fixed-rate senior notes due December 2028	140,000	150,000
	1,759,673	1,861,520
Total debt	3,891,666	3,862,628
Short-term debt and current maturities of convertible notes, long-term debt and lease financing obligations	(23,976)	(103,715)
Long-term debt and lease financing obligations, less current maturities	$3,867,690	$3,758,913

RITE AID CORPORATION AND SUBSIDIARIES
NOTES TO CONSOLIDATED FINANCIAL STATEMENTS (continued)
For the Years Ended February 28, 2004, March 1, 2003 and March 2, 2002

(In thousands, except per share amounts)

2004 Transactions:

New Credit Facility: On May 28, 2003, the Company replaced its senior secured credit facility with a new senior secured credit facility. The new facility consists of a $1,150,000 term loan and a $700,000 revolving credit facility, and will mature on April 30, 2008. The proceeds of the loans made on the closing of the new credit facility were, among other things, used to repay the outstanding amounts under the old facility and to purchase the land and buildings at the Company's Perryman, MD and Lancaster, CA distribution centers, which had previously been leased through a synthetic lease arrangement. On August 4, 2003, the Company amended and restated the senior secured credit facility, which reduced the interest rate on term loan borrowings under the senior secured credit facility by 50 basis points.

Borrowings under the new facility currently bear interest either at LIBOR plus 3.00% for the term loan and 3.50% for the revolving credit facility, if the Company chooses to make LIBOR borrowings, or at Citibank's base rate plus 2.00% for the term of the loan and 2.50% for the revolving credit facility. The Company is required to pay fees of 0.50% per annum on the daily unused amount of the revolving facility. Amortization payments of $2,875 related to the term loan will begin on May 31, 2004, and continue on a quarterly basis until February 28, 2008, with a final payment of $1,104,000 due April 30, 2008.

Substantially all of Rite Aid Corporation's wholly-owned subsidiaries guarantee the obligations under the new senior secured credit facility. The subsidiary guarantees are secured by a first priority lien on, among other things, the inventory, accounts receivable and prescription files of the subsidiary guarantors. Rite Aid Corporation is a holding company with no direct operations and is dependent upon dividends, distributions and other payments from its subsidiaries to service payments under the new senior secured credit facility. Rite Aid Corporation's direct obligations under the new senior secured credit facility are unsecured.

The new senior secured credit facility allows for the issuance of up to $150,000 in additional term loans or additional revolver availability. The Company may request the additional loans at any time prior to the maturity of the senior secured credit facility, provided that the Company is not in default of any terms of the facility, nor is in violation of any financial covenants. The new senior secured credit facility allows the Company to have outstanding, at any time, up to $1,000,000 in secured debt in addition to the senior secured credit facility. At February 28, 2004, the remaining additional permitted secured debt under the new senior credit facility is $197,975. The Company has the ability to incur an unlimited amount of unsecured debt, if the terms of such unsecured indebtedness comply with certain terms set forth in the credit agreement and subject to the Company's compliance with certain financial covenants. If the Company issues unsecured debt that does not meet the credit agreement restrictions, it reduces the amount of available permitted secured debt. The new senior secured credit facility also allows for the repurchase of any debt with a maturity prior to April 30, 2008, and for a limited amount of debt with a maturity after April 30, 2008, based upon outstanding borrowings under the revolving credit facility and available cash at the time of the repurchase.

The new senior secured credit facility contains customary covenants, which place restrictions on incurrence of debt, the payment of dividends, mergers, liens and sale and leaseback transactions. The new senior secured credit facility also requires us to meet various financial ratios and limits capital expenditures. For the twelve months ending February 26, 2005, the covenants require us to maintain a maximum leverage ratio of 6.05:1. Subsequent to February 26, 2005, the ratio gradually decreases to 3.8:1 for the twelve months ending March 1, 2008. We must also maintain a minimum interest coverage ratio of 2.05:1 for the twelve months ending February 26, 2005. Subsequent to February 26, 2005, the ratio gradually increases to 3.25:1 for the twelve months ending March 1, 2008. In addition, we must maintain a minimum fixed charge ratio of 1.10:1 for the twelve months ending February 26,

RITE AID CORPORATION AND SUBSIDIARIES
NOTES TO CONSOLIDATED FINANCIAL STATEMENTS (continued)
For the Years Ended February 28, 2004, March 1, 2003 and March 2, 2002

(In thousands, except per share amounts)

2005. Subsequent to February 26, 2005, the ratio gradually increases to 1.25:1 for the twelve months ending March 1, 2008. Capital expenditures are limited to $386,085 for the fiscal year ending February 26, 2005, with the allowable amount increasing in subsequent years.

The Company was in compliance with the covenants of the new senior secured credit facility and its other debt instruments as of February 28, 2004. With continuing improvements in operating performance, the Company anticipates that it will remain in compliance with its debt covenants. However, variations in operating performance and unanticipated developments may adversely affect the Company's ability to remain in compliance with the applicable debt covenants.

The new senior secured credit facility provides for customary events of default, including nonpayment, misrepresentation, breach of covenants and bankruptcy. It is also an event of default if any event occurs that enables, or which with the giving of notice or the lapse of time would enable, the holder of the Company's debt to accelerate the maturity of debt having a principal amount in excess of $25,000.

The Company's ability to borrow under the senior secured credit facility is based on a specified borrowing base consisting of eligible accounts receivable, inventory and prescription files. At February 28, 2004, the term loan was fully drawn and the Company had no outstanding draws on the revolving credit facility. At February 28, 2004, the Company had additional borrowing capacity of $584,804, net of outstanding letters of credit of $115,196.

As a result of the placement of the new senior secured credit facility, the Company recorded a loss on debt modification in fiscal 2004 of $43,197 (which included the write-off of previously deferred debt issue costs of $35,120).

On October 1, 2003, the Company paid, at maturity, its remaining outstanding balance on the 6.0% dealer remarketable securities.

In May 2003, the Company issued $150,000 aggregate principal amount of 9.25% senior notes due 2013. These notes are unsecured and effectively subordinate to the Company's secured debt. The indenture governing the 9.25% senior notes contains customary covenant provisions that, amount other things, include limitations on the Company's ability to pay dividends, make investments or other restricted payments, incur debt, grant liens, sell assets and enter into sale lease-back transactions.

In April 2003, the Company issued $360,000 aggregate principal amount of 8.125% senior secured notes due 2010. The notes are unsecured, unsubordinated obligations to Rite Aid Corporation and rank equally in right of payment with all other unsecured, unsubordinated indebtedness. The Company's obligations under the notes are guaranteed, subject to certain limitations, by subsidiaries that guarantee the obligations under our new senior secured credit facility. The guarantees are secured, subject to the permitted liens, by shared second priority liens, with the holders of the Company's 12.5% senior notes and the Company's 9.5% senior secured notes, granted by subsidiary guarantors on all of their assets that secure the obligations under the new senior secured credit facility, subject to certain exceptions. The indenture governing the Company's 8.125% senior secured notes contains customary covenant provisions that, among other things, include limitations on our ability to pay dividends, make investments or other restricted payments, incur debt, grant liens, sell assets and enter into sales lease-back transactions.

RITE AID CORPORATION AND SUBSIDIARIES
NOTES TO CONSOLIDATED FINANCIAL STATEMENTS (continued)
For the Years Ended February 28, 2004, March 1, 2003 and March 2, 2002

(In thousands, except per share amounts)

During fiscal 2004 the Company repurchased the following securities:

Debt Repurchased	Principal Amount Repurchased	Amount Paid	(Gain)/ loss
6.0% fixed rate senior notes due 2005	$ 37,848	$ 36,853	$ (865)
7.125% notes due 2007	124,926	120,216	(4,314)
6.875% senior debentures due 2013	15,227	13,144	(1,981)
7.7% notes due 2027	5,000	4,219	(715)
6.875% fixed rate senior notes due 2028	10,000	7,975	(1,895)
12.5% senior secured notes due 2006	10,000	11,275	1,888
Total	$203,001	$193,682	$(7,882)

2003 Transactions:

Senior Secured Notes: The Company issued $300,000 of 9.5% senior secured notes due 2011 in February 2003. The notes were unsecured, unsubordinated obligations of the Company and rank equally in right of payment with all of the Company's other unsecured, unsubordinated indebtedness. The Company's obligations under the notes are guaranteed, subject to certain limitations, by subsidiaries that guarantee the obligations under the senior secured credit facility. The guarantees are secured, subject to the permitted liens, by shared second priority liens with the holders of the 12.5% senior notes and the 8.125% senior secured notes, granted by subsidiary guarantors on all assets that secure the Company's obligations under the senior secured credit facility, subject to certain limitations. Proceeds from these notes were used to redeem all the $149,500 of the Company's senior secured (shareholders) notes due 2006 as well as to fund other debt repurchases and general corporate purposes.

Repurchase of Debt: The Company repurchased $25,425 of its 6.0% dealer remarketable securities due 2003, $118,605 of its 6.0% notes due 2005, and $15,000 of its 7.125% notes due 2007 during fiscal 2003. In addition to the debt repurchases noted above, the Company retired $150,500 of its 5.25% convertible subordinated notes at maturity in September 2002, and made quarterly mandatory repayments on the senior secured credit facility term loan totaling $27,500 during fiscal 2003. These fiscal 2003 transactions resulted in a gain of $13,628 on debt retirements and modifications.

2002 Refinancing and Other Transactions:

On June 27, 2001, the Company completed a major financial restructuring that extended the maturity dates of the majority of its debt to 2005 or beyond, provided additional equity and converted a portion of its debt to equity. These transactions are described below:

Senior Secured Credit Facility: The Company entered into a new $1,900,000 senior secured credit facility. This facility was replaced by the new senior secured credit facility discussed above.

High Yield Notes: The Company issued $150,000 of 11.25% senior notes due July 2008. These notes are unsecured and are effectively subordinate to the secured debt of the Company.

Debt for Debt Exchange: The Company exchanged $152,025 of its existing 10.5% senior secured notes due 2002 for an equal amount of 12.5% senior notes due September 2006. In addition, holders of these notes received warrants to purchase 3,000 shares of Company common stock at $6.00 per share. On June 29, 2001, the warrant holders exercised these warrants, on a cashless basis, and as a result approximately 982 shares of common stock were issued.

During the third quarter of fiscal 2004, the Company recorded a non-recurring income tax benefit, driven by the approval by the Congressional Joint Committee on Taxation on the conclusions of the Internal Revenue Service examination of the Company's federal tax returns for the fiscal years 1996 through 2000.

During the first quarter of fiscal 2004, the Company recorded a loss on debt modification of $43,197 related to the placement of its new senior secured credit facility.

During the fourth quarter of fiscal 2003, the Company incurred $78,277 in store closing and impairment charges. The Company also recorded a $27,700 million credit related to the elimination of several liabilities for former executives and a $19,502 million reduction of its LIFO reserve related to a lower level of inflation than originally estimated.

During the second quarter of fiscal 2003, the Company incurred $58,223 in store closing and impairment charges. In the first quarter of fiscal 2003, the company incurred a charge of $20,000 to reserve for probable loss related to the U.S. Attorney's investigation of former management's business practices. The Company also recorded a tax benefit of $44,011 related to a tax law change that increased the carryback period from two years to five for certain net operating losses.

20. Financial Instruments

The carrying amounts and fair values of financial instruments at February 28, 2004 and March 1, 2003 are listed as follows:

	2004		2003	
	Carrying Amount	Fair Value	Carrying Amount	Fair Value
Variable rate indebtedness	$1,150,000	$1,150,000	$1,372,500	$1,372,500
Fixed rate indebtedness	$2,558,497	$2,640,995	$2,313,942	$2,027,603

Cash, trade receivables and trade payables are carried at market value, which approximates their fair values due to the short-term maturity of these instruments.

The following methods and assumptions were used in estimating fair value disclosures for financial instruments:

LIBOR-based borrowings under credit facilities:

The carrying amounts for LIBOR-based borrowings under the credit facilities, term loans and term notes approximate their fair values due to the short-term nature of the obligations and the variable interest rates.

Long-term indebtedness:

The fair values of long-term indebtedness is estimated based on the quoted market prices of the financial instruments. If quoted market prices were not available, the Company estimated the fair value based on the quoted market price of a financial instrument with similar characteristics.

Continental Airlines, Inc.—Leases

Continental Airlines, Inc. is a major United States air carrier engaged in the business of transporting passengers, cargo and mail. They are the fifth largest United States airline (as measured by the number of scheduled miles flown by revenue passengers, known as revenue passenger miles, in 2003). Together with ExpressJet Airlines, Inc. (operating as Continental Express), from which they purchase seat capacity, and the wholly owned subsidiary, Continental Micronesia, Inc., Continental serves 228 airports worldwide at December 31, 2003.

Learning Objectives

- Understand the economic incentives of leasing versus buying assets.
- Interpret lease footnotes and discussion of commitments and contingencies.
- Relate lease footnote disclosures to balance sheet data.
- Understand the balance sheet and income statement effects of lease accounting.
- Perform present value calculations relating to lease obligations.
- Create pro-forma financial statements to capitalize leases previously treated as operating.
- Understand the economic consequences and quality of earnings issues related to lease accounting.

Refer to the 2003 financial statements of Continental Airlines Inc.

✧ Concepts ✧

a. Why do companies lease assets rather than buy them?

b. What is an operating lease? What is a capital lease? What is a direct financing lease? What is a sales-type lease? (*Hint*: if your textbook does not cover these lease complexities, use your favorite internet search engine to find definitions and examples.)

c. Why do accountants distinguish between different types of leases?

✧ Process ✧

d. Consider Continental's operating lease payments and the information in Note 6, Leases.

   i. Provide the summary journal entry that Continental made during fiscal 2003 for operating lease payments. Assume that half of the expense recorded on the income statement for landing fees and other rentals, pertains to landing fees.

   ii. Provide the summary journal entry that Continental will make to record the anticipated operating lease payments for the year ended December 31, 2004 (that is, in the *next* fiscal year).

e. The 2003 balance sheet shows "Owned property and equipment – Flight equipment" totaling $6,574 million and "Capital leases – Flight Equipment" of $107. What do these amounts represent? How many jet aircraft does each comprise?

f. Note 1 provides information about owned aircrafts' residual value and useful lives. Assume that Continental uses 30 years for owned aircrafts' useful lives. Recalculate depreciation on these aircraft for 2003. Prepare the journal entry to record this depreciation. State any other assumptions you make.

g. Consider the information in Note 1 concerning aircraft under capital lease. Assume that capital leases generally have terms of 20 years. Recalculate amortization on these leased aircraft for 2003. Prepare the journal entry to record this amortization. State any other assumptions you make.

h. Note 6, Leases, indicates that the present value of capital lease obligations is $323. Explain where this figure is found on Continental's balance sheet.

✧ Analysis ✧

i. Consider the future minimum lease payments made under the capital leases disclosed in Note 6, Leases. Assume that all lease payments are made on December 31 of the respective years. Also assume that payments made later than 2008 are made evenly over 10 years. That is, lease payments of $47.3 million will be made on December 31, 2009 through 2018, inclusive.

  i. Estimate the average interest rate for these leases. (*Hint*: Use the internal rate of return—IRR—function on a financial calculator or spreadsheet.)

  ii. Based on your calculation of the average interest rate, approximate the interest expense related to these leases for the year that will end December 31, 2004. Use the effective interest rate method. Under the effective interest rate method, interest expense is calculated as the present value of capital lease obligations measured at the beginning of each year times the average interest rate (the one you calculated in part i *i.* above).

  iii. How much cash will be paid for these leases in fiscal 2004?

  iv. Provide the journal entry to record the lease payment of December 31, 2004 based on your answers to parts i *ii.* and *iii.*

  v. Based on your journal entry in part i *iv.*, what portion of the Capital Lease liability is current as of December 31, 2003? Speculate as to why your estimate differs from the "current maturities of capital leases" in Note 6?

j. Consider how the financial statements would look had Continental capitalized all of its operating leases (that is, the aircraft and non-aircraft). Make the following assumptions:

- Continental enters into the leases on December 31, 2003 and annual payments are made at the end of each fiscal year beginning December 31, 2004.
- The implicit interest rate in these leases is 12%.
- Payments for "Later years" are made on December 31 each year for ten years.

  i. Calculate the present value of the future minimum lease payments.

  ii. Prepare the journal entry to capitalize these leases at December 31, 2003.

  iii. What would Continental have reported as the cost of "Equipment and Property Under Capital Leases: Flight equipment" at December 31, 2003? As "Total assets"?

  iv. What would Continental have reported as "Long-Term Debt and Capital Leases" at December 31, 2003? As "Total current liabilities"? And as total liabilities?

  v. What incentives does Continental Airlines Inc.'s management have to report its aircraft leases as operating leases? Comment on the effect of leasing on the quality of Continental's financial reporting.

k. Refer to your solution to part *j*. Had Continental capitalized their operating leases, key financial ratios would have been affected for 2003. Discuss how the current ratio, return on assets, return on equity, and debt to equity ratio would have been impacted. State any assumptions you make. Is it true that the decision to capitalize will always yield weaker ratios?

l. Note 1 reveals that Continental assumes a 15% residual value for its planes and a useful life of between 25 and 30 years. By comparison, Delta Airlines assumes residual values as low as 5% and an average useful life of 20 years for owned aircraft. Which company has the more conservative depreciation policy? Had Continental Airlines adopted the same policy as Delta Airlines, how much depreciation would Continental have recorded in 2003? Compare this to the depreciation you calculated in part f above. Comment on the net income effect of Continental's policy choices.

CONTINENTAL AIRLINES, INC.
Form 10-K report
ITEM 2. PROPERTIES.

Flight Equipment

As shown in the following table, our operating aircraft fleet consisted of 355 mainline jets and 224 regional jets at December 31, 2003, excluding aircraft out of service. The regional jets are leased by ExpressJet from us and are operated by ExpressJet.

Aircraft Type	Total Aircraft	Owned	Leased	Firm Orders	Options	Seats in Standard Configuration	Average Age
777-200ER	18	6	12	-	1	283	4.3
767-400ER	16	14	2	-	-	235	2.3
767-200ER	10	9	1	-	-	174	2.8
757-300	4	4	-	5	-	210	2.0
757-200	41	13	28	-	-	183	6.9
737-900	12	8	4	3	24	167	2.3
737-800	81	26	55	40	35	155	3.6
737-700	36	12	24	15	24	124	5.0
737-500	63	15	48	-	-	104	7.7
737-300	51	14	37	-	-	124	17.3
MD-80	23	6	17	-	-	141	17.8
Mainline jets	355	127	228	63	84		7.6
ERJ-145XR	54	-	54	50	100	50	1.0
ERJ-145	140	18	122	-	-	50	3.6
ERJ-135	30	-	30	-	-	37	3.3
Regional jets	224	18	206	50	100		2.9
Total	579	145	434				5.8

As of December 31, 2003, we had the following mainline aircraft out of service:

Aircraft Type	Total Aircraft	Owned	Leased
DC 10-30	5	2	3
MD-80	14	9	5
737-300	2	-	2
Total	21	11	10

[Continental explains elsewhere that there are another 40 turboprop aircraft—32 leased, 8 owned—that are out of service.]

CONTINENTAL AIRLINES, INC.
CONSOLIDATED STATEMENTS OF OPERATIONS

(In millions, except per share data)

	Year Ended December 31,		
	2003	2002	2001
Operating Revenue:			
Passenger	$8,135	$7,862	$8,457
Cargo, mail and other	735	540	512
	8,870	8,402	8,969
Operating Expenses:			
Wages, salaries and related costs	3,056	2,959	3,021
Aircraft fuel	1,255	1,023	1,229
Aircraft rentals	896	902	903
Landing fees and other rentals	620	633	581
Maintenance, materials and repairs	509	476	568
Depreciation and amortization	444	444	467
Booking fees, credit card discounts and sales	377	380	445
Passenger servicing	297	296	347
Regional capacity purchase, net	153	-	-
Commissions	148	212	364
Other	988	1,135	1,193
Security fee reimbursement	(176)	-	-
Stabilization Act grant	-	12	(417)
Fleet impairment losses and other special charges	100	242	124
	8,667	8,714	8,825
Operating Income (Loss)	203	(312)	144
Nonoperating Income (Expense):			
Interest expense	(393)	(372)	(311)
Interest capitalized	24	36	57
Interest income	19	24	45
Gain on dispositions of ExpressJet Holdings shares	173	-	-
Equity in the income (loss) of affiliates	23	8	(20)
Other, net	152	(15)	(45)
	(2)	(319)	(274)
Income (Loss) before Income Taxes and Minority Interest	201	(631)	(130)
Income Tax Benefit (Expense)	(114)	208	35
Minority Interest	(49)	(28)	-
Net Income (Loss)	$ 38	$ (451)	$ (95)

CONTINENTAL AIRLINES, INC.
CONSOLIDATED BALANCE SHEETS
(In millions, except for share data)

	December 31,	
ASSETS	2003	2002
Current Assets:		
Cash and cash equivalents	$ 999	$ 983
Restricted cash and cash equivalents	170	62
Short-term investments	431	297
Accounts receivable, net of allowance for doubtful receivables of $19 and $30	403	378
Spare parts and supplies, net of allowance for obsolescence of $98 and $98	191	248
Deferred income taxes	157	165
Note receivable from ExpressJet Holdings, Inc.	67	-
Prepayments and other	168	145
Total current assets	2,586	2,278
Property and Equipment:		
Owned property and equipment:		
Flight equipment	6,574	6,762
Other	1,195	1,275
	7,769	8,037
Less: Accumulated depreciation	1,784	1,599
	5,985	6,438
Purchase deposits for flight equipment	225	269
Capital leases:		
Flight equipment	107	117
Other	297	262
	404	379
Less: Accumulated amortization	126	118
	278	261
Total property and equipment	6,488	6,968
Routes	615	615
Airport operating rights, net of accumulated amortization of $293 and $268	259	287
Intangible pension asset	124	144
Investment in affiliates	173	89
Note receivable from ExpressJet Holdings, Inc.	126	-
Other assets, net	278	260
Total Assets	$10,649	$10,641

CONTINENTAL AIRLINES, INC.
CONSOLIDATED BALANCE SHEETS
(In millions, except for share data)

LIABILITIES AND STOCKHOLDERS' EQUITY	2003	2002
Current Liabilities:		
Current maturities of long-term debt and capital leases	$ 422	$ 493
Accounts payable	840	930
Air traffic liability	957	882
Accrued payroll	281	285
Accrued other liabilities	366	336
Total current liabilities	2,866	2,926
Long-Term Debt and Capital Leases	5,558	5,471
Deferred Income Taxes	446	413
Accrued Pension Liability	678	723
Other	309	329
Commitments and Contingencies		
Minority Interest	-	7
Redeemable Preferred Stock of Subsidiary	-	5
Stockholders' Equity:		
Preferred stock - $.01 par, 10,000,000 shares authorized; one share of Series B issued and outstanding, stated at par value	-	-
Class B common stock - $.01 par, 200,000,000 shares authorized; 91,507,192 and 91,203,321 shares issued	1	1
Additional paid-in capital	1,401	1,391
Retained earnings	948	910
Accumulated other comprehensive loss	(417)	(395)
Treasury stock -25,471,881 and 25,442,529 shares, at cost	(1,141)	(1,140)
Total stockholders' equity	792	767
Total Liabilities and Stockholders' Equity	$10,649	$10,641

The accompanying Notes to Consolidated Financial Statements are an integral part of these statements.

CONTINENTAL AIRLINES, INC.
CONSOLIDATED STATEMENTS OF CASH FLOWS
(In millions)

	Year Ended December 31,		
	2003	2002	2001
Cash Flows from Operating Activities:			
Net income (loss)	$ 38	$ (451)	$ (95)
Adjustments to reconcile net income (loss) to cash from operations:			
Deferred income taxes	101	(179)	(40)
Depreciation and amortization	444	444	467
Fleet disposition/impairment losses	100	242	61
Gains on sales of investments	(305)	-	-
Equity in the (income) loss of affiliates	(23)	(8)	20
Other, net	(36)	12	31
Changes in operating assets and liabilities:			
(Increase) decrease in accounts receivable	(25)	(23)	73
(Increase) decrease in spare parts and supplies	4	4	(20)
Increase (decrease) in accounts payable	(19)	(79)	(8)
Increase (decrease) in air traffic liability	75	(132)	(111)
Increase (decrease) in other	(12)	124	189
Net cash provided by (used in) operating activities	342	(46)	567
Cash Flows from Investing Activities:			
Capital expenditures	(205)	(539)	(568)
Purchase deposits paid in connection with future aircraft deliveries	(29)	(73)	(432)
Purchase deposits refunded in connection with aircraft delivered	81	219	337
Purchase of short-term investments	(134)	(56)	(96)
Proceeds from sales of ExpressJet Holdings, net	134	447	-
Proceeds from sales of Internet-related investments	76	-	-
Proceeds from disposition of property and equipment	16	9	11
Other	53	(43)	(26)
Net cash used in investing activities	(8)	(36)	(774)

CONTINENTAL AIRLINES, INC.
CONSOLIDATED STATEMENTS OF CASH FLOWS
(In millions)

Cash Flows from Financing Activities:			
Proceeds from issuance of long-term debt, net	559	596	436
Payments on long-term debt and capital lease obligations	(549)	(383)	(367)
Purchase of common stock	-	-	(451)
Proceeds from issuance of common stock	5	23	241
Increase in restricted cash to collateralize letters of credit	(108)	(32)	(22)
Other	-	-	(11)
Net cash (used in) provided by financing activities	(93)	204	(174)
Impact on cash of ExpressJet deconsolidation	(225)	-	-
Net Increase (Decrease) in Cash and Cash Equivalents	16	122	(381)
Cash and Cash Equivalents - Beginning of Period	983	861	1,242
Cash and Cash Equivalents - End of Period	$ 999	$ 983	$ 861

Supplemental Cash Flows Information:			
Interest paid	$ 374	$ 345	$ 314
Income taxes paid (refunded)	$ 13	$ (31)	$ (4)
Investing and Financing Activities Not Affecting Cash:			
Property and equipment acquired through the issuance of debt	$ 120	$ 908	$ 707
Capital lease obligations incurred	$ 22	$ 36	$ 95
Contribution of ExpressJet stock to pension plan	$ 100	$ -	$ -

The accompanying Notes to Consolidated Financial Statements are an integral part of these statements.

CONTINENTAL AIRLINES, INC.

NOTE 1 - SUMMARY OF SIGNIFICANT ACCOUNTING POLICIES (excerpts)
g. Property and Equipment -

Property and equipment are recorded at cost and are depreciated to estimated residual values over their estimated useful lives using the straight-line method. Jet aircraft are assumed to have an estimated residual value of 15% of original cost; other categories of property and equipment are assumed to have no residual value. The estimated useful lives for our property and equipment are as follows:

	Estimated Useful Life
Jet aircraft and simulators	25 to 30 years
Buildings and improvements	10 to 30 years
Food service equipment	6 to 10 years
Maintenance and engineering equipment	8 years
Surface transportation and ground equipment	6 years
Communication and meteorological equipment	5 years
Computer software	3 to 10 years
Capital lease - flight and ground equipment	Lease Term

NOTE 6 - LEASES

We lease certain aircraft and other assets under long-term lease arrangements. Other leased assets include real property, airport and terminal facilities, sales offices, maintenance facilities, training centers and general offices. Most aircraft leases include both renewal options and purchase options. The purchase options are generally effective at the end of the lease term at the then-current fair market value. Our leases do not include residual value guarantees. At December 31, 2003, the scheduled future minimum lease payments under capital leases and the scheduled future minimum lease rental payments required under operating leases, that have initial or remaining noncancelable lease terms in excess of one year, are as follows (in millions):

	Capital Leases	Operating Leases	
Year ending December 31,		Aircraft	Non-aircraft
2004	$ 44	$ 897	$ 360
2005	46	975	362
2006	39	864	365
2007	40	833	367
2008	45	811	354
Later years	473	6,988	5,675
Total minimum lease payments	687	$11,368	$7,483
Less: amount representing interest	364		
Present value of capital leases	323		
Less: current maturities of capital leases	25		
Long-term capital leases	$298		

At December 31, 2003, Continental had 469 aircraft under operating leases and seven aircraft under capital leases, including aircraft subleased to ExpressJet. These operating leases have remaining lease terms ranging up to 21 ½ years. Projected sublease income to be received from ExpressJet, not included in the above table, is approximately $3.7 billion.

International Speedway Corporation—Deferred Taxes

International Speedway Corporation (ISC) dates back nearly 50 years, when Bill France Racing, Inc. signed the initial contract to secure the land for construction of Daytona International Speedway. Today, ISC is a leader in motorsports entertainment with 12 owned and operated motorsports facilities the U.S., as well as a 37.5% interest in Chicagoland Speedway and Route 66 Raceway. ISC manages over a million grandstand seats and has a presence in 6 of the USA's top 10 media markets. Nearly 80% of the U.S. population lives within 400 miles of ISC facilities.

Learning Objectives

- Understand the concepts underlying deferred income tax accounting.
- Interpret the income tax note to the financial statements.
- Use deferred tax asset and liability information to infer balances for tax purposes.
- Consider the tax consequences when revenue recognition differs for accounting and tax purposes.

Refer to the 2003 financial statements of International Speedway Corporation.

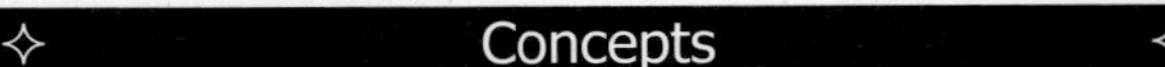

a. Explain in general terms why the company reports deferred income taxes as part of their total income tax expense. Why don't companies simply report their current tax bill as their income tax expense?

b. Explain in general terms what deferred tax assets and deferred tax liabilities represent.

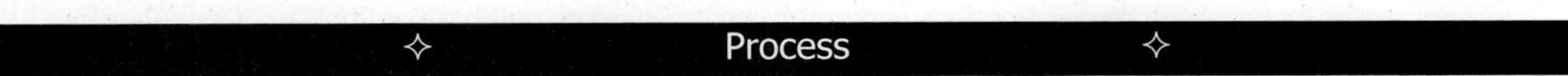

c. According to Note 8—Federal and State Income Taxes, ISC had a net deferred tax liability balance of $113,414 at November 30, 2003. Explain where that balance is found on the balance sheet.

d. What journal entry did ISC record for income tax expense in fiscal 2003?

e. The largest component of the deferred tax liability relates to "Amortization and depreciation."

   i. Explain how this deferred tax liability component arose.

   ii. Use the table below and information from the balance sheet and Note 8, to estimate ISC's net property and equipment (Net P&E) for tax purposes. Begin with step 1 and work up. For step 2, assume that the deferred tax liability was calculated with the company's 2003 effective tax rate.

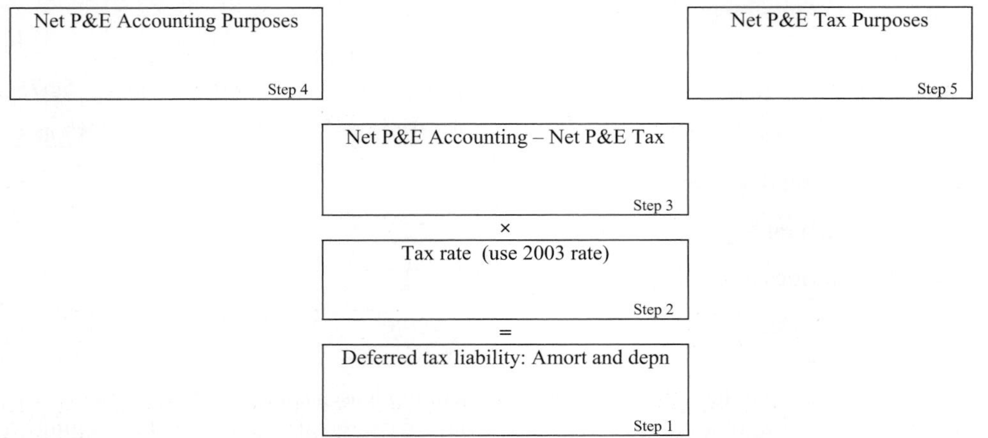

f. According to Note 1—Description of the Business, Basis of Presentation and Summary of Significant Accounting Policies, ISC's revenue recognition policy is:

REVENUE RECOGNITION/DEFERRED INCOME: Admission income and all race-related revenue is earned upon completion of an event and is stated net of admission and sales taxes collected. Advance ticket sales and all race-related revenue on future events are deferred until earned. Revenues from the sale of merchandise to retail customers, internet and catalog sales, and direct sales to dealers are recognized at the time of the sale.

Kansas Speedway Corporation ("KSC") offers Founding Fan Preferred Access Speedway Seating ("PASS") agreements, which give purchasers the exclusive right and obligation to purchase KSC season-ticket packages for certain sanctioned racing events annually for thirty years under specified terms and conditions. Among the conditions, licensees are required to purchase all season-ticket packages when and as offered each year. Founding Fan PASS agreements automatically terminate without refund should owners not purchase any offered season tickets.

Net fees received under PASS agreements are deferred and are amortized into income over the expected life of the PASS.

i. Why doesn't ISC record admission revenue when event tickets are purchased and paid for?

ii. Assume that for tax purposes cash received from ticket sales is considered current period taxable revenue. How would receiving cash for tickets for the 2004 Daytona 500 auto race affect ISC's deferred tax assets and liabilities? Assume the tickets are sold in fiscal 2003.

iii. Assume that the balance sheet item Deferred income, in the current liabilities section, relates entirely (and in equal amounts) to advance tickets sold to the Daytona 500 auto race to be held on February 15, 2004 and the Pepsi 400 auto race to be held on July 3, 2004, both at the Daytona International Speedway. Assume further that for tax purposes 10% of advance ticket receipts are immediately taxable and the remainder is taxable when the auto races take place.

Calculate the deferred tax asset or liability associated with the deferred revenue ISC recorded during fiscal 2003.

Assume that during the first quarter of 2004, a further $10 million of tickets were sold, all for the Pepsi 400. Provide the journal entry to record the sale of the tickets.

Provide the adjusting entry that ISC will record at the end of first quarter 2004 to record the previously deferred revenues that were earned that quarter. Also provide the journal entry to adjust the deferred tax liability related to deferred revenues. Assume that the company's 39% tax rate remains unchanged.

Now assume that during the second quarter of fiscal 2004 no further advanced tickets were sold. However, a tax-law change was enacted lowering ISC's tax rate to 37%. Provide the adjusting journal entry related to the deferred tax asset associated with deferred income that ISC will record at the end of the second quarter.

g. One of ISC's deferred tax assets is labeled "Loss carryforwards."

i. What is a loss carryforward? How does it meet the definition of an asset?

ii. If ISC's loss carryforwards were expected to expire unused, would the related deferred tax assets still meet the definition of an asset?

h. One of ISC's deferred tax liabilities is labeled "Equity investments." Explain how accounting for investments in other companies using the equity method can give rise to deferred tax liabilities.

CONSOLIDATED BALANCE SHEETS

	November 30, 2002	November 30, 2003
	(In Thousands)	
ASSETS		
Current Assets:		
Cash and cash equivalents	$ 109,263	$ 223,973
Short-term investments	200	201
Receivables, less allowance of $1,500 in 2002 and 2003	30,557	37,996
Inventories	4,799	5,496
Prepaid expenses and other current assets	3,784	4,078
Total Current Assets	148,603	271,744
Property and Equipment, net	859,096	884,623
Other Assets:		
Equity investments	31,152	33,706
Goodwill	92,542	92,542
Other	24,578	21,177
	148,272	147,425
Total Assets	$ 1,155,971	$ 1,303,792
LIABILITIES AND SHAREHOLDERS' EQUITY		
Current Liabilities:		
Current portion of long-term debt	$ 5,775	$ 232,963
Accounts payable	17,506	15,739
Deferred income	98,315	106,998
Income taxes payable	3,939	6,877
Other current liabilities	10,968	13,928
Total Current Liabilities	136,503	376,505
Long-Term Debt	309,606	75,168
Deferred Income Taxes	74,943	113,414
Long-Term Deferred Income	11,709	11,894
Other Long-Term Liabilities	885	346
Commitments and Contingencies	-	-
Shareholders' Equity:		
Class A Common Stock, $.01 par value, 80,000,000 shares authorized; 25,319,221 and 28,359,173 issued and outstanding in 2002 and 2003, respectively	253	283
Class B Common Stock, $.01 par value, 40,000,000 shares authorized; 27,867,456 and 24,858,610 issued and outstanding in 2002 and 2003, respectively	279	249
Additional paid-in capital	693,463	694,719
Retained (deficit) earnings	(67,641)	34,602
Accumulated other comprehensive loss	(874)	(333)
	625,480	729,520
Less unearned compensation-restricted stock	3,155	3,055
Total Shareholders' Equity	622,325	726,465
Total Liabilities and Shareholders' Equity	$ 1,155,971	$ 1,303,792

See accompanying notes

CONSOLIDATED STATEMENTS OF OPERATIONS

	Year Ended November 30,		
	2001	2002	2003
	(In Thousands, Except Per Share Amounts)		
REVENUES:			
Admissions, net	$ 214,494	$ 213,255	$ 210,535
Motorsports related income	238,208	259,609	284,902
Food, beverage and merchandise income	70,575	70,396	74,199
Other income	5,233	7,292	6,109
	528,510	550,552	575,745
EXPENSES:			
Direct expenses:			
Prize and point fund monies and NASCAR sanction fees	87,859	97,290	107,821
Motorsports related expenses	98,458	99,441	102,231
Food, beverage and merchandise expenses	38,251	38,109	41,250
General and administrative expenses	79,953	80,325	85,773
Depreciation and amortization	54,544	41,154	44,171
Homestead-Miami Speedway track reconfiguration	-	-	2,829
	359,065	356,319	384,075
Operating income	169,445	194,233	191,670
Interest income	3,446	1,211	1,821
Interest expense	(26,505)	(24,277)	(23,179)
Equity in net income from equity investments	2,935	1,907	2,553
Minority interest	992	-	-
Income before income taxes and cumulative effect of accounting change	150,313	173,074	172,865
Income taxes	62,680	66,803	67,417
Income before cumulative effect of accounting change	87,633	106,271	105,448
Cumulative effect of accounting change—company operations	-	(513,827)	-
Cumulative effect of accounting change—equity investment	-	(3,422)	-
Net income (loss)	$ 87,633	$ (410,978)	$ 105,448
Basic earnings per share before cumulative effect of accounting change	$ 1.65	$ 2.00	$ 1.99
Cumulative effect of accounting change	-	(9.75)	-
Basic earnings (loss) per share	$ 1.65	$ (7.75)	$ 1.99
Diluted earnings per share before cumulative effect of accounting change	$ 1.65	$ 2.00	$ 1.98
Cumulative effect of accounting change	-	(9.74)	-
Diluted earnings (loss) per share	$ 1.65	$ (7.74)	$ 1.98
Dividends per share	$ 0.06	$ 0.06	$ 0.06
Basic weighted average shares outstanding	52,996,660	53,036,552	53,057,077
Diluted weighted average shares outstanding	53,076,828	53,101,535	53,133,282

See accompanying notes

CONSOLIDATED STATEMENTS OF CASH FLOWS

	Year Ended November 30,		
	2001	2002	2003
		(In Thousands)	
OPERATING ACTIVITIES			
Net income (loss)	$ 87,633	$ (410,978)	$ 105,448
Adjustments to reconcile net income (loss) to net cash provided by operating activities:			
Cumulative effect of accounting change	-	517,249	-
Depreciation and amortization	54,544	41,154	44,171
Deferred income taxes	27,177	29,461	38,471
Homestead-Miami Speedway track reconfiguration	-	-	2,829
Amortization of unearned compensation	1,619	1,485	1,695
Amortization of financing costs	1,566	1,332	294
Undistributed income from equity investments	(2,935)	(1,907)	(2,553)
Minority interest	(992)	-	-
Other, net	722	(1,634)	(37)
Changes in operating assets and liabilities			
Receivables, net	(3,226)	(5,415)	(7,439)
Inventories, prepaid expenses and other current assets	3,394	2,209	(990)
Accounts payable and other current liabilities	1,815	2,873	1,040
Income taxes payable	-	4,544	2,939
Deferred income	(10,631)	(1,759)	8,868
Net cash provided by operating activities	160,686	178,614	194,736
INVESTING ACTIVITIES			
Capital expenditures	(98,379)	(53,521)	(72,587)
Proceeds from affiliate	-	4,045	4,075
Proceeds from short-term investments	400	400	400
Purchases of short-term investments	(400)	(400)	(400)
Proceeds from asset disposals	722	3,836	178
Proceeds from STAR bonds	-	5,589	-
Proceeds from restricted investments	33,930	1,263	-
Acquisition, net of cash acquired	(3,878)	-	-
Equity investments	(1,202)	-	-
Advances to affiliate	(1,500)	-	-
Other, net	(1,647)	(1,533)	(1,552)
Net cash used in investing activities	(71,954)	(40,321)	(69,886)
FINANCING ACTIVITIES			
Payment of long-term debt	(5,165)	(9,225)	(5,775)
Cash dividends paid	(3,190)	(3,191)	(3,193)
Reacquisition of previously issued common stock	(965)	(831)	(352)
Deferred financing fees	-	-	(820)
Payments under credit facilities	(71,000)	(90,000)	-
Proceeds under credit facilities	12,000	-	-
Proceeds from interest rate swap	-	3,213	-
Net cash used in financing activities	(68,320)	(100,034)	(10,140)
Net increase in cash and cash equivalents	20,412	38,259	114,710
Cash and cash equivalents at beginning of period	50,592	71,004	109,263
Cash and cash equivalents at end of period	$ 71,004	$ 109,263	$ 223,973

See accompanying notes

NOTES TO CONSOLIDATED FINANCIAL STATEMENTS, NOVEMBER 30, 2003

NOTE 8 - FEDERAL AND STATE INCOME TAXES

Deferred income taxes reflect the net tax effects of temporary differences between the carrying amounts of assets and liabilities for financial reporting purposes and the amounts used for income tax purposes.

Significant components of the provision for income taxes for the years ended November 30, are as follows (in thousands):

	2001	2002	2003
Current tax expense:			
Federal	$ 31,560	$ 29,441	$ 24,480
State	3,944	7,902	4,466
Deferred tax expense (benefit):			
Federal	23,986	29,526	36,329
State	3,190	(66)	2,142
Provision for income taxes	$ 62,680	$ 66,803	$ 67,417

The reconciliation of income tax computed at the federal statutory tax rates to income tax expense for the years ended November 30, are as follows (percent of pre-tax income):

	2001	2002	2003
Income tax computed at federal statutory rates	35.0%	35.0%	35.0%
State income taxes, net of federal tax benefit	3.1	3.6	3.1
Nondeductible goodwill	2.8	-	-
Other, net	0.8	-	0.9
	41.7%	38.6%	39.0%

NOTE 8 - FEDERAL AND STATE INCOME TAXES (continued)

The components of the net deferred tax assets (liabilities) at November 30 are as follows (in thousands):

	2002	2003
Amortization and depreciation	$ 48,138	$ 38,527
Deferred revenues	4,412	4,315
Loss carryforwards	2,672	2,840
Deferred expenses	2,645	2,454
Accruals	987	2,062
Compensation related	1,373	1,505
Other	275	199
Deferred tax assets	60,502	51,902
Amortization and depreciation	(130,916)	(157,664)
Equity investment	(4,210)	(7,322)
Other	(319)	(330)
Deferred tax liabilities	(135,445)	(165,316)
Net deferred tax liabilities	$ (74,943)	$ (113,414)

The Company has recorded deferred tax assets related to various state net operating loss carryforwards totaling approximately $69.3 million, that expire in varying amounts beginning in fiscal 2020.

NOTE 9 - CAPITAL STOCK

The Company's authorized capital includes 80 million shares of Class A Common Stock, par value $.01 ("Class A Common Stock"), 40 million shares of Class B Common Stock, par value $.01 ("Class B Common Stock"), and 1 million shares of Preferred Stock, par value $.01 ("Preferred Stock"). The shares of Class A Common Stock and Class B Common Stock are identical in all respects, except for voting rights and certain dividend and conversion rights as described below. Each share of Class A Common Stock entitles the holder to one-fifth (1/5) vote on each matter submitted to a vote of the Company's shareholders and each share of Class B Common Stock entitles the holder to one (1) vote on each such matter, in each case including the election of directors. Holders of Class A Common Stock and Class B Common Stock are entitled to receive dividends at the same rate if and when declared by the Board of Directors out of funds legally available therefrom, subject to the dividend and liquidation rights of any Preferred Stock that may be issued and outstanding. Class A Common Stock has no conversion rights. Class B Common Stock is convertible into Class A Common Stock, in whole or in part, at any time at the option of the holder on the basis of one share of Class A Common Stock for each share of Class B Common Stock converted. Each share of Class B Common Stock will also automatically convert into one share of Class A Common Stock if, on the record date of any meeting of the shareholders, the number of shares of Class B Common Stock then outstanding is less than 10% of the aggregate number of shares of Class A Common Stock and Class B Common Stock then outstanding.

The Board of Directors of the Company is authorized, without further shareholder action, to divide any or all shares of the authorized Preferred Stock into series and fix and determine the designations, preferences and relative rights and qualifications, limitations, or restrictions thereon of any series so established, including voting powers, dividend rights, liquidation preferences, redemption rights and conversion privileges. No shares of Preferred Stock are outstanding. The Board of Directors has not authorized any series of Preferred Stock, and there are no plans, agreements or understandings for the authorization or issuance of any shares of Preferred Stock.

Bethlehem Steel Corporation—Retirement Obligations

Bethlehem Steel Corporation is the nation's second largest integrated steel producer with revenues of about $3.5 billion and shipments of 7.5 million tons of steel products in 2002. Founded in 1904 by Charles M. Schwab, Bethlehem Steel employs about 11,000 and produces a wide variety of steel mill products including hot-rolled, cold-rolled and coated sheets, tin mill products, carbon and alloy plates, rail, specialty blooms, carbon and alloy bars. Principal markets include automotive, construction, machinery and equipment, appliance, containers, service centers, and rail. The company has been operating under Chapter 11 of the U.S. Bankruptcy Code since October 2001. In March 2003, the company signed an asset purchase agreement to sell substantially all of its assets to International Steel Group (ISG) of Cleveland, Ohio.

Learning Objectives

- Read and understand pension and Other Post-Employment Benefits (OPEB) footnote terminology.
- Understand and account for the difference between expensing and funding pension obligations.
- Evaluate the impact of actuarial assumptions on pension expense and obligations.
- Understand how current rules smooth pension costs and can lead to pension income.

Refer to the 2001 Bethlehem Steel Corporation financial statements and selected notes.

 **Concepts** 

a. There are two general types of pension plans—defined benefit plans and defined contribution plans.

   i. How do these two types of plans differ? Which type does Bethlehem Steel have?

   ii. Explain how the matching principle applies to pension accounting.

   iii. What makes a pension plan's obligation increase or decrease from one period to the next?

   iv. What makes a pension plan's assets increase or decrease from one period to the next?

   v. List some of the assumptions that are made in order to account for pensions.

b. Bethlehem Steel provides healthcare and other benefits to retirees. These other post-employment benefits are known as OPEB.

   i. Explain how the matching principle applies to OPEB.

   ii. What makes an OPEB obligation increase or decrease from one period to the next?

   iii. What makes an OPEB plan's assets increase or decrease from one period to the next?

   iv. List some of the assumptions that are made in order to account for OPEB.

 **Process** 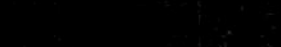

c. Consider Bethlehem Steel's pension plan obligation.

   i. What is the present value at November 30, 2001 of the pension benefits that Bethlehem has promised its employees? Where on the balance sheet is the pension obligation? At what amount? Note: although Bethlehem Steel has a December 31 year end, the actuarial valuation of the pension plan takes place as of November 30 each year.

   ii. Is the Bethlehem Steel pension plan under-funded or over-funded at December 31, 2001? At December 31, 2000?

   iii. Briefly explain the items listed under the caption "Unrecognized:" in the pension footnote. When, if ever, will these unrecognized gains and losses appear in Bethlehem Steel's financial statements?

d. Consider Bethlehem Steel's pension expense.

   i. What are the components of Bethlehem Steel's pension expense?

   ii. What amount did Bethlehem Steel record for pension expense in the income statement for 2001?

✧ Analysis ✧

e. Pension and OPEB accounting require management to make a number of estimates about investment returns, discount rates, and future costs.

   i. Consider Bethlehem Steel's pension plan assets. Estimate the actual return (in percentage terms) that the plan assets earned in 2001. How does that return compare to the expected return?

   ii. During 2001, Bethlehem Steel changed the discount rate used to calculate its projected pension benefit obligation from 8% to 7 1/8%. Which footnote numbers does this rate change affect?

   iii. Bethlehem Steel now projects compensation rate increases of 3%. How would the 2001 pension footnote have been different had the 2000 compensation rate assumption been used?

f. Comment on the trend in pension and OPEB expense at Bethlehem Steel. How have these expenses affected operating income over the past three years? Do you consider this trend persistent? That is, do you expect it to continue?

g. Read the accompanying article, Pension Accounting Whoppers, from the October 20, 2002 *New York Times*.

   i. The article indicates that many companies report pension income instead of pension expense. Explain how current GAAP allows that to take place, especially in a "down" (stock) market.

   ii. Under current GAAP, a variety of changes in the value of pension plan obligations and pension plan assets are amortized, or smoothed, into earnings over time. The International Accounting Standards Board and the Financial Accounting Standards Board are considering changes in pension accounting that would require that year-to-year changes in the value of plan assets and benefit obligations be included in reported earnings for the year. Assume the position of Chief Financial Officer for Bethlehem Steel and provide arguments for and against such a move. What position would you counsel the standard setters to take? Would your advice change if you were an investor? Why or why not?

h. Bethlehem Steel filed for protection under Chapter 11 of the U.S. Bankruptcy Code on October 15, 2001.

   i. How did Bethlehem Steel's external auditors modify their opinion about the company's financial statements in light of the bankruptcy filing?

   ii. If the going concern assumption did not hold, how would the financial statements differ?

The New York Times
nytimes.com

October 20, 2002

Pension Accounting Whoppers

For all of this year's accounting scandals, one of the most perilous financial minefields may still lie ahead — corporate America's management of traditional pension plans covering some 45 million Americans. The fate of these funds in the boom-to-bust financial cycle is at once a glaring accounting scandal and a looming threat to the economy.

First, the scandal. Accounting rules allow companies to estimate their pension funds' average annual return over time, and report that amount as profit, regardless of what actually takes place. This has provided an artificial means for companies to pad their reported earnings — the bottom line that determines top executives' bonuses. Many blue-chip companies' financial statements continue to assume 9 or 10 percent returns, even now in the middle of the most severe bear market in decades.

Over all, it is estimated that 50 of America's largest companies counted $54.4 billion of pension fund gains as profits last year, when they in fact lost $35.8 billion. The accounting rules made it very easy for corporate managers to legally distort their numbers, to their benefit and to the detriment of shareholders.

Phantom earnings. Sound familiar? In a year when Americans have learned just how corrosive other accounting fictions can be to the financial markets' integrity — ostensibly independent offshore partnerships come to mind — such wishful bookkeeping can no longer be tolerated.

The Financial Accounting Standards Board, the body that sets accounting rules, should heed the call of investment advocates like Warren Buffett and California's controller, Kathleen Connell, who have been clamoring to put an end to this practice. If necessary, Congress should intervene. The overhaul of accounting standards must be aimed at revealing an enterprise's true state of affairs, and forcing a separate disclosure of more intangible projections. This will narrow managers' ability to manipulate their results.

The looming threat for the economy lies in the fact that once companies are done reaping the benefits of their accounting fictions, they do ultimately have to face up to the reality of what this bear market has done to their pension funds. In the boom years of the late 1990's, companies didn't need to deposit any new cash in these funds to keep them fully funded. But now they find themselves with glaring pension fund deficits, as they did in previous down markets.

Wall Street analysts and debt-rating agencies are concerned that more and more companies across a broad range of industries will have to invest in their underfunded pension funds when they can least afford it. General Motors and Lucent are two major companies that recently took big hits to address shortfalls.

The broader concern for the economy, particularly if the stock market and interest rates remain depressed, is that this trend could help feed a potentially vicious circle. Companies facing pension liabilities could refrain from new capital investments, thereby depressing the stock market further. But nothing is gained by having fictitious accounting sugarcoat this looming threat.

Consolidated Statements of Operations

(Dollars in millions, except per share data)	Year Ended December 31 2001	2000	1999
Net Sales	$ 3,334.3	$ 4,094.4	$ 4,023.2
Costs and Expenses:			
Cost of sales	3,468.6	3,816.6	3,822.1
Depreciation and amortization (Note A)	253.1	260.3	257.5
Selling, administration and general expense	106.4	113.0	122.2
Unusual items (Note C)	372.3	(20.9)	-
Total Costs and Expenses	4,200.4	4,169.0	4,201.8
Loss from Operations before Reorganization Items	(866.1)	(74.6)	(178.6)
Reorganization Items (Note B)	(8.1)	-	-
Financing Income (Expense):			
Interest and other financing costs (Notes A, B and E)	(93.3)	(75.4)	(51.9)
Interest income	1.9	6.6	8.3
Loss Before Income Taxes	(965.6)	(143.4)	(222.2)
Benefit (Provision) for Income Taxes (Note D)	(984.0)	25.0	39.0
Net Loss	(1,949.6)	(118.4)	(183.2)
Dividend Requirements on Preferred and Preference Stock	40.5	40.7	41.2
Net Loss Applicable to Common Stock	$ (1,990.1)	$ (159.1)	$ (224.4)
Net Loss per Common Share (Note K):			
Basic and Diluted	$ (15.30)	$ (1.21)	$ (1.72)

The accompanying Notes are an integral part of the Consolidated Financial Statements.

Consolidated Balance Sheets

(Dollars in millions, except per share data)	December 31 2001	2000
Assets		
Current Assets:		
Cash and cash equivalents (Note A)	$ 104.0	$ 109.7
Receivables (Note E)	350.4	152.1
Inventories (Notes A and E)		
Raw materials and supplies	259.5	303.3
Finished and semifinished products	465.8	570.9
Total Inventories	725.3	874.2
Other current assets	22.8	10.4
Total Current Assets	1,202.5	1,146.4
Investments and Miscellaneous Assets	129.6	136.1
Property, Plant and Equipment, less accumulated depreciation of $4,367.6 and $4,363.5 (Note A)	2,686.9	2,870.5
Deferred Income Tax Asset - net (Note D)	-	985.0
Goodwill (Notes A and C)	-	329.0
Intangible Pension Asset (Note G)	225.0	-
Total Assets	$ 4,244.0	$ 5,467.0
Liabilities and Stockholders' Equity (Deficit)		
Current Liabilities:		
Accounts payable	$ 150.1	$ 355.1
Accrued employment costs	34.4	137.2
Other postretirement benefits (Note G)	3.5	175.0
Accrued taxes (Note D)	14.4	59.7
Debt and capital lease obligations - current (Note E)	19.3	55.4
Other current liabilities	49.9	144.8
Total Current Liabilities	271.6	927.2
Long-term Debt and Capital Lease Obligations (Note E)	628.2	798.0
Deferred Gain (Note F)	103.2	126.2
Pension Liability (Note G)	-	442.0
Other Postretirement Benefits (Note G)	37.8	1,780.0
Other Long-term Liabilities	5.6	273.6
Liabilities Subject to Compromise (Note B)	4,878.1	-
Stockholders' Equity (Deficit) (Notes H, I and J):		
Preferred Stock -- at $1 per share par value (aggregate liquidation preference of $467.9); Authorized 20,000,000 shares	11.4	11.6
Preference Stock -- at $1 per share par value (aggregate liquidation preference of $70.6); Authorized 20,000,000 shares	2.0	2.1
Common Stock -- at $1 per share par value; Authorized 250,000,000 Issued 135,780,069 and 134,623,707 shares	135.8	134.6
Common Stock -- Held in treasury 4,898,134 and 4,850,953 shares at cost	(65.9)	(65.7)
Additional paid-in capital	1,908.2	1,926.8
Accumulated other comprehensive income	(833.0)	-
Accumulated deficit	(2,839.0)	(889.4)
Total Stockholders' Equity (Deficit)	(1,680.5)	1,120.0
Total Liabilities and Stockholders' Equity (Deficit)	$ 4,244.0	$ 5,467.0

The accompanying Notes are an integral part of the Consolidated Financial Statements.

Consolidated Statements of Cash Flows

(Dollars in millions)	2001	2000	1999
	Year Ended December 31		
Operating Activities:			
Net Loss	$ (1,949.6)	$ (118.4)	$ (183.2)
Adjustments for items not affecting cash from operating activities:			
Deferred income taxes (Note D)	984.0	(26.0)	(39.0)
Depreciation and amortization (Note A)	253.1	260.3	257.5
Unusual items (Note C)	372.3	(20.9)	-
Recognition of deferred gains	(22.7)	(17.1)	(18.6)
Reorganization items (Note B)	8.1	-	-
Litigation recovery	13.0	-	-
Other - net	(1.9)	19.1	28.8
Working capital (excluding investing and financing activities):			
Receivables - operating	9.6	81.2	(65.7)
Receivables - financing (Note E)	(212.0)	-	70.0
Inventories	148.7	(9.4)	175.7
Accounts payable	25.1	(45.2)	10.8
Employment costs and other	(4.6)	1.0	(24.7)
Funding Postretirement Benefits (Note G):			
Pension less (more) than expense	94.5	29.0	(5.0)
Retiree healthcare and life insurance benefits less than expense	83.0	134.0	20.0
Cash Provided from (used by) Operations Before Reorganization Items	(199.4)	287.6	226.6
Reorganization Items	(8.1)	-	-
Cash Provided from (used by) Operating Activities	(207.5)	287.6	226.6
Investing Activities:			
Capital expenditures	(89.2)	(224.3)	(557.0)
Cash proceeds from asset sales and other	47.5	128.0	177.0
Cash Used for Investing Activities	(41.7)	(96.3)	(380.0)
Financing Activities:			
Borrowings (Note E)	408.8	132.3	249.7
Debt and capital lease payments (Note E)	(108.9)	(226.7)	(65.1)
Cash dividends paid (Note J)	(20.2)	(40.4)	(40.4)
Other payments	(36.2)	(41.3)	(29.2)
Purchase of Common Stock	-	(4.9)	-
Cash Provided from (Used for) Financing Activities	243.5	(181.0)	115.0
Net Increase (Decrease) in Cash and Cash Equivalents	(5.7)	10.3	(38.4)
Cash and Cash Equivalents - Beginning of Period	109.7	99.4	137.8
- End of Period	$ 104.0	$ 109.7	$ 99.4
Supplemental Cash Flow Information:			
Interest paid, net of amount capitalized	$ 92.5	$ 68.8	$ 46.1
Income taxes paid (received) - net (Note D)	(1.4)	1.4	0.7
Capital lease obligations incurred	5.2	5.3	7.9
Debt assumed in purchase combination	18.9	-	-

The accompanying Notes are an integral part of the Consolidated Financial Statements.

A. ACCOUNTING POLICIES

Reorganization Under Chapter 11 - On October 15, 2001, Bethlehem and 22 of its wholly owned subsidiaries filed voluntary petitions for reorganization under chapter 11 of the United States Bankruptcy Code. See Note B, *Reorganization Under Chapter 11* for a discussion of the filing and its impact on these financial statements.

Principles of Consolidation - The consolidated financial statements include the accounts of Bethlehem Steel Corporation and all majority owned subsidiaries and joint ventures.

Cash and Cash Equivalents - Cash equivalents consist primarily of overnight investments, certificates of deposit and other short-term, highly liquid instruments generally with original maturities at the time of acquisition of three months or less. Cash equivalents are stated at cost plus accrued interest, which approximates market.

Inventories - Inventories are valued at the lower of cost (principally FIFO) or market.

Property, Plant and Equipment - Property, plant and equipment is stated at cost. Maintenance, repairs and renewals that neither materially add to the value of the property nor appreciably prolong its life are charged to expense. Gains or losses on dispositions of property, plant and equipment are recognized in income. Interest is capitalized on significant construction projects and totaled none in 2001, $12 million in 2000 and $26 million in 1999.

Our property, plant and equipment by major classification is:

(Dollars in Millions)	December 31	
	2001	2000
Land (net of depletion)	$ 30.3	$ 31.2
Buildings	666.0	677.4
Machinery and equipment	6,224.3	6,295.6
Accumulated depreciation	(4,367.6)	(4,363.5)
	2,553.0	2,640.7
Construction-in-progress	133.9	229.8
Total	$ 2,686.9	$ 2,870.5

Depreciation - Depreciation is based upon the estimated useful lives of each asset group. That life is 18 years for most steel producing assets. Steel producing assets, other than blast furnace linings, are depreciated on a straight-line basis adjusted by an activity factor. This factor is based on the ratio of production and shipments for the current year to the average production and shipments for the current and preceding four years at each operating location. Annual depreciation after adjustment for this activity factor is not less than 75% or more than 125% of straight-line depreciation. Depreciation after adjustment for this activity factor was $24 million less than straight-line in 2001, $9 million less than straight-line in 2000 and $10 million less than straight-line in 1999. Through December 31, 2001, $29 million less accumulated depreciation has been recorded under this method than would have been recorded under straight-line depreciation. The cost of blast furnace linings is depreciated on a unit-of-production basis.

Amortization - Goodwill was amortized over a 30-year life using the straight-line method. Amortization was $12 million in 2001, 2000 and 1999. See Note C, *Asset Impairment and Unusual Items.*

Asset Impairment - We periodically evaluate the carrying value of long-lived assets when events and circumstances warrant such a review. A long-lived asset is considered impaired when the anticipated undiscounted future cash flows from a logical grouping of assets is less than its carrying value. In that event, we recognize a loss equal to the amount by which the carrying value exceeds the fair market value of assets less any estimated disposal costs. See Note C, *Asset Impairment and Unusual Items.*

Foreign Currency, Interest Rate and Commodity Price Risk Management - On January 1, 2001, we adopted FASB Statement No. 133, *Accounting for Derivative Instruments and Hedging Activities.* Adopting this standard had no effect on net income. Amounts recognized on the balance sheet at adoption were subsequently recorded in earnings.

Periodically, we enter into financial contracts to manage risks. We use foreign currency exchange contracts to manage the cost of firm purchase commitments for capital equipment or other purchased goods and services denominated in a foreign currency. We use interest rate swap agreements to fix the interest rate on certain floating rate financings. We use commodity contracts to fix the cost of a portion of our annual requirements for natural gas, zinc and other metals. Generally, foreign currency and commodity contracts are for periods of less than a year. At December 31, 2001, we had no open derivative financial contracts.

Environmental Expenditures - Environmental expenditures that increase the life or efficiency of property, plant and equipment, or that will reduce or prevent future environmental contamination are capitalized. Expenditures that relate to existing conditions caused by past operations and have no significant future economic benefit are expensed. Environmental expenses are accrued at the time the expenditure becomes probable and the cost can be reasonably estimated. We do not discount any recorded obligations for future remediation expenditures to their present value nor do we record recoveries of environmental remediation costs from insurance carriers and other third parties, if any, as assets until their receipt.

Revenue Recognition - We recognize substantially all revenues when products are shipped to customers and all substantial risks of ownership change.

Use of Estimates - In preparing these financial statements, we make estimates and use assumptions that affect some of the reported amounts and disclosures. See, for example, Note B, *Reorganization Under Chapter 11*; Note D, *Taxes*; Note F, *Commitments and Contingent Liabilities*; and Note G, *Postretirement Benefits.* In the future, actual amounts received or paid could differ from those estimates.

Reclassifications - Presentation of certain amounts in prior years have been revised to be consistent with the current year.

New Accounting Pronouncements - During 2001, the Financial Accounting Standards Board issued Statement No. 143 *Accounting for Asset Retirement Obligations.* The Statement requires the recognition of a liability and an asset for the estimated cost of disposal as part of the initial cost of a long-lived asset and subsequent amortization of the asset to expense using a systematic and rationale method. Bethlehem will adopt this Statement on January 1, 2003 and currently cannot reasonably estimate the effect of adoption of this Statement on our financial position or results of operations.

During 2001 the Financial Accounting Standards Board issued Statement No. 144, *Accounting for the Impairment or Disposal of Long-Lived Assets.* This Statement establishes a single accounting approach for measuring impairment of long-lived assets, including a segment of a business accounted for as a discontinued operation whether sold or disposed of by other means. Bethlehem adopted this Statement on January 1, 2002, and it had no financial impact.

B. REORGANIZATION UNDER CHAPTER 11

On October 15, 2001, Bethlehem Steel Corporation and 22 of its wholly owned subsidiaries (collectively, the Debtors) filed voluntary petitions for reorganization under chapter 11 of the United States Bankruptcy Code (the Code) in the United States Bankruptcy Court for the Southern District of New York (the Court). The wholly owned subsidiaries that did not file for chapter 11 reorganization are not material in relation to Bethlehem's consolidated financial position and results of operations. Bethlehem continues to manage its properties and operate its businesses in the under Sections 1107 and 1108 of the Code as a debtor-in-possession.

These consolidated financial statements have been prepared in conformity with generally accepted accounting principles on a going concern basis, which contemplates continuity of operations, realization of assets and payment of liabilities. Under bankruptcy law, actions by creditors to collect indebtedness owed by the Debtors prior to October 15, 2001 (pre-petition) are stayed and certain other pre-petition contractual obligations may not be enforced against the Debtors. As a result of the chapter 11 filing, there is no assurance that the carrying amounts of the assets will be realized or that liabilities will be settled for amounts recorded. Bethlehem also is continuing to pursue various strategic alternatives including, among other things, possible consolidation opportunities, joint ventures with other steel operators, a stand-alone plan of reorganization and liquidation of part or all of Bethlehem's assets. Such alternatives are in an early stage and have not been implemented, nor can there be any assurance that any such alternatives will be implemented. After further consideration of such alternatives and negotiations with various parties in interest, Bethlehem expects to present a chapter 11 plan, which will likely cause a material change to the carrying amount of assets and liabilities in the financial statements.

Due to material uncertainties, it is not possible to predict the length of time the Debtors will operate under chapter 11 protection, the outcome of the reorganization in general, the effect of the reorganization on the Debtors' businesses or the recovery by creditors of the Debtors and equity holders of Bethlehem.

These consolidated financial statements have been prepared in accordance with the AICPA's Statement of Position 90-7 *Financial Reporting by Entities in Reorganization Under the Bankruptcy Code* (SOP 90-7). SOP 90-7 provides for segregating pre-petition liabilities that are subject to compromise, identifying all transactions and events that are directly associated with the reorganization of the Debtors and discontinuing interest accrual on unsecured or undersecured debt.

Except for secured debt and capital lease obligations, all recorded pre-petition liabilities of the Debtors have been classified as liabilities subject to compromise. The Court authorized, but did not require, payments of certain pre-petition wages, employee benefits and other obligations. Net changes in pension, other postemployment benefits and certain other accrued liabilities since October 15, 2001, are included in liabilities subject to compromise. Payments of approximately $108 million have been made on liabilities subject to compromise, primarily for wages, active and retiree health care benefits and for other employee related costs. Liabilities subject to compromise at December 31, 2001 follows:

(Dollars in millions)	**Dec. 31, 2001**
Other postemployment benefits	$ 2,005.7
Pension liability	1,624.0
Unsecured debt	526.7
Accounts payable	220.8
Accrued employment costs	270.6
Other accrued liabilities	152.8
Accrued taxes and interest	77.5
Total	$ 4,878.1

Net costs resulting from reorganization of the businesses have been reported in the statement of earnings separately as reorganization items. For the year ended December 31, 2001, the following have been incurred:

(Dollars in millions)	**2001**
Professional fees	$ 7.1
Losses from termination of contracts	1.4
Interest income	(0.4)
Total	$ 8.1

Interest on unsecured debt that was not charged to earnings for the period from October 15 to December 31, 2001 was approximately $9 million.

G. POSTRETIREMENT BENEFITS

We have noncontributory defined benefit pension plans that provide postretirement benefits for substantially all our employees. Defined benefits are based on years of service and the five highest consecutive years of pensionable earnings during the last ten years prior to retirement or a minimum amount based on years of service. We fund annually the amount required under ERISA minimum funding standards plus additional amounts as appropriate based on liquidity. In addition, we currently provide other postretirement benefits (OPEB) for health care and life insurance to most employees and their dependents.

The following sets forth the plans' funded status at our valuation date together with certain actuarial assumptions used and the amounts recognized in our consolidated balance sheets and income statements:

(Dollars in millions)	Pension		OPEB	
	2001	**2000**	**2001**	**2000**
Change in benefit obligation:				
Projected benefit obligation - beginning of year	$ 6,060	$ 6,115	$ 2,775	$ 2,750
Current service cost	60	64	13	12
Interest cost	463	468	213	212
Actuarial adjustments	469	(3)	223	(8)
Other	32	3	12	1
Benefits / administration fees paid	(589)	(587)	(205)	(192)
Projected benefit obligation - November 30	6,495	6,060	3,031	2,775
Change in plan assets:				
Fair value of plan assets - beginning of year	5,735	6,090	90	100
Actual return on plan assets	(393)	213	1	9
Employer contributions	8	27	-	-
Benefits / administration fees paid	(597)	(595)	(74)	(19)
Fair value of plan assets - November 30	4,753	5,735	17	90
Unfunded projected benefit obligation	1,742	325	3,014	2,685
Unrecognized:				
Net actuarial gain (loss)	(958)	432	(960)	(767)
Initial net obligation	(2)	(37)	-	-
Prior service from plan amendments	(223)	(281)	(12)	(18)
December - net	7	3	5	55
Accrued expense	566	442	2,047	1,955
Balance Sheet Accounts:				
Current and long-term liabilities	$ -	$ 442	$ 41	$ 1,955
Liabilities subject to compromise	1,624	-	2,006	-
Adjustments to recognize minimum pension liability:				
Accumulated other comprehensive income	(833)	-	-	-
Intangible pension asset	(225)	-	-	-
Accrued expense	$ 566	$ 442	$ 2,047	$ 1,955

Under applicable accounting principles, we are required to record a minimum pension liability equal to the unfunded pension obligation of $1,624 million. The difference between the unfunded accumulated and projected benefit obligations represents the projected salary assumption used for actuarial purposes. Those applicable accounting principles require that any excess of the minimum liability over the accrued expense be recorded as an intangible asset up to the unamortized past service costs with the balance charged to other comprehensive income.

(Dollars in millions)	Pension			OPEB		
	2001	2000	1999	2001	2000	1999
Components of net expense:						
Current service cost	$ 60	$ 64	$ 60	$ 13	$ 12	$ 11
Interest cost	463	468	405	213	212	158
Expected return on plan assets	(520)	(557)	(496)	(1)	(7)	(7)
Other	8	-	-	3	-	-
Amortizations:						
Initial net obligation	34	34	34	-	-	-
Plan amendments	50	50	29	2	2	-
Actuarial (gain) loss	-	(12)	-	34	38	23
PBGC, Multiemployer, other	8	8	8	7	7	15
Net expense	$ 103	$ 55	$ 40	$ 271	$ 264	$ 200
Assumptions:						
Expected return on plan assets	9 1/2%	9 1/2%	8 3/4%	8 %	8 %	6 3/4%
Discount rate - expense	8 %	8 %	6 3/4%	8 %	8 %	6 3/4%
Discount rate - projected obligation	7 1/8%	8 %	8 %	7 1/8%	8 %	8 %
Rate of compensation increase	3 %	2.9%	2.9%	3 %	2.9%	2.9%
Trend rate						
-beginning next year	n/a	n/a	n/a	8.8%	8.6%	9 1/2%
-ending rate	n/a	n/a	n/a	4.8%	4.8%	4.8%
-ending year	n/a	n/a	n/a	2010	2010	2010

A one-percentage-point change in assumed health care cost trend rates would have an effect of $20 million on the total service and interest cost components of the 2002 other postretirement benefits expense and of $245 million on the November 30, 2001 projected benefit obligation for other postretirement benefits.

Report of Independent Auditors

To the Board of Directors and
Stockholders of
Bethlehem Steel Corporation:

In our opinion, the consolidated financial statements listed in the accompanying index present fairly, in all material respects, the financial position of Bethlehem Steel Corporation and its subsidiaries ("Bethlehem") at December 31, 2001 and 2000, and the results of their operations and their cash flows for each of the three years in the period ended December 31, 2001 in conformity with accounting principles generally accepted in the United States of America. In addition, in our opinion, the financial statement schedule listed in the accompanying index presents fairly, in all material respects, the information set forth therein when read in conjunction with the related consolidated financial statements. These financial statements and financial statement schedule are the responsibility of the company's management; our responsibility is to express an opinion on these financial statements and financial statement schedule based on our audits. We conducted our audits of these statements in accordance with auditing standards generally accepted in the United States of America, which require that we plan and perform the audit to obtain reasonable assurance about whether the financial statements are free of material misstatement. An audit includes examining, on a test basis, evidence supporting the amounts and disclosures in the financial statements, assessing the accounting principles used and significant estimates made by management, and evaluating the overall financial statement presentation. We believe that our audits provide a reasonable basis for our opinion.

The accompanying consolidated financial statements have been prepared assuming that Bethlehem will continue as a going concern, which contemplates continuity of the company's operations and realization of its assets and payments of its liabilities in the ordinary course of business. As more fully described in the notes to the consolidated financial statements, on October 15, 2001, Bethlehem filed a voluntary petition for reorganization under Chapter 11 of the United States Bankruptcy Code. The uncertainties inherent in the bankruptcy process and the company's recurring losses from operations raise substantial doubt about Bethlehem's ability to continue as a going concern. Bethlehem is currently operating its business as a Debtor-in-Possession under the jurisdiction of the Bankruptcy Court, and continuation of the company as a going concern is contingent upon, among other things, the confirmation of a Plan of Reorganization, the company's ability to comply with all debt covenants under the existing debtor-in-possession financing agreements, and Bethlehem's ability to generate sufficient cash from operations and obtain financing sources to meet its future obligations. If no reorganization plan is approved, it is possible that the company's assets may be liquidated. The consolidated financial statements do not include any adjustments to reflect the possible future effects on the recoverability and classification of assets or the amount and classification of liabilities that may result from the outcome of these uncertainties.

/s/ PricewaterhouseCoopers LLP

Philadelphia, Pennsylvania
January 30, 2002

The Dow Chemical Company—Treasury Stock

The Dow Chemical Company is a global science and technology based company that develops and manufactures a portfolio of chemicals, plastics and agricultural products and services for customers in 162 countries around the world. With annual sales of $19 billion, Dow conducts its operations through 14 global businesses employing 39,200 people. The company has 123 manufacturing sites in 32 countries and supplies more than 2,400 products grouped within six operating segments: PERFORMANCE PLASTICS (Adhesives, Sealants and Coatings; Engineering Plastics; Epoxy Products and Intermediates; Fabricated Products; and Polyurethanes), PERFORMANCE CHEMICALS (Specialty Chemicals; Emulsion Polymers), AGRICULTURAL PRODUCTS (Dow AgroSciences LLC); PLASTICS (Polyethylene, Polystyrene, Polypropylene, Insite Technology); CHEMICALS; and HYDROCARBONS AND ENERGY.

Learning Objectives

- Explain how companies account for treasury stock transactions.
- Explain why treasury stock is treated as a contra-equity account and not as an asset.
- Consider the effect of treasury stock transactions on the effective ownership of the company.

Refer to The Dow Chemical Company's 1999 financial statements and Note L—Stockholders' Equity.

Concepts

a. Common stock is classified as authorized, issued, and outstanding.

   i. How many shares of common stock is Dow authorized to issue?

   ii. How many shares of common stock has Dow actually issued at December 31, 1999?

   iii. How many shares of Dow common stock are outstanding at December 31, 1999?

   iv. Why do companies repurchase their own shares?

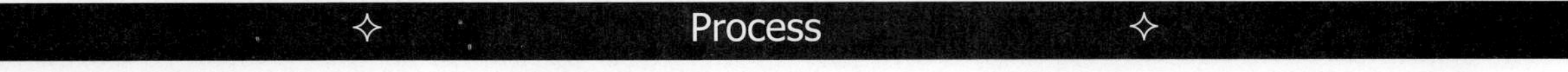

Process

b. During 1999, Dow repurchased a number of its own common shares on the open market. The company reissued some of these "treasury shares" in 1999.

   i. How many shares of its own common stock did Dow repurchase on the open market during 1999?

   ii. How much did Dow pay, in total and per share, on average, for its stock during 1999?

   iii. How many shares of treasury stock did Dow reissue in connection with its employee stock option programs in 1999?

   iv. For what other reason did Dow reissue treasury stock during 1999? Approximately how many shares of stock did Dow reissue in conjunction with this transaction?

c. Describe the method Dow uses to account for its treasury stock transactions. Prepare a single journal entry that summarizes Dow's treasury stock *purchase* activity in 1999.

d. Provide definitions of the financial statement elements "asset" and "shareholders' equity." Where are the treasury shares classified in Dow's consolidated balance sheet? Based on how Dow uses these shares, the treasury shares appear to embody an expected future economic benefit. Why doesn't Dow disclose its treasury stock as an asset?

Analysis

e. In recent years, a number of chemical companies have merged to take advantages of efficiencies in production and distribution and to acquire product lines that enhance their offerings. Some of the mergers are friendly, others are not. Assume that German chemical company BASF has acquired a 6% interest in The Dow Chemical Company and that as of December 31, 1999 BASF wishes to own 10% of Dow's outstanding common stock.

   i How many shares would BASF have to purchase on the open market to acquire a 10% interest in the company? What journal entry would Dow prepare to record the purchase of stock by BASF? (Assume the average stock price for this transaction was $\$133^5/_8$.)

   ii. Now assume that Dow's Board of Directors supports BASF's bid to become a 10% shareholder. How many shares of its own common stock would Dow have to repurchase on the open market to result in a 10% stake for BASF? What journal entry would Dow prepare in this case? (Again, assume that the average stock price for this transaction was $\$133^5/_8$ per share.)

Consolidated Statements of Income

In millions, except for per share amounts	1999	1998	1997
Net Sales	**$18,929**	$18,441	$20,018
Cost of sales	**14,302**	13,799	14,679
Research and development expenses	**845**	807	785
Selling, general and administrative expenses	**1,530**	1,666	1,880
Amortization of intangibles	**146**	88	61
Purchased in-process research and development charges	**6**	349	–
Special charges	**94**	458	–
Insurance and finance company operations, pretax income	**127**	112	113
Equity in earnings of nonconsolidated affiliates	**82**	64	75
Sundry income – net	**261**	916	436
Earnings before Interest, Income Taxes and Minority Interests	**2,476**	2,366	3,237
Interest income	**121**	139	182
Interest expense and amortization of debt discount	**431**	493	471
Income before Income Taxes and Minority Interests	**2,166**	2,012	2,948
Provision for income taxes	**766**	685	1,041
Minority interests' share in income	**69**	17	99
Preferred stock dividends	**5**	6	6
Net Income Available for Common Stockholders	**$ 1,326**	$ 1,304	$ 1,802
Share Data			
Earnings per common share – basic	**$ 6.02**	$ 5.83	$ 7.81
Earnings per common share – diluted	**5.93**	5.76	7.70
Common stock dividends declared per share	**3.48**	3.48	3.36
Weighted-average common shares outstanding – basic	**220.1**	223.5	230.6
Weighted-average common shares outstanding – diluted	**224.4**	227.3	234.8

See Notes to Financial Statements.

In millions	December 31 1999	1998
Assets		
Current Assets		
Cash and cash equivalents	**$ 506**	$ 123
Marketable securities and interest-bearing deposits	**706**	267
Accounts and notes receivable:		
Trade (net of allowance for doubtful receivables – 1999: $107; 1998: $93)	**2,631**	2,787
Other	**1,983**	1,750
Inventories:		
Finished and work in process	**2,264**	2,245
Materials and supplies	**522**	565
Deferred income tax assets – current	**235**	303
Total current assets	**8,847**	8,040
Investments		
Investment in nonconsolidated affiliates	**1,359**	1,311
Other investments	**2,872**	2,191
Noncurrent receivables	**390**	424
Total investments	**4,621**	3,926
Property		
Property	**24,276**	24,435
Less accumulated depreciation	**15,786**	15,988
Net property	**8,490**	8,447
Other Assets		
Goodwill (net of accumulated amortization – 1999: $351; 1998: $246)	**1,834**	1,641
Deferred income tax assets – noncurrent	**597**	684
Deferred charges and other assets	**1,110**	1,092
Total other assets	**3,541**	3,417
Total Assets	**$25,499**	$23,830

See Notes to Financial Statements.

Consolidated Balance Sheets

In millions, except for share amounts	December 31 1999	1998
Liabilities and Stockholders' Equity		
Current Liabilities		
Notes payable	**$ 692**	$ 1,526
Long-term debt due within one year	**343**	300
Accounts payable:		
Trade	**1,782**	1,682
Other	**1,087**	981
Income taxes payable	**178**	290
Deferred income tax liabilities – current	**38**	71
Dividends payable	**213**	192
Accrued and other current liabilities	**1,962**	1,800
Total current liabilities	**6,295**	6,842
Long-Term Debt	**5,022**	4,051
Other Noncurrent Liabilities		
Deferred income tax liabilities – noncurrent	**839**	747
Pension and other postretirement benefits – noncurrent	**1,843**	1,903
Other noncurrent obligations	**2,219**	2,283
Total other noncurrent liabilities	**4,901**	4,933
Minority Interest in Subsidiaries	**408**	532
Preferred Securities of Subsidiary	**500**	–
Temporary Equity		
Preferred stock at redemption value (authorized 250,000,000 shares of $1.00 par value each; issued Series A – 1999: 1,316,440; 1998: 1,360,813)	**114**	117
Guaranteed ESOP obligation	**(64)**	(74)
Total temporary equity	**50**	43
Stockholders' Equity		
Common stock (authorized 500,000,000 shares of $2.50 par value each; issued 1999 and 1998: 327,125,854)	**818**	818
Additional paid-in capital	**1,321**	718
Retained earnings	**13,445**	12,887
Accumulated other comprehensive income	**(251)**	(347)
Treasury stock at cost (shares 1999: 103,844,216; 1998: 106,749,081)	**(7,010)**	(6,647)
Net stockholders' equity	**8,323**	7,429
Total Liabilities and Stockholders' Equity	**$25,499**	$23,830

See Notes to Financial Statements.

Consolidated Statements of Stockholders' Equity

In millions	1999	1998	1997
Common Stock			
Balance at beginning and end of year	**$ 818**	$ 818	$ 818
Additional Paid-in Capital			
Balance at beginning of year	**718**	532	307
Issuance of treasury stock at more than cost	**550**	121	162
Proceeds from sales of put options and other	**53**	65	63
Balance at end of year	**1,321**	718	532
Retained Earnings			
Balance at beginning of year	**12,887**	12,357	11,323
Net income before preferred stock dividends	**1,331**	1,310	1,808
Preferred stock dividends declared	**(5)**	(6)	(6)
Common stock dividends declared	**(768)**	(774)	(768)
Balance at end of year	**13,445**	12,887	12,357
Accumulated Other Comprehensive Income			
Unrealized Gains on Investments			
Balance at beginning of year	**130**	316	192
Unrealized gains (losses)	**160**	(186)	124
Balance at end of year	**290**	130	316
Cumulative Translation Adjustments			
Balance at beginning of year	**(414)**	(429)	(363)
Translation adjustments	**(64)**	15	(66)
Balance at end of year	**(478)**	(414)	(429)
Minimum Pension Liability			
Balance at beginning of year	**(63)**	(33)	(22)
Adjustments	**–**	(30)	(11)
Balance at end of year	**(63)**	(63)	(33)
Treasury Stock			
Balance at beginning of year	**(6,647)**	(5,935)	(4,301)
Purchases	**(429)**	(742)	(1,655)
Sales of treasury shares in open market	**39**	–	–
Issuance to employees and employee plans	**27**	21	30
Reclassification related to put options	**–**	9	(9)
Balance at end of year	**(7,010)**	(6,647)	(5,935)
Net Stockholders' Equity	**$ 8,323**	$ 7,429	$ 7,626

See Notes to Financial Statements.

Consolidated Statements of Comprehensive Income

In millions	1999	1998	1997
Net Income Available for Common Stockholders	**$ 1,326**	$ 1,304	$ 1,802
Other Comprehensive Income, Net of Tax (Tax amounts shown below for 1999, 1998, 1997)			
Unrealized gains on investments:			
Unrealized holding gains (losses) during the period (less tax of $123, $(66), $56)	**206**	(193)	124
Less: Reclassification adjustments for net amounts included in net income (less tax of $(27), $4, $0)	**(46)**	7	–
Cumulative translation adjustments (less tax of $(47), $47, $(23))	**(64)**	15	(66)
Minimum pension liability adjustments (less tax of $0, $(17), $(9))	**–**	(30)	(11)
Total other comprehensive income (loss)	**96**	(201)	47
Comprehensive Income	**$ 1,422**	$ 1,103	$ 1,849

See Notes to Financial Statements.

Consolidated Statements of Cash Flows

In millions	1999	1998	1997
Operating Activities			
Net income available for common stockholders	**$ 1,326**	$ 1,304	$ 1,802
Adjustments to reconcile net income to net cash provided by operating activities:			
Depreciation and amortization	**1,301**	1,305	1,297
Purchased in-process research and development charges	**6**	349	–
Provision for deferred income tax	**154**	(15)	150
Undistributed earnings of nonconsolidated affiliates	**(2)**	(16)	(21)
Minority interests' share in income	**69**	17	99
Net gain on sales of consolidated companies	**(26)**	(726)	(189)
Net gain on sales of property	**(57)**	(47)	(49)
Other net (gain) loss	**(85)**	10	(39)
Changes in assets and liabilities that provided (used) cash:			
Accounts receivable	**(5)**	564	(275)
Inventories	**79**	52	56
Accounts payable	**157**	(10)	193
Other assets and liabilities	**75**	159	521
Cash provided by operating activities	**2,992**	2,946	3,545
Investing Activities			
Capital expenditures	**(1,412)**	(1,546)	(1,198)
Proceeds from sales of property	**115**	96	117
Purchases of consolidated companies	**(441)**	(808)	(1,692)
Proceeds from sales of consolidated companies	**38**	1,300	907
Purchases from outside investors in limited partnerships	**–**	(210)	(909)
Proceeds from outside investors in limited partnership	**–**	200	–
Investments in nonconsolidated affiliates	**(100)**	(75)	(218)
Purchases of investments	**(4,136)**	(1,722)	(1,920)
Proceeds from sales of investments	**3,296**	1,670	1,630
Cash used in investing activities	**(2,640)**	(1,095)	(3,283)
Financing Activities			
Changes in short-term notes payable	**(749)**	(206)	700
Payments on long-term debt	**(342)**	(549)	(665)
Proceeds from issuance of long-term debt	**1,353**	218	238
Purchases of treasury stock	**(429)**	(742)	(1,655)
Proceeds from sales of common stock	**616**	142	192
Purchase of subsidiary preferred stock	**(102)**	–	–
Proceeds from issuance of preferred securities of subsidiary	**500**	–	108
Distributions to minority interests	**(36)**	(33)	(72)
Dividends paid to stockholders	**(771)**	(786)	(758)
Cash provided by (used in) financing activities	**40**	(1,956)	(1,912)
Effect of Exchange Rate Changes on Cash	**(9)**	(7)	(18)
Summary			
Increase (decrease) in cash and cash equivalents	**383**	(112)	(1,668)
Cash and cash equivalents at beginning of year	**123**	235	1,903
Cash and cash equivalents at end of year	**$ 506**	$ 123	$ 235

See Notes to Financial Statements.

K. Limited Partnerships and Preferred Securities of Subsidiary

In July 1999, a newly formed consolidated foreign subsidiary of the Company issued $500 of preferred securities in the form of preferred partnership units. The units provide a distribution of 7.965 percent, are mandatorily redeemable in 2009, and may be called at any time by the subsidiary. The preferred partnership units have been classified as "Preferred Securities of Subsidiary" in the consolidated balance sheet.

In April 1993, three wholly owned subsidiaries of the Company contributed assets with an aggregate fair value of $977 to Chemtech Royalty Associates L.P. (Chemtech), a then newly formed Delaware limited partnership. In 1993, outside investors acquired limited partner interests in Chemtech totaling 20 percent in exchange for $200.

In early 1998, a subsidiary of the Company purchased the limited partner interests of the outside investors in Chemtech for a fair value of $210 in accordance with windup provisions in the partnership agreement. The limited partnership was renamed Chemtech II L.P. (Chemtech II). In June 1998, the Company contributed assets with an aggregate fair value of $783 (through a wholly owned subsidiary) to Chemtech II, and an outside investor acquired a limited partner interest in Chemtech II totaling 20 percent in exchange for $200.

Chemtech II is a separate and distinct legal entity from the Company and its affiliates, and has separate assets, liabilities, business and operations. The partnership has a general partner, a wholly owned subsidiary of the Company, which directs business activities and has fiduciary responsibilities to the partnership and its other members.

The outside investor in Chemtech II receives a cumulative annual priority return of $13 on its investment and participates in residual earnings.

Chemtech II will not terminate unless a termination or liquidation event occurs. The outside investor may cause such an event to occur in the year 2003. In addition, the partnership agreement provides for various windup provisions wherein subsidiaries of the Company may purchase at any time the limited partner interest of the outside investor. Upon windup, liquidation or termination, the partners' capital accounts will be redeemed at current fair values.

In December 1991, three wholly owned subsidiaries of the Company contributed assets with an aggregate market value of $2 billion to DowBrands L.P., a then newly formed Delaware limited partnership. Outside investors made cash contributions of $45 in December 1991 and $855 in June 1992 in exchange for an aggregate 31 percent limited partner interest in DowBrands L.P. In July 1997, the outside investors' limited partnership interests in DowBrands L.P. were purchased by subsidiaries of the Company for $909.

For financial reporting purposes, the assets (other than intercompany loans, which are eliminated), liabilities, results of operations and cash flows of the partnerships and subsidiaries are included in the Company's consolidated financial statements, and the outside investors' limited partner interests are reflected as minority interests.

L. Stockholders' Equity

In 1997, the Board of Directors of the Company authorized, subject to certain business and market conditions, the purchase of up to 20,000,000 shares of the Company's common stock. On August 3, 1999, the Board of Directors terminated its 1997 authorization to repurchase Dow stock due to the pending merger with Union Carbide. The total number of shares purchased under the 1997 authorization was 16,185,000. From time to time, the Company utilizes options as part of its stock repurchase program. The Company's potential repurchase obligation related to these options is reclassified from stockholders' equity to temporary equity.

The number of treasury shares purchased, pursuant to authorization of the Board of Directors in 1997 and prior years, was 3,734,000 in 1999, 8,099,000 in 1998 and 19,538,000 in 1997. The number of treasury shares issued to employees under option and purchase programs was 3,192,000 in 1999, 3,008,000 in 1998 and 3,875,000 in 1997. In December 1999, the Company sold 3,500,000 shares of common stock held in treasury in the open market for $431 to facilitate the accounting treatment of the merger with Union Carbide as a pooling-of-interests, which is a condition to the completion of the merger.

There are no significant restrictions limiting the Company's ability to pay dividends.

Gross undistributed earnings of nonconsolidated affiliates included in retained earnings were $315 at December 31, 1999 and $247 at December 31, 1998.

Reserved Treasury Stock at December 31

Shares (000's)	**1999**	1998	1997
Stock option plans	**15,892**	15,155	13,784
Employees' stock purchase plans	**1,177**	888	932
Total shares reserved	**17,069**	16,043	14,716

Xilinx Inc.—Employee Stock Options

Xilinx, Inc. designs, develops, and markets complete programmable logic solutions, including advanced integrated circuits, software design tools, predefined system functions delivered as intellectual property cores, design services, customer training, field engineering and technical support. Customers are electronic equipment manufacturers primarily in the telecommunications, networking, computing, industrial, and consumer markets. Products are sold globally through a direct sales management organization and through franchised domestic and foreign distributors.

Learning Objectives
- Discuss the economic and organizational issues surrounding employee stock options.
- Understand the accounting method choices for employee stock options.
- Read and understand an employee stock option footnote.

Refer to the 2002 financial statements of Xilinx Inc. and note 10, Stockholders' Equity.

 **Concepts** 

a. Consider the Employee Stock Option Plans.

   i. Explain, in your own words, how this plan works. What incentives does this plan provide for Xilinx employees?

   ii. Explain briefly the following terms used in note 10: grant date, exercise price, expiry date, vesting period, options granted, options exercised, and options forfeited.

b. Consider the Employee Qualified Stock Purchase Plan. Explain, in your own words, how this plan works. What incentives does this plan provide for Xilinx employees? How do these incentives differ from the incentives created under the Employee Stock Option Plans?

c. Explain the difference between the intrinsic-value method and the fair-value method of accounting for employee stock options.

✧ **Process** 

d. The table on page 40 of the Xilinx 2002 financial statements explains changes in the number of outstanding (unexercised) options during the year.

   i. How many options were granted during the year? What was the average exercise price of these new options? Compare this price to the average price in 2001. What can we conclude from this comparison?

   ii. How many options were exercised during the year? How much cash did Xilinx receive from the exercise of these options? Where does this cash appear on the statement of cash flows? *Hint*: it is included with other share activity and not shown as its own separate cash-flow line item.

   iii. How many options expired worthless during the year? Why would employees not exercise all the options they held?

e. Did Xilinx use the intrinsic value method or the fair-value method to account for employee stock options granted during the year? What journal entry did Xilinx record for compensation expense related to employee stock options granted in fiscal 2002?

✧ Analysis ✧

f. Consider the last paragraph of note 10. What is the average fair value of options granted during the year ended March 31, 2002? Compare this to the average exercise price of the options granted during the year (part *d. i.* above). Why are these two numbers different?

g. What did Xilinx report as net income / loss for the years ended March 31, 2002 and March 31, 2001? What would Xilinx have reported as net income / loss in each of the years, had the company used fair-value method to account for employee stock options? Calculate the difference. What does this difference represent? Is the difference material? If you were an analyst interested in valuing Xilinx's stock, which numbers would be more relevant? Why?

h. Refer to the article, Balancing act between jobs and profits, that appeared in the January 22, 2003 issue of the *Financial Times*. Assume that you are Wim Roelandts, the CEO of Xilinx Inc. You are aware that the Financial Accounting Standards Board issued a rule (FAS 123R) that will require all companies to expense the fair value of employee stock options by third-quarter 2005. Prepare a brief letter to the FASB explaining Xilinx's opinion of this new rule.

i. Each year Xilinx receives a tax benefit related to employee stock options. This benefit arises because firms may deduct as an expense for tax purposes, the intrinsic value of options *exercised* each year.

   i. What tax benefit did Xilinx receive during the year ended March 31, 2002? *Hint*: the benefit is reported on Xilinx's statement of shareholders' equity and in the operating section of the statement of cash flows.

   ii. Verify the 2002 tax benefit. To do this, first calculate the intrinsic value of options *exercised* during the year ended March 31, 2002 and then apply the appropriate tax rate. Recall that an option's intrinsic value is the difference between its exercise price and the fair-value of the stock. Assume that the weighted average exercise price of options granted in 2002 provides a good measure of the fair-value of Xilinx stock when options were exercised during the year. Further assume that the federal statutory tax rate of 35% is an appropriate rate for Xilinx.

   iii. Under the new FASB rules, firms must report any tax benefits that are credited to additional paid-in capital, in the *financing* section (and no longer in the *operating* section) of the statement of cash flows (as well as in the statement of shareholders' equity). What effect will this have on firms' statement of cash flows? In your opinion, will this change improve employee stock option disclosures? Why or why not?

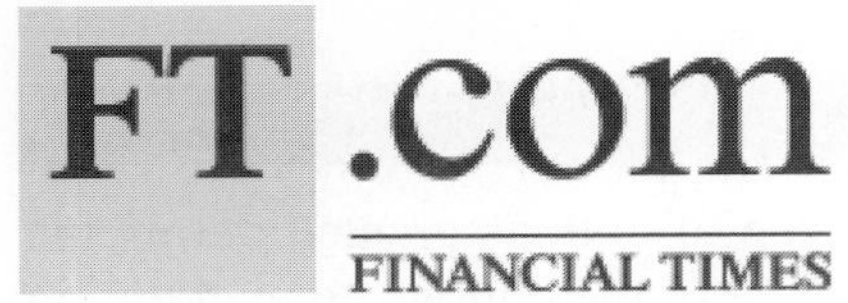

INSIDE TRACK

Balancing act between jobs and profits

By Simon London
Financial Times; January 22, 2003

Xilinx is in many ways the archetypal Silicon Valley company. It has a low-rise campus headquarters, employs an army of electrical engineers and has just gone through an eye-watering boom-to-bust business cycle.

But the company's response to the technology melt-down of 2001 and 2002 was far from typical. While almost all of its peers were handing out pink slips by the hundred, Xilinx managed to avoid job losses. Adversity was met instead with an imaginative programme of pay cuts, sabbaticals and salary-for-equity swaps.

This was good news for employees, of course. But it is no secret that some shareholders would have liked to see deeper cuts. So why has Xilinx tried to buck the trend? "In management you have to have a balance between the interests of all stakeholders—investors, customers and employees. You cannot focus on one stakeholder to the detriment of another," explains Wim Roelandts, the company's Belgian-born chief executive.

Such talk is tantamount to treason in most American boardrooms. Conventional wisdom holds that the job of a CEO is to deliver maximum returns to shareholders. Looking after employees and customers, while good business, is just a means to this end. But then Mr Roelandts is not a conventional CEO. The bluff 57-year-old is a product of both his European roots and, importantly, a 30-year career at Hewlett-Packard before taking the top job at Xilinx in 1996.

Under founders Bill Hewlett and David Packard, HP developed a distinctive and humane approach to management, including a long-standing policy of avoiding job cuts. While the company has in recent years ditched or adapted many of these principles, the legacy of the "HP way" lives on.

Xilinx has three former HP executives on its board, including John Doyle, a former head of human resources at the computer giant.

"I grew up with a no lay-offs policy at HP," says Mr Doyle. "So while we had rigorous discussions [within Xilinx] about how to respond to the downturn, we were never looking at the issues just from the point of view of shareholders."

The first signs of trouble in Xilinx's main business—supplying "programmable" microchips used in everything from networking equipment to consumer electronics—came in early 2001. Revenues fell to $400m (£250m) in the first quarter of the year from $450m in the last three months of 2000. It was clear that worse was to come. After discussions with the board, however, Mr Roelandts told employees that the company would dismiss employees only as a last resort. He also said, however, that Xilinx would have to remain profitable.

To satisfy these apparently conflicting objectives, a sliding scale of pay cuts was introduced. Mr Roelandts's base salary was cut by 20 per cent, vice-presidents lost 15 per cent, senior managers 10 per cent and so on. The average pay cut was 6 per cent; the lowest-paid workers lost nothing.

No further action would have been necessary if trading conditions had stabilised. Alas, they did not. In the summer of 2001, things went from bad to worse. Then the terrorist attacks of September 11 2001 threatened to bring the US economy to a grinding halt. Revenues in the second quarter of 2001 fell to $289m, followed by a decline to $224m in the three months to the end of September. Thus Xilinx's top line halved in less than a year.

But still Mr Roelandts was determined to avoid job losses. Further initiatives included offering employees the opportunity to take an unpaid sabbatical of up to a year and a scheme that allowed employees to swap a portion of their salary for stock options. In total, these measures shaved 10 per cent from Xilinx's gross expenses, enough to keep in it the black for all but a single quarter.

But why the effort? No one would have blamed the company for cutting jobs in the face of such a startling collapse in demand. The stock price might even have responded positively to signs that costs were being cut.

The stakeholder ethos at board level was certainly a factor. But good old-fashioned pragmatism was also at work. While many companies claim that people are their most valuable asset, at Xilinx it is an incontrovertible fact. "Listen, 75 per cent of our people are knowledge workers, university-trained, most of them engineers working on future products," explains Mr Roelandts. "The decision to avoid lay-offs was a better business decision. It protected the people who work on the future; it kept their minds free to continue to innovate. No one can innovate when they are worried about their job."

On this view, the interests of employees and shareholders were not in conflict at all. Over the long term, investors will benefit from the no-job-losses policy as Xilinx's happy engineers produce a stream of new products. It is just a question of patience. John Doyle says: "All these interests come together if you take a long enough time horizon. At Hewlett-Packard, Bill and Dave's time horizon was infinite—they wanted to be in business essentially forever."

The snag is that investors tend to be less patient than during Bill Hewlett's and Dave Packard's heyday. Other technology companies that tried to avoid substantial job losses in the current downturn, such as Sun Microsystems, were eventually put under pressure by Wall Street to make deep cuts.

So how has Mr Roelandts been able to resist? Xilinx's status as a "fabless" company—one that designs chips but outsources production and much else besides—is a crucial factor. Because it operates neither expensive manufacturing facilities nor a direct sales force, most of its costs are variable. A company with a higher proportion of fixed costs would have fallen swiftly into the red.

In addition, Mr Roelandts's message to shareholders even before the downturn was that retaining engineering talent was one of his primary goals. At the height of the dotcom bubble, when virtually everyone in Silicon Valley seemed on the verge of joining a start-up, Xilinx lost only about 5 per cent of its workforce each year. The average for the valley as a whole was closer to 25 per cent. This was not achieved by offering glitzy benefits. Xilinx has never had an on-campus massage parlour or even a crèche. Trustworthy management, interesting work and a collegiate atmosphere are more important, says Peg Wynn, vice-president of human resources.

The success of the policy of no job losses in the eyes of employees became clear earlier this month when Xilinx won fourth place in the "100 Best Places to Work" ranking published by Fortune magazine. While companies nominate themselves for inclusion in the ranking, scores are based on confidential feedback from employees. Notably, Xilinx was the highest-placed listed company in this year's ranking, beaten only by three privately owned corporations.

Whether the approach will be as pleasing for shareholders remains to be seen. By protecting employees through the downturn, Mr Roelandts hopes to be able to pull ahead of competitors such as Altera and Lattice in product development and sales. He says: "We'll see what happens. But so far we have not missed project deadlines, projects did not get delayed and we have gained 15 points of market share during this down cycle."

The stock market is less convinced: Xilinx shares have performed almost exactly in line with Altera since the downturn began.

Vindication—or vilification—of Mr Roelandts's singular management style will come over the next two to three years as Xilinx's fortunes unfold. Indeed, the company announced quarterly results yesterday. Proof that nice guys don't always finish last? Watch this space.

ITEM 8. FINANCIAL STATEMENTS AND SUPPLEMENTARY DATA

XILINX, INC.

CONSOLIDATED STATEMENTS OF OPERATIONS

(In thousands, except per share amounts)	Years ended March 31, 2002	2001	2000
Net revenues	$ 1,015,579	$ 1,659,358	$ 1,020,993
Costs and expenses:			
Cost of revenues	557,884	679,402	384,038
Research and development	204,752	213,195	123,584
Sales, general and administrative	228,759	274,093	186,619
Amortization of goodwill and other intangibles	42,998	17,915	—
Impairment loss on intangible assets and equipment	25,336	—	—
Write-off of acquired in-process research and development	—	90,700	4,560
Total operating costs and expenses	1,059,729	1,275,305	698,801
Operating income (loss)	(44,150)	384,053	322,192
Capital gain from merger of United Silicon Inc. with United Microelectronics Corp	—	—	674,728
Write-down of the United Microelectronics Corp investment	(191,852)	(362,124)	—
Altera lawsuit settlement	19,400	—	—
Interest income and other, net	23,705	39,339	27,361
Interest expense	(57)	(165)	(9)
Income (loss) before provision for (benefit from) taxes on income and equity in income of joint venture	(192,954)	61,103	1,024,272
Provision for (benefit from) taxes on income	(79,347)	25,845	378,006
Income (loss) before equity in income of joint venture	(113,607)	35,258	646,266
Equity in income of joint venture	—	—	6,184
Net income (loss)	**$ (113,607)**	**$ 35,258**	**$ 652,450**
Net income (loss) per share:			
Basic	$ (0.34)	$ 0.11	$ 2.06
Diluted	$ (0.34)	$ 0.10	$ 1.90
Shares used in per share calculations:			
Basic	333,556	328,196	316,724
Diluted	333,556	353,345	343,479

See accompanying notes

XILINX, INC.
CONSOLIDATED BALANCE SHEETS

(In thousands, except per share amounts)	*March 31,* 2002	2001
ASSETS		
Current assets:		
Cash and cash equivalents	$ 230,336	$ 208,693
Short-term investments	279,381	162,091
Accounts receivable, net of allowances for doubtful accounts, customer returns and pricing adjustments of $13,375 and $14,975 in 2002 and 2001, respectively	148,432	172,768
Inventories	79,289	342,453
Deferred income taxes	142,026	151,530
Prepaid expenses and other current assets	119,289	64,344
Total current assets	998,753	1,101,879
Property, plant and equipment, at cost:		
Land	86,291	86,742
Buildings	289,919	218,234
Machinery and equipment	233,047	222,687
Furniture and fixtures	37,530	26,961
	646,787	554,624
Accumulated depreciation and amortization	(197,017)	(137,448)
Net property, plant and equipment	449,770	417,176
Long-term investments	289,727	288,972
Investment in United Microelectronics Corp.	380,362	430,894
Intangible assets, less accumulated amortization of $96,017 and $41,863 in 2002 and 2001, respectively	134,674	198,611
Other assets	82,074	64,664
Total Assets	$2,335,360	$2,502,196
LIABILITIES AND STOCKHOLDERS' EQUITY		
Current liabilities:		
Accounts payable	$ 36,731	$ 104,674
Accrued payroll and related liabilities	33,883	28,776
Income taxes payable	37,897	62,443
Deferred income on shipments to distributors	69,781	130,501
Other accrued liabilities	17,548	24,016
Total current liabilities	195,840	350,410
Deferred tax liabilities	235,780	233,470
Commitments and contingencies		
Stockholders' equity:		
Preferred stock, $.01 par value; 2,000 shares authorized; none issued and outstanding	—	—
Common stock, $.01 par value; 2,000,000 shares authorized; 336,188 shares issued and outstanding at March 31, 2002; 331,140 shares issued and outstanding at March 31, 2001	3,361	3,311
Additional paid-in capital	719,747	725,626
Retained earnings	1,107,281	1,257,083
Treasury stock, at cost	(8,197)	(70,584)
Accumulated other comprehensive income	81,548	2,880
Total stockholders' equity	1,903,740	1,918,316
	$2,335,360	$2,502,196

See accompanying notes

XILINX, INC.
CONSOLIDATED STATEMENTS OF CASH FLOWS

(In thousands)	*Years ended March 31,* 2002	2001	2000
Increase (decrease) in cash and cash equivalents			
Cash flows from operating activities:			
Net income (loss)	$(113,607)	$35,258	$652,450
Adjustments to reconcile net income (loss) to net cash provided by operating activities:			
Depreciation and amortization	106,097	80,755	40,889
Amortization of deferred compensation	10,981	4,465	—
Net (gain) loss on sale of available-for-sale securities	(9,572)	(7,380)	1,600
Impairment loss on intangible assets	14,925	—	—
Impairment loss on equipment	10,411	—	—
Other-than-temporary loss on investments	4,322	2,046	—
Write-off of acquired in-process research and development	—	90,700	4,560
Write-down (gain) related to United Microelectronics Corp investment	191,852	362,124	(674,728
Provision for deferred income taxes	(1,403)	(154,350)	254,444
Undistributed earnings of joint venture	—	—	(6,184
Changes in assets and liabilities:			
Accounts receivable	24,336	(37,720)	(68,578
Inventories	245,943	(186,708)	2,160
Prepaid expenses and other current assets	(39,550)	6,387	(31,201
Deferred income taxes	10,906	145,340	22,537
Other assets	(20,076)	(53,070)	(13,540
Accounts payable	(67,943)	44,244	33,035
Accrued liabilities	(1,031)	3,592	13,054
Income taxes payable	(77,378)	(132,939)	(30,824
Tax benefit from exercise of stock options	52,401	159,025	112,143
Deferred income on shipments to distributors	(60,720)	15,498	29,293
Total adjustments	394,501	342,009	(311,340
Net cash provided by operating activities	280,894	377,267	341,110
Cash flows from investing activities:			
Purchases of available-for-sale securities	(1,085,053)	(2,389,366)	(2,506,365
Proceeds from sale or maturity of available-for-sale securities	962,207	2,652,456	2,240,293
Proceeds from maturity of held-to-maturity securities	—	—	34,358
Purchases of property, plant and equipment	(94,883)	(222,670)	(143,746
Assets obtained (purchased) with acquisitions	—	4,243	(22,750
Net cash provided by (used in) investing activities	(217,729)	44,663	(398,210
Cash flows from financing activities:			
Acquisition of treasury stock	(125,580)	(402,796)	(5,289
Proceeds from issuance of common stock	81,088	81,802	84,315
Proceeds from sale of put options	2,970	22,209	10,038
Net cash provided by (used in) financing activities	(41,522)	(298,785)	89,064
Net increase in cash and cash equivalents	21,643	123,145	31,964
Cash and cash equivalents at beginning of year	208,693	85,548	53,584
Cash and cash equivalents at end of year	$ 230,336	$ 208,693	$ 85,548
Schedule of non-cash transactions:			
Issuance of treasury stock under employee stock plans	$188,575	$332,212	$10,400
Supplemental disclosures of cash flow information:			
Income taxes paid	$ 13,865	$ 7,691	$ 11,881
Interest paid	$ 57	$ 165	$ 9

See accompanying notes

XILINX, INC.
CONSOLIDATED STATEMENTS OF STOCKHOLDERS' EQUITY

Three years ended March 31, 2002 *(In thousands)*	*Common Stock Outstanding*		*Additional Paid-in Capital*	*Retained Earnings*	*Treasury Stock*	*Accumulated Other Comprehensive Income (Loss)*	*Total Stockholders' Equity*
	Shares	*Amount*					
Balance at March 31, 1999	312,486	$3,124	$291,669	$607,060	$(5,112)	$(17,423)	$879,318
Components of comprehensive income:							
Net income	—	—	—	652,450	—	—	652,450
Unrealized gain on available-for-sale securities, net of taxes of $18,313	—	—	—	—	—	26,073	26,073
Cumulative translation adjustment	—	—	—	—	—	17,606	17,606
Total comprehensive income							696,129
Issuance of common shares Under employee stock plans	13,272	131	84,184	—	—	—	84,315
Acquisition of treasury stock	(246)	—	—	—	(5,288)	—	(5,288)
Issuance of treasury stock Under employee stock plans	—	—	(10,400)	—	10,400	—	—
Put option premiums	—	—	10,038	—	—	—	10,038
Tax benefit from exercise of Stock options	—	—	112,143	—	—	—	112,143
Balance at March 31, 2000	325,512	3,255	487,634	1,259,510	—	26,256	1,776,655
Components of comprehensive income:							
Net income	—	—	—	35,258	—	—	35,258
Unrealized loss on available-for-sale securities, net of tax benefit of $2,316	—	—	—	—	—	(22,831)	(22,831)
Cumulative translation adjustment	—	—	—	—	—	(545)	(545)
Total comprehensive income							11,882
Issuance of common shares Under employee stock plans	9,382	93	82,737	—	—	—	82,830
Acquisition of treasury stock	(6,373)	(63)	—	—	(402,797)	—	(402,860)
Issuance of treasury stock Under employee stock plans	—	—	(294,528)	(37,685)	332,213	—	—
Issuance of shares for RocketChips	2,619	26	288,322	—	—	—	288,348
Put option premiums	—	—	22,209	—	—	—	22,209
Deferred compensation-RocketChips	—	—	(19,773)	—	—	—	(19,773)
Tax benefit from exercise of Stock options	—	—	159,025	—	—	—	159,025
Balance at March 31, 2001	331,140	3,311	725,626	1,257,083	(70,584)	2,880	1,918,316
Components of comprehensive loss:							
Net loss	—	—	—	(113,607)	—	—	(113,607)
Unrealized gain on available-for-sale securities, net of taxes of $57,458	—	—	—	—	—	79,180	79,180
Cumulative translation adjustment	—	—	—	—	—	(512)	(512)
Total comprehensive loss							(34,939)
Issuance of common shares Under employee stock plans	7,022	70	80,148	—	—	—	80,218
Acquisition of treasury stock	(2,161)	(22)	—	—	(126,188)	—	(126,210)
Issuance of treasury stock Under employee stock plans	—	—	(152,380)	(36,195)	188,575	—	—
Issuance of shares for RocketChips	187	2	—	—	—	—	2
Put option premiums	—	—	2,970	—	—	—	2,970
Deferred compensation-RocketChips	—	—	8,483	—	—	—	8,483
Deferred compensation-other	—	—	2,499	—	—	—	2,499
Tax benefit from exercise of Stock options	—	—	52,401	—	—	—	52,401
Balance at March 31, 2002	336,188	$3,361	$719,747	$1,107,281	$(8,197)	$81,548	$1,903,740

See accompanying notes

Note 9. Comprehensive Income (Loss)

Comprehensive income (loss) is defined as the change in equity of a company during a period resulting from certain transactions and other events and circumstances, excluding transactions resulting from investments by owners and distributions to owners. The difference between net income (loss) and comprehensive income (loss) for the Company is from foreign currency translation adjustments and unrealized gains or losses on our available-for-sale securities.

The components of comprehensive income (loss) are as follows:

		March 31,	
(in thousands)	*2002*	*2001*	*2000*
Net income (loss)	$(113,607)	$ 35,258	$ 652,450
Cumulative translation adjustment	(512)	(545)	17,606
Unrealized gain (loss) on available-for-sale securities, net of tax	82,592	(22,594)	26,343
Reclassification adjustment for gains on available-for-sale securities, net of tax, included in earnings	(3,412)	(237)	(270)
Comprehensive income (loss)	$ (34,939)	$ 11,882	$ 696,129

The components of accumulated other comprehensive income are as follows:

		March 31,	
(in thousands)	*2002*	*2001*	*2000*
Cumulative translation adjustment	$(1,106)	$ (594)	$ (49)
Unrealized gain on available-for-sale securities, net of tax	82,654	3,474	26,305
Accumulated other comprehensive income	$81,548	$ 2,880	$ 26,256

Note 10. Stockholders' Equity

Preferred Stock

The Company's Certificate of Incorporation authorized 2 million shares of undesignated preferred stock. The preferred stock may be issued in one or more series. The Board of Directors is authorized to determine or alter the rights, preferences, privileges and restrictions granted to or imposed upon any wholly unissued series of preferred stock. As of March 31, 2002 and 2001 no preferred shares were issued or outstanding.

Treasury Stock

The Board of Directors has approved stock repurchase programs enabling the Company to repurchase its common stock. We have reissued treasury shares for employee stock option exercises and Employee Qualified Stock Purchase Plan requirements. During fiscal 2002 and 2001, we repurchased a total of 2.2 million and 6.4 million shares of common stock for $126.2 million and $402.9 million, respectively. In fiscal 2002 and 2001, 3.5 million and 5.0 million shares were reissued, respectively. As of March 31, 2002, we held 0.04 million shares of treasury stock in conjunction with the stock repurchase program.

Put Options

During fiscal 2002 and 2001, we sold put options that entitle the holder of each option to sell to us, by physical delivery, one share of common stock at specified prices. The cash proceeds from the sale of put options of $3.0 million and $22.2 million for fiscal 2002 and 2001, respectively, have been included in additional paid-in capital following the provisions of Emerging Issues Task Force Issue No. 00-19, "Accounting for Derivative Financial Instruments Indexed to, and Potentially Settled in, a Company's Own Stock." As of March 31, 2002, 0.3 million shares of common stock were subject to future issuance under outstanding put options with expiration dates through August 2002, with strike prices ranging from $40 to $45 per share.

Performance Equity-linked Redemption Quarterly-pay Securities (PERQS)

During fiscal 2002 and 2001, we purchased $5.5 million and $1.1 million, respectively, of Performance Equity-linked Redemption Quarterly-pay Securities (PERQS). The securities pay 9% interest per year and mature on December 30, 2002. At maturity, the PERQS will be converted into shares of Xilinx common stock. The exchange ratio will be one-fifth of a share of Xilinx common stock for each PERQS. As of March 31, 2002, the Company held 0.63 million PERQS. The total cost of the PERQS of $6.6 million and $1.1 million as of March 31, 2002 and 2001, respectively, is included in treasury stock on the balance sheet.

Stockholder Rights Plan

In October 1991, we adopted a stockholder rights plan (which expired on October 4, 2001) and declared a dividend distribution of one preferred stock purchase right for each outstanding share of common stock. The rights would have become exercisable based upon the occurrence of certain conditions including acquisitions of Company stock. In the event one of the conditions was triggered, each right entitled the registered holder to purchase a number of shares of preferred stock of the Company or, under limited circumstances, of the acquirer. The rights were redeemable at the Company's option, under certain conditions, for $.01 per right.

Employee Stock Option Plans

Under existing stock option plans (Option Plans), options reserved for future issuance to employees and directors of the Company total 71.1 million shares as of March 31, 2002. Options to purchase shares of our common stock under the Option Plans are granted at 100% of the fair market value of the stock on the date of grant. Options granted to date expire ten years from date of grant and vest at varying rates over two or four years.

A summary of our Option Plans activity, and related information are as follows:

Years ended March 31,	*2002*		*2001*		*2000*	
	Shares (000)	*Weighted Average Exercise Price*	*Shares (000)*	*Weighted Average Exercise Price*	*Shares (000)*	*Weighted Average Exercise Price*
Outstanding at beginning of year	54,425	$19.98	55,333	$ 12.19	63,158	$9.50
Granted	9,804	35.34	7,814	63.51	4,149	37.24
Exercised	(6,359)	9.10	(8,008)	7.41	(10,997)	6.03
Forfeited	(1,101)	40.80	(714)	33.26	(977)	13.74
Outstanding at end of year	56,769	$23.45	54,425	$19.98	55,333	$12.19
Shares available for grant	15,160		23,862		17,153	

The above table does not include additional shares which become available under a formula set forth in the stockholder approved 1997 Stock Plan. That formula provides that on the first day of each fiscal year, an additional number of shares become available for issuance equal to the lesser of 20 million shares or 4% of the number of shares outstanding as of the end of the prior fiscal year, as adjusted with respect to shares repurchased by the Company during the year and as adjusted for splits, stock dividends and certain other changes to the outstanding capital stock of the Company.

The following information relates to options outstanding and exercisable under the Option Plans at March 31, 2002:

	Options Outstanding			Options Exercisable	
Range of Exercise Prices	*Options Outstanding (000)*	*Weighted Average Remaining Contractual Life (Years)*	*Weighted Average Exercise Price*	*Options Exercisable (000)*	*Weighted Average Exercise Price*
$ 0.57 - $ 5.43	5,686	2.18	$ 3.83	5,685	$ 3.83
$ 5.62 - $ 8.25	7,346	3.77	$ 7.64	7,306	$ 7.65
$ 8.31 - $ 9.97	9,285	5.66	$ 9.58	8,984	$ 9.58
$ 9.98 - $14.22	7,519	5.15	$11.95	7,386	$11.97
$14.50 - $18.78	1,268	6.91	$17.83	806	$17.66
$19.27 - $21.81	6,188	7.00	$21.67	4,448	$21.67
$23.53 - $33.13	5,971	8.82	$32.18	1,638	$31.10
$33.19 - $41.40	6,611	8.87	$37.70	1,751	$36.96
$41.55 - $77.63	5,853	8.26	$65.53	2,475	$67.50
$79.69 - $96.63	1,042	8.31	$89.03	442	$89.27
$ 0.57 - $96.63	56,769	6.20	$23.45	40,921	$16.74

At March 31, 2001, 37.5 million options were exercisable at an average price of $11.94. At March 31, 2000, 33.6 million options were exercisable at an average price of $8.37.

Employee Qualified Stock Purchase Plan

Under our 1990 Employee Qualified Stock Purchase Plan (Stock Purchase Plan), qualified employees can elect to have up to 15 percent of their annual earnings withheld, up to a maximum of $21,250, to purchase our common stock at the end of six-month enrollment periods. The purchase price of the stock is 85% of the lower of the fair market value at the beginning of the twenty-four month offering period or at the end of each six-month purchase period. Almost all employees are eligible to participate. Under this plan, 0.7 million and 1.4 million shares were issued during 2002 and 2001, respectively, and 7.3 million shares were available for future issuance at March 31, 2002.

Stock-Based Compensation

As permitted under SFAS No. 123, "Accounting for Stock-Based Compensation", we have elected to continue to follow Accounting Principles Board Opinion No. 25, "Accounting for Stock Issued to Employees" (APB 25) and related interpretations in accounting for our stock-based awards to employees. Under APB 25, the Company generally recognizes no compensation expense with respect to such awards.

Pro forma information regarding net income (loss) and earnings (loss) per share is required by SFAS 123 and has been determined as if we had accounted for awards to employees under the fair value method of SFAS 123. The fair value of stock options and stock purchase plan rights under the Option Plans and Stock Purchase Plan was estimated as of the grant date using the Black-Scholes option pricing model. The Black-Scholes model was originally developed for use in estimating the fair value of traded options and requires the input of highly subjective assumptions including expected stock price volatility. Our stock options and stock purchase plan rights have characteristics significantly different from those of traded options, and changes in the subjective input assumptions can materially affect the fair value estimate. The fair value of stock options and stock purchase plan rights granted in fiscal years 2002, 2001 and 2000 were estimated at the date of grant assuming no expected dividends and the following weighted average assumptions.

	Stock Options			*Stock Purchase Plan Rights*		
Years ended March 31,	*2002*	*2001*	*2000*	*2002*	*2001*	*2000*
Expected life (years)	3.50	3.50	3.50	0.50	0.50	0.50
Expected stock price volatility	0.76	0.71	0.65	0.95	0.79	0.67
Risk-free interest rate	3.8%	5.9%	5.8%	3.3 %	5.6%	5.3%

For purposes of pro forma disclosures, the estimated fair value of stock-based awards is amortized against pro forma net income over the stock-based awards' vesting period. Had we accounted for stock-based awards to employees under SFAS 123, our net income (loss) would have been $(227.9) million, $(100.2) million, and $560.3 million in 2002, 2001, and 2000, respectively. Basic net income (loss) per share would have been $(0.68), $(0.31), and $1.73 in 2002, 2001, and 2000, respectively, while diluted net income (loss) per share would have been $(0.68), $(0.31), and $1.60, respectively.

Calculated under SFAS 123, the weighted-average fair value of the stock options granted during 2002, 2001, and 2000 was $19.22, $37.91, and $18.87 per share, respectively. The weighted-average fair value of stock purchase rights granted under the Stock Purchase Plan during 2002, 2001, and 2000 were $16.13, $27.31, and $18.19 per share, respectively.

Note 11. Income Taxes

The provision for (benefit from) taxes on income consists of the following:

(In thousands)		*Years ended March 31,* 2002	2001	2000
Federal:	Current	$ (84,315)	$131,903	$ 97,019
	Deferred	24,227	(124,263)	196,172
		(60,088)	7,640	293,191
State:	Current	3,227	21,678	15,851
	Deferred	(25,630)	(30,087)	58,272
		(22,403)	(8,409)	74,123
Foreign:	Current	3,144	26,614	10,692
Total		$ (79,347)	$ 25,845	$ 378,006

The tax benefits associated with stock option exercises and the employee stock purchase plan resulted in a tax benefit of $52.4 million, $159.0 million, and $112.1 million, for fiscal years 2002, 2001, and 2000, respectively. Such benefits are credited to additional paid-in capital when realized. The Company has Federal and state tax loss and tax credit carryforwards of approximately $120 million and $46 million respectively. If unused, these tax loss carryforwards and $31 million of the tax credit carryforwards will expire in 2005 through 2022. Pretax income from foreign operations was $14.4 million, $281.5 million, and $106.4 million for fiscal years 2002, 2001, and 2000, respectively. Unremitted foreign earnings that are considered to be permanently invested outside the United States and on which no U.S. taxes have been provided, accumulated to approximately $199 million as of March 31, 2002. The residual U.S. tax liability, if such amounts were remitted, would be approximately $49.8 million.

The provision for income taxes reconciles to the amount obtained by applying the Federal statutory income tax rate to income (loss) before provision for taxes as follows:

(In thousands)	*Years ended March 31,* 2002	2001	2000
Income (loss) before provision for taxes	$(192,954)	$ 61,103	$1,024,272
Federal statutory tax rate	35%	35%	35%
Computed expected tax	$ (67,534)	$ 21,386	$ 358,495
State taxes net of federal benefit	(14,562)	(5,468)	48,180
Tax exempt interest	(3,667)	(6,734)	(5,472)
Foreign earnings at lower tax rates	8,784	(9,488)	(15,370)
In-process research and development charge	-	31,745	-
Amortization of goodwill	9,884	4,143	-
Tax credits	(13,235)	(10,640)	(6,095)
Other	983	901	(1,732)
Provision for (benefit from) taxes on income	$ (79,347)	$ 25,845	$ 378,006

Wachovia Corporation—Marketable Securities

Wachovia Corporation, with a history dating back to 1879, is a major bank holding company with dual headquarters in Winston-Salem, North Carolina, and Atlanta, Georgia. At December 31, 1999, with assets of \$67.353 billion and market capitalization of \$13.723 billion, Wachovia ranked 16th among U.S. banks. Wachovia offers credit and deposit services, insurance, investment and trust products, capital markets, wealth management and information services to consumers, primarily in the Southeast. The company also provides global banking solutions to corporate clients through locations in Chicago, London, New York, Sao Paulo, Hong Kong and Tokyo.

Learning Objectives

- Interpret footnote disclosures of investment securities and analyze investment security accounts.
- Distinguish between securities classified as trading, available-for-sale, and held-to-maturity.
- Infer and prepare mark-to-market journal entries.
- Understand and critique the accounting treatment for marketable securities under SFAS No. 115.

Refer to the 1999 Financial Statements and notes for Wachovia Corporation.

Concepts

a. Consider "Trading" securities.

   i. In general, what are trading securities?

   ii. How would a company record \$1 of dividends or interest received from trading securities?

   iii. If the market value of trading securities increased by \$1 during the reporting period, what journal entry would the company record?

b. Consider securities classified as "Available-for-Sale."

   i. In general, what are securities available-for-sale?

   ii. How would a company record \$1 of dividends or interest received from securities available-for-sale?

   iii. If the market value of securities available-for-sale increased by \$1 during the reporting period, what journal entry would the company record?

c. Consider securities "Held-to-maturity."

   i. In general, what are these securities? Why are equity securities never classified as held-to-maturity?

   ii. If the market value of securities held-to-maturity increased by \$1 during the reporting period, what journal entry would the company record?

Process

d. Consider the "Trading account assets" on Wachovia's Balance Sheet.

   i. What is the balance in this account on December 31 1999? What is the market value of these securities on that date?

   ii. Assume that the 1999 unadjusted trial balance for "Trading account assets" was \$820,501. What adjusting journal entry would Wachovia make to adjust this account to market value? Ignore any income tax effects for this part.

e. Consider the balance sheet account "Securities available-for-sale."

   i. What is the 1999 year-end balance in this account?

   ii. What is the December 31, 1999 market value of these securities? What is the amortized cost of these securities? What does "amortized cost" represent? How does "amortized cost" compare to the original cost of the securities?" What does the difference between the market value and the amortized cost represent?

   iii. Assume that the December 31, 1999 unadjusted trial balance for "Securities available-for-sale" was $7,192,800. (The company adjusts the securities available-for-sale account periodically during the year and the unadjusted trial balance above reflects prior adjustments). Prepare the adjusting journal entry required to mark this portfolio to market at year end. Ignore deferred taxes for this part.

f. Consider the balance sheet account "Securities held-to-maturity."

   i. What is the 1999 year-end balance in this account? What is the amortized cost of these securities?

   ii. What is the market value of Wachovia's "Securities held-to-maturity?"

   iii. Assume that on January 1, 1999, Wachovia purchased on the open market, 30-year Treasury bonds with aggregate face value of $1 million. Wachovia intends to hold the bonds until they mature in 25 years. The bonds have a coupon rate of 5% but when Wachovia purchased the bonds, the prevailing market rate of interest (that is, the effective interest rate) was 6%. If interest is paid annually on December 31, what price did Wachovia pay for these bonds on January 1, 1999? Prepare the journal entry to record the purchase. Calculate the interest income Wachovia recorded during 1999 on these bonds. (Note: interest income is calculated using the effective interest rate method. Under this method, interest income each period, is equal to the net book value of the bonds at the beginning of the year times the *effective* interest rate. Cash received is equal to the face value of the bond times the coupon rate.) What is the amortized cost of these bonds at December 31, 1999? What is the market value of these bonds at December 31, 1999 if the prevailing market rate of interest at that date is 6.25%?

   iv. What will the amortized cost of the bonds be on December 31, 2024 (i.e., at maturity)? What will the market value of the bonds be on that date? State any assumptions you make.

Analysis

g. Consider the statements of shareholders' equity and the item labeled "Comprehensive (loss) income." This account captures the year-over-year changes in all assets and liabilities that are not reflected in income for the year (other than transactions with the shareholders during the year). For example, Wachovia's unrealized increases and decreases in the market value of available-for-sale securities are included in total assets at the end of the year. Yet, these increases or decreases are not included in Net income for the year. They are however, included in "Comprehensive income" for the year. The line item labeled "Accumulated comprehensive (loss) income" is the accumulation of many years' comprehensive income.

   i. What is the 1999 year-end balance in the "Accumulated comprehensive income" account? The 1998 balance? Explain, in general terms, why the account balance changed so drastically during 1999.

   ii. What do you conclude about the interest rate environment in 1999 compared to 1998?

   iii. What would Wachovia have reported as Net income in 1999 had the company classified "Securities available-for-sale" as "Trading account assets?" That is, what is Wachovia's "Comprehensive income" for the year?

iv. As a user of Wachovia's financial statements, do you consider comprehensive income an important number? What information can you glean from comprehensive income above and beyond net income?

h. Early versions of SFAS No. 115 would have required all marketable securities to be carried at market value on the balance sheet.

i. Prepare a brief argument against this method of accounting.

ii. Now, prepare a brief argument in support of this method of accounting.

iii. Which position would you have supported if you had been CFO of Wachovia in 1998? In 1999? How would your answer differ if you were an investor?

WACHOVIA CORPORATION

CONSOLIDATED STATEMENT OF INCOME

	1999	1998	1997
Interest Income			
Loans, including fees	$ 4,000,541	$ 3,873,404	$ 3,455,296
Securities available-for-sale	504,470	597,557	625,139
Securities held-to-maturity:			
State and municipal	11,673	15,044	16,452
Other investments	79,919	95,952	87,632
Interest-bearing bank balances	7,390	12,988	5,230
Federal funds sold and securities purchased under resale agreements	30,696	25,803	22,319
Trading account assets	32,131	44,497	50,317
Total interest income	4,666,820	4,665,245	4,262,385
Interest Expense			
Domestic deposits	1,156,113	1,224,046	1,216,229
Foreign deposits	109,082	135,659	87,320
Total interest on deposits	1,265,195	1,359,705	1,303,549
Short-term borrowed funds	457,161	563,846	478,162
Long-term debt	474,378	390,662	387,107
Total interest expense	2,196,734	2,314,213	2,168,818
Net Interest Income	2,470,086	2,351,032	2,093,567
Provision for loan losses	298,105	299,480	264,949
Net interest income after provision for loan losses	2,171,981	2,051,552	1,828,618
Other Income			
Service charges on deposits	369,646	334,980	306,231
Fees for trust services	216,392	199,949	175,549
Credit card income	255,243	171,127	162,234
Investment fees	235,350	61,556	53,290
Capital markets income	170,771	130,083	49,522
Electronic banking	88,626	74,257	64,640
Mortgage fees	33,213	44,929	23,544
Other operating income	240,882	211,238	170,758
Total other operating revenue	1,610,123	1,228,119	1,005,768
Securities gains	10,894	20,442	1,454
Total other income	1,621,017	1,248,561	1,007,222
Other Expense			
Salaries	1,020,384	874,750	742,106
Employee benefits	199,902	180,603	163,051
Total personnel expense	1,220,286	1,055,353	905,157
Net occupancy expense	151,282	138,636	116,654
Equipment expense	198,062	153,007	139,792
Personal computer disposal charge	0	0	67,202
Merger-related charges	19,309	85,312	220,330
Other operating expense	661,686	564,024	517,586
Total other expense	2,250,625	1,996,332	1,966,721
Income before income tax	1,542,373	1,303,781	869,119
Income tax expense	531,152	429,611	276,313
Net Income	$ 1,011,221	$ 874,170	$ 592,806

WACHOVIA CORPORATION

CONSOLIDATED BALANCE SHEET
$ IN THOUSANDS

	December 31 1999	December 31 1998
Assets		
Cash and due from banks	$ 3,475,004	$ 3,800,265
Interest-bearing bank balances	184,904	109,983
Federal funds sold and securities purchased under resale agreements	761,962	675,470
Trading account assets	870,304	664,812
Securities available-for-sale	7,095,790	7,983,648
Securities held-to-maturity	1,048,724	1,383,607
Loans, net of unearned income	49,621,225	45,719,222
Less allowance for loan losses	(554,810)	(547,992)
Net loans	49,066,415	45,171,230
Premises and equipment	953,832	901,681
Due from customers on acceptances	111,684	348,955
Other assets	3,783,918	3,083,191
Total assets	$67,352,537	$64,122,842
Liabilities		
Domestic deposits:		
Demand	$ 8,730,673	$ 8,768,271
Interest-bearing demand	4,527,711	4,980,715
Savings and money market savings	13,760,479	12,641,766
Savings certificates	8,701,074	8,982,396
Large denomination certificates	3,154,754	3,344,553
Total domestic deposits	38,874,691	38,717,701
Interest-bearing foreign deposits	2,911,727	2,277,028
Total deposits	41,786,418	40,994,729
Federal funds purchased and securities sold under repurchase agreements	5,372,493	5,463,418
Commercial paper	1,658,988	1,359,382
Other short-term borrowed funds	3,071,493	1,912,262
Long-term debt	7,814,263	7,596,727
Acceptances outstanding	111,684	348,955
Other liabilities	1,878,741	1,109,137
Total liabilities	61,694,080	58,784,610
Shareholders' Equity		
Preferred stock, par value $5 per share: Authorized 50,000,000 shares; none outstanding	0	0
Common stock, par value $5 per share: Authorized 1,000,000,000 shares; issued and outstanding 201,812,295 shares in 1999 and 202,986,100 shares in 1998	1,009,061	1,014,931
Capital surplus	598,149	669,244
Retained earnings	4,125,524	3,571,617
Accumulated comprehensive (loss) income	(74,277)	82,440
Total shareholders' equity	5,658,457	5,338,232
Total liabilities and shareholders' equity	$67,352,537	$64,122,842

WACHOVIA CORPORATION

CONSOLIDATED STATEMENTS OF SHAREHOLDERS' EQUITY (EXCERPTS)

$ IN THOUSANDS, EXCEPT PER SHARE

	Common Stock		Capital	Retained	Accumulated Other Comprehensive	
	Shares	Amount	Surplus	Earnings	Income (Loss)	Total
Year Ended December 31, 1998						
Balance at beginning of year	$ 205,926,632	$ 1,029,633	$ 974,803	$ 3,098,767	$ 71,098	$ 5,174,301
Comprehensive income:						
Net income				874,170		874,170
Other comprehensive income:						
Unrealized holding gains on securities available-for-sale (net of deferred tax expense of $16,233)					23,802	23,802
Less reclassification adjustment for gains realized in net income (net of tax expense of $7,982)					(12,460)	(12,460)
Comprehensive invome				874,170	11,342	885,512
Cash dividends declared -- $1.86 a share				(381,798)		(381,798)
Common stock issued pursuant to:						
Stock option and employee benefit plans	2,211,599	11,058	102,540			113,598
Dividend reinvestment plan	301,992	1,510	22,885			24,395
Acquisitions	1,127,723	5,639	77,674			83,313
Common stock acquired	(6,581,846)	(32,909)	(508,093)			541,002
Miscellaneous			(565)	(19,522)		(20,087)
Balance at end of year	202,986,100	$ 1,014,931	$ 669,244	$ 3,571,617	$ 82,440	$ 5,338,232
Year Ended December 31, 1999						
Balance at beginning of year	202,986,100	$ 1,014,931	$ 669,244	$ 3,571,617	$ 82,440	$ 5,338,232
Comprehensive income:						
Net income				1,011,221		1,011,221
Other comprehensive income:						
Unrealized holding losses on securities available-for-sale (net of deferred tax benefit of $92,356)					(149,636)	(149,636)
Less reclassification adjustment for gains realized in net income (net of tax expense of $3,813)					(7,081)	(7,081)
Comprehensive invome				1,011,221	(156,717)	854,504
Cash dividends declared -- $2.06 a share				(418,447)		(418,447)
Common stock issued pursuant to:						
Stock option and employee benefit plans	1,252,596	6,263	111,308			117,571
Dividend reinvestment plan	282,947	1,414	21,692			23,106
Acquisitions	4,801,987	24,010	399,059			423,069
Note conversions	3,065	15	235			250
Common stock acquired	(7,514,400)	(37,572)	(603,357)			(640,929)
Miscellaneous			(32)	(38,867)		(38,899)
Balance at end of year	201,812,295	$ 1,009,061	$ 598,149	$ 4,125,524	$ (74,277)	$ 5,658,457

WACHOVIA CORPORATION

NOTES TO FINANCIAL STATEMENTS

Note A—Accounting Policies (excerpts)

Trading Instruments—The Corporation maintains trading positions in both derivative and nonderivative (or cash) financial instruments. Trading cash instruments are held for distribution through retail sales or in anticipation of market movements and are carried at fair value. Gains and losses, both realized and unrealized, are included in capital markets income. Interest revenue arising from cash financial instruments is included in interest income-trading account assets. Trading cash instruments are comprised primarily of securities backed by the U.S. Treasury and various federal agencies and state and local governmental bodies.

Securities Held-to-Maturity and Available-for-Sale—Management determines the appropriate classification of debt securities at the time of purchase. Debt securities are classified as held-to-maturity when the Corporation has the positive intent and ability to hold the securities to maturity. Held-to-maturity securities are stated at amortized cost.

Debt securities not classified as held-to-maturity or trading and marketable equity securities are classified as available-for-sale and are stated at fair value. Unrealized gains and losses, net of tax, on available-for-sale securities are included in accumulated other comprehensive income—a separate component of shareholders' equity.

The amortized cost of debt securities classified as held-to-maturity or available-for-sale is adjusted for amortization of premiums and accretion of discounts to maturity, or in the case of mortgage-backed securities, over the estimated life of the security. Such amortization is included in interest income from securities. The specific identification method is used to determine realized gains and losses on sales of securities, which are reported as securities gains and losses.

Note D—Securities

The aggregate amortized cost, fair value and gross unrealized gains and losses of securities as of December 31 were as follows:

1999	Amortized Cost	Unrealized Gains	Unrealized Losses	Fair Value
Held-to-Maturity				
US Treasury & other agencies	$ 402,828	$ 2	$ 11,437	$ 391,393
State and municipal	204,289	12,863	401	216,751
Mortgage-backed	399,803	12,142	689	411,256
Other	41,804	15	69	41,750
	$1,048,724	$25,022	$ 12,596	$1,061,150
Available-for-Sale				
US Treasury & other agencies	$2,833,744	$10,881	$ 45,625	$2,799,000
State and municipal	56,138	1,054	197	56,995
Mortgage-backed	3,781,281	7,604	85,921	3,702,964
Other	186,228	20	2,976	183,272
Equity	356,799	0	3,240	353,559
	$7,214,190	$19,559	$137,959	$7,095,790

1998	Amortized Cost	Unrealized Gains	Unrealized Losses	Fair Value
Held-to-Maturity				
US Treasury & other agencies	$ 518,063	$ 6,662	$ 3	$ 524,722
State and municipal	176,768	19,521	0	196,289
Mortgage-backed	610,328	31,669	5	641,992
Other	78,448	677	2	79,123
	$1,383,607	$ 58,529	$ 10	$1,442,126
Available-for-Sale				
US Treasury & other agencies	$3,123,663	$ 83,895	$ 1,991	$3,205,567
State and municipal	60,964	3,199	2	64,161
Mortgage-backed	4,159,464	50,641	3,351	4,206,754
Other	333,442	2,250	1,983	333,709
Equity	171,632	1,825	0	173,457
	$7,849,165	$141,810	$ 7,327	$7,983,648

Chico's FAS, Inc.—Marketable Securities

Chico's FAS, Inc. is a specialty retailer of exclusively designed, private label, sophisticated, casual-to-dressy clothing, complementary accessories and other non-clothing gift items under the Chico's and White House | Black Market brand names.

Learning Objectives

- Interpret footnote disclosures of investment securities and analyze investment security accounts.
- Infer and prepare marketable securities transactions and mark-to-market journal entries.
- Perform a basic analysis and interpretation of the components of financial performance.

Refer to the Chico's FAS financial statements for the year ended January 31, 2004.

 Concepts 

a. Why might Chico's hold marketable securities? How does Chico's make money from these marketable securities?

b. What is the balance sheet value of Chico's marketable securities at January 31, 2004? What sort of marketable securities are these? How does Chico's classify these marketable securities?

c. What is the fair market value of Chico's marketable securities at January 31, 2004? The original cost? Explain how Chico's accounts for the difference between fair market value and original cost.

 Process 

d. Prepare T-accounts for Chico's marketable securities as well as for the shareholders' equity account, "Accumulated other comprehensive income." Using the statement of cash flows and the balance sheet, reconcile the activity in the two accounts for the period February 2, 2003 to January 31, 2004.

e. Prepare the journal entries that Chico's must have made to record the purchase and sale of new marketable securities during the year.

f. Prepare the journal entry that Chico's must have made to adjust its marketable securities to fair market value at January 31, 2004.

g. Assume that the "cash paid for interest" reported on the statement of cash flows represents Chico's interest expense each year. Prepare the journal entry to record interest income and expense for the year ended January 31, 2004.

✧ Analysis 

h. At January 31, 2004, what proportion of Chico's total assets do marketable securities represent? In your opinion, is this proportion too low? Too high? Explain.

i. Return on assets (ROA) measures the profitability of an entity's assets without regard to how those assets are financed. ROA is calculated as:

$$ROA = \frac{\text{Net Income} + [(1 - \text{tax rate}) \times \text{Interest Expense}]}{\text{Total Assets}}$$

Approximate Chico's tax rate by dividing the tax provision (expense) by income before income tax. Using year-end balances, calculate Chico's ROA for the years ending January 31, 2004 and February 2, 2003. Comment on the trend.

j. Calculate ROA for the years ending January 31, 2004 and February 2, 2003 for Chico's marketable securities separately. Use your calculation of gross interest income from part *g* as net income in the numerator of the ROA calculation. (*Hint*: interest earned on municipal bonds is not taxable and interest expense is not associated with these assets.)

k. Calculate ROA for the years ending January 31, 2004 and February 2, 2003 for Chico's other assets (assets other than marketable securities). Use your calculation of gross interest income from part *g* to adjust net income in the numerator. Assume that interest expense pertains entirely to these other assets. Comment on the trend.

CHICO'S FAS, INC. AND SUBSIDIARIES
CONSOLIDATED BALANCE SHEETS

(In thousands)

ASSETS	January 31, 2004	February 1, 2003
Current Assets:		
Cash and cash equivalents	$ 15,676	$ 8,753
Marketable securities, at market	104,453	91,195
Receivables, less allowances for sales returns of $288 and $304, respectively	6,368	2,226
Inventories	54,896	44,908
Prepaid expenses	8,655	6,223
Deferred taxes	7,525	7,125
Total current assets	197,573	160,430
Property and Equipment:		
Land and land improvements	5,976	5,166
Building and building improvements	25,014	19,668
Equipment, furniture and fixtures	100,589	71,769
Leasehold improvements	99,806	78,792
Total property and equipment	231,385	175,395
Less accumulated depreciation and amortization	(57,660)	(36,686)
Property and equipment, net	173,725	138,709
Deferred Taxes	—	92
Goodwill	60,114	—
Other Intangible Assets	34,043	—
Other Assets, Net	5,399	2,313
	$ 470,854	$ 301,544

LIABILITIES AND STOCKHOLDERS' EQUITY	January 31, 2004	February 1, 2003
Current Liabilities:		
Accounts payable	$ 27,796	$ 24,991
Accrued liabilities	43,187	29,698
Current portion of deferred liabilities	599	171
Total current liabilities	71,582	54,860
Noncurrent Liabilities:		
Deferred liabilities	12,713	6,551
Deferred taxes	11,724	—
Total noncurrent liabilities	24,437	6,551
Commitments and Contingencies		
Stockholders' Equity:		
Common stock, $.01 par value; 200,000 shares authorized and 87,537 and 85,282 shares issued and outstanding, respectively	875	853
Additional paid-in capital	98,586	63,986
Retained earnings	275,339	175,109
Accumulated other comprehensive income	35	185
Total stockholders' equity	374,835	240,133
	$ 470,854	$ 301,544

The accompanying notes are an integral part of these consolidated statements.

CHICO'S FAS, INC. AND SUBSIDIARIES
CONSOLIDATED STATEMENTS OF INCOME

(In thousands, except per share amounts)

	FISCAL YEAR ENDED		
	January 31, 2004	**February 1, 2003**	**February 2, 2002**
Net sales by Company stores	$ 737,918	$ 508,492	$ 362,443
Net sales by catalog and Internet	22,780	16,070	10,203
Net sales to franchisees	7,801	6,546	5,439
Net sales	768,499	531,108	378,085
Cost of goods sold	297,477	209,770	153,937
Gross profit	471,022	321,338	224,148
General, administrative and store operating expenses	289,118	199,495	146,611
Depreciation and amortization	21,130	15,050	10,001
Income from operations	160,774	106,793	67,536
Interest income, net	888	883	507
Income before income taxes	161,662	107,676	68,043
Income tax provision	61,432	40,917	25,856
Net income	$ 100,230	$ 66,759	$ 42,187
PER SHARE DATA:			
Net income per common share – basic	$ 1.16	$ 0.80	$ 0.52
Net income per common and common equivalent share – diluted	$ 1.14	$ 0.78	$ 0.50
Weighted average common shares outstanding – basic	86,403	83,309	80,365
Weighted average common and common equivalent shares outstanding – diluted	88,142	86,032	83,778

The accompanying notes are an integral part of these consolidated statements.

CHICO'S FAS, INC. AND SUBSIDIARIES
CONSOLIDATED STATEMENTS OF STOCKHOLDERS' EQUITY

(In thousands)

	Common Stock		Additional		Accumulated	
		Par	Paid-in	Retained	Other Comprehensive	
	Shares	Value	Capital	Earnings	Income	Total
BALANCE, February 3, 2001	78,747	$ 788	$ 18,323	$ 66,163	$ 47	$ 85,321
Net income	—	—	—	42,187	—	42,187
Unrealized gain on marketable securities, net	—	—	—	—	55	55
Comprehensive income						42,242
Issuance of common stock	2,834	28	7,675	—	—	7,703
Stock option compensation	—	—	45	—	—	45
Tax benefit of stock options exercised	—	—	8,184	—	—	8,184
BALANCE, February 2, 2002	81,581	816	34,227	108,350	102	143,495
Net income	—	—	—	66,759	—	66,759
Unrealized gain on marketable securities, net	—	—	—	—	83	83
Comprehensive income						66,842
Issuance of common stock	3,701	37	7,210	—	—	7,247
Tax benefit of stock options exercised	—	—	22,549	—	—	22,549
BALANCE, February 1, 2003	85,282	853	63,986	175,109	185	240,133
Net income	—	—	—	100,230	—	100,230
Unrealized loss on marketable securities, net	—	—	—	—	(150)	(150)
Comprehensive income						100,080
Issuance of common stock	2,255	22	19,474	—	—	19,496
Tax benefit of stock options exercised	—	—	15,126	—	—	15,126
BALANCE, January 31, 2004	87,537	$ 875	$ 98,586	$ 275,339	$ 35	$ 374,835

The accompanying notes are an integral part of these consolidated statements.

CHICO'S FAS, INC. AND SUBSIDIARIES
CONSOLIDATED STATEMENTS OF CASH FLOWS

(In thousands)

	FISCAL YEAR ENDED		
	January 31, 2004	February 1, 2003	February 2, 2002
CASH FLOWS FROM OPERATING ACTIVITIES:			
Net income	$ 100,230	$ 66,759	$ 42,187
Adjustments to reconcile net income to net cash provided by operating activities —			
Depreciation and amortization, cost of goods sold	1,970	1,093	406
Depreciation and amortization, other	21,130	15,050	10,001
Stock option compensation	—	—	45
Deferred tax expense (benefit)	1,336	(1,651)	(1,816
Tax benefit of options exercised	15,126	22,549	8,184
Deferred rent expense, net	1,874	1,482	883
Loss on impairment and disposal of property and equipment	3,746	1,315	1,445
(Increase) decrease in assets, net of effects of acquisition —			
Receivables, net	(1,953)	(143)	915
Inventories	(4,658)	(16,002)	(4,511
Prepaid expenses and other, net	(1,281)	(1,691)	(1,835
(Decrease) increase in liabilities, net of effects of acquisition —			
Accounts payable	(3,175)	9,000	3,134
Accrued liabilities	11,035	11,046	6,454
Total adjustments	45,150	42,048	23,305
Net cash provided by operating activities	145,380	108,807	65,492
CASH FLOWS FROM INVESTING ACTIVITIES:			
Purchases of marketable securities	(166,855)	(134,918)	(56,396
Proceeds from sale of marketable securities	153,447	84,235	30,245
Acquisition, net of cash acquired	(87,636)	—	—
Purchases of property and equipment	(52,300)	(64,742)	(37,437
Net cash used in investing activities	(153,344)	(115,425)	(63,588
CASH FLOWS FROM FINANCING ACTIVITIES:			
Proceeds from issuance of common stock	15,231	7,247	7,703
Payments on capital leases	(344)	—	—
Principal payments on debt	—	(5,155)	(66
Deferred finance costs	—	(98)	(78
Net cash provided by financing activities	14,887	1,994	7,559
Net increase (decrease) in cash and cash equivalents	6,923	(4,624)	9,463
CASH AND CASH EQUIVALENTS, Beginning of period	8,753	13,377	3,914
CASH AND CASH EQUIVALENTS, End of period	$ 15,676	$ 8,753	$ 13,377
SUPPLEMENTAL DISCLOSURES OF CASH FLOW INFORMATION:			
Cash paid for interest	$ 142	$ 285	$ 610
Cash paid for income taxes	$ 47,855	$ 19,200	$ 17,658
NON-CASH INVESTING AND FINANCING ACTIVITIES:			
Common stock issued in acquisition	$ 4,266	—	—

The accompanying notes are an integral part of these consolidated statements.

e following table presents unaudited pro forma results of operations for the fiscal years ended January 31,)04 and February 1, 2003 as if the acquisition of The White House had occurred on February 2, 2003 d February 3, 2002, respectively. The unaudited pro forma information presented below is for illustrative rposes only and is not indicative of results that would have been achieved or results which may be achieved the future:

	Fiscal 2003	Fiscal 2002
Net sales	$ 817,474	$ 598,064
Net income	101,021 (1)	70,060
Net income per common share:		
Basic	$ 1.17	$ 0.84
Diluted	$ 1.14	$ 0.81

ncludes approximately $2.7 million (pre-tax) of nonrecurring charges related to the acquisition recorded by The White House in its iistorical results prior to September 5, 2003.

PROPERTY AND EQUIPMENT IMPAIRMENT:

ring fiscal 2003, the Company decided to conclude the Pazo test concept and initiated the closing/conversion process for the 10 zo stores. As of January 31, 2004, this process has essentially been completed. In connection with the decision to conclude e Pazo test concept, the Company completed an impairment review of Pazo's property and equipment. Upon completion of the view, the Company determined that the carrying value of certain Pazo assets exceeded their future undiscounted cash flows. As esult, the Company recorded an impairment charge of $2.9 million during fiscal 2003. The provision for the asset impairment included in general, administrative and store operating expenses in the accompanying consolidated statements of income.

MARKETABLE SECURITIES:

arketable securities classified as available-for-sale consisted of the following:

	January 31, 2004	February 1, 2003
Municipal bonds, cost	$ 104,418	$ 91,010
Municipal bonds, fair value	104,453	91,195
Unrealized gain	$ 35	$ 185

ring fiscal 2003, the Company recorded a net unrealized loss of approximately $0.2 million. The Company believes that the realized loss is as a result of short-term swings in interest rates and that the unrealized loss is temporary. At January 31, 2004, proximately 44 percent of the Company's marketable securities mature within one year, 4 percent between one and five years, 5 rcent between five and ten years, and the remainder with maturities greater than ten years will mature by 2032.

BCE Inc.—Investments in Other Companies

BCE (Bell Canada Enterprises) is a management holding corporation whose core businesses are the provision of telecommunications services and the manufacture of telecommunications equipment. BCE has the largest number of registered shareholders of any Canadian corporation and its common shares are listed on exchanges in Canada, the United States, Europe, and Japan.

Learning Objectives

- Understand the accounting for investments in the shares of other companies.
- Trace transactions affecting the investment account through the financial statements.
- Explain how a change in effective ownership affects the accounting for the investment.

Refer to the 1990 financial statements of BCE Inc. The annual report of BCE Inc. indicates that the company has investments in the equity securities of Bell Canada, Northern Telecom, Bell-Northern Research, Montreal Trust, TransCanada PipeLines, Maritime Telegraph and Telephone Company, and many others.

Concepts

a. Why does BCE own shares in so many other companies?

b. When BCE owns between 20 and 50% of the voting shares of other companies, it refers to the companies as "associated companies."

  i. What accounting method does BCE use to account for its investments in associated companies?

  ii. Explain in general terms how this method works.

c. Indicate where associated company earnings and dividends are reflected on each of BCE's financial statements.

Process

d. Provide the journal entries BCE made in 1990 to record the earnings of and the dividends received from its associated companies.

e. Refer to note 4(b) and explain how a change in BCE's effective interest (i.e., percentage ownership) in Encor Inc. led them to change their method of accounting for this investment. How does BCE now account for its shares in Encor?

f. Is this considered a "change in accounting principle"? Should the new method be applied retroactively or prospectively?

BCE INC.

CONSOLIDATED INCOME STATEMENT
For the Year Ended December 31
($ Millions)

	1990	1989	1988
Telecommunications services			
Operating revenues	$8,468	$8,011	$7,092
Operating expenses	6,284	5,976	5,254
Net revenues—telecommunications services	2,184	2,035	1,838
Telecommunications equipment manufacturing			
Revenues (note 1)	7,851	7,161	6,598
Cost of revenues	4,707	4,340	3,903
Selling, general, administrative and other expenses	2,357	2,198	2,203
Restructuring costs (note 2)	—	—	242
	7,064	6,538	6,348
Net revenues—telecommunications equipment manufacturing	787	623	250
Financial services			
Revenues—Investment and loan income	1,387	851	—
Revenues—Fees and commissions	188	134	—
	1,575	985	—
Less: Interest expense	1,208	730	—
Operating expenses	306	197	—
	1,514	927	—
Net revenues—financial services	61	58	—
Other operations			
Operating revenues	479	524	755
Operating expenses	452	506	715
Net revenues—other operations	27	18	40
Total revenues	3,059	2,734	2,128
Other income (expense)			
Equity in net income of associated companies (note 4)	155	173	38
Allowance for funds used during construction	41	39	41
Interest—long-term debt	(730)	(661)	(573)
Interest—other debt	(222)	(208)	(138)
Unrealized foreign currency gains (losses) (notes 1 and 24)	(3)	2	2
Miscellaneous—net (note 8)	(176)	156	152
	(935)	(499)	(478)
Income before income taxes and minority interest	2,124	2,235	1,650
Income taxes (note 7)	628	733	634
Income before minority interest	1,496	1,502	1,016
Minority interest	349	301	163
Income from continuing operations	1,147	1,201	853
Loss from discontinued real estate operations (note 3)	—	(440)	(7)
Net income (note 24)	1,147	761	846
Dividends on preferred shares	85	37	5
Net income applicable to common shares	$1,062	$ 724	$ 841

The important differences between Canadian and United States generally accepted accounting principles affecting the consolidated income statement are described and reconciled in note 24.

BCE INC.

CONSOLIDATED BALANCE SHEET
At December 31

	1990	1989
Assets		
Current assets		
Cash and temporary cash investments	$ 308	$ 141
Accounts receivable (note 11)	3,930	3,611
Inventories (note 13)	1,043	1,100
Other (principally prepaid expenses)	480	463
	5,761	5,315
Financial services		
Short-term securities	1,028	936
Loans receivable (note 14-a)	9,442	8,349
Bonds, stocks and other investments (note 14-b)	1,493	1,457
	11,963	10,742
Investments		
Associated companies (at equity) (notes 1 and 4)	2,338	2,904
Other investments (notes 4 and 5)	948	736
	3,286	3,640
Property, plant, and equipment		
At cost (note 15)	29,087	26,946
Less: Accumulated depreciation	10,513	9,655
	18,574	17,291
Other assets		
Long-term notes and receivables	1,333	1,304
Deferred charges—unrealized foreign currency losses, less amortization	15	—
Other deferred charges	373	283
Cost of shares in subsidiaries in excess of underlying net assets, less amortization (note 1)	682	686
	2,403	2,273
Total assets	$41,987	$39,261

On behalf of the Board of Directors:

Marcel Belanger
Director

R.M. Barford
Director

Donald R. Newman
Vice-President and Comptroller

BCE INC.
CONSOLIDATED BALANCE SHEET
At December 31

	1990	1989
Liabilities and Shareholders' Equity		
Current liabilities		
Accounts payable	$ 2,659	$ 2,501
Advance billing and payments	183	162
Dividends payable	217	215
Taxes accrued	180	169
Interest accrued	297	291
Debt due within one year (note 16)	1,878	2,342
	5,414	5,680
Financial services		
Demand deposits (note 14-c)	1,071	1,041
Investment certificates and borrowing (note 14-c)	10,655	9,359
	11,726	10,400
Long-term debt		
Long-term debt (note 17)	7,431	7,005
Deferred credits		
Income taxes	2,425	2,430
Other	389	448
	2,814	2,878
Minority interest in subsidiary companies		
Preferred shares	1,309	1,262
Common shares	1,968	1,630
	3,277	2,892
Preferred shares		
Preferred shares (note 18) (Includes $579 million redeemable at option of holders, not before 1995 (1989—$200 million))	1,235	858
Common shareholders' equity		
Common shares (note 19)	5,407	5,276
Common shares purchase warrants (note 20)	39	—
Contributed surplus	1,034	1,034
Retained earnings	3,727	3,448
Foreign exchange adjustment (note 21)	(117)	(210)
	10,090	9,548
Commitments and contingent liabilities (note 12)		
Total liabilities and shareholders' equity	$41,987	$39,261

BCE INC.

CONSOLIDATED STATEMENT OF CHANGES IN FINANCIAL POSITION

For the years ended December 31 ($ millions)	1990	1989	1988
Cash and temporary cash investments were provided from (used for)			
Operations	$ 3,481	$ 2,774	$ 2,578
Investments	(4,173)	(5,059)	(3,946)
Financing	1,870	3,332	2,022
Dividends declared	(1,011)	(919)	(811)
Increase (decrease) in cash and temporary cash investments	167	128	(157)
Cash and temporary cash investments at beginning of year	141	13	170
Cash and temporary cash investments at end of year	$ 308	$ 141	$ 13

Cash Provided from (Used for) Operations			
Income from continuing operations	$ 1,147	$ 1,201	$ 853
Items not affecting cash			
Depreciation	2,018	1,813	1,598
Minority interest	349	301	163
Deferred income taxes	70	88	188
Equity in net income of associated companies lower than (in excess of) dividends received	(49)	(69)	56
Allowances for funds used during construction	(41)	(39)	(41)
Other items	68	(74)	(94)
Changes in working capital other than cash and debt			
(Increase) decrease in current assets:			
Accounts receivable	(319)	(463)	(256)
Inventories	57	(29)	(31)
Other current assets	(17)	(123)	(161)
Income and other taxes receivable	—	103	(31)
Increase (decrease) in current liabilities:			
Accounts payable	158	83	270
Advance billing and payments	21	(269)	69
Dividends payable	2	6	27
Taxes accrued	11	166	(79)
Interest accrued	6	79	47
Net cash provided from operations	$ 3,481	$ 2,774	$ 2,578

Cash Provided from (Used for) Investments			
Capital expenditures (net)	(3,312)	(3,191)	(3,052)
Investments—Acquisition of Montreal Trustco Inc.	—	(874)	—
—Other	(372)	(526)	(1,064)
Sales of investments in TCPL and Encor (notes 4-a and 4-b)	710	—	—
Long-term notes and receivables	(29)	6	(98)
Net securities and loans—Financial services			
Short-term securities	(92)	313	—
Loans receivable	(1,093)	(661)	—
Bonds, stocks and other investments	(36)	(275)	—
Other items	51	149	268
Net cash used for investments	$(4,173)	$(5,059)	$(3,946)

BCE INC.

CONSOLIDATED STATEMENT OF CHANGES IN FINANCIAL POSITION (CONTINUED)

For the years ended December 31 ($ millions)	1990	1989	1988
Cash Provided from (Used for) Financing			
Proceeds from long-term debt	656	1,233	1,179
Reduction of long-term debt	(372)	(239)	(443)
Issue of preferred shares	371	847	—
Issue of common shares			
Common shareholder purchase plans	126	132	159
Acquisition of Montreal Trustco Inc.	—	336	—
Issues of preferred and common shares by subsidiaries to minority shareholders	236	463	190
Redemption of preferred shares by subsidiaries	(79)	(51)	(11)
Notes payable and bank advances	(358)	61	1,127
Net deposits and borrowings—Financial services			
Demand deposits	30	80	—
Investment certificates and borrowings	1,296	560	—
Other items	(36)	(90)	(179)
Net cash provided from financing	$ 1,870	$ 3,332	$ 2,022
Dividends Declared			
By BCE Inc.			
Preferred shares	(85)	(37)	(5)
Common shares	(769)	(743)	(705)
By subsidiaries to minority shareholders	(157)	(139)	(101)
Total dividends declared	$(1,011)	$ (919)	$ (811)

BCE INC.

CONSOLIDATED STATEMENT OF RETAINED EARNINGS

For the years ended December 31 ($ millions)	1990	1989	1988
Balance at beginning of year	$ 3,448	$ 3,477	$ 3,345
Net income	1,147	761	846
	4,595	4,238	4,191
Deduct:			
Dividends			
Preferred shares	85	37	5
Common shares	769	743	705
	854	780	710
Costs related to issuance and redemption of share capital of BCE Inc. and of subsidiaries	14	10	4
	868	790	714
Balance at end of year	$ 3,727	$ 3,448	$ 3,477

BCE INC.
NOTES TO CONSOLIDATED FINANCIAL STATEMENTS

1. Accounting Policies

The financial statements have been prepared in accordance with Canadian generally accepted accounting principles and all figures are in Canadian dollars. These statements conform in all material respects with International Accounting Standards. Certain previously reported figures have been reclassified to conform with the current presentation.

With respect to the consolidated financial statements of BCE, the important differences between Canadian and United States generally accepted accounting principles are described and reconciled in note 24.

Consolidation
The consolidated financial statements include the accounts of all majority-owned subsidiaries, either direct or indirect, with the exception of BCE Development Corporation (BCED) (see note 3). The financial subsidiaries of Northern Telecom Limited (Northern Telecom) are also fully consolidated. The investments in associated companies (20% to 50% owned) are accounted for by the equity method.

At December 31, 1990, the direct and indirect subsidiaries of BCE (100% owned, unless otherwise indicated) included Bell Canada, Tele-Direct (Publications) Inc., Northern Telecom Limited (53.1%), Montreal Trustco Inc., BCE Telecom International Inc. (formerly BCE Information Services Inc.), NewTel Enterprises Limited (55.7%), Telebec Ltée, Northern Telephone Limited (99.9%), Northwestern Inc., Bell Canada International Inc. and BCE Mobile Communications Inc. (69.7%).

The excess of cost of shares over acquired equity (goodwill) of subsidiary and associated companies is being amortized to earnings on a straight-line basis over its estimated life. The amortization, over periods up to 40 years, amounted to $68 million in 1990 (1989-$59 million, 1988-$45 million).

Telecommunications equipment purchased by Bell Canada and the other telecommunications subsidiaries of BCE, from Northern Telecom and its subsidiaries, is reflected in BCE's consolidated balance sheets at the cost to the purchasing companies, and is included in telecommunications equipment manufacturing revenues in the consolidated income statement. To the extent that any income related to these revenues, and those from associated companies, has not been offset by depreciation or other operating expenses, it remains in consolidated retained earnings and consolidated income. This practice is generally followed with respect to activities of regulated industries. All other significant intercompany transactions have been eliminated in the consolidated financial statements.

Telecommunications equipment manufacturing revenues comprise:

($ millions)	1990	1989	1988
Revenues from			
Bell Canada	$1,477	$1,495	$1,416
Other telecommunications subsidiary and associated companies of BCE	266	238	181
Revenues from others	6,108	5,428	5,001
Total	$7,851	$7,161	$6,598

4. Investments in Associated Companies

BCE uses the equity method of accounting for investments in companies where ownership by BCE, or a subsidiary, ranges from 20% to 50%. Under this accounting method, BCE's proportional share of income of such companies, from the dates of their acquisition, net of amortization of excess purchase price over net assets acquired, is taken into income and added to the cost of investments. Income received from these companies reduces the carrying amounts of the investments.

Three-Year Summary of Investments in Associated Companies:

($ millions)	TCPL* (a)	STC PLC (c)	MT&T and Bruncor Inc. (d)	Memotec Data Inc. (e)	Quebecor Inc. (f)	Other companies	Total
1988							
Balance-January 1, 1988	$ 998	$1,247	$176	$209	$ —	$119	$2,749
Cost of investments	134	40	9	20	80	13	296
Equity income (loss)	(65)	63	23	6	2	9	38
Income received	(50)	(26)	(15)	(1)	(1)	(1)	(94)
Currency translation	(17)	(163)	—	(2)	—	—	(182)
Sale of investments	—	—	—	—	—	(57)	(57)
Balance-December 31, 1988	$1,000	$1,161	$193	$232	$81	$ 83	$2,750
1989							
Cost of investments	237	—	10	4	—	12	263
Equity income	62	78	21	3	3	6	173
Income received	(51)	(29)	(16)	(5)	(1)	(2)	(104)
Currency translation and other adjustments	(12)	(152)	—	—	(1)	(13)	(178)
Balance-December 31, 1989	$1,236	$1,058	$208	$234	$82	$ 86	$2,904
1990							
Cost of investments	8	—	7	5	1	14	35
Equity income	52	60	21	—	16	6	155
Income received	(45)	(35)	(17)	(6)	(1)	(2)	(106)
Currency translation and other adjustments	1	186	—	(2)	(1)	(16)	168
Sale of investments	(498)	—	—	—	—	—	(498)
Transfer of Encor (b)	(320)	—	—	—	—	—	(320)
Balance-December 31, 1990	$ 434	$1,269	$219	$231	$97	$ 88	$2,338

* Includes Encor Inc. to July 1990; see (b) on the following page.

4. Investments in Associated Companies (continued)

(a) TCPL (excerpt)

At December 31, 1990, BCE owned approximately 24.4% of common shares (37,647,081 shares) of TransCanada PipeLines Limited (TCPL) (1989-48.9% (74,611,977 shares), 1988-49.1% (73,896,249 shares)), while at the same date warrants to purchase 37,500,000 TCPL common shares from BCE were also outstanding.

The reduction in ownership in 1990 reflects the sale of 37,500,000 TCPL common shares, as part of units, by BCE to a group of underwriters pursuant to an underwriting agreement entered into in September 1990. The units offered by BCE consisted of 37,500,000 TCPL common shares sold on an installment basis and warrants to purchase a further 37,500,000 TCPL common shares from BCE at $17.50 per share for a total exercise price of $656 million. The purchase price for the TCPL common shares is payable in two installments for a total consideration of $618.8 million (excluding underwriters' fee and expenses of issue). The warrants were sold for an aggregate consideration of $18.7 million (excluding underwriters' fee and expenses of issue) and expire on December 15, 1992. The first installment of $309.4 million for the common shares and $18.7 million for the warrants was received on October 1, 1990, and the remaining $309.4 million is due by October 1, 1991. BCE realized a gain of $149 million ($120 million after tax) on the 37,500,000 TCPL common shares and the warrants sold as part of the units.

Equity income of TCPL was based on 24.4% ownership from October 1, 1990.

(b) Encor

As a result of a restructuring of TCPL, which became effective on May 2, 1989, TCPL distributed to its common shareholders one common share of a recapitalized Encor Inc. (Encor) for each common share of TCPL they owned. As a result of that distribution, BCE received 48.9% of the outstanding Encor common shares.

At December 31, 1990, BCE owned approximately 19.3% of common shares (29,702,130 shares) of Encor, compared with 48.9% (74,253,930 shares) at December 31, 1989, and 100% of the redeemable convertible preferred shares of Encor convertible into 74,618,433 common shares which were acquired on May 2, 1989. At December 31, 1990, warrants to purchase from BCE 29,701,200 Encor common shares were also outstanding. The reduction in ownership reflects the sale by BCE, in July 1990, of units consisting of 44,551,800 Encor common shares and warrants to purchase 29,701,200 Encor common shares from BCE at $2.65 per share for a total exercise price of $79 million. BCE's common shareholding was reduced to 29,702,130 common shares of Encor prior to exercise of the warrants. The net proceeds received in July 1990 amounted to $99 million. The warrants expire on January 21, 1992.

Commencing with the third quarter of 1990, BCE no longer accounts for its common share investment in Encor by the equity method. Therefore, the carrying value of the remaining investments in common shares after the above-mentioned sale ($79 million) and preferred shares of Encor have been transferred to Other investments.

Boston Beer & Lion Brewery—Financial Statement Analysis

Boston Beer is the largest craft brewer by volume in the United States. In 1996, the company sold 1,213,000 barrels of beer, which it believes to be more than the next five largest craft brewers combined. The company's business strategy is to continue to lead the craft-brewed beer market by creating and offering a wide variety of the highest quality full-flavored beers, while increasing sales through new product introductions and substantial trade and consumer awareness programs, supported by a large, well trained and rapidly expanding field sales organization.

The Lion Brewery, Inc., is a brewer and bottler of brewed beverages, including malta, specialty beers and specialty soft drinks. Malta is a non-alcoholic brewed beverage which the company produces for major Hispanic food distribution companies primarily for sale in the eastern United States. Specialty beers are brewed by the company both for sale under its own labels and on a contract basis for other marketers of craft beer brands. The company also produces specialty soft drinks, including all-natural brewed ginger beverages, on a contract basis for third parties and brews beer for sale under company-owned labels for the local market at popular prices.

Learning Objectives

- Read and compare financial statements for two companies in the same industry.
- Consider how different strategic choices lead to different financial statement relationships.
- Perform an analysis of financial information using common-size balance sheets and income statements, ratios, and other comparative techniques.
- Critically evaluate two companies based on financial information and form recommendations.

Refer to the 1996 financial statements and Form 10-K excerpts of the Boston Beer Company and the Lion Brewery Inc. *Note*: both companies received unqualified audit opinions from their auditors.

Analysis

a. Prior to reading the financial statements, review the background information about each company. This information was extracted from each company's Form 10-K. On the basis of these descriptions what differences in the financial statements of the two companies do you expect? That is, as a result of the companies' strategic operating, investing, and financing decisions, how would you expect major financial statement relationships to differ?

b. A company's financial statements can be analyzed in many ways. Return on equity (ROE) is a widely-used measure of profitability that compares the profit the company made during the period (net income) to the resources invested in the company (shareholders' equity). The DuPont model systematically breaks ROE into components. One form of the model is:

$$ROE = \frac{NI}{EBT} \times \frac{EBT}{EBIT} \times \frac{EBIT}{Sales} \times \frac{Sales}{Total\ Assets} \times \frac{Total\ Assets}{Common\ Equity}$$

where NI is net income, EBT is earnings before tax, and EBIT is earnings before interest and tax.

- NI / EBT measures the proportion of earnings before tax that is kept by the company.
- EBT / EBIT measures the effect of interest; it indicates the proportion of earnings before interest and tax that is retained after paying interest. It should be considered together with the leverage component (Total Assets / Common Equity). Further analysis of this component includes average interest rates on debt (and on investments if interest expense is reported net of interest income).
- EBIT / Sales measures the company's operating return on sales; it can be broken down into further subcomponents such as the gross margin percent. Preparing common-size income

statements will help you analyze this component. This component and the next form the 'guts' of the model—did the managers operate the firm profitably?

- Sales / Total Assets measures asset utilization; it can be broken down into further subcomponents such as accounts receivable turnover, inventory turnover, and plant asset turnover. This is another key component—did the managers use the assets efficiently?
- Total Assets / Common Equity measures the effect of leverage on ROE. Note that this ratio equals 1 + the debt-equity ratio (i.e., Total Liabilities / Total Common Equity). Subcomponents include the current and quick ratios. Together with the interest component of ROE, you can look at times interest earned and other fixed charge ratios.

Note that once the common terms cancel ROE is Net Income divided by the firm's Common Equity (the book value of what the shareholders have invested and reinvested in the firm). ROE, its components, and further subcomponents can be compared across time, firms, and to expectations, making it a very powerful tool.

Calculate ROE and the five subcomponents, above, for both companies for 1995 and 1996.

c. Refer to your ROE decomposition from *b*.

   i. What trends do you notice in the ROE subcomponents for each firm over time?

   ii. Evaluate which firm is more profitable. Consider profitability in terms of overall ROE, operating return on sales (and insights from common-size income statements), and return on assets.

   iii. Which firm is more efficient in its use of assets? Consider efficiency in terms of total asset turnover, receivables turnover (and average collection period), inventory turnover (and average holding period), payables turnover (and average time to payment), cash conversion cycle (i.e., receivables days + inventory days – payables days), and fixed asset turnover. Are there any adjustments that could be made to enhance the interpretation of Boston Beer's total asset turnover?

   iv. Are the companies likely to meet their debts as they come due? Consider ratios such as the current ratio, the quick ratio, and the debt-equity ratio. Also consider interest costs and the times interest earned ratio. Is there any "off-balance sheet" financing that will constrain future cash flow? Consider operating leases, equity investments, guarantees, and so on.

   v. Evaluate each firm's tax rate. Do they appear reasonable? Does one firm have an advantage over the other?

   vi. Are the differences you expected in part *a*. apparent?

d. Assess the cash flow of each company. Are cash flows from operations a source or a use of cash? How are operations and investments being financed? What differences do you note?

e. Consider the future prospects of both companies and evaluate the risks they face. Which company demonstrates the most potential to increase its owners' wealth through operations? Why? Are there any unusual or non-recurring items that need to be considered in your analysis? That is, are the earnings of high quality? Are the earnings persistent?

f. As a potential investor, are either of these companies worth seeking further information about? What sort of information would you want?

THE BOSTON BEER COMPANY, INC.

Item 1. Business

General

Boston Beer is the largest craft brewer by volume in the United States In fiscal 1996, the Company sold 1,213,000 barrels of beer, which it believes to be more than the next five largest craft brewers combined.

The Company's net sales have grown from $29.5 million in 1991 to $191.1 million in fiscal 1996, representing a compounded annual growth rate of 46%. The Company's net sales increased 26% in 1996 from 1995.

In 1996, in addition to its flagship brand, Samuel Adams Boston Lager, the Company brewed seventeen beers under the Boston Beer Company name: Boston Ale, Lightship, Cream Stout, Honey Porter, Scotch Ale, Double Bock, Triple Bock, Octoberfest, Winter Lager, Old Fezziwig, Cherry Wheat, Summer Ale, Cranberry Lambic, Golden Pilsner, and three beers brewed under the LongShot label. The Company also sells beer brewed under the Oregon Original brand name through a separate sales organization and utilizes both separate and shared brewing operations. The Company brews its beer under contract at five breweries located in Pittsburgh, Pennsylvania, Lehigh Valley, Pennsylvania, Portland, Oregon, Rochester, New York, and Cincinnati, Ohio. Effective March 1, 1997, the Company, through an affiliate, Samuel Adams Brewery Company, Ltd., acquired the equipment and other brewery-related personal property of The Schoenling Brewing Company in Cincinnati, Ohio and leased the real estate on which the brewery is located. The Company intends to purchase the real estate of the Cincinnati brewery once certain pre-conditions have been satisfied. …

Industry Background

The Company is the largest brewer by volume in the craft-brewing/micro-brewing segment of the U.S. brewing industry. The terms craft brewer and micro-brewer are often used interchangeably by consumers and within the industry to mean a small, independent brewer whose predominant product is brewed with only traditional brewing processes and ingredients. Craft brewers include contract brewers, small regional brewers, and brewpubs. Craft beers are full-flavored beers brewed with higher quality hops, malted barley, yeast, and water, and without adjuncts such as rice, corn, or stabilizers, or with water dilution used to lighten beer for mass production and consumption. The Company estimates that in 1996 the craft brew segment accounted for approximately 4.7 million barrels. Over the five- year period ended December 31, 1996, craft beer shipments have grown at a compounded annual rate of approximately 39%, while total U.S. beer industry shipments have remained substantially level.

The primary cause for the rapid growth of craft-brewed beers is consumers' rediscovery of and demand for more traditional, full-flavored beers. Before Prohibition, the U.S. beer industry consisted of hundreds of small breweries that brewed such full-flavored beers. Since the end of Prohibition, U.S. brewers have shifted production to milder, lighter beers, which use lower cost ingredients, and can be mass-produced to take advantage of economies of scale in production and advertising. This shift toward these mass-produced beers has coincided with extreme consolidation in the beer industry. Today, three major brewers control over 75% of all U.S. beer shipments. …

In response to increased consumer demand for more flavorful beers, the number of craft-brewed beers has increased dramatically. Currently there are more than 500 craft brewers. In addition to the many independent brewers and contract brewers, the three major brewers (Anheuser-Busch, Inc., Miller Brewing Co., and Coors Brewing Co.) have all entered this fast-growing market, either through developing their own specialty beers or by acquiring in whole or part, or forming partnerships with existing craft brewers. It should be noted that in the last four months of 1996, the growth of the craft beer market has slowed materially. This slow down in growth may be accelerating in early 1997.

Business Strategy

The Company's business strategy is to continue to lead the craft-brewed beer market by creating and offering a wide variety of the highest quality full-flavored beers, while increasing sales through new product introductions and substantial trade and consumer awareness programs, supported by a large, well trained and rapidly expanding field sales organization. This strategy is detailed below.

Quality Assurance

The Company employs nine brewmasters and retains a world recognized brewing authority as consulting brewmaster to monitor the Company's contract brewers. Over 125 test, tastings, and evaluations are typically required to ensure that each batch of Samuel Adams conforms to the Company's standards. Its brewing department is supported by a quality control lab at the Company's small brewery in Boston. In order to assure that its customers enjoy only the freshest beer, the Company requires its contract brewers to include a "freshness" date on its bottles of Samuel Adams products. Boston Beer was among the first craft brewers to follow this practice. For Samuel Adams products, the Company uses only higher quality hops grown in Europe and in England.

Contract Brewing

The Company believes that its strategy of contract brewing, which utilizes the excess capacity of other breweries, gives the Company flexibility as well as quality and cost advantages over its competitors. The Company carefully selects breweries with (i) the capability of utilizing traditional brewing methods, and (ii) first rate quality control capabilities throughout brewing, fermentation, finishing, and packaging. By using the current excess capacity at other breweries, the Company has avoided potential start up problems of bringing a new brewery on line. Furthermore, by brewing in multiple locations, the Company can reduce its distribution costs and deliver fresher beer to its customers than other craft brewers with broad distribution from a single brewery. While the Company currently plans to continue its contract-brewing strategy, it has, as discussed above, acquired an existing brewery in Cincinnati and will also regularly evaluate the economic and quality issues involved with acquiring other breweries, as well as continuing with its contract brewing arrangements. It should be noted that the acquisition of the assets of the Cincinnati brewery and the subsequent ownership of the brewery assets will cause an erosion of the Company's consolidated gross profit margin and that on a line of business basis, the Cincinnati operation is expected to show a loss.

The Company currently has contracts with five brewers, one of whom is an affiliate of the Company, to produce its Samuel Adams lines of beers in the U.S., each of which is described in greater detail below. The Company believes that its current contract brewers have capacity, to which the Company has access, to brew annually approximately one and one half times as much of the Company's beer as the Company sold during 1996.

The Company continues to brew its Samuel Adams Boston Lager at each of its contract brewers but does not brew each of its other products at each contract brewer. Therefore, at any particular time, the Company may be relying on only one supplier for its products other than Samuel Adams Boston Lager. …

Strong Sales and Distribution Presence

Boston Beer sells its products through a dynamic sales force, which the Company believes is the largest of any craft brewer and one of the largest in the domestic beer industry. The Company sells its beer through wholesale distributors, which then sell to retailers such as pubs, restaurants, grocery chains, package stores, and other retail outlets. The Company's sales force has a high level of product knowledge, and is trained in the details of the brewing process. Its sales force receives selling skills training each year from outside training experts. Sales representatives typically carry hops, barley, and other samples to educate wholesale and retail buyers as to the quality and taste of its beers. The Company has developed strong relationships with its distributors and retailers, many of which have benefited from the Company's premium pricing strategy and rapid growth.

Products

The Company's product strategy is to create and offer a world class variety of traditional beers and to promote the Samuel Adams product line. At the end of 1996, the Company marketed twelve year-round and 6 seasonal beers under the Samuel Adams and LongShot brand names. … The Company's Samuel Adams Boston Lager has historically accounted for the majority of the Company's sales. …

The Company uses its Boston brewery to develop new types of innovative and traditional beers and to supply draft beer for the local market. Product development entails researching market needs and competitive products, sample brewing, and market taste testing.

In 1994, the Company formed the Oregon Ale and Beer Company ("Oregon Ale and Beer") to develop and market Pacific Northwest style beers. Oregon Ale and Beer markets its beers under the Oregon Original brand through a sales force separate from that which sells Samuel Adams' styles. Oregon Original ales have been brewed in Oregon at two breweries, one in Lake Oswego and the other in Portland. …

Sales and Marketing

The Company's products are sold to independent distributors by a large field sales. With few exceptions, the Company's products are not the primary brands in the distributor's portfolio. Thus, the Company, in addition to competing with other beers for a share of the consumer's business, competes with other beers for a share of the distributor's attention, time, and selling efforts. The Company considers its distributors its primary customers and is focused on the relationship it has with its distributors.

In addition to this distributor focus, the Company has set up its sales organization to include on-premise and retail account specialists. This is designed to develop and strengthen relations at the chain headquarter level, and to provide educational and promotional programs aimed at distributors, retailers, and consumers, in each channel of distribution.

The Company has also historically engaged in extensive media campaigns, primarily radio. In addition, its sales force complements these efforts by engaging in sponsorships of cultural and community events, local beer festivals, industry-related trade shows, and promotional events at local establishments for sampling and awareness. All of these efforts are designed to stimulate consumer demand by educating consumers, retailers, and distributors, on the qualities of beer. The Company uses a wide array of point-of-sale items (banners, neons, umbrellas, glassware, display pieces, signs, menu stands, etc.) designed to stimulate impulse sales and continued awareness. It should be noted that this rate of increase in sales versus prior periods is slowing for the Company as well as for the market.

Competition

The craft-brewed and high-end segments of the U.S. beer market are highly competitive due to continuing product proliferation from craft brewers and the recent introduction of specialty beers by national brewers. Recent growth in the sales of craft-brewed beers has increased competition and, as a result, the Company's growth rate compared to the preceding years is declining. The Company's products also compete generally with other alcoholic beverages, including other segments of the beer industry and low alcohol products. The Company competes with other beer and beverage companies not only for consumer acceptance and loyalty but also for shelf and tap space in retail establishments and for marketing focus by the Company's distributors and their customers, all of which also distribute and sell other beers and alcoholic beverage products. The principal methods of competition in the craft-brewed segment of the beer industry include product quality and taste, brand advertising, trade and consumer promotions, pricing, packaging, and the development of new products. The competitive position of the Company is enhanced by its uncompromising product quality, its development of new beer styles, innovative point of sale materials, a large motivated sales force, tactical introduction of seasonal beers and pricing strategies generating above-average profits to distributors and retailers.

The Company expects competition with craft brewers to increase as new craft brewers emerge and existing craft brewers expand their capacity and distribution. While some of the smaller micro-brewers and craft brewers have already left the marketplace due to the intense competition in the marketplace which they were unable to withstand with their oftentimes limited resources, new entrants into the market continue and competition, overall, is high. In addition, large brewers have developed or are developing niche brands and are acquiring small brewers to compete in the craft-brewed segment of the domestic beer market. These competitors may have substantially greater financial resources, marketing strength, and distribution networks than the Company.

The Company competes directly with regional specialty brewers such as Sierra Nevada Brewing Company, Pyramid Brewing Company, Anchor Brewing Company, other contract brewers such as Pete's Brewing Company, Massachusetts Bay Brewing, foreign brewers such as Heineken, Molson, Corona, Amstel, and Becks, and other regional craft brewers and brewpubs. Niche beers produced by affiliates of certain major domestic brewers such as Anheuser-Busch, Incorporated, Miller Brewing Co., and Coors Brewing Co., also compete with the Company's products.

The Company believes that with the bulk of its production of beers being produced as a contract brewer, it has competitive advantages over the regional craft brewers because of its higher quality, greater flexibility, and lower initial capital costs. Its use of contract brewing frees up capital for other uses and allows the Company to brew its beer closer to major markets around the country, providing fresher beer to customers and affording lower transportation costs. The Company's recent purchase of a brewery in Cincinnati where it previously contract-brewed its beers, will continue to provide certain logistical advantages while at the same time providing the Company with added flexibility of production through its ownership which complements its strategy of contract brewing. The Company also believes that its products enjoy competitive advantages over foreign beers, including lower transportation costs, no import charges, and superior product freshness. …

Taxation

The federal government and each of the states levy excise taxes on alcoholic beverages, including beer. For brewers producing no more than 2,000,000 barrels of beer per calendar year, the federal excise tax is $7.00 per barrel on the first 60,000 barrels of beer removed for consumption or sale during a calendar year, and $18.00 per barrel for each barrel in excess of 60,000. For brewers producing more than 2,000,000 barrels of beer in a calendar year, the federal excise tax is $18.00 per barrel. As the brewer of record of its beers, the Company has been able to take advantage of this reduced tax on the first 60,000 barrels of its beers produced. Individual states also impose excise taxes on alcoholic beverages in varying amounts, which have also been subject to change. The state excise taxes are usually paid by the Company's distributors. …

Item 6. Selected Financial Data

THE BOSTON BEER COMPANY, INC.
SELECTED FINANCIAL DATA

	Dec. 28 1996	Dec. 31 1995	Dec. 31 1994	Dec. 31 1993	Dec. 31 1992	Dec. 31 1991
	Year Ended					
	(in thousands, except per share, per barrel and employee data)					
Income Statement Data:						
Sales	$213,879	$169,362	$128,077	$85,758	$53,343	$32,302
Less excise taxes	22,763	18,049	13,244	8,607	5,165	2,845
Net sales	191,116	151,313	114,833	77,151	48,178	29,457
Cost of Sales	95,786	73,847	52,851	35,481	22,028	13,039
Gross Profit	95,330	77,466	61,982	41,670	26,150	16,418
Advertising, promotional, and selling expenses	70,131	60,461	46,503	32,669	21,075	12,105
General and administrative	12,042	7,585	6,593	4,105	3,306	2,247
Total operating expenses	82,173	68,046	53,096	36,774	24,381	14,352
Operating income	13,157	9,420	8,886	4,896	1,769	2,066
Other income (expense), net	1,714	959	199	(2)	(124)	23
Income before income taxes	14,871	10,379	9,085	4,894	1,645	2,089
Provision (benefit) for income taxes *	6,486	(2,195)	–	–	–	–
Net income	$8,385	$12,574	$9,085	$4,894	$1,645	$2,089
Income before income taxes		$10,379	$9,085	$4,894	$1,645	$2,089
Pro forma income taxes (unaudited) **	–	4,483	3,765	2,040	691	859
Pro forma net income (unaudited) **		$5,896	$5,320	$2,854	$954	$1,230
Statistical Data:						
Barrels sold	1,213	961	714	475	294	174
Net sales per barrel	$158	$158	$161	$162	$164	$169
Employees	253	196	138	110	87	69
Net sales per employee	$755	$772	$832	$701	$554	$427
Balance Sheet Data at period end:						
Working capital	$47,769	$45,266	$3,996	$8,173	$6,169	$6,053
Total assets	$96,553	$76,690	$31,776	$24,054	$15,780	$11,981
Total long term debt	$1,800	$1,875	$1,950	$2,000	$2,050	$2,100
Total partners/ stockholders' equity	$64,831	$54,798	$6,600	$8,854	$6,434	$5,954
Dividends	–	–	–	–	–	–

* In 1995, the Company recorded a one-time tax benefit of $1,960,000 upon change in tax status of the entity, and a tax benefit of $235,000 for the period November 21, 1995 to December 31, 1995.

** Reflects pro forma provisions for income taxes using statutory federal and state corporate income tax rates that would have been applied had the Company been required to file income tax returns during the indicated period. See Note B of notes to the consolidated financial statements.

*** Reflects weighted average number of common and common equivalent shares of the Class A and Class B Common Stock assumed to be outstanding during the respective periods. For the years ended December 31, 1995 and December 31, 1994, shares reflect pro forma weighted average numbers. See Note B of notes to the consolidated financial statements.

THE BOSTON BEER COMPANY, INC.
CONSOLIDATED BALANCE SHEETS
(in thousands, except share data)

	December 28, 1996	December 31, 1995
Assets		
Current Assets:		
Cash & cash equivalents	$ 5,060	$ 1,877
Short term investments	35,926	34,730
Accounts receivable	18,109	16,265
Allowance for doubtful accounts	(1,930)	(175)
Inventories	13,002	9,280
Prepaid expenses	674	437
Deferred income taxes	2,968	1,011
Other current assets	3,882	1,858
Total current assets	77,691	65,283
Restricted investments	611	602
Equipment and leasehold improvements, at cost	21,043	9,690
Accumulated depreciation	(6,412)	(3,531)
Deferred income taxes	151	1,777
Other assets	3,469	2,869
Total assets	$ 96,553	$ 76,690
Liabilities and Stockholders' Equity		
Current Liabilities:		
Accounts payable	$ 17,783	$ 9,793
Accrued expenses	12,064	10,149
Current maturities of long-term debt	75	75
Total current liabilities	29,922	20,017
Long-term debt, less current maturities	1,800	1,875
Commitments and Contingencies (Note I)	–	–
Stockholders' Equity:		
Class A Common Stock, $.01 par value; 20,300,000 shares authorized; 15,972,058, and 15,643,664 issued and outstanding as of December 28, 1996 and December 31, 1995, respectively	160	156
Class B Common Stock, $.01 par value; 4,200,000 shares authorized; 4,107,355 issued and outstanding as of December 28, 1996 and December 31, 1995, respectively	41	41
Additional paid-in-capital	55,391	53,482
Unearned compensation	(363)	(509)
Unrealized loss on investments in marketable securities	(442)	–
Unrealized gain on forward exchange contract	31	–
Retained earnings	10,013	1,628
Total stockholders' equity	64,831	54,798
Total liabilities and stockholders' equity	$ 96,553	$ 76,690

The accompanying notes are an integral part of the financial statements.

THE BOSTON BEER COMPANY, INC.

CONSOLIDATED STATEMENTS OF INCOME
(in thousands, except per share data)

	For the Years Ended		
	December 28, 1996	December 31, 1995	December 31, 1994
Sales	$ 213,879	$ 169,362	$ 128,077
Less excise taxes	22,763	18,049	13,244
Net sales	191,116	151,313	114,833
Cost of sales	95,786	73,847	52,851
Gross profit	95,330	77,466	61,982
Operating expenses:			
Advertising, promotional and selling expenses	70,131	60,461	46,503
General and administrative expenses	12,042	7,585	6,593
Total operating expenses	82,173	68,046	53,096
Operating income	13,157	9,420	8,886
Other income (expense):			
Interest income	1,932	452	429
Interest expense	(236)	(250)	(233)
Other income, net	18	757	3
Total other income	1,714	959	199
Income before income taxes	14,871	10,379	9,085
Provision (benefit) for income taxes	6,486	(2,195)	–
Net income	$ 8,385	$ 12,574	$ 9,085
Pro forma data (unaudited) (Note B):			
Income before pro forma income taxes		10,379	9,085
Pro forma income tax expense		4,483	3,765
Pro forma net income		$ 5,896	$ 5,320
Net income per common and common equivalent share	$ 0.41	$ 0.33 *	$ 0.29 *
Weighted average number of common and common equivalent shares	20,352	17,949 *	18,171 *

* Pro forma, see Note B.

The accompanying notes are an integral part of the financial statements.

THE BOSTON BEER COMPANY, INC.

CONSOLIDATED STATEMENTS OF CASH FLOWS
(in thousands)

	For the Years Ended		
	December 28, 1996	December 31, 1995	December 31, 1994
Cash flows from operating activities:			
Net income	$ 8,385	$ 12,574*	$ 9,085*
Adjustments to reconcile net income to net cash provided by operating activities:			
Depreciation and amortization	3,030	1,565	925
(Gain) loss on disposal of fixed asset	(4)	38	21
Bad debt expense	1,832	(557)	391
Stock option compensation expense	186	250	280
Changes in assets & liabilities:			
Accounts receivable	(1,921)	(5,473)	(2,339)
Inventory	(3,722)	(1,525)	(4,049)
Prepaids expense	(237)	64	(285)
Other current assets	(1,993)	(753)	(593)
Deferred taxes	(331)	(2,195)	—
Other assets	(743)	(2,459)	(172)
Accounts payable	7,990	(494)	6,353
Accrued expenses	3,291	1,405	3,673
Total adjustments	7,378	(10,134)	4,205
Net cash provided by operating activities:	15,763	2,440	13,290
Cash flows for investing activities:			
Purchases of fixed assets	(11,359)	(4,268)	(2,621)
Proceeds on disposal of fixed assets	4	45	—
(Purchases) maturities of government securities	2,648	(27,027)	(2,624)
Purchase of marketable securities	(4,286)	—	—
Purchase of restricted investments	(1,225)	(612)	(1,171)
Maturities of restricted investments	1,216	615	1,145
Net cash used in investing	(13,002)	(31,247)	(5,271)
Cash flows from financing activities:			
Proceeds from issuance of common stock	—	49,691	—
Proceeds from exercise of stock option plans	560	—	—
Proceeds from sale under stock purchase plan	40	—	—
Repurchase of shares under employee investment and incentive share plans	(103)	—	—
Principal payments on long-term debt	(75)	(50)	(50)
Partners' distributions	—	(19,055)	(11,619)
Net cash provided by (used for) financing activities	422	30,586	11,669
Net increase (decrease) in cash and cash equivalents	3,183	1,779	(3,650)
Cash and cash equivalents at beginning of period	1,877	98	3,748
Cash and cash equivalents at end of period	$ 5,060	$ 1,877	$ 98
Supplemental disclosure of cash flow information:			
Interest paid	$ 224	$ 252	$ 236
Taxes paid	$ 5,992	—	—

* Net income for the fiscal year ended December 31, 1995 is before pro forma income taxes. See Note B.
The accompanying notes are an integral part of the financial statements.

THE BOSTON BEER COMPANY, INC.
NOTES TO THE CONSOLIDATED FINANCIAL STATEMENTS (excerpts)

A. Basis of Presentation:

The Boston Beer Company, Inc. (the "Company"), is engaged in the business of marketing and selling beer and ale products throughout the United States and in select international markets. On November 20, 1995, in connection with the initial public offering of the Company's stock effected that date, the non-corporate limited partners transferred their respective partnership interests to the Company and the owners of the general partner and corporate limited partners transferred their respective ownership interests in such entities to the Company. In exchange, the transferors received an aggregate of 16,641,740 shares of the Company's common stock on a pro rata basis, based on their then respective percentage equity interests in the Partnership. The aforementioned transactions are collectively referred to hereinafter as the "Recapitalization."

B. Summary of Significant Accounting Policies:

Fiscal Year
Effective in fiscal 1996, the Company changed its fiscal year to end on the last Saturday in December. The impact on the current year of two fewer days of operations was not material.

Principles of Consolidation
The consolidated financial statements include the accounts of the Company, its subsidiaries, and the Partnership. All intercompany accounts and transactions have been eliminated.

Revenue Recognition
Revenue is recognized when goods are shipped to customers. Accounts receivable balances are reflected net of an allowance for uncollectible accounts of approximately $1,930,000 and $175,000 at December 28, 1996 and December 31, 1995, respectively.

Short Term Investments and Restricted Investments
Short term investments consist primarily of U.S. Government securities and marketable equity securities with original maturities beyond three months and less than twelve months. All short term investments have been classified as available-for-sale and are reported at fair value with unrealized gains and losses included in stockholders' equity. Fair value is based on quoted market prices as of December 28, 1996.

Restricted investments consist solely of the unexpended proceeds from the debt as discussed in Note G. These investments, consisting of treasury notes which mature within one year, are expected to be held to maturity and accordingly are valued at amortized cost, which approximates fair value.

Inventories
Inventories, which consist principally of hops, bottles, and packaging, are stated at the lower of cost, determined on a first-in, first-out (FIFO) basis, or market.

Equipment and Leasehold Improvements
Equipment and leasehold improvements are recorded at cost. Expenditures for maintenance, repairs, and renewals are charged to expense; major improvements are capitalized. Upon retirement or sale, the cost of the assets disposed of and the related accumulated depreciation are removed from the accounts and any resulting gain or loss is included in the determination of net income. Provision for depreciation is computed on the straight-line method based upon the estimated useful lives of the underlying assets as follows:

Kegs and equipment	3 to 10 years
Office equipment and furniture	3 to 5 years
Leasehold improvements	5 years, or the life of the lease, whichever is shorter

Deposits
The Company recognizes a liability for estimated refundable deposits in kegs and for unclaimed deposits on bottles which are subject to state regulations. A liability for refundable deposits (redemptions) on reusable bottles in 1995 was not recorded, nor was there an offsetting adjustment to inventory. As of December 28, 1996, the Company recorded an estimated liability of $587,000, with an offsetting adjustment to cost of goods sold for re-used glass which had not been redeemed as of the end of the year. The Company recorded this liability to recognize that the re-used glass may not be placed back into production in the future. Total redemptions associated with reusable bottles during the years ended December 28, 1996, December 31, 1995, and 1994 were $3,053,000, $1,441,000, and $1,402,000 respectively.

Fair Value of Financial Instruments
The carrying amount of the Company's long term debt, including current maturities, approximates fair value because the interest rates on these instruments change with market interest rates. The carrying amounts for accounts receivable and accounts payable approximate their fair values due to the short term maturity of these instruments.

Advertising and Sales Promotions
Advertising and sales promotional programs are charged to expense during the period in which they are incurred. Total advertising and sales promotional expense for the years ended December 28, 1996, December 31, 1995, and 1994, were $35,730,000, $35,039,000, and $27,598,000 respectively.

Purchase Commitments
The Company recognizes losses on hops purchase commitments when amounts from the sale price of the related product are expected to be less than the cost of the product. The Company has not historically experienced any losses related to hops purchase commitments.

Forward Exchange Contracts
Unrealized gains and losses on contracts designated as hedges of existing assets and liabilities are accrued as exchange rates change and are recorded as a component of Stockholders' Equity. Realized gains and losses are recognized in income as contracts expire.

Stock-Based Compensation
Statement of Financial Accounting Standards No. 123 "Accounting for Stock-Based Compensation" ("SFAS 123"), requires the Company to either elect expense recognition or the disclosure-only alternative for stock-based employee compensation. SFAS 123 has been adopted in the Company's 1996 financial statements with comparable disclosures for the prior year. The Company has reviewed the adoption and impact of SFAS 123, and has elected to adopt the disclosure-only alternative and accordingly this standard has no impact on the Company's results of operations or its financial position.

Income Taxes
The Company records income taxes under the liability method whereby deferred tax assets and liabilities are determined based on differences between financial reporting and tax bases of assets and liabilities, and are measured by applying enacted tax rates for the taxable years in which those differences are expected to reverse.

Pro Forma Income Taxes (unaudited)
The financial statements of the Company for the periods prior to the Recapitalization do not include a provision for income taxes because the taxable income of the Company, up until the effective date of the Recapitalization, is included in the income tax returns of the Partnership's partners and former Subchapter S corporation's shareholder. The statements of income include a pro forma income tax provision on taxable income for financial statement purposes using an estimated effective federal and state income tax rate which would have resulted if the Partnership and Subchapter S corporation had filed a corporate income tax return during those periods.

Earnings Per Share
Earnings per share is based on the weighted average number of shares outstanding during the period after consideration of the dilutive effect, if any, for stock options. Fully diluted net income per share has not been presented as the amount would not differ significantly from those presented.

New Accounting Pronouncements
In February, 1997, the Financial Accounting Standards Board issued Statement of Financial Accounting Standards No. 128, "Earnings Per Share" (SFAS 128), which is effective for fiscal years that end after December 15, 1997, including interim periods. Earlier application is not permitted. However, an entity is permitted to disclose pro forma earnings per share amounts computed using SFAS 128 in the notes to financial statements in periods prior to adoption. The Statement requires restatement of all prior-period earnings per share data presented after the effective date. SFAS 128 specifies the computation, presentation, and disclosure requirements for earnings per share and is substantially similar to the standard recently issued by the International Accounting Standards Committee entitled International Accounting Standards, "Earnings Per Share" (IAS 33). The Company plans to adopt SFAS 128 in 1997 and has not yet determined the impact.

C. Short Term Investments:

Short term investments consist of marketable equity securities having a cost of $4,286,000 and a market value of $3,844,000, which resulted in an unrealized loss of $442,000 at December 28, 1996. The Company did not have any investments in marketable equity securities as of December 31, 1995. In addition, the Company has investments in

U.S. Government securities having a cost of $32,082,000 and $34,730,000 at December 28, 1996 and December 31, 1995, respectively, which approximates fair value.

D. Inventories:

	December 28, 1996	December 31, 1995
	(in thousands)	
Raw material, principally hops	$ 12,677	$ 8,543
Work in process	—	518
Finished goods	325	219
	$ 13,002	$ 9,280

E. Equipment and Leasehold Improvements:

	December 28, 1996	December 31, 1995
	(in thousands)	
Kegs and equipment	$ 16,457	$ 7,012
Office equipment and furniture	3,527	1,623
Leasehold improvements	1,059	1,055
	$ 21,043	$ 9,690
Less accumulated depreciation	6,412	3,531
	$ 14,631	$ 6,159

The Company recorded depreciation expense related to these assets of $2,886,000, $1,565,000, and $925,000 for the years ended December 28, 1996, December 31, 1995, and December 31, 1994, respectively.

F. Accrued Expenses:

	December 28, 1996	December 31, 1995
	(in thousands)	
Advertising	$ 4,019	$ 4,451
Keg deposits	1,813	1,276
Employee wages and reimbursements	1,906	1,586
Point of sale related accruals	1,288	1,000
Other accrued liabilities	3,038	1,836
	$ 12,064	$ 10,149

For the year ended December 28, 1996, the Company included $1,117,000 of accrued freight costs in accounts payable. For the year ended December 31, 1995, $1,189,000 of freight costs previously recognized as a component of accrued expenses were reclassified to accounts payable.

G. Long-Term Debt and Line of Credit:

Long-Term Debt

During 1988, the Company entered into a $2,200,000 loan with the Massachusetts Industrial Finance Authority ("MIFA"), which matures July 15, 2007. As of December 28, 1996, the loan requires scheduled annual principal payments as follows:

	(in thousands)
1997	$ 75
1998	75
1999	100
2000	100
2001	100
Thereafter	1,425
	1,875
Less: current portion	75
Total long-term debt	$ 1,800

Interest accrues at 11.5 % and is paid semiannually. The proceeds from the MIFA loan were used to fund approximately $1,500,000 of engineering and design efforts, which were subsequently abandoned in 1989, and to acquire approximately $200,000 of various assets for the brewery. The unexpended proceeds referenced in Note B were restricted to the further development of the Company's Boston brewery, a leased facility. All assets acquired with the proceeds of the loan are reflected as equipment or leasehold improvements. The loan is collateralized by the related fixed assets and any unexpended proceeds which approximated, including interest, $611,000 and $602,000 at December 28, 1996 and December 31, 1995, respectively.

The loan agreement contains various covenants, the most restrictive of which is that the Company's equity may not be less than $700,000 as of the end of each fiscal year, and the debt to equity ratio of the Company may not exceed 4 to 1 at the end of any fiscal year. As of December 28, 1996, the Company's equity was $65,000,000 and the debt to equity ratio was .03 to 1.

Line of Credit
On May 2, 1995, the Company entered into an unsecured Revolving Line of Credit Agreement (the "Agreement") with a bank providing for borrowings of up to $14,000,000 at either the bank's prime rate (8.25% at December 28, 1996) or the applicable Libor Rate plus .50% for terms of 30, 60, or 90 days. The Company pays a commitment fee of .15% of the unused portion of the line. The Agreement, which expires on May 1, 1997, requires the Company to maintain certain financial ratios related to tangible net worth, interest coverage, and profits, and restricts the Company's ability to incur additional indebtedness, incur certain liens and encumbrances, make investments in other persons, engage in a new business, or enter into sale and leaseback transactions. The Agreement also contains certain events of default, including the failure of the Company's president to control and be actively engaged on a full-time basis in the business of the Company. As of December 28, 1996 and December 31, 1995, no borrowings were outstanding thereunder.

H. Income Taxes:

Income Taxes
Effective with the Recapitalization described in Note A, the Company became subject to federal and state income taxes. The historical income tax benefit reflects the recording of a one-time tax benefit of $1,960,000 upon the change in tax status of the entity as required by SFAS 109, and a tax benefit of $235,000 for the period from November 21 to December 31, 1995.

Significant components of the Company's deferred tax assets and liabilities as of December 28, 1996 and December 31, 1995 are as follows:

(in thousands)

	1996			1995		
	Current	Long-Term	Total	Current	Long-Term	Total
Deferred Tax Assets:						
Incentive/investment unit and option plans	$ 11	$ 1,052	$ 1,063	$ 21	$ 1,856	$1,877
Accrued expenses not currently deductible	943	—	943	467	—	467
Reserves	1,828	—	1,828	88	—	88
Deferred Compensation	—	90	90	—	65	65
Net operating loss	—	—	—	334	—	334
Other	250	(2)	248	101	—	101
Total deferred tax assets	3,032	1,140	4,172	1,011	1,921	2,932
Deferred tax liabilities:						
Depreciation	—	(814)	(814)	—	(144)	(144)
Tax installment sale	(64)	(175)	(239)	—	—	—
Net deferred tax assets	$2,968	$ 151	$3,119	$1,011	$ 1,777	$2,788

The deferred tax asset balance at December 31, 1995 includes a $593,000 net deferred tax asset of the corporate limited partners recorded upon the Recapitalization.

Based upon prior earnings history and expected future taxable income, the Company does not believe that a valuation allowance is required for the net deferred tax asset.

Significant components of the income tax provision (benefit) for income taxes for the years ended December 28, 1996 and December 31, 1995 are as follows:

(in thousands)

	1996	1995
Current:		
Federal	$ 5,261	—
State	1,556	—
Total current	6,817	—
Deferred:		
Federal	(251)	$ (1,667)
State	(80)	(528)
Total deferred	$ (331)	$ (2,195)
Total income tax expense (benefit)	$ 6,486	$ (2,195)

The reconciliation of income tax computed at statutory rates to actual income tax expense for the years ended December 28, 1996 and December 31, 1995, are as follows:

	1996	1995
Statutory rate	35.0%	35.0%
State income tax, net of federal benefit	6.5	(1.8)
Permanent differences	1.2	0.3
Income for the period prior to the Recapitalization not subject to tax	—	(36.9)
Deferred tax asset resulting from change in tax status	—	(15.9)
Other	0.9	(1.8)
	43.6%	(21.1%)

At December 31, 1995, the Company had a tax net operating loss carryforward of approximately $765,000, which arose during the period from November 21 to December 31, 1995, which was fully utilized in 1996.

I. Commitments and Contingencies:

Lease Commitments
The Company has various operating lease agreements primarily involving real estate. Terms of the leases include purchase options, renewals, and maintenance costs, and vary by lease. These lease obligations expire at various dates through 2001.

Minimum annual rental payments under these agreements are as follows:

	(in thousands)
1997	$ 802
1998	673
1999	668
2000	565
2001	565
Thereafter	—
	$ 3,273

Rent expense for the years ended December 28, 1996, December 31, 1995, and 1994 was approximately $512,000, $340,000, and $276,000 respectively.

Distribution
The Company's two largest distributors each accounted for approximately 6% of the Company's net sales.

License Agreement
The Company signed a contract in March, 1996, with a major beverage company with respect to a transaction in which that company will license and sell a new craft brew beer whose trademark and trade names are owned by the Company. The Company is expected to expense up to $750,000 in 1997 and 1998, principally to cover marketing expenses to aid the introduction of this new beer and will, in return, receive a royalty on sales after a certain period of time. The Company will also provide certain technical assistance. The agreement also sets forth the circumstances in which the relationship can be terminated and the terms on which rights to the product will revert to the Company or may be reacquired by the Company. There can be no assurance that any contemplated royalty will be earned by the Company.

Litigation
In early 1996, Boston Brewing Company, Inc. ("Boston Brewing"), an affiliate of both Boston Beer Company Limited Partnership and The Boston Beer Company, Inc., had an action filed against it by one of its distributors, such action having been filed in a court in England. The action contains a claim for damages of an alleged breach of a Distributorship Agreement between Boston Brewing and the plaintiff. The action is being vigorously defended by the Company and at present is in the discovery stage.

In addition, the Company is subject to legal proceedings and claims which arise in the ordinary course of business. In the opinion of management, the amount of ultimate liability with respect to these actions will not materially affect the financial position or results of operations of the Company.

J. Common Stock:

Initial Public Offering
On November 20, 1995, the Company completed an initial public offering and sold an aggregate of 3,109,279 shares of Common Stock, of which 990,000 shares were sold for $15.00 per share in a best efforts offering and 2,119,279 shares were sold for $20.00 in an underwritten offering, resulting in net proceeds, after deducting underwriting discounts and expenses, of $49,691,000. In addition, as described in Note A, upon Recapitalization the owners of the general and corporate limited partners transferred their respective ownership interests to the Company. In exchange, the transferors received an aggregate of 16,641,740 shares of the Company's common stock on a pro rata

basis based on their then respective equity interest in the Partnership. The total number of shares of Class A and Class B Common Stock outstanding after completion of the offering was 19,751,019.

K. Financial Instruments:

During 1996, the Company entered into a forward exchange contract to reduce exposure to currency movements affecting existing foreign currency denominated assets, liabilities, and firm commitments. The contract duration matches the duration of the currency position. The future value of the contract and the related currency position is subject to offsetting market risk resulting form foreign currency exchange rate volatility. The carrying amounts of the contract and the unrealized gain recognized as a component of Stockholders' Equity totaled $1,195,000 and $31,070, respectively, at December 28, 1996. There were no realized gains or losses on the contract as of December 28, 1996.

L. Related Party Transactions:

At December 31, 1995, borrowings of $150,000 under a recourse note due on December 31, 1997 from the Company's Chief Operating Officer were outstanding. The note bears interest based on the applicable federal rate. This note was repaid in its entirety during 1996.

The Company has a deferred compensation agreement with its Chief Operating Officer which calls for specific payments upon retirement on or after April 1, 2000 with pro-rated annual payments called for upon early retirement. The Company has expensed approximately $59,000, $56,000, and $49,000 for the three years ended December 28, 1996, December 31, 1995 and 1994, respectively.

N. Sale of Distribution Rights:

In September 1995, the Company sold its distribution rights to a major metropolitan area and associated receivables and inventories for approximately $1,200,000 and the assumption of certain deposit liabilities and truck leases. On closing approximately $420,000 was paid in cash with the remainder in the form of a note which is payable in equal monthly installments of $13,000 plus interest at 10% per annum. This transaction resulted in a gain to the Company of approximately $807,000 and is included in other income. The sale of the distribution rights is not expected to result in any significant change in future operations of the Company when compared to historical results.

O. Subsequent Event:

Effective March 1, 1997, the Company acquired all of the equipment and other brewery-related personal property from the Schoenling Brewing Company and leased the real estate on which the brewery is situated. In addition, subject to the satisfaction of certain pre-conditions, the Company has agreed to purchase the real estate on which the brewery is located. The acquisition of the brewery assets and real estate will be accounted for under the purchase method of accounting. The purchase price allocation has not yet been determined.

P. Valuation and Qualifying Accounts:

The information required to be included in Schedule II, Valuation and Qualifying Accounts, for the years ended December 31, 1994, 1995, and December 28, 1996 is as follows:

	Balance at Beginning of Period	Additions Charged to Costs and Expenses (in thousands)	Net Additions (Deductions)	Balance At End of Period
Allowance for Doubtful Accounts				
1994	$ 146	47	(11)	182
1995	182	107	(114)	175
1996	175	1,832	(77)	1,930
Inventory Reserves				
1994	$ 457	381	(590)	248
1995	248	782	(1,014)	16
1996	16	2,860	(386)	2,490

Deductions from allowance for doubtful accounts represent the write-off of uncollectible balances whereas deductions from inventory reserves represent inventory destroyed in the normal course of business.

THE LION BREWERY, INC.

ITEM 1. BUSINESS

GENERAL

The Lion Brewery, Inc. ("The Lion Brewery" or the "Company") is a producer and bottler of brewed beverages, including malta, specialty beers and specialty soft drinks. The Lion Brewery was incorporated in Pennsylvania on April 5, 1933. The Company is the dominant producer of malta in the continental United States. Specialty beers, generally known as craft beers, are brewed by the Company both for sale under its own label and on a contract basis. Craft beers are distinguishable from other domestically produced beers by their fuller flavor and adherence to traditional European brewing styles. In 1996, the Company produced a flavored, alcoholic, malt based brew under contract. The Company also produces specialty soft drinks, including all-natural brewed ginger beverages, on a contract basis for third parties. The Lion Brewery also brews beer for sale under traditional Company owned labels for the local market at popular prices.

The Company's growth strategy is to rapidly expand its production and marketing of specialty beers, while maintaining the growth in its non-alcoholic beverages. By owning and operating its own brewery and with its significant brewing and packaging experience, the Company believes it is well positioned to optimize the quality and consistency of its products as well as to formulate new products. The Company plans to increase sales of its specialty beer labels through increased penetration of these brands in its existing markets, expansion into contiguous regional markets, new product introductions, increased marketing efforts and additions to brewing and bottling capacity.

The Company's original specialty beers—1857 Premium Lager, Liebotschaner Cream Ale and Stegmaier Porter—are reminiscent of the Company's rich beer brewing heritage. Since the brewhouse was built at the turn of the century in Wilkes-Barre, Pennsylvania, The Lion Brewery is the beneficiary of a long brewing tradition. The Company's flagship line of distinctive full-flavored beers are marketed under the Brewery Hill name. The Company currently produces seven styles of beer under the Brewery Hill label, two of which are seasonal flavors. Brewery Hill PennCenntenial Lager was recently introduced in November 1996 along with our winter seasonal, Brewery Hill Caramel Porter.

The Company established its reputation as a quality leader in the rapidly growing craft beer market by winning three Gold Medals at the Great American Beer Festival. The Lion Brewery's 1857 Premium Lager was voted Best American Premium Lager in 1994 and Liebotschaner Cream Ale won back to back gold medals in the American Lager Cream Ale Category in 1994 and 1995. … In addition, craft beers and specialty soft drinks brewed by the Company under contract have won several awards.

COMPANY HISTORY AND INDUSTRY BACKGROUND

The brewhouse in which the Company continues to brew its products was built at the turn of the century in Wilkes-Barre, Pennsylvania. At that time, the U.S. brewing industry comprised nearly 2,000 breweries, most of which were small operations that produced distinctive beers for local markets. The Company was incorporated as The Lion, Inc. in April 1933 to operate the brewery, which was one of the fewer than 1,000 breweries to reopen following Prohibition. Over the ensuing decades, lighter, less distinctively flavored beers appealing to broad segments of the population and supported by national advertising programs became prevalent. These beers use lower cost ingredients and are mass produced to take advantage of economies of scale. This shift toward mass produced beers coincided with extreme consolidation in the beer industry. In keeping with this consolidation trend, the Company purchased other labels including the Stegmaier brands, which had been produced on Brewery Hill in Wilkes-Barre since 1857. Of the more than 60 breweries existing in eastern Pennsylvania 50 years ago, only two, including the Lion Brewery, remain. Today, according to industry sources, approximately 90% of all domestic beer shipments come from the four largest domestic brewers.

Beginning in the mid 1980s and continuing in the 1990s, a number of domestic craft brewers began selling higher quality, more full-flavored beers, usually in local markets, as a growing number of consumers began to migrate away from less flavorful mass-marketed beers towards greater taste and broader variety, mirroring similar trends in other beverage and food categories. As an established regional specialty brewer, the Lion Brewery believes it is well-positioned to benefit from this shift in consumer preferences. In 1995, according to industry sources, the craft beer segment increased to approximately 3.8 million barrels, representing approximately 2.1% of the 180 million barrel, $50 billion retail domestic beer market. Over the five year period ended December 31, 1995, craft beer shipments increased at a compound annual rate of approximately 40%, while shipments in the total U.S. beer industry remained relatively flat. Industry analysts have attributed this flat overall beer consumption to a variety of factors, including increased concerns about the health consequences of consuming alcoholic beverages, safety consciousness and concerns about drinking and driving; a trend toward a diet including lighter, lower calorie beverages such as diet soft drinks, juices and sparkling water products; the increased activity of anti-alcohol consumer protection groups; an increase in the minimum drinking age from 18 to

21 years in all states; the general aging of the population; and increased federal and state excise taxes. Today the top three national brewers have entered into this fast growing craft segment by introducing their own specialty beers and/or by acquiring or investing in smaller regional craft brewers.

Before the emergence of the market opportunity in specialty beer, the Lion Brewery diversified into other products to sustain operations and continue to utilize its brewhouse and bottling facility. The Company's strategic entry into malta production in 1982 has resulted in the Company becoming the dominant producer of malta in the continental United States. Malta was originally developed many years ago by German brewers operating in the Caribbean area. The brewers developed malta by blending the excess molasses production from sugar with grain mash. Malta is still popular throughout the Caribbean and South America. In addition to malta, the Company also diversified into producing premium soft drinks in 1991.

BUSINESS STRATEGY

The Company intends to enhance its position as a leading producer of specialty brewed beverages by rapidly expanding production and marketing of craft beers and other malt based premium products; while maintaining the growth of its nonalcoholic brewed beverages. Key elements of the Company's business strategy are to:

Produce High Quality Brewed Beverages. The Company is committed to producing a variety of full-flavored brewed beverages. The Company employs a Head Brewmaster, an assistant brewmaster and a brewing assistant and retains a world recognized brewing authority to ensure the high quality and consistency of its products. To monitor the quality of its products, the Company maintains its own quality control laboratory staffed with two full-time quality control technicians and submits its products for analysis to the Seibel Institute of Technology, an independent laboratory, on a continuous basis. To monitor freshness, the Company dates each bottle and case with the date and time of its bottling. The Company brews its craft beers according to traditional styles and methods, selecting and using only high quality ingredients.

Brew Products in Company-Owned and Operated Facilities. The Company owns and operates its own brewing facility, which enables the Company to optimize the quality and consistency of its products, to achieve the greatest control over its production costs and to formulate new brewed products. The Company believes that its ability to engage in new product development through onsite experimentation in its brewhouse and to continuously monitor and control product quality in its own facilities are competitive advantages.

Expand Distribution of Craft Beers. The Company distributes craft beer under its own labels through a network of wholesale distributor relationships. Currently the Company distributes its products in twelve states, although the majority of its sales remain concentrated in Pennsylvania. The Company intends its penetration in existing markets and to enter new markets by increasing the size of its sales force and its marketing efforts. The Company chooses wholesaler distributors that the Company believes will best promote and sell the brands. The Company, through on site tours and presentations, actively educates its distributors in the total brewing process and the growing craft beer industry.

Introduce New Products. The Company is committed to developing and introducing new products to appeal to the strong consumer interest in full-flavored craft beers. The Company's diversified product mix and brewing expertise enhance its ability to create successful new products. The Company believes that new product introductions have helped the Company gain consumer awareness in its existing markets. Currently, the Company markets seven craft beers under the Brewery Hill label. In 1996, the Company introduced Brewery Hill Pale Ale in March, Brewery Hill Cherry Wheat; its summer seasonal, in May, Brewery Hill PennCenntenial Lager and Brewery Hill Caramel Porter; a winter seasonal, in November. The Company is also is developing new soft drink products for its contract customers.

Increase Production Capacity and Efficiency. The Company is in the process of increasing its annual production capacity from 340,000 to 400,000 barrels based upon its anticipated product mix. This expansion will modify its existing seven ounce bottling line to also accommodate 12 oz. bottles, the bottle size for most of the Company's products. In addition, The Company has increased its fermentation and lagering capacity with the relining of nine storage tanks. The Company also completed an upgrade of a boiler and is in the process of adding a malt storage and elevation system.

PRODUCTS

The Lion Brewery's diversified product portfolio consists of a variety of styles of malta, craft beers and specialty brewed beverages and soft drinks, including all-natural brewed ginger beverages, and popularly priced beer sold under traditional Company-owned labels. The Company distributes its products in glass bottles and kegs and its products are dated to monitor freshness. …

The Company also brews many distinctive craft beers and other specialty malt beverages under contract for other labels. Some of these customers are microbreweries and brewpubs that need additional brewing capacity to meet their production requirements and which typically provide their own recipes. In other instances, the Company formulates beer and specialty malt beverages for customers marketing their own labels. Most of these contract brewing customers provide their own packaging and labels. The Company arranges shipment to distributors F.O.B. the Company's warehouse and handles invoicing as a service to these customers. …

The Lion Brewery craft beer and specialty malt beverages produced for sale under its own labels and under contract for others accounted for approximately 14% and 10% of its annual barrel shipments and 19% and 12% of its net sales in fiscal 1996 and 1995, respectively.

SPECIALTY SOFT DRINKS. The Lion Brewery first began blending and bottling specialty soft drinks in 1987. The Company currently produces specialty soft drinks under contract for five customers including:

- Reed's. In June 1991, the Lion Brewery began producing for this customer Reed's All Natural Ginger Beer, a soft drink based on brewed ginger root. The Lion is currently the sole brewer of beverages sold under the Reed's label. Sales of this product line grew 48% and 44% in fiscal 1996 and 1995, respectively. This product was originally developed and produced in a small microbrewery in Colorado and the Company believes that Reed's is the leading brewed soft drink in health food stores. …
- Mad River. The Company produces eleven varieties of premium all natural blended soft drinks for Mad River. The product is sold to consumers primarily in resort locations and in upscale specialty food stores.
- The Company also produces specialty soft drinks for Goya Foods, Vitarroz and Virgil's. Specialty soft drinks accounted for approximately 12% and 10% of the Lion Brewery's barrel shipments and 9% and 8% of its net sales in fiscal 1996 and 1995, respectively.

POPULAR PRICED BEER. The Company brews beer for sale at popular prices in local markets under several traditional Company-owned brands. A majority of this beer is bottled in 16 oz. returnable bottles. The Company is intentionally reducing its production of popular priced beer in conjunction with a general decline in market demand for lower priced beer marketed in 16 oz. returnable bottles and in recognition of the significantly greater profitability for the Company using its production capacity for craft beer. Popular priced beer accounted for approximately 6% and 7% of barrel shipments and 4% and 5% of net sales in fiscal 1996 and 1995, respectively. …

SALES AND MARKETING

The Lion Brewery's four largest malta customers, Goya Foods, Vitarroz, Cerveceria India and 7-Up/RC Puerto Rico, accounted for 95% of the Company's total malta sales for fiscal 1996 and 1996. Mr. Lawson, the Company's Chief Executive Officer, is primarily responsible for selling and marketing these and the Company's other contract accounts. The Head Brewmaster and the Vice President of Logistics are also actively involved with these customer relationships in discussing product recipes, new product formulations, production scheduling and delivery. …

The Company's strategy is to increase its penetration into its existing markets while expanding to other markets. This strategy will be implemented by further developing the existing distributor relationships and establishing new distributors in target markets. The Company anticipates significantly increasing its sales and marketing efforts by hiring additional sales personnel and increasing public brand name exposure through print, outdoor and electronic advertising on a selective basis. …

EXCERPT FROM MANAGEMENT'S DISCUSSION AND ANALYSIS

Operating Data

	Year Ended September 30,					
	Percent of Net Sales			Net Sales Per Barrel		
	1996	1995	1994	1996	1995	1994
Malta	67.8%	75.0%	78.6%	$ 80	$ 78	$ 73
Beer:						
Craft:						
Company label	6.7	4.9	1.2	127	110	83
Contract	12.4	7.4	6.7	99	84	74
	19.1	12.3	7.9			
Popular priced	3.7	5.0	6.8	55	55	54
Total beer	22.8	17.3	14.7			
Specialty soft drinks	9.4	7.7	6.7	64	62	59
	100.0%	100.0%	100.0%	$ 80	$ 76	$ 71

THE LION BREWERY, INC.

BALANCE SHEETS
SEPTEMBER 30, 1996 AND 1995

	1996	1995
Assets		
Current assets:		
Cash and cash equivalents	$1,992,000	$ 0
Accounts receivable, less allowance for doubtful accounts of $157,000 and $129,000 at September 30, 1996 and 1995, respectively	2,001,000	2,476,000
Inventories	2,128,000	2,003,000
Prepaid expenses and other assets	190,000	277,000
Total current assets	6,311,000	4,756,000
Property, plant & equipment, net of accumulated depreciation of $1,684,000 and $1,122,000 at September 30, 1996 and 1995, respectively	3,600,000	3,254,000
Goodwill, net of accumulated amortization of $475,000 and $311,000 at September 30, 1996 and 1995, respectively	6,039,000	6,203,000
Deferred financing costs and other assets, net of accumulated amortization of $144,000 at September 30, 1995	4,000	228,000
	$15,954,000	$14,441,000
Liabilities and Shareholders' Equity		
Current liabilities:		
Current portion of long-term debt	$ 0	$ 1,745,000
Accounts payable	1,663,000	1,978,000
Accrued expenses	839,000	478,000
Refundable deposits	205,000	171,000
Income taxes payable	178,000	330,000
Total current liabilities	2,885,000	4,702,000
Long-term debt, less current portion	0	6,131,000
Net pension liability	243,000	218,000
Deferred income taxes	206,000	351,000
Total liabilities	3,334,000	11,402,000
Warrants	0	722,000
Shareholders' equity:		
Common stock, $.01 par value; 10,000,000 shares authorized; 3,885,052 and 1,851,183 shares issued and outstanding at September 30, 1996 and 1995, respectively	39,000	19,000
Additional paid-in capital	10,612,000	1,304,000
Adjustment to reflect minimum pension liability, net of deferred income taxes	(42,000)	(10,000)
Retained earnings	2,011,000	1,004,000
Total shareholders' equity	12,620,000	2,317,000
Total liabilities and shareholders' equity	$ 15,954,000	$ 14,441,000

The accompanying notes to financial statements are an integral part of these balance sheets.

THE LION BREWERY, INC.

STATEMENTS OF INCOME

FOR THE YEARS ENDED SEPTEMBER 30, 1996 AND 1995

	Year ended September 30, 1996	1995
Gross sales	$26,983,000	$25,175,000
Less excise taxes	544,000	382,000
Net sales	26,439,000	24,793,000
Cost of sales	19,939,000	18,834,000
Gross profit	6,500,000	5,959,000
Operating expenses:		
Delivery	824,000	827,000
Selling, advertising and promotional expenses	1,240,000	782,000
General and administrative	1,373,000	1,336,000
	3,437,000	2,945,000
Operating income	3,063,000	3,014,000
Interest expense and amortization of debt discount, net	520,000	1,042,000
Income before provision for income taxes and extraordinary item	2,543,000	1,972,000
Provision for income taxes	1,125,000	921,000
Income before extraordinary item	1,418,000	1,051,000
Extraordinary item, net of income tax benefit of $228,000	(322,000)	(0)
Net income	1,096,000	1,051,000
Warrant accretion	89,000	300,000
Net income available to common shareholders	$ 1,007,000	$ 751,000
Income per share before extraordinary item	$ 0.47	$ 0.40
Extraordinary item - loss per share	(0.11)	(0.00)
Net income per share	$ 0.36	$ 0.40
Shares used in per share calculation	2,835,000	1,898,000

The accompanying notes to financial statements are an integral part of these statements.

THE LION BREWERY, INC.

STATEMENTS OF CASH FLOWS
FOR THE YEARS ENDED SEPTEMBER 30, 1996 AND 1995

	1996	1995
Cash flows from operating activities:		
Net income	$1,096,000	$1,051,000
Adjustments to reconcile net income to net cash provided by operating activities		
Extraordinary item	550,000	0
Depreciation and amortization	830,000	947,000
Bad debt expense	12,000	36,000
Provision for inventory reserve	75,000	45,000
Benefit for deferred income taxes	(145,000)	(132,000)
Loss on disposal of equipment	0	2,000
Changes in assets and liabilities:		
(Increase) decrease in:		
Accounts receivable	463,000	153,000
Inventories	(200,000)	(212,000)
Prepaid expenses and other assets	87,000	23,000
Increase (decrease) in:		
Accounts payable, accrued expenses and refundable deposits	80,000	248,000
Income taxes payable	(152,000)	330,000
Pension liability	(7,000)	(16,000)
Net cash provided by operating activities	2,689,000	2,475,000
Cash flows from investing activities:		
Proceeds from sale of equipment	0	12,000
Purchase of equipment	(908,000)	(319,000)
Net cash used in investing activities	(908,000)	(307,000)
Cash flows from financing activities:		
Net proceeds from sale of common stock	9,466,000	0
Repurchase of common stock	(950,000)	0
Deferred financing costs	0	(25,000)
Issuance of long term debt	0	500,000
Net reductions in line of credit	(721,000)	(1,860,000)
Repayment of long term debt	(7,584,000)	(924,000)
Net cash provided by (used in) financing activities	211,000	(2,309,000)
Net increase (decrease) in cash and cash equivalents	1,992,000	(141,000)
Cash and cash equivalents, beginning of year	0	141,000
Cash and cash equivalents, end of year	$1,992,000	$ 0
Supplementary disclosure of cash flow information:		
Cash paid for:		
Interest	$ 516,000	$ 951,000
Income taxes	$1,183,000	$ 672,000

The accompanying notes to financial statements are an integral part of these statements.

THE LION BREWERY, INC.

NOTES TO FINANCIAL STATEMENTS (excerpts)

1. BASIS OF PRESENTATION AND DESCRIPTION OF THE BUSINESS

The Lion Brewery, Inc. (the Company), formerly The Lion, Inc., is a brewer and bottler of brewed beverages, including malta, specialty beers and specialty soft drinks. Malta is a non-alcoholic brewed beverage which the Company produces for major Hispanic food distribution companies primarily for sale in the eastern United States. Specialty beers, generally known as craft beers, are brewed by the Company both for sale under its own labels and on a contract basis for other marketers of craft beer brands. Craft beers are distinguishable from other domestically produced beers by their fuller flavor and adherence to traditional European brewing styles. The Company also produces specialty soft drinks, including all-natural brewed ginger beverages, on a contract basis for third parties. The Lion Brewery also brews beer for sale under traditional Company-owned labels for the local market at popular prices.

The Company was incorporated in Pennsylvania on April 5, 1933. On October 4, 1993, Lion Partners Company, L.P. (the Partnership) acquired shares of common stock of the Company for $2,100,000. Prior to this transaction, the Partnership had no affiliation with the Company. The Company then redeemed shares of common stock for $6,983,000 (of which $2,500,000 was payable in a note), including $1,008,000 of direct acquisition costs. After these transactions, the Partnership owned 81% of the common stock of the Company.

The Company accounted for these transactions as a purchase by the Partnership whereby the cost of acquiring 81% of the Company was pushed down to establish a new accounting basis which is reflected in the accompanying financial statements. The Company allocated the cost of the acquisition of 81% of the Company to the assets acquired and liabilities assumed based on their fair values and carried over 19% of the historical cost at the date of the acquisition. The purchase price was $8,677,000 and was allocated to tangible assets ($8,782,000) and liabilities ($6,619,000). The excess of the purchase price over net assets acquired of $6,514,000 was assigned to goodwill.

2. SUMMARY OF SIGNIFICANT ACCOUNTING POLICIES

Revenue Recognition

Revenue is generally recognized upon shipment. For products brewed under beer and soft drink contracts, revenue is generally recognized upon completion of production.

Inventories

Inventories are stated at the lower of cost or market determined on a first-in, first-out method (FIFO).

Property, Plant and Equipment

Property, plant and equipment are recorded at cost and are depreciated using the straight-line method over the useful lives of the assets. All significant additions and improvements are capitalized and repairs and maintenance charges are expensed as incurred. The new accounting pronouncement on impairment of long lived assets had no impact on the Company's financial statements. Estimated useful lives for the assets are as follows:

	Years
Buildings	20
Machinery and equipment	3-10
Kegs and bottles	3-7

Income taxes

The Company recognizes deferred tax assets and liabilities for the estimated future tax effects of events based on temporary differences between financial statement and tax basis of assets and liabilities using enacted tax rates in effect in the years the differences are expected to be reversed. Valuation allowances are established when necessary to reduce deferred tax assets to the amounts expected to be realized. Income tax expense is comprised of current taxes payable and the change in deferred tax assets and liabilities during the year.

Intangible Assets

The excess of the cost of the acquired assets over their fair values is being amortized using the straight-line method over forty years. The Company continually evaluates the remaining estimated useful lives and the recoverability of its intangible assets utilizing the undiscounted cash flow method.

Product and Customer Concentrations

The sale of malta, beer and soft drinks has accounted for all of the Company's sales, with malta accounting for 68% and 75% for the years ended September 30, 1996 and 1995. The Company's top three customers accounted for 60% and 68% of sales in fiscal 1996 and 1995. Accounts receivable from these three customers totaled $1,712,000 and $1,831,000 at September 30, 1996 and 1995. The Company's largest customer accounted for 27% and 30% of sales in fiscal 1996 and 1995. The Company does maintain contracts with several of its top customers; however there are no minimum purchase requirements. The Company does not have a contract with its largest customer. The length of such contracts range from two to four years. The decision by a major customer to switch production of its contract beverages from the Company to another brewer, or to build facilities to brew its own product, could have a materially adverse effect on the Company's financial results.

Excise Taxes
The U.S. federal government currently imposes an excise tax of $18 per barrel on every barrel of beer produced for consumption in the United States. However, any brewer with production under 2 million barrels per year pays a federal excise tax of $7 per barrel on the first 60,000 barrels it produces annually. Individual states also impose excise taxes on alcoholic beverages in varying amounts. The Company records the excise tax as a reduction of gross sales in the accompanying financial statements.

Net Income Per Share
Net income per share is computed using the weighted average number of common and dilutive common equivalent shares outstanding during the period. Common equivalent shares consist of stock options and warrants (using the treasury stock method for all periods presented). Accretion relating to the Company's warrants (see Note 11) is deducted in computing income applicable to common stock.

Stock split
In January 1996, the Company's Board of Directors amended the Company's Articles of Incorporation to effect a 3,091.33 for 1 stock split. All common shares and per share amounts in the accompanying financial statements have been adjusted retroactively to give effect to the stock split.

Financial Instruments
Financial instruments that potentially subject the Company to credit risk consist principally of trade receivables. The fair value of accounts receivable approximates carrying value.

3. INVENTORIES
Inventories consist of the following:

	1996	1995
Raw materials	$163,000	$ 176,000
Finished goods	673,000	663,000
Supplies	1,292,000	1,164,000
	$2,128,000	$ 2,003,000

4. PROPERTY, PLANT AND EQUIPMENT
Property, plant and equipment consist of the following:

	1996	1995
Land and building	$ 1,024,000	$ 1,014,000
Machinery and equipment	4,038,000	3,167,000
Kegs and bottles	222,000	195,000
	5,284,000	4,376,000
Less accumulated depreciation	1,684,000	1,122,000
	$ 3,600,000	$3,254,000

5. ACCRUED EXPENSES
Accrued expenses consist of the following:

	1996	1995
Payroll and related accruals	$ 427,000	$ 346,000
Other accruals	412,000	132,000
	$ 839,000	$ 478,000

6. INCOME TAXES
The provision for income taxes is as follows:

	1996	1995
Current:	$ 786,000	$ 755,000
Federal	256,000	298,000
State	1,042,000	1,053,000
Deferred:		
Federal	(105,000)	(102,000)
State	(40,000)	(30,000)
	(145,000)	(132,000)
	$ 897,000	$ 921,000

The principal items accounting for the difference between income taxes computed at the statutory rate and the provision for income taxes reflected in the statements of income are as follows:

	1996	1995
United States statutory rate	35%	35%
State taxes (net of federal tax benefit)	7	9
Nondeductible expenses - goodwill amortization	3	3
	45%	47%

Components of the Company's deferred tax balances are as follows:

	1996	1995
Deferred tax assets:		
Benefit accruals	$ 235,000	$ 160,000
Accounts receivable	71,000	53,000
Inventories	96,000	46,000
Other	–	18,000
	402,000	277,000
Deferred tax liabilities:		
Property, plant and equipment	559,000	628,000
Other	49,000	–
	608,000	628,000
	$ 206,000	$ 351,000

7. DEBT

Debt at September 30, 1995 consists of the following:

	1995
Revolving credit loan	$ 721,000
Term loan	1,019,000
Senior subordinate notes	3,631,000
Junior subordinate notes	2,500,000
Other	5,000
	7,876,000
Current portion	1,745,000
	$6,131,000

On May 2, 1996, the Company completed an initial public offering of equity securities. A portion of the proceeds were used to repay indebtedness of the Company (See Note 12). The extraordinary item recorded in 1996 consists of prepayment penalties of $160,000, unamortized debt discounts of $213,000 and the write-off of unamortized deferred financing costs of $177,000 related to the early extinguishment of debt, net of an income tax benefit of $228,000.

The Company is currently negotiating a $5,000,000 revolving line of credit and a $2,500,000 revolving equipment line of credit. Both facilities would be unsecured and interest will be paid monthly based upon either the Bank's prime rate minus 1/2%, LIBOR plus 75 basis points or the Bank's offered rate. There can be no assurance that such agreement will be finalized.

8. PENSION PLANS

The Company maintains a noncontributory defined benefit pension plan covering nonunion employees. The plan provides benefits based on years of service and compensation levels. The Company's funding policy for these plans is predicted on allowable limits for federal income tax purposes.

The components of net periodic pension cost for the defined benefit plan are as follows:

	1996	1995
Service cost - benefits earned during the period	$ 30,000	$ 24,000
Interest cost on projected benefit obligation	36,000	36,000
Actual return on plan assets	(23,000)	(39,000)
Net amortization and deferral	19,000	38,000
Effect of settlement	–	15,000
Net pension expense	$ 62,000	$ 74,000

Assumptions used in the accounting for the defined benefit plan are as follows as of September 30, 1996 and 1995:

Weighted average discount rate	8.5%
Expected long-term rate of return on assets	9.0
Average salary increase	5.0

The following table sets forth the funded status and the net pension liability included in the balance sheet for the defined benefit plan:

	1996	1995
Actuarial present value of benefit obligation:		
Accumulated benefit obligation (including vested benefits of $392,000 and $327,000)	$ 403,000	$ 340,000
Projected benefit obligation	438,000	413,000
Plan assets at fair value	160,000	122,000
Projected benefit obligation in excess of plan assets	(278,000)	(291,000)
Unrecognized net loss	111,000	87,000
Adjustment required to recognize minimum liability	(76,000)	(14,000)
Net pension liability recognized in balance sheet	$ 243,000	$ 218,000

The Company also participates in a multi-employer pension plan which provides defined benefits to union employees. Contributions are based on a fixed amount per hour worked. Pension cost aggregated $162,000 and $142,000 for the years ended September 30, 1996 and 1995, respectively.

9. COMMITMENTS AND CONTINGENCIES

The Company leases warehouse facilities and equipment under noncancelable operating leases. Future minimum lease payments under these leases are:

1997	$234,000
1998	246,000
1999	187,000
2000	136,000
2001	102,000

Rent expense for all leased facilities amounted to $294,000 in 1996 and $249,000 in 1995.

The Company has entered into employment agreements with the Company's President and Chief Financial Officer at annual base salaries aggregating $235,000. Bonuses are determined at the discretion of the Board of Directors. The contracts also provide for up to 2 years severance in the case of involuntary termination.

The Company is engaged in certain legal and administrative proceedings incidental to its normal course of business activities. Management believes the outcome of these proceedings will not have a material adverse effect on the Company's financial position or results of operations.

10. RELATED PARTY TRANSACTIONS

The Company obtained covenants not to compete from two selling employee/shareholders for an aggregate of $600,000 payable in annual installments of $100,000 over a six year noncompete period, one covenant ending in October, 1999 and the other ending in October, 2000.

11. STOCK OPTION PLANS AND WARRANTS

The senior subordinated noteholders received warrants for the purchase of 291,565 shares of the Company's common stock having a nominal exercise price. The loan agreement provides that the noteholders may put these warrants to the Company and accordingly, the warrants were accreted to the estimated redemption price. During fiscal 1996 and 1995, accretion of $89,000 and $300,000, respectively, was recorded and charged to retained earnings. The warrants were exercised in December 1995. The Company used $950,000 of the net proceeds of the initial public offering to repurchase 132,696 shares of common stock issued upon the exercise of the warrants.

12. PUBLIC OFFERING AND PREFERRED STOCK AUTHORIZATION

On May 2, 1996, the Company completed an initial public offering of 1,875,000 shares of common stock for $6.00 per share, including the partial exercise of the over-allotment option. The proceeds of the initial public offering, including the partial exercise of the over-allotment option, net of the underwriting commissions and expenses totaled $9,466,000. A portion of these proceeds were used to repay indebtedness of the Company of $7,948,000 and to retire 132,696 shares of Common Stock, in connection with the termination of a loan agreement, at a cost of $950,000.

In connection with this offering, the Company issued warrants to the underwriters to purchase up to 135,000 shares of common stock at an exercise price of $7.20, which are exercisable for a period of five years from the date of the offering. The holders have certain rights to obtain the registration of these shares under the Securities Act.

Grupo Casa Saba SA de CV—Inflation Accounting

With more than 109 years of experience, Grupo Casa Saba is one of Mexico's leading distributors of pharmaceutical, health and beauty products. The company's extensive nationwide distribution network can deliver products anywhere in Mexico in less than 12 hours. In addition, they distribute complementary products like general merchandise and exclusive lines, along with books, magazines and other publications. Casa Saba shares trade on the Mexican Bolsa and the New York Stock Exchange under the ticker SAB.

Learning Objectives

- Understand the impact of inflation on the financial statements
- Explain the basic procedures used to adjust financial statements for the effect of inflation.
- Explain how financial statement analysis differs when the information is inflation adjusted.

Refer to the 2001 financial statements of Grupo Casa Saba.

✧ Concepts ✧

a. There are two types of price changes that affect financial statements: general price changes (i.e., inflation) and specific price changes (i.e., the relative value of what is being measured). Describe in general terms how each of these price changes influence the measurement of assets, liabilities, revenues and expenses in unadjusted historical cost financial statements.

b. Describe the difference between a monetary (or nominal) item and a real item. Provide examples of each from Grupo Casa Saba's balance sheets.

c. Refer to Note 3(c). How do Casa Saba's financial statements take into account the effect of inflation?

d. Briefly explain what the income statement item "Gain on monetary position" represents. In 2001, was this item a gain or a loss?

✧ Process ✧

e. The annual inflation rate used to adjust financial statements in Mexico was 4.4% in 2001, 9.0% in 2000, and 12.3% in 1999. What net sales did Casa Saba report in their 2000 annual report for the year 2000? What total assets did they report in their annual report for the year 2000.

f. Refer to Note 6 of the Casa Saba annual report. Why is the restatement for land about four times the original cost while the restatement for computer equipment is only about one time the original cost?

g. Assume that on January 1, 2001, Grupo Casa Saba purchased land for $4 million. If the rate of inflation used to adjust the financial statements in 2001 was 4.4%, what journal entry did Casa Saba prepare to adjust that land at December 31, 2001?

h. Using disclosures in Note 3(c), explain how the revenue from a cash sale (monetary revenue) that occurred in July 2001 would be adjusted for inflation in the 2001 income statement.

i. Refer to Note 3(c). Explain how a unit of inventory originally purchased in October 2000 and sold in July 2001 (nonmonetary expense) would be adjusted for inflation in the 2001 income statement.

j. According to Note 3(c), what are the two sources of "net loss on restatement"?

✧ Analysis ✧

k. What issues arise when you compare the financial statements of a Mexican company, like Grupo Casa Saba, with those of companies that do not adjust for inflation? How would you address those issues?

 We thank Ross Jennings for developing this case.

CONSOLIDATED BALANCE SHEETS

Grupo Casa Saba, S. A. de C. V. and Subsidiaries

As of December 31, 2000 and 2001

(Amounts stated in thousands of 2001 year-end constant Mexican Pesos)

ASSETS

	2000	2001
CURRENT:		
Cash and cash equivalents	$ 242,480	$ 90,266
Accounts receivable, net	2,310,016	2,693,992
Inventories, net	2,349,126	2,666,736
Prepaid expenses	12,021	10,010
Total current assets	4,913,643	5,461,004
PROPERTY AND EQUIPMENT, net	1,022,504	950,228
OTHER ASSETS, net	67,231	58,753
GOODWILL, net	269,158	242,369
Total assets	$ 6,272,536	$ 6,712,354

LIABILITIES

	2000	2001
CURRENT:		
Current maturities of long-term debt	$ 75,690	$ 304,000
Trade accounts payable	3,009,379	3,117,168
Other payables and accrued liabilities	41,585	43,046
Employee profit sharing	5,521	216
Total current liabilities	3,132,175	3,464,430
LONG-TERM DEBT	634,952	379,000
DEFERRED INCOME TAX	90,239	245,008
Total liabilities	3,857,366	4,088,438
STOCKHOLDERS' EQUITY:		
Capital stock	871,295	871,295
Premium on stock sold	674,448	674,448
Reserve for share repurchases	823,563	823,563
Retained earnings	928,113	1,333,658
Net loss on restatement	(850,697)	(1,047,496)
Accrued deferred income tax effect	(31,552)	(31,552)
Total stockholders' equity	2,415,170	2,623,916
Total liabilities and stockholders' equity	$ 6,272,536	$ 6,712,354

The accompanying notes are an integral part of these consolidated financial statements

CONSOLIDATED STATEMENTS OF INCOME

Grupo Casa Saba, S. A. de C. V. and Subsidiaries

For the years ended December 31, 2000 and 2001

(Amounts stated in thousands of 2001 year-end constant Mexican Pesos, except per share data)

	2000	2001
NET SALES	$ 16,263,609	$ 16,236,673
COST OF SALES	14,572,845	14,498,030
Gross profit	1,690,764	1,738,643
OPERATING EXPENSES:		
Selling	447,289	449,143
Administrative	643,938	654,821
Severance payments to personnel	8,919	–
	1,100,146	1,103,964
Operating income	590,618	634,679
COMPREHENSIVE COST OF FINANCING, net:		
Interest income	(8,202)	(2,466)
Interest expense	215,308	176,272
Exchange gain, net	(70)	(872)
Gain on monetary position	(126,074)	(31,212)
	80,962	141,722
OTHER INCOME, net	(17,243)	(30,253)
Income before provisions	526,899	523,210
PROVISIONS FOR:		
Income tax	–	34,806
Asset tax	9,245	–
Deferred income tax	96,464	82,744
	105,709	117,550
Employee profit sharing	5,520	115
	111,229	117,665
Net income	$ 415,670	$ 405,545
Net income per share	$ 1.561	$ 1.523
Weighted average shares outstanding (in millions)	266,321	266,321

The accompanying notes are an integral part of these consolidated financial statements.

CONSOLIDATED STATEMENTS OF STOCKHOLDERS' EQUITY

Grupo Casa Saba, S. A. de C. V. and Subsidiaries

For the years ended December 31, 2000 and 2001

(Amounts stated in thousands of 2001 year-end constant Mexican Pesos)

	Capital stock		Premium on stock sold
	Historical	Restated	
BALANCES AS OF JANUARY 1, 2000	$ 167,903	$ 703,392	$ 674,448
Comprehensive income	–	–	–
BALANCES AS OF DECEMBER 31, 2000	167,903	703,392	674,448
Comprehensive income	–	–	–
BALANCES AS OF DECEMBER 31, 2001	$ 167,903	$ 703,392	$ 674,448

The accompanying notes are an integral part of these consolidated financial statements.

Reserve for shares repurchase		Retained earnings		Net loss on restatement		Accrued deferred income tax effect		Total
$	823,563	$	512,443	$	(736,800)	$	–	$	2,144,949
	–		415,670		(113,897)		(31,552)		270,221
	823,563		928,113		(850,697)		(31,552)		2,415,170
	–		405,545		(196,799)		–		208,746
$	823,563	$	1,333,658	$	(1,047,496)	$	(31,552)	$	2,623,916

CONSOLIDATED STATEMENTS OF CHANGES IN FINANCIAL POSITION

Grupo Casa Saba, S. A. de C. V. and Subsidiaries

For the years ended December 31, 2000 and 2001

(Amounts stated in thousands of 2001 year-end Mexican Pesos)

	2000	2001
OPERATING ACTIVITIES:		
Net income	$ 415,670	$ 405,545
Add - Non cash items:		
Depreciation and amortization	104,945	100,135
Allowance for doubtful accounts	21,002	30,285
Loss on sale of property and equipment	4,201	11,415
Deferred income tax	96,464	82,744
	642,282	630,124
Changes in assets and liabilities:		
(Increase) decrease in:		
Accounts receivable	(509,437)	(414,261)
Inventories	(708,826)	(514,409)
Prepaid expenses	14,013	2,011
Trade accounts payable	893,786	107,789
Other payables and accrued liabilities	(82,889)	1,461
Income tax	(1,206)	-
Employee profit sharing	5,520	(5,305)
	(389,039)	(822,714)
Net cash provided by (used in) operating activities	253,243	(192,590)
INVESTING ACTIVITIES:		
Additions of property and equipment, net of retirements	(19,646)	8,926
Increase (decrease) in other assets	29,200	(4,919)
Net cash provided by investing activities	9,554	4,007
FINANCING ACTIVITIES:		
Bank loans, net of payments made	(95,840)	2,308
Effect in change of bank loans due to the restatement	(76,850)	(29,950)
Initial accrued effect of deferred income tax	(37,776)	–
Deferred income tax	–	72,025
Net cash (used in) provided by financing activities	(210,466)	44,383
Net increase (decrease) in cash and cash equivalents	$ 33,223	$ (152,214)
Cash and cash equivalents at beginning of year	209,257	242,480
Cash and cash equivalents at end of year	$ 242,480	$ 90,266
Supplementary information:		
Income tax and asset tax paid	$ 23,311	$ 37,783
Interest paid	$ 209,914	$ 179,835

The accompanying notes are an integral part of these consolidated financial statements.

the shares in the amount of $1,300 ($1,357 at year-end constant Mexican Pesos) is reflected in the income statement as "Other income" for the year then ended.

g. On July 13, 2000, the subsidiary Casa Saba S, S. A. de C. V. was incorporated. Its corporate name was subsequently changed to Distribuidora Casa Saba, S.A. de C.V.("Distribuidora Saba"). Effective December 2000, this subsidiary renders services related to the purchase, storage and sale of medicines, pharmaceutical products and toiletries, as well as transportation services, to Casa Saba.

h. Effective November 18, 2000, the subsidiary Inmobiliaria Tarik, S.A. de C.V. changed its corporate name to Servicios Corporativos Saba, S.A. de C.V. ("Servicios Corporativos Saba"). Effective December 2000, this subsidiary renders, among other services, specialized personnel services to Casa Saba. These services consist of administrative, legal, accounting, tax, finance, treasury, and electronic data processing services.

i. In December 2001, as a part of an internal reorganization of the operations of the Group, the management thereof entered into the agreements discussed below to strengthen its corporate structure, as well as to facilitate the transactions carried out by some of the consolidated subsidiaries that comprise it. Those agreements do not change the consolidated financial position of the Group in any way as of December 31, 2001.

- Through a stock purchase agreement dated December 17, 2001, the Company sold 100% of its equity stake in Inmuebles Visosil, S.A. de C.V. (Visosil). This equity stake represented 20.7% of the issued and outstanding capital stock of Visosil. That sale was made to Casa Saba in order to have absolute control of Visosil concentrated in Casa Saba. The aggregate purchase price amounted to $274,000 at year-end constant Mexican Pesos. That amount reduced the liability that the Company had payable to Casa Saba. That transaction generated a loss amounting to $6,798 at year-end constant Mexican Pesos, the amount of which was eliminated in the income statement, in accordance with the basis of consolidation described in Note 3) below. By a resolution adopted at the General Ordinary Stockholders´ Meeting held on July 2, 2001, Visosil had previously approved a capital stock increase that was fully paid by Casa Saba. As a result of the foregoing, Casa Saba held 79.2% of the issued and outstanding capital stock of Visosil at that date.

- Through a stock purchase agreement dated December 17, 2001, the Company sold 100% of its equity stake in Drogueros. This equity stake represented 99.9% of the issued and outstanding capital stock of Drogueros. That sale was made to Visosil in order to have absolute control of Drogueros concentrated in Visosil. The aggregate purchase price amounted to $300,000 at year-end constant Mexican Pesos. That amount reduced the liability that the Company had payable to Visosil. That transaction generated a loss amounting to $8,323 at year-end constant Mexican Pesos, the amount of which was eliminated in the income statement, in accordance with the basis of consolidation described in Note 3) below.

3. Significant accounting policies:

a. Use of estimates

Preparing the accompanying financial statements requires the Group's management to make certain estimates and assumptions that affect the reported amount of some assets and liabilities, and disclosure of contingent assets and liabilities at the date of the financial statements, as well as the reported amount of revenues and expenses incurred during the periods. Actual results can differ from these estimates.

b. Basis of consolidation

The Group's financial statements are presented on a consolidated basis under Mexican GAAP. The Group's consolidated financial statements reflect the results of operations of the Company and those of its subsidiaries (controlled directly or indirectly, acquired, newly incorporated or disposed subsidiaries) from the date on which they were acquired and/or incorporated up to the date when they were sold and/or at the year-end of the latest year reported. All significant intercompany balances and transactions have been eliminated from the Group's consolidated financial statements. The Group holds substantially all of the issued and outstanding capital stock of each of its consolidated subsidiaries referred to in Note 2) above.

c. Recognition of the impact of inflation on the financial information

In accordance with Bulletin B-10 "Recognition of the Impact of Inflation on Financial Information" as amended ("Bulletin B-10"), the Group restates its consolidated financial statements in terms of the purchasing power of the currency as of the end of the latest period reported, thereby comprehensively recognizing the impact of inflation. Consequently, the amounts of the financial statements for both the current year and prior year are comparable since all amounts are stated in terms of Mexican Pesos of the same purchasing power. Accordingly, all prior year financial statement amounts presented herein differ from those originally reported to restate changes in Mexican Pesos of purchasing power since the prior year.

The impact of inflation on the financial information is recognized in accordance with Bulletin B-10 by applying the following procedures:

i) The amounts of the accompanying consolidated financial statements and the accompanying notes are presented for comparative purposes in Mexican Pesos in purchasing power as of December 31, 2001, by applying the inflation factor derived from the National Consumer Price Index (the "NCPI").

ii) Revenues and expenses related to monetary items are restated from the month in which they occur up to year-end, by applying the inflation factor derived from the NCPI. Expenses related to nonmonetary items (cost of sales and depreciation) are restated as of the date on which inventories are sold, and/or the time when property and equipment are depreciated, based on the restated value of those assets, and from the date they were expensed up to year-end, based on the applicable NCPI factor.

iii) Gain or loss on monetary position represents the result of holding monetary assets and liabilities whose purchasing power is affected by inflation. Gain or loss on monetary position is determined by applying the NCPI to the consolidated average net monetary position at the beginning of each month, which amount is subsequently restated in terms of the purchasing power of the Mexican Peso at fiscal year-end by applying the relevant restatement factor. As of December 31, 2000 and 2001, the Group's consolidated monetary position represented a gain in the amount of $126,074 and $31,212, respectively, the effect of which is included in the statements of income for these periods in the line item "Comprehensive cost of financing".

iiv) Inventories are initially recorded at acquisition cost. They are subsequently restated to their replacement value. Restated inventory values do not exceed net realizable values. Cost of sales is restated to replacement value when products are sold and are restated from the month in which they occur up to year-end of the latest year reported, by applying the inflation factor derived from the NCPI .

v) Property and equipment are initially recorded at acquisition cost. Effective 1998, those fixed assets, along with their depreciation, are restated based on the "adjustments due to changes in the general price level method" by applying the NCPI: (i) on the value determined by an appraisal performed by independent experts as of December 31, 1996 (except for Drogueros, as discussed in Note 6) hereinbelow), and (ii) on the historical cost of acquisitions made subsequent to that date.

Depreciation is calculated on the restated value of fixed assets, by using the straight-line method based on the remaining economic useful lives thereof. The remaining economic useful lives were estimated by independent experts as of December 31, 1996, as well as by the Group for acquisitions made subsequent to that date.

vi) Goodwill is restated based on the NCPI.

vii) Stockholders' equity is restated based on the NCPI to maintain stockholders' equity in constant Mexican Pesos of purchasing power, in accordance with the age of the original contributions and the earnings or losses generated. The restatement of stockholders' equity represents the amount necessary to maintain shareholders' investment in terms of year-end purchasing power of the currency of the lasted year reported.

viii) The net loss on restatement represents the accumulated monetary effect at the date on which the financial statements were adjusted for the first time (restated to 2001 year-end Mexican Pesos), plus the surplus or deficit generated from comparing the restatement of nonmonetary assets based on replacement values and the restatement made by applying the NCPI. Effective 1997, that surplus or deficit is only generated by restating inventories to replacement value above or below the NCPI. As of December 31, 2000 and 2001, a loss was generated in the amounts of $113,897 and $196,799, respectively.

d. Cash and cash equivalents

Cash consists basically of non-interest bearing bank deposits. Cash equivalents are comprised mainly of short-term investments (highly liquid that have a ninety day term of maturity or less when acquired) in banking institutions payable on demand, at variable interest rates. Investments are valued at market value (cost plus accrued interest).

e. Allowance for doubtful accounts

The allowance for doubtful accounts represents the Group's estimate of the probable loss inherent to all receivables considering: (i) the general historical trend of payment performance of customers, and (ii) factors surrounding the credit risk of specific customers.

f) Goodwill

Goodwill derived from acquiring shares of capital stock of subsidiary companies at a price exceeding that of their book value is amortized over the term during which the Group's management estimates that the additional benefits of such investments will be generated, without exceeding twenty years. Book value is substantially equal to the "fair value" of the net assets acquired as a result of their restatement through the acquisition date. As of December 31, 2000 and 2001, the amount of the amortization of goodwill expensed amounted to $21,453 ($22,397 at year-end constant Mexican Pesos) and $21,232, respectively.

g) Labor obligations

i) Members of the Group that have personnel recognize the obligations for retirement pensions and seniority premiums derived from defined benefit plans for all their employees in accordance with the Federal Labor Law, as well as the schemes that have been established for each plan. Seniority premiums are granted for a voluntary separation of personnel, after completing fifteen years of service , and calculated based on the number of years worked. Retirement pensions are granted to all personnel having completed at least ten years of service and have reached sixty-five years of age. Members of the Group are required to pay certain severance benefits only to employees that are dismissed without proper cause. These payments (which are made to employees during the normal course of operations), for non-substitute indemnification of a retirement are expensed when paid, since during the normal course of operations it is impracticable to estimate the number of employees that will be dismissed.

Projected benefit obligations, unamortized items, and the net periodic cost applicable to retirement pensions and seniority premiums, are determined by using the "projected unit credit method", in conformity with Bulletin D-3, "Labor Obligations".

Members of the Group with employees have created a fund in an irrevocable trust in a financial institution. The purpose of this fund is to meet the labor obligations referred to above. Contributions to the fund determined based on actuarial computations in 2000 and 2001 at nominal value were $3,219 and $4,000, respectively. As of December 31,2000 and 2001, fund assets consisted primarily of equity securities, as well as investments in fixed income securities issued by Mexican companies, that are traded on the Mexican Stock Market

ii) As discussed in Note 2) above, during 2000 Casa Saba restructured its operations internally. In connection with this restructuring , Casa Saba terminated some operating and administrative personnel. Severance payments made by Casa Saba to such personnel are reflected in the income statement for the year ended December 31, 2000 under the line item "severance payments to personnel". In addition, they further streamline and increase the efficiency of its operations, effective December 2000, Casa Saba transferred all of its personnel to two of its consolidated subsidiaries, Servicios Corporativos Saba and Distribuidora Saba. These subsidiaries render specialized services to Casa Saba, which are described in Note 2). All of the acquired labor benefits and rights of the employees and workers of Casa Saba were transferred to these consolidated subsidiaries in accordance with the Federal Labor Law. These events did not have a significant impact on the determination and recording of the labor obligations determined by independent actuaries.

iii) The relevant information of the study performed by independent actuaries, with regard to the pension plan and seniority premiums of the Members of the Group with employees is summarized below. The rates referred to below with regard to the actuarial assumptions are stated in real terms (nominal rates at market discounted for inflation). The amounts in the tables below have not been restated to Mexican Pesos in purchasing power as of December 31, 2001. They are presented at nominal value such as disclosed by independent actuaries.

4. Accounts receivable:

	2000	2001
Trade receivables	$ 2,188,181	$ 2,655,910
Allowance for doubtful accounts	(72,657)	(92,312)
	2,115,524	2,563,598
Value added tax recoverable	29,902	33,506
Income tax recoverable	124,258	67,019
Other	40,332	29,869
	$ 2,310,016	$ 2,693,992

5. Inventories:

	2000	2001
Pharmaceutical products	$ 1,364,503	$ 1,530,932
Beauty care products	258,444	604,230
Books and magazines	143,712	197,684
Stationery	7,793	743
Electric appliances	24,117	9,662
Groceries	6,688	–
Other	9,927	23,120
	1,815,184	2,366,371
Estimate for slow-moving magazines inventory	(28,775)	(20,928)
	1,786,409	2,345,443
Merchandise-in-transit	562,717	321,293
	$ 2,349,126	$ 2,666,736

Merchandise-in-transit applies mainly to pharmaceutical products. The title has been transferred to the Group.

6. Property and equipment:

	2000	2001		
	Total	Original cost	Resta-tement	Total
Building	$ 720,836	$ 243,670	$ 468,820	$ 712,490
Machinery and equipment	74,868	35,989	39,971	75,960
Transportation equipment	212,364	82,715	103,758	186,473
Office equipment	117,833	42,599	76,988	119,587
Computer equipment	213,297	106,554	109,303	215,857
	1,339,198	511,527	798,840	1,310,367
Less-Accumulated depreciation	(573,728)	(269,727)	(341,330)	(611,057)
	765,470	241,800	457,510	699,310
Land	257,006	50,323	200,565	250,888
Construction-in-progress	28	27	3	30
	$ 1,022,504	$ 292,149	$ 658,078	$ 950,228

The restatement of property and equipment of the subsidiary Drogueros, whose net replacement value as of December 31, 2000 and 2001 is included in the foregoing summary, amounts to $116,206 and $109,424, respectively. That restatement was determined by applying the NCPI to the historical value of the property and equipment of Drogueros from their respective dates of acquisition.

The average annual depreciation rates for 2000 and 2001 were as follows:

Buildings and improvements	2.10%
Machinery and equipment	6.09%
Transportation and equipment	10.15%
Furniture and fixtures	6.50%
Computer equipment	11.15%

7. Related party balances and transactions:

i) As of December 31, 2000 and 2001, payable balances to related parties Xtra Inmuebles, S.A. de C.V. and Pastas Molisaba, S.A. de C.V. amounted to $1,612 ($1,683 at year-end constant Mexican Pesos) and $219, respectively. Those balances derived from property leased and miscellaneous articles purchased are included in the balance sheet under the line item "Other payables and accrued liabilities". Through 2000 and 2001, the leases expensed amounted to $2,415 ($2,521 at year-end constant Mexican Pesos) and $3,720, respectively. During 2001, the miscellaneous articles expensed amounted $201.

During 2000 and 2001, the Group had no other related party agreement, except for the balances and transactions referred to above.

As of December 31, 1999, related party balances and transactions were as follows:

		Accounts Receivable	Accounts Payables
Balances			
Debir	(*)	$ 1,092,732	$ –
Principia	(*)	340,464	–
		1,433,196	–
Other		3,302	–
Lemans Refaccionaria de Autopartes, S.A. de C.V.		–	1,200
		$ 1,463,498	$ 1,200

	Revenues	Expenses
Transactions		
Rent	$ 789	$ –
Interest	303,814	–
Fees	384	5,296
Office supplies	–	11,397
Leases and services	–	2,841
Purchases	–	19,250
Fixed asset purchases	–	3,158
Communication services	–	4,020
	$ 304,987	$ 45,962